The Perfect Calm

The Titanic Disaster

A Case Study in Root Cause Analysis

By
William Christiansen

Copyright © 2016
by William Christiansen

All rights reserved. No part of this publication may be reproduced or transmitted in any form or by any means, electronic, or mechanical, including photocopying, recording, or any information storage and retrieval system, without permission in writing from the publisher.

Cover and Interior Book Design by Deb Christiansen

ISBN 9781508469063

Published by
Books For Dessert
P.O. Box 563
Schoolcraft, MI 49087
www.booksfordessert.com

Printed in the United States of America

This book is for Deb, my wife,
because she believed I could write it.

Icebergs

"The polar regions of the earth are covered with a thick, moving ice-cap, forming 'glaciers.' The ends of these glaciers are all the time pushing out from the land until they overhang far into the sea. In time, as these overhanging parts are beaten by storms and wore upon by the action of the water, great masses are broken off. Thousands of these fragments, broken off from the southwest coast of Greenland, are caught and held for a time by the floe-ice in the land-locked waters between Baffin's Bay and Greenland. When the southwest wind unlocks the Arctic gates, these fragments of glaciers break from their moorings and sail southward, a magnificent fleet of hundreds of icebergs.

"While the greater part never get farther than the Labrador coast and northern Newfoundland, a small number, helped on by wind and current, make their way into the gulf of St Lawrence or sail on to the southward, to be watched for by anxious sea-captains, as the single remaining terror of all those monsters, real and fabled, that once filled the sea.

"What hope has any ship moving at the rate of twenty-two knots an hour against a mass of ice rising to a height of a hundred feet, reaching down to a depth of a thousand, and extending over the sea for a mile? The *Titanic* answered, *None*."

~ 1918, Our Wonder World, A Library of Knowledge in Ten Volumes

Contents

Icebergs 5

Preface 9

Part One

Chapter 1
White Star Line and the Largest Steamship Ever Built 13

Chapter 2
Lifeboats for an Unsinkable Ship 20

Chapter 3
Preparing for the Maiden Voyage 26

Chapter 4
The Crew and Staff of the Titanic 29

Chapter 5
Sailing Day 34

Photos I
Titanic, Crew, and Passengers 51

Chapter 6
The Atlantic Voyage 61

Chapter 7
Icebergs and Warnings 73

Chapter 8
Into the Perfect Calm - Prelude to Collision 82

Chapter 9
Iceberg Right Ahead 93

Chapter 10
Immediate Aftermath 103

Chapter 11
Keep the Bad News Quiet 118

Chapter 12
Distress Calls and Rockets 125

Chapter 13
Aboard the Carpathia 134

Chapter 14
Loading and Launching the Lifeboats 144

Chapter 15
Aboard the Californian 178

Chapter 16
Titanic's Last Minutes 187

Chapter 17
One Lifeboat Returns 201

Chapter 18
Rescue 220

Chapter 19
The World Learns of Disaster 228

Chapter 20
Search and Recovery 238

Chapter 21
The Inquiries 242

Part One Epilogue
    Survived And Perished 248

Photos II
    Iceberg and Aftermath 276

Part Two

Chapter 22
    Root Cause Analysis Primer 284

Chapter 23
    Define and Measure 306

Chapter 24
    Collision with an Iceberg – Root Cause Analysis 322

Chapter 25
    The Titanic Sank After The Collision – Root Cause Analysis 350

Chapter 26
    1503 Perish – Root Cause Analysis 360

Chapter 27
    Improve and Control 407

Chapter 28
    Findings of the American and British Inquiries 412

Part Two Epilogue
    Preventing Another Disaster 421

Index 425

Preface

The British luxury liner was the largest craft ever conceived. She was the latest thing in the art of shipbuilding and absolutely no money was spared in her construction. At 800 feet and displacing 75,000 tons, she was considered one of the greatest works of men. Built using the latest technology including the use of 19 watertight compartments, only 10 of which were needed to stay afloat, she was considered "unsinkable." An unsinkable ship shouldn't need lifeboats but she carried the minimum required by law, less than half of the number needed for the passengers she carried on that fateful April voyage.

Her indestructible folly and the essential need for lifeboats was exposed by a starboard collision with an iceberg at 25 knots, 400 miles from Newfoundland, when the unsinkable liner sank in the cold North Atlantic. So was the fate of the fictional ship *Titan* in American author Morgan Robertson's novella, *Futility*, published in 1898.

Fourteen years later, 400 miles from Newfoundland, the futility of a very real ship's dilemma was captured by many ships in range of only her wireless signal. "*CQD* (Come Quick Danger)... *SOS* (Save Our Souls) ...we have struck iceberg...sinking fast...Position 41.46 N. 50.14 W. ... *CQD* ... *SOS*."

This was the desperate message repeated by *Titanic's* Senior Marconi Wireless Operator to any ship that could hear it–many did–and come to their assistance in time. None could.

Late on the night of April 14, 1912, in a remarkably perfect calm on the North Atlantic, the *RMS Titanic* collided with a massive iceberg and sank in less than three hours. At the time, 2215 passengers and crew were aboard the *Titanic* for her maiden voyage to the United States. Only 712 survived to complete the voyage aboard the *Carpathia*, the first ship to arrive at daybreak the following morning.

In the 100 plus years that have passed since that cold and cruel night much has been learned about the *Titanic's* only voyage. Hitting an iceberg was the obvious incident that brought on this tragedy, but the underlying causes of the *Titanic's* demise, and the resulting loss of life, have been hypothesized, investigated, and debated for over a century. The investigation started with the United States Senate Inquiry the day after survivors landed in New York and was followed by the British Wreck Commissioner's Inquiry when they returned to England. Newspapers in both countries printed facts, rumors, survivor accounts, and opinions that swayed public opinion and further fueled public outrage. As the story unfolded, many questions demanded answers:

- How could the *Titanic* strike an iceberg in the perfectly calm conditions of the night?
- Was a missing key a key cause for not seeing the iceberg in time?
- Did a coal fire doom the *Titanic*?

- Did Captain Smith have all the ice warnings?
- After striking the iceberg, why did the unsinkable *Titanic* sink?
- Why were only 712 lives saved?
- What prevented the nearby liner, *Californian,* from helping?

As a root cause analysis practitioner and instructor of root cause analysis techniques at a Fortune 100 company's largest manufacturing facility, I was curious to see how the techniques would hold up when used to analyze this century old disaster. I began using the *Titanic* disaster as the example incident for my root cause analysis class and this proved to be a popular topic. Everyone, it seems, knows the story of the *Titanic* and many have a favorite theory on why she sank. The structured root cause analysis techniques, using information that was known at that time, allowed the students to identify multiple root causes associated with the *Titanic* disaster. Most left class confident that, if they could identify root causes for the sinking of the *Titanic*, they could use the techniques and tools to identify root causes for problems in their department.

Many books have been written that tell the whole or some facet of the story of the *Titanic*. The aim of this book is to tell the story in an engaging way, then present and use proven root cause analysis techniques to analyze the *Titanic* disaster.

Readers only interested in the story of the *Titanic* should thoroughly enjoy Part One of this book which tells the story from the building of the luxury liner and her unsinkable perception, through the maiden voyage, the collision with an iceberg, and the tragic aftermath. Newspaper stories and survivors' own published accounts are used to describe the tragedy and its aftermath and much of the story is also told through testimony given at the U.S. and British Inquiries. Portions of the story, including dialog not attributed to testimony or a published account, are dramatizations that assist with the storytelling. While these dramatizations do not alter recognized and accepted facts, I leave it to the reader to determine if any of the testimony and printed accounts from the period contain dramatizations that stretch the truth.

Those interested in root cause analysis methods that can be used by a wide variety of industries will also want to read Part Two of this book. Part Two identifies proven and practical root cause analysis techniques and includes a method to analyze the root causes of Human Performance issues. These techniques are then used to analyze and identify root causes of the *Titanic* disaster using the information presented throughout the story and additional testimony from the U.S. and British Inquiries. In order to demonstrate that these root cause analysis techniques work, without the benefit of 100 years to investigate, the focus will be on what was known and could be determined in the aftermath of the tragedy. This includes analysis of Human Performance; what people did to cause, or failed to do to prevent, the wreck of the *Titanic* and the disastrous aftermath. Part Two readers will also find my conclusions as to the root causes of the *Titanic* disaster—identified through the use of the root cause analysis methods described.

The *Titanic* story and root cause analysis case studies presented in this book are intended to entertain and to educate. Some *Titanic* scholars and enthusiasts may disagree with debatable parts of the timeline and facts presented. Some may also disagree with the conclusions and the root causes identified, while still others will be certain in their belief that there are root causes that went unidentified. Whether you agree with or dispute the root causes identified, it is my belief that the root cause analysis process presented in this book provides the opportunity for all issues to be identified and debated during an incident investigation.

This book would not have been started or finished without the help and encouragement of my publisher, editor, best friend, and wife Deb Christiansen. Her questions, suggestions, and insights were invaluable. Deb's editing and boutique publishing expertise then proceeded to turn this project into the book you are reading. Enjoy.

William Christiansen
January 2016

Part One

Maiden Voyage of the Unsinkable *Titanic*

Great Mechanical Marvels, Building a Giant Liner

"... In both the *Olympic* and the *Titanic* three million steel rivets, weighing in all 1200 tons, have been employed to bind the massive steel plates, insuring the greatest stability; and the rudder of each vessel weighs 100 tons, yet will be moved by electricity almost as lightly as a feather.
"Because of the enormous size of the ships, the accommodations, both as regards the several public apartments, including tennis-courts, sun-parlors, swimming-pools, etc., and the passenger staterooms, are exceptionally spacious, while the beauty and luxury of the appointments surpass anything of the kind heretofore attempted."

~ 1912, Book of Wonders and Curious Things

Chapter 1

WHITE STAR LINE AND THE LARGEST STEAMSHIP EVER BUILT

Thomas Henry Ismay, owner of White Star Line, formed the Oceanic Steam Navigation Company in 1869 and established White Star Line as a high-class steamship service in the Atlantic passenger trade. In 1891 Joseph Bruce Ismay, the eldest son of Thomas and Margaret Ismay, became a partner in the business at age 28.

Joseph Bruce Ismay was born in Crosby, near Liverpool on December 12, 1862. He was educated at Elstree School, an English preparatory school, and at Harrow, an independent school for boys in the town of Harrow, in north-west London. After Harrow the young Ismay was tutored in France for a year before apprenticing with his father's company. He then spent a year abroad and upon his return was assigned to White Star's New York office. A capable tennis player, Ismay, at 22, and his partner won the Gentlemen's Doubles Championship of New South Wales in 1885. In 1888 Ismay married Julia Florence Schieffelin, the eldest daughter of George R. Schieffelin of New York. The Ismays had two sons and two daughters. Ismay moved the family to England in 1891, the year he was made a partner in his father's firm. He took over the business after his father's death in 1899.

The firm thrived under the direction of J. Bruce Ismay and in 1901 he negotiated terms under which the White Star Line was purchased by U.S. financier J. Pierpont Morgan for $32,000,000. J.P. Morgan combined White Star Line with other shipping acquisitions to form a shipping trust called the International Mercantile Marine (IMM). Ismay remained the largest White Star shareholder and White Star ships would continue under the British flag with British crews, but American interests essentially controlled the company. In 1904 J.P. Morgan named J. Bruce Ismay President and Managing Director of International Mercantile Marine.

In the summer of 1907 Bruce and Florence Ismay dined at the London home of Lord William J. Pirrie, a partner and chairman of the Belfast shipbuilding firm Harland & Wolff and a director of International Mercantile Marine. Over drinks and cigars Ismay and Pirrie discussed the recent success of the Cunard Line's large and fast *Lusitania* and *Mauretania*. The men concurred that speed was not the most important consideration for capturing the immigrant trade which was their main source of income. They instead would create the largest ships to maximize steerage capacity and while Third Class accommodations would be comfortable, to attract wealthy and prosperous travelers, First and Second Class accommodations would be the most luxurious in existence.

Three ships would be built for the Oceanic Steam Navigation Company (White Star Line) by Harland & Wolff under the supervision of Lord William J. Pirrie. Following White Star's propensity to use names that end in "*ic*" for their ships (e.g. *Baltic, Majestic*), the first ship would be called the *Olympic* and the ships would be identified as Olympic-class liners. The second ship would be her sister ship *Titanic*. Construction would occur almost simultaneously and take place at the Harland & Wolff Queen's Island shipyard. The plan called for construction of the third ship, originally named *Gigantic* but later changed to *Britannic,* to start after the *Olympic* was completed.

With J.P. Morgan's full support Bruce Ismay is granted complete control of the ultimate decisions of design, equipment, and decoration during the construction of *Olympic* and *Titanic*. The ships will be built on a cost-plus basis using the best available materials and the best known technology.

In his testimony for the British Wreck Commissioner's Inquiry J. Bruce Ismay described the nature of White Star's ship construction contract with Harland & Wolff.

> **British Wreck Commissioner's Inquiry** – Testimony of J. Bruce Ismay, examined by Attorney General Sir Rufus Isaacs.
>
> 18279. Now, I want you just to tell me about the building of the "Olympic" and the "Titanic," two sister vessels. I am not going to ask you the details of the construction, I am going to keep that for skilled witnesses, and those who have had more to do with it and who know – but generally speaking, first of all, have you any financial interest by way of shareholding or otherwise in the firm of Harland & Wolff?
> Ismay – Absolutely none.
>
> 18280. Or any of those which take an active part in the management of the Oceanic Steam Navigation Company?
> Ismay – I do not quite follow you there. For instance, Lord Pirrie, who is a Director of the Oceanic Steam Navigation Company, is also a Director of Harland & Wolff, but he is the only gentleman that has an interest in both the Company and the shipbuilding yard.
>
> 18281. That is what I thought. Now one other general question with regard to the construction of vessels by Harland & Wolff; are they constructed under contract at a lump sum in the ordinary course, or are they constructed at cost price plus a percentage?
> Ismay – Cost price, plus a percentage. We build no ships by contract at all.
>
> 18282. So that what it amounts to, if I follow you correctly, is, that there is no limit placed by you upon the cost of the vessel?
> Ismay – Absolutely none. All we ask them to do is to produce us the

very finest ship they possibly can; the question of money has never been considered at all.

Designing and Building the Very Finest Ship

Alexander Carlisle, Lord Pirrie's brother-in-law, is the General Manager and Chairman of the Managing Directors at Harland & Wolff. He is also their Chief Naval Architect. Carlisle starts drawing up plans for the *Olympic* and, on September 17, 1908, the Harland & Wolff Directors order both the shipyard and the engine works to begin preparations for construction.

Hull number 400 for the *Olympic* is laid down on December 16, 1908. On March 31, 1909 hull 401 is laid for the *Titanic*. Harland & Wolff is Belfast's largest employer with over 12,000 workers engaging in the construction of the *Olympic* and *Titanic*. The shipyard workers put in 9 hour days on weekdays and half days on Saturday for around $10 a week, the high side of the average pay for the period. The ships are constructed of overlapping steel plates held together with millions of rivets. The plates and rivets are made of the best available steel. Most of the rivets are installed by hydraulic rams but hard to reach areas are riveted by the men using hammers in the traditional method.

After completing the original designs Alexander Carlisle retires from the firm in June, 1910. He is succeeded by Lord Pirrie's nephew, Thomas Andrews, as the Chief Naval Architect and Managing Director of the design department at Harland & Wolff.

Thomas Andrews Jr., born in Comber, Northern Ireland on February 7, 1873, is one of four sons of wealthy mill owners Right Hon. Thomas Andrews and Eliza Pirrie. In 1884 Andrews was accepted into the Royal Belfast Academical Institution, but left school at the age of sixteen and joined his uncle's business as a premium apprentice. He worked his way up through various departments and eventually became a Harland & Wolff managing director in charge of ship design. In 1901 he became a member of the Institution of Naval Architects. On June 24, 1908 he married Helen Reilly Barbour and two years later the couple had a daughter, Elizabeth who is known as Elba.

The family resides on Windsor Avenue, in Belfast but Andrews returns to County Down on weekends to play cricket and sail on Strangford Lough.

As a manager and a boss Thomas Andrews is fair and concerned about his colleagues and workers. He has worked on the *Celtic, Cedric, Baltic,* and *Adriatic* and is ready to take on the *Titanic* when Carlisle retires. The *Titanic* is now Andrew's ship. He will oversee every detail of construction and outfitting and sail on her maiden voyage to America.

The Royal Mail Steamer *Titanic*

When completed the *RMS Titanic* will be the largest movable object ever constructed. It will be longer than the height of the world's tallest building. Estimated to cost $7,500,000 no expense will be spared in making *Titanic* the largest most luxurious liner ever built.

The *Titanic* will be powered by 29 boilers and 159 furnaces that will consume up to 650 tons of coal a day to produce the 50,000 horsepower necessary to drive the 3 screw propellers. She will have a top cruising speed of 24 knots.

White Star Line's *RMS Titanic*

- Length — 882.6 feet
- Beam — 92.6 feet
- Height — 104.0 feet – Keel (bottom) to Bridge
  175.0 feet – Keel to top of Funnels
- Weight — 46,328 tons
- Displaces — 66,000 tons
- 3 Anchors — 31 tons
- Coal capacity — 8,000 tons
- Maximum capacity — 3,547 people

Planned amenities include a gymnasium with the latest exercise equipment, a Squash Racquet Court, Turkish bath, swimming pool, barber shop, and an À la Carte Restaurant.

The *Titanic* plan boasts ten decks. From top to bottom, bow (front) to stern (rear), they are:

The Boat Deck – The Boat Deck is the top deck and features the ship's four massive funnels towering 60 feet above the deck. The first three funnels vent steam from the boiler rooms while the fourth is a non-functioning funnel added to enhance the overall appearance of the massive liner. A portion of the deck is open promenade for First Class passengers and also contains the officer's deckhouse. The Bridge is situated on the forward end of this deck with the middle section enclosed in glass to keep the weather out. The Wheelhouse is directly behind the enclosed section of the Bridge and is also enclosed to protect the compass and master panel for the watertight doors. The Navigation Room is just behind the Wheelhouse on the starboard (right) side followed by the Captain's and Officer's quarters and their own private promenade deck. Continuing back from the Officer's quarters and behind the front funnel on the starboard side are the Marconi rooms consisting of an office, a bedroom, and a silent room for sending and receiving transmissions. Next is the First Class Grand Staircase with its huge glass and wrought iron dome designed to allow natural light to flood the open staircase all the way down to D Deck where it originates. Three elevators from E Deck also reach the Boat Deck as their top stop.

The second funnel is just aft (toward the back of the ship) of the Grand Staircase with the gymnasium located next to the funnel's boiler casing on the port (left) side. The raised roof of the First Class lounge follows. This roof contains a skylight and extends to the boiler casing for the third funnel and the Officer's mess on the port side. Running along both sides of the ship from the private Officer's promenade to the end of the third funnel is the First Class promenade. In good weather rich industrialists, famous authors and artists, and other elite, powerful, or simply the well-to-do that can afford First Class accommodations, will stroll this promenade and no doubt admire the vast ocean they are crossing.

The next deckhouse holds machinery and storage followed by the dome over the aft First Class Grand Staircase. This staircase dome also allows natural light to illuminate the open staircase down to C Deck where it originates. The dome is part of the raised roof level that covers the First Class Smoking Room. On top of this roof is the deckhouse containing the casing and fourth funnel. Surrounding this area is the Second Class promenade which is accessible from B Deck.

The Boat Deck will also hold enough lifeboats to comply with current law but not so many that the deck and promenades will be robbed of space or be inconvenient for First Class passengers.

A Deck – Also called the Promenade Deck, this deck is for First Class passengers and includes a promenade facing the bow overlooking the Well Deck two decks below. This promenade extends back along each side of the ship to the aft end where it overlooks the aft Well Deck. The forward half of both side promenades would later be enclosed with large glass windows after passengers from the *Olympic* complained of water spray from the bow reaching this part of the deck. This will be the only visible difference between the sister ships.

This deck contains one of the magnificent bases of the forward Grand Staircase, as well as First Class staterooms, the First Class Lounge, the Reading and Writing Room, the Library, the aft Grand Staircase, and the First Class Smoking Room. The Verandah Cafe and Palm Court Cafe for First Class passengers are also located on A Deck.

B Deck – The B Deck level includes the Forecastle Deck (small raised deck at the bow), the Bridge Deck, and the Poop Deck (raised deck at the stern). The Forecastle Deck is the top deck at the forward end of the ship running from the bow a short distance to the opening for the Well Deck one level below. The forward mast rises 101 feet from the Forecastle Deck tilting back slightly toward the stern. The top 15 feet of this mast is made of teak wood. The remainder of the mast is built out of steel and includes a 50 foot ladder inside the mast to reach the crow's nest where a pair of Lookout men will scan the ocean ahead for any sign of danger. The four wires that are the Marconi radio antenna stretch from the forward mast to the aft mast 92 feet above the A Deck. After the forward Well Deck opening the Bridge Deck extends back to the aft Well Deck opening. This deck contains the First Class entrance gangways that lead to the spectacular forward Grand Staircase with its candelabra and iron-framed glass dome visible two decks above. This deck also contains First Class cabins and the two Grand Promenade Suites each containing their own bathroom, servant quarters, and a private, enclosed promenade. The Cafe Parisian and First Class À la Carte Restaurant follow the First Class Grand Staircase. After the First Class section is the Second Class entrance, bar, and Smoking Room. The Poop Deck completes the B Deck level in the stern of the ship. This open deck is available to Third Class passengers and contains the Docking Bridge and equipment necessary to dock the ship.

C Deck – The C Deck, also called the Shelter Deck, is the lowest deck with open access to the outside. The forward enclosed portion of the deck contains crew galley and mess, crew hospital, and the gear used to raise and lower the anchor. The open forward Well Deck follows with electric cargo cranes and the hatch cover. This deck also serves as a Third Class promenade. Between the forward and aft Well Decks this deck contains the forward Grand Staircase and First Class cabins as well as cabins for Pursers, Stewardesses, and medical staff. C Deck also includes the Barbershop, Purser's Office, and the saloon for maids, valets, postal workers, and the Marconi Operators. The originating base of the aft First Class Grand Staircase follows, then the Second Class library, and enclosed promenade follow the First Class area. Then comes the aft open Well Deck with its cargo cranes that will also serve as an open-air Third Class promenade. After the aft Well Deck is the Third Class Smoking Room on the port side and on the starboard side the Third Class General Room where nightly celebrations will be held by the steerage passengers lucky enough to be making their way to America's promise aboard the *Titanic*. Completing the C Deck level is a section containing the capstan gear (revolving anchor chain cylinder for raising and lowering an anchor) and the top of the ship's rudder.

D Deck – Known as the Saloon Deck this is the largest deck and contains accommodations for all passenger classes and crew. First Class access to this deck is by way of the Grand Staircase and elevators. D Deck also includes the First Class Dining Saloon, First Class Pantry, First and Second Class galleys, the Second Class Dining Saloon, as well as the bakery and the butcher shop.

E Deck – This deck is called the Upper Deck and has accommodations for the crew and all three passenger classes. This deck contains the originating base of the forward Grand Staircase and can also be accessed using the elevators. E Deck is the highest level that contains some watertight bulkheads. The two forward compartments and the last five contain the bulkheads with watertight doors that are manually operated by the crew. The watertight bulkheads do not extend to this deck level for eight amidship (middle portion of the ship) compartments leaving the middle of the ship wide open at this deck level. This is not considered a problem because the ship will stay afloat with the first four compartments flooded or with any two of the larger amidship compartments flooded.

F Deck – The F or Middle Deck is the lowest level deck that will be completely above the waterline. This deck contains the Third Class Dining Saloon and most of the Third Class accommodations with some Second Class cabins and crew dormitories. F Deck also contains First Class amenities including the Turkish Bath and Saltwater Swimming Pool.

G Deck – Called the Lower Deck this deck is the lowest deck that contains accommodations for passengers and crew. The bow and stern sections of this deck are above the waterline but the amidship sections are below the waterline with compartments five through twelve being vertical continuation of the boiler rooms, coal bunkers, and engine rooms that have their foundation on the ships double hull bottom. The bow end of G Deck contains four compartments that house the chain locker in the first compartment and crew accommodations in the second. The second compartment is also the base for two open spiral staircases used by the crew to access the upper decks. The third compartment is an open bunk area for unaccompanied Third Class male passengers that can only be accessed from the deck above. The fourth compartment back from the bow contains the Post Office and the Squash Racket Court.

Orlop Deck – The Orlop Deck is completely below the waterline and is considered the lowest deck on the ship. Passengers are not allowed on this deck. Like G Deck it has compartments in the bow and stern but the middle compartments are vertical continuations of the watertight bulkheads between the boiler rooms, coal bunkers, and engine rooms. Watertight doors on this level are closed by hand. From the bow back, the forward three compartments contain anchor chain stowage, cargo stowage, and motor vehicle stowage. The Post Office's mail sorting room is located in compartment four. On this deck, and the Tank Top, Coal Trimmers and Firemen will do the hard and dirty work of moving and burning up to 650 tons of coal a day to power the boilers and produce the horsepower necessary to propel the ship.

Tank Top – The Tank Top is not considered a deck but is the top of the ship's double bottom hull. The Tank Top is the foundation for the boilers, coal bunkers, engines, and other equipment. This is the only level with watertight doors that can be closed manually by the crew, automatically with a flotation device, or electronically from the bridge.

The plans call for the *Titanic* to be built with identical dimensions as her Sister ship *Olympic,* but the *Titanic* will have structural additions, and more staterooms and suites, making her heavier than the *Olympic*. Fully fitted, *Titanic* will be the largest, most luxurious ship in the world and no foreseeable ocean-going calamity will sink her.

Chapter 2

Lifeboats for an Unsinkable Ship

Watertight Compartments

Harland & Wolff's Lord Pirrie design the Olympic-class liners to be the safest ships to ever take to the sea. They are built with a cellular double-bottom hull with five feet between the inner and outer steel skins. The hull is subdivided with fifteen transverse bulkheads, creating sixteen compartments from the bow to the stern (Figure 2 - 1). The first two of these vertical bulkheads in the bow and the last six in the stern divide the E Deck reaching the Saloon Deck above. The bulkheads are one deck lower in the middle portion of the ship with those bulkheads dividing the F Deck. The watertight compartments, although extending above the waterline, are still open at the top and are far from being truly "watertight" in the way the name suggests. Extending the bulkheads any higher would compromise passenger space as well as limit crew movement throughout the ship. Large watertight doors are built into each bulkhead so each compartment can be isolated in the event of an emergency. At the lowest level below the waterline the watertight doors can be closed electronically from the bridge. The watertight doors on the other decks are closed manually using a special key. With the watertight doors closed, the ship can stay afloat with the first four compartments flooded or with any two of the larger amidship compartments flooded. Even with more compartments breached White Star believes the ship would survive long enough for the passengers and crew to be rescued.

The transverse bulkheads creating the watertight compartments along with the double bottom hull are the design features that lead to the "unsinkable" designation for the sister ships. The *Olympic* and *Titanic* aren't the first ships to use a transverse bulkhead design or the first to be given the unsinkable tag. The *RMS Adriatic* was the fourth of White Star Line's big four when she entered service in 1907. Stories about her at the time say she "appears almost unsinkable," based on her watertight compartments.

An incident demonstrating the value of watertight compartments was that of White Star's steamship *Suevic*, which ran upon rocks during a gale on the English coast in 1907. The bow was badly crushed but the watertight compartments kept water from flooding the entire vessel. All passengers and crew were rescued by local villagers who spotted the ship's distress rockets. Eventually the *Suevic* was separated into two parts with carefully placed dynamite charges. The watertight bulkhead held and the aft half of the ship was released and floated free. The damaged bow was left on the rocks and the remaining stern half of the vessel proceeded in reverse, under her own steam, to Belfast for repair.

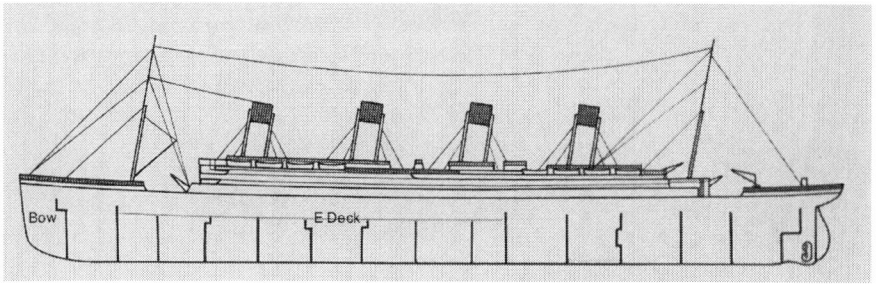

Figure 2 - 1, *Titanic's* hull showing traverse bulkheads

Practically Unsinkable

The unsinkable decree originated in 1910 with White Star Line's own publicity brochure for their sister ships *Olympic* and *Titanic*. The brochure states, "…and as far as it is possible to do so, these two wonderful vessels are designed to be unsinkable." White Star later insisted that the words used in the publicity brochure only point to *Olympic* and *Titanic* being designed to be unsinkable, not that it was claiming they were unsinkable.

It didn't matter. In 1911 articles in the *Irish News*, the *Belfast Morning News*, and *Shipbuilder* magazine contain reports describing the system of watertight compartments and electronic watertight doors. Public opinion concludes that for all practical and foreseeable sea going calamities, the *Titanic* will be "practically unsinkable." Soon enough "practically" is dropped from the general vernacular as the unsinkable myth continues to perpetuate in the public's mind.

"God himself could not sink this ship!" was alleged to have been the answer given by a deck hand when asked if *Titanic* was really unsinkable. The deck hand would be proven cruelly wrong early on the morning of April 15, 1912.

British Board of Trade Regulations

The *Titanic* may be unsinkable but The Merchant Shipping Act 1894 is in effect and must be followed.

> From The Merchant Shipping Act 1894, Section 427, Rules as to life-saving appliances
> (1) The Board of Trade may make rules (in this Act called rules for life-saving appliances) with respect to all or any of the following matters; namely,—
> (a) The arranging of British ships into classes, having regard to the

services in which they are employed, to the nature and duration of the voyage, and to the number of persons carried;

(b) The number and description of the boats, life-boats, life-rafts, life-jackets, and life-buoys to be carried by British ships, according to the class in which they are arranged, and the mode of their construction, also the equipments to be carried by the boats and rafts, and the methods to be provided to get the boats and other life-saving appliances into the water which methods may include oil for use in stormy weather; and

(c) The quantity, quality, and description of buoyant apparatus to be carried on board British ships carrying passengers, either in addition to or in substitution for boats, life-boats, life-rafts, life-jackets, and life-buoys.

(2) All such rules shall be laid before Parliament so soon as may be after they are made, and shall not come into operation until they have lain for forty days before both Houses of Parliament during the session of Parliament; and on coming into operation shall have effect as if enacted in this Act.

(3) Rules under this section shall not apply to any fishing boat for the time being entered in the fishing boat register under Part IV of this Act.

A table specifying requirements relating to life-saving appliances, issued in accordance with section 427 of the 1894 Act, base the requirements for the number of lifeboats on the tonnage of a ship. Ships over 10,000 tons are required to carry 16 lifeboats with a total capacity of 1060 people. At a projected 46,000 tons with a capacity of 3,547 passengers and crew the *Titanic* will need to carry the maximum required – 16 lifeboats.

Welin Quadrant Davits

Several meetings take place between Harland & Wolff and the White Star Line to discuss design details for the *Olympic* and *Titanic*. At one of these meetings Harland & Wolff's Chief Naval Architect, Alexander Carlisle, recommends the use of davits designed to handle four lifeboats. With sixteen davit pairs installed, each ship could carry up to four times the number of lifeboats required by British Board of Trade regulations. His design is approved and the davits will be built by the Welin Quadrant Davit Company.

> **British Wreck Commissioner's Inquiry** – Testimony of Alexander Carlisle, examined by Mr. Butler Aspinall.
> 21267. I will direct your attention to statements in the interview which were suggested and cross-examined to, in the case of one or more of the witnesses who were called. This is the statement: "When working out the designs of the 'Olympic' and the 'Titanic' I put my ideas before

the davit constructors, and got them to design me davits which would allow me to place, if necessary, four lifeboats on each pair of davits, which would have meant a total of over 40 boats. Those davits were fitted in both ships, but though the Board of Trade did not require anything more than the 16 lifeboats, 20 boats were supplied." I will stop there for one moment. The paragraph opens thus: "When working out the designs of the 'Olympic' and the 'Titanic.'" At that time did you occupy a position in the builder's firm?

Carlisle – I was chairman of the managing directors and general manager of the whole works.

21268. At the present moment I think you have retired from business?

Carlisle – I retired on the 30th of June, 1910.

21269. Did you take part in working out the designs of the "Olympic" and the "Titanic"? Deal with the "Titanic."

Carlisle – Yes, they were entirely designed practically by Lord Pirrie. The details, the decorations, the equipments, and general arrangements all came under me.

21270. Did you put your ideas before the davits constructors?

Carlisle – I did.

21271. Who would that be?

Carlisle – Welin's Quadrant Davit Company.

Examined by Mr. Clement Edwards.

21385. You recalled an occasion when you produced that plan at a meeting at which Lord Pirrie was present, and Mr. Sanderson, and Mr. Ismay?

Carlisle – Yes.

…21402. Now do you remember what Mr. Ismay said in regard to this proposal that there should be equipment for this number of boats?

Carlisle – He quite agreed that it would be a good thing to make preparations for supplying the larger number of boats.

21403. (The Commissioner.) Now do be accurate. Do you mean to say that he thought it was desirable that a larger number of boats should be supplied, or that there should be what Mr. Edwards correctly calls an equipment for a larger number of boats? They are two different things.

Carlisle – I take it at that first interview it was merely the davits for carrying four boats.

The Hull Launch

On May 31, 1911 over 100,000 people gather to watch the launch of *Titanic's* hull. J.P. Morgan, Bruce Ismay, Lord and Lady Pirrie, and other dignitaries watch from a grandstand constructed for the occasion. *Titanic* is the largest man-made object ever moved and tons of tallow, soap, and train oil are used to grease the wooden slipway bed to protect the freshly painted hull against the three-tons-per-square-inch pressure. As the launch time nears the workers knock away the posts holding the hull in place, leaving only mechanical triggers holding the *Titanic*. When the foreman signals his men to stand clear they gather and after the count comes up one short, they find James Dobbins with his leg pinned under a collapsed beam. Just past noon, shortly after Dobbins is pulled free, three rockets are fired to warn nearby ships to stay clear of the launch area. *Titanic* is then released to the cheers of the crowd as she eases down the slipway into the River Lagan. The launch takes 62 seconds. James Dobbins takes 24 hours to die of his injuries becoming *Titanic's* seventh construction-related fatality.

Outfitting the *Titanic* will take another 10 months. The use of Welin Quadrant Davits for the lifeboats will allow White Star Line to equip the *Titanic* with up to 64 wooden lifeboats if they choose to, or if the British Board of Trade requires it.

Titanic – A Lifeboat in Herself

Prior to his retirement in 1910, Alexander Carlisle proposes that each of the 16 davit pairs be equipped with 3 standard lifeboats each, resulting in 48 lifeboats for each Olympic-class liner. Carlisle's proposal is not adopted, and ultimately the decision is made to only include slightly more lifeboat capacity than required by outdated British Board of Trade regulations. *Titanic's* 16 davit-mounted wooden lifeboats will include two emergency clippers, designed to hold 40 people each, and 14 standard lifeboats, designed to hold 65 people each. An additional four collapsible canvas-sided boats, with a capacity of 47 people each, are also planned to bring the total lifeboat capacity to 1178 people. The *Titanic* will exceed the minimum lifeboat requirement by ten percent. This is not nearly enough lifeboats for all the passengers and crew but isn't considered a problem for a ship thought to be unsinkable.

> **British Wreck Commissioner's Inquiry** – Testimony of J. Bruce Ismay, examined by Mr. Harbinson.
> 18748. I gather from you, in answer to the Attorney-General, that you yourself gave the instructions for the building of the "Titanic" and the "Olympic"?
> Ismay – Yes.
> 18749. I think to Harland and Wolff?
> Ismay – Yes.
> 18750. These ships constituted a departure as regards magnitude?
> Ismay – They did.
> 18751. Did your company carefully consider this new departure?
> Ismay – Certainly.

18752. And, of course, in considering them you considered the question of the floatability of these ships in cases of accident or emergency?
Ismay – We did.

18753. And also, of course, the accommodation that they would provide for an additional number of passengers?
Ismay – Yes.

18754. Did you give any special consideration to the question of providing additional lifeboat accommodation to cope with the additional number of passengers that you proposed to carry?
Ismay – I do not think any special attention was given to that.

18755. Would not that have been a consideration that should have specially engaged you?
Ismay – I think the position was taken up that the ship was looked upon as practically unsinkable; she was looked upon as being a lifeboat in herself.

18756. That is owing to the transverse bulkheads?
Ismay – No; to the bulkheads and the power of flotation she had in case of accident.

18757. I understand that you considered that either of these steamers would float with two adjacent watertight compartments full?
Ismay – Two of the largest compartments full.

18758. If that were so, and you considered those boats practically as lifeboats themselves and unsinkable, on that theory it was not necessary to carry any lifeboats at all?
Ismay – Yes, because we might have to use them to pick up a crew from another ship.

18759. It was practically for that purpose you carried lifeboats?
Ismay – Or landing, in the case of the ship going ashore.

18760. You did not consider having them for the purpose of saving the crew and passengers carried?
Ismay – No, I do not think so.

Chapter 3

Preparing for the Maiden Voyage

The *Olympic/Hawke* Collision

On September 18, 1911 White Star Line announces that *Titanic* will depart on her maiden voyage on March 20, 1912. Two days later in the English channel the *Olympic*, departing for her fifth trip across the Atlantic, collides with the British warship *HMS Hawke*.

The *Hawke* is conducting routine maneuvers when the two ships come too close together and the *Hawke* is sucked into the side of the *Olympic* by the water surge of the much larger vessel. Being a warship the *Hawke's* bow is filled with concrete in order to ram and sink enemy ships. The resulting collision breaches two of *Olympic's* watertight compartments and her starboard propeller shaft is also damaged. But she does not sink. Reports of *Olympic's* survival after being rammed by a ship designed to ram and sink other vessels further bolsters the belief that Olympic class vessels are indeed unsinkable.

Titanic is forced to give up a propeller shaft and her dry dock for repairs to the *Olympic* but eventually White Star Line chooses a new date for the maiden voyage. The *Titanic*, the world's largest, most luxurious, and safest liner will depart Southampton for New York on April 10, 1912.

Sea Trials

Titanic takes on coal in Belfast in preparation for her sea trials and maiden voyage. After being postponed for a day due to high winds, the sea trials commence on April 2, 1912. Tugs assist *Titanic* through the Victoria Channel to Belfast Lough. All equipment, including the Marconi wireless, is tested. After speed and handling trials, including turning and stop-start maneuvers, running tests commence about 2:00 p.m.. *Titanic* travels about 40 miles, at an average speed of 18 knots, in the open Irish Sea. The sea trials last less than a day and with all tests meeting Board of Trade standards, Francis Carruthers signs the paperwork and notes, "Good for one year from today 2.4.12."

The *Titanic* then completes the 570 mile trip from Belfast to Southampton, her port of embarkation, arriving just after midnight on April 4th. *Titanic* docks at White Star's Berth 44 to begin provisioning and staffing for her maiden voyage.

Provisioning in Southampton

An additional 5892 tons of coal is loaded in Southampton, most of it taken from the *Olympic* and other company ships due to a shortage caused by the just settled coal strike. Cargo arrives and is loaded into holds using cranes and winches with a final count of 11,500 separate pieces weighing 559 tons. The vast array of general cargo includes ostrich feathers, tennis balls, oak beams, straw hats, grandfather clocks, olive oil, and mercury.

April 5th is Good Friday and the *Titanic* is proudly "dressed" displaying her flags and pennants for the first and only time as a salute to the people of Southampton. April 7th is Easter Sunday and no work takes place on the *Titanic*.

With a few days remaining before the voyage Harland & Wolff's Thomas Andrews, the ship's builder, oversees and scrutinizes the final preparations for the maiden voyage. On April 8th enough fresh food to serve 2200 for seven days is loaded and includes 40,000 eggs, 6000 pounds of butter, 200 barrels of flour, 7000 heads of lettuce, 40 tons of potatoes, and 1750 quarts of ice cream. The ship will carry 126,000 pounds of meat, poultry, and fish along with 1500 bottles of wine, 20,000 bottles of beer, and 850 bottles of assorted spirits to, depending on accommodation class, accompany the fine food or wash down the grub. An additional reserve of 17 cases of cognac, 70 cases of wine and 191 cases of liquor are included on the cargo manifest.

The Coalbunker Fire

At some point after coal is loaded in Belfast, or in Southampton, a fire breaks out in coalbunker 10 next to the watertight bulkhead that separates Boiler Room 5 from Boiler Room 6. Once the ship is underway the coal must be used and the bunker emptied to extinguish the fire.

> **British Wreck Commissioner's Inquiry** – Testimony of Lead Fireman Frederick Barrett, examined by Mr. Pringle.
> 2330. You told us there was some fire in that bunker?
> Barrett – Yes.
> 2331. Soon after you left port?
> Barrett – Yes.
> 2332. Is it a very uncommon thing for fire to get into a coal bunker in that way?
> Barrett – It is not an uncommon thing.
> 2333. It happens sometimes?
> Barrett – Yes.
> 2334. I suppose the proper order is to have that actual bunker emptied as soon as possible?
> Barrett – Yes.

2335. And, therefore, that was all right?
Barrett – Yes.

The smoldering fire, although contained in the coalbunker, is nonetheless a concern to be dealt with but not one to be shared with the passengers.

Chapter 4

THE CREW AND STAFF OF THE TITANIC

Over 900 non-passengers are needed aboard the *Titanic* for her maiden voyage. This number includes the Officers and deck crew, the non-sailing White Star crew, and non-White Star contracted staff.

White Star Line recruits the majority of the crew in Southampton. White Star also decides on a last minute Officer substitution bringing in Chief Officer Henry T. Wilde from the *Olympic*. This causes the current Chief Officer and First Officer to each move down a rank and bumps Second Officer David Blair off the ship.

Charles Lightoller later described the situation in his book: *Lightoller – Titanic and Other Ships*.

> "Unfortunately whilst in Southampton, we had a reshuffle amongst the Senior Officers. Owing to the *Olympic* being laid up, the ruling lights of the White Star Line thought it would be a good plan to send the Chief Officer of the *Olympic*, just for the one voyage, as Chief Officer of the *Titanic*, to help, with his experience of her sister ship. This doubtful policy threw both Murdoch and me out of our stride; and, apart from the disappointment of having to step back in our rank, caused quite a little confusion. Murdoch from Chief, took over my duties as First, I stepped back on Blair's toes, as Second, and picked up the many threads of his job, whilst he – luckily for him as it turned out – was left behind. The other officers remained the same. However, a couple of days in Southampton saw each of us settled in our new positions and familiar with our duties."

The Captain and Officers of the *Titanic*

Captain Edward J. Smith – Ship's Master, age 62. Smith is an experienced Master with 38 years at sea. He joined White Star in 1880 gaining his first command in 1887. He became commodore of the White Star fleet in 1904 and it has become routine for Smith to command the newest ships, including the *Adriatic* and the *Olympic*, on their maiden voyages. Smith's quiet splendor is reassuring to the point that some passengers will only make the Atlantic crossing in a ship commanded by him. As a Commander in the Royal Naval Reserve, Smith has the distinction of being able to fly the Blue Duster of the

R.N.R., while most ships fly the merchant marine's Red Duster. Smith's annual salary contains a $200 no-collision bonus clause. Smith is married to Eleanor and they have a young daughter Helen Melville. The family lives in Portswood, Southampton.

Mr. Henry T. Wilde – Chief Officer, age 38. Wilde went to sea as a young apprentice and in due course earned his second mate's certificate and soon thereafter his masters certificate. He joined the White Star Line as a junior officer and served on a number of ships, mainly in the Liverpool to New York, and Australian routes. Wilde was also a Lieutenant in the Royal Naval Reserve. He became Chief Officer of the *Olympic* in 1911 under the command of Captain Edward J. Smith. Wilde may have been expecting to remain as Chief Officer on the *Olympic* under new skipper Captain Herbert James Haddock or may have expected his own command but is instead selected as a last minute addition to the *Titanic* as Chief Officer.

Later, before leaving Queenstown, Chief Officer Wilde shares his misgivings about the new ship in a letter to his sister, "I still don't like this ship…I have a queer feeling about it."

Mr. William T. Murdoch – First Officer, age 39. Murdoch joined the White Star Line after serving on several sailing vessels. He served aboard the *Medic* and the *Runic* on the Australian run and later transferred to the Atlantic steamers *Arabic*, *Adriatic*, *Oceanic*, and *Olympic*. Murdoch transferred from the *Olympic* to be Chief Officer of the *Titanic* but as sailing day approaches he is replaced by Henry T. Wilde and bumped to First Officer.

Mr. Charles H. Lightoller – Second Officer, age 38. Lightoller began his seagoing career at age 13. By the time he was 21, he had already survived a shipwreck, a fire at sea, and a cyclone. After nearly succumbing to malaria Lightoller left the sea for the Klondike Gold Rush in 1898. Unsuccessful as a prospector he was back in England in 1899 and joined the White Star Line in 1900. Lightoller's early years on the Atlantic run were spent mostly on the *Majestic* under the command of Captain Edward J. Smith. Lightoller sailed as *Titanic's* First Officer for the sea trials but he also moves down in rank after Wilde is made Chief Officer.

Mr. David Blair – Second Officer (replaced). Blair sailed on the *Titanic* from Belfast as Second Officer and intended to continue to New York but is considered too senior to be a Third Officer and is bumped off in Southampton by Chief Officer Wilde's appointment. In his rush to leave Blair forgets to leave a key with Charles Lightoller who is replacing him as Second Officer. The key Blair carries away is the key to the locker containing the lookout men's binoculars.

Mr. Herbert "Bert" Pitman – Third Officer, age 34. Pitman joined the Merchant Navy in 1895 at the age of 18. He received nautical training in the navigation department of the Merchant Venturers' Technical College and passed his examination for second mate in 1900, first mate in 1902, and qualified as a master mariner in August 1906. He then joined the White Star Line and served as Fourth, Third, and Second Officer on the *Dolphin*, *Majestic*, and the *Oceanic*. Pitman joined the *Titanic* with the other officers on April 2nd for sea trials in Belfast Lough. Pitman is the only officer who is not in the Royal Naval Reserve.

Mr. Joseph Boxhall – Fourth Officer, age 28. Boxhall is from a family with a strong seafaring tradition; his grandfather had been a mariner, his uncle was a Trinity House buoymaster and Board of Trade official, and his father, Captain Joseph Boxhall, was a respected master with the Wilson Line. Boxhall joined his first ship in 1899 and earned his Second Mate's Certificate in 1903 before joining the Wilson Line. By 1907 he had earned his Master's and Extra-Master's certification and joined the White Star Line in November. While serving aboard the *Oceanic* as Sixth Officer in 1908 he met Charles Lightoller, the only *Titanic* officer he knew prior to joining the ship in Belfast.

Mr. Harold G. Lowe – Fifth Officer, age 29. Lowe ran away from home at the age of 14 to start his seafaring career. After serving along the West African coast for five years he joined White Star only fifteen months prior to joining the *Titanic*. He had served as Third Officer on the *Belgic* and the *Tropic*. *Titanic's* maiden voyage will be Lowe's first trip across the North Atlantic.

Mr. James Moody – Sixth Officer, age 24. Moody graduated from the King Edward VII Nautical School in London and passed his Master's Examination in April 1911. He was transferred from the *Oceanic* and joined the *Titanic* in Belfast. Moody, as Sixth Officer, will earn about $37.00 per month.

The Sailing Crew

The Deck Crew – *Titanic's* Sailing Deck Crew totals 60 and includes:

- An Able Officer with seniority and rank over all the crew except the officers.

- Able Bodied Seamen (ABS) with seniority over other crew members. They see to the day-to-day operation of the ship and are trained to operate the lifeboat davits and man the lifeboats.

- Boatswains are experienced seamen that manage the deck lines, deck cranes, winches, etc. on deck.

- A Master-at-Arms and an assistant who, along with Chief Officer Wilde, possess the only keys to the firearms cabinet.

- Six Quartermasters, who are highly trained seamen, work the bridge, steer the ship, manage signal flags, and stand bridge watch to assist the Duty Officer with general navigation.

- Six Lookouts. These Able Bodied Seamen work in pairs and alternate two hour shifts for an extra five shillings a month.

The Non-Sailing White Star Crew

The *Titanic's* non-Sailing crew totals 767 and includes:

The Guarantee Group – The nine-member guarantee group are considered members of the crew but are assigned passenger accommodations. Headed by the ship's designer, Thomas Andrews, the group is responsible for overseeing any unfinished work and fixing any problems that might arise during the voyage.

The Engineering Crew
- 25 Engineers along with 10 electricians and boilermakers are responsible for keeping the engines, generators, and other mechanical equipment on the *Titanic* running. The highest paid members of the crew, they have the education and technical expertise to operate, maintain, and repair the engineering plant.
- 13 Stoker Foremen direct over 163 firemen (Stokers) who keep a constant supply of coal flowing into Titanic's 159 furnaces servicing her 29 boilers.
- 73 Coal Trimmers manage the coal piles in the coal bunkers and keep the right amount of coal flowing to the Stokers. Coal Trimmers are the lowest paid of the engineering crew with the nastiest working conditions. They endure extreme heat and coal dust while laboring with shovels and wheelbarrows.
- 33 Greasers work the turbine and reciprocating engine rooms alongside the engineers. They are responsible for maintaining and supplying oil and lubricants to all the mechanical equipment.
- Six Mess Hall Stewards man the crew's kitchen to cook for and serve the crew.

The Victualling Crew
- Two Pursers supervise the Victualling Department and are the direct link between passengers and the ship's officers.
- Four Clerks work in the Purser's Office to deal with passenger inquiries and requests.
- Stewards are responsible for no fewer than 57 different functions in each class dining saloon, public rooms, cabins and recreational facilities.
- Stewardesses primarily serve the women passengers. 20 Stewardesses and one matron brings to 21 the number of female crew on *Titanic's* maiden voyage.
- Galley and Kitchen staff including chefs, cooks, bakers, butchers, and scullions (dishwashers) work in the kitchens of each class to provide meals for the passengers.

The Non-White Star Staff

Staff not employed by White Star Line totals 91 and includes:
- Two Wireless Telegraphy Operators, employed by the Marconi Company, send and receive wireless messages for passengers and crew.
- Five Postal Clerks, three American, two British, supervise and process all incoming and outgoing mail on board the ship.
- The Orchestra's eight members are employed by the Liverpool firm of C.W. and F.N. Black, who contract with all of the steamship companies to provide musicians.
- 68 Private Restaurant staff employees operate the First Class À la Carte restaurant located on B Deck.

The night before voyage, April 9th, most of the officers spend the night aboard ship and keep their assigned watch.

Chapter 5

Sailing Day

Southampton, England

On the morning of April 10th Captain Edward J. Smith arrives by taxi at the Southampton docks. He is accompanied by his wife Eleanor and twelve-year-old daughter Helen who routinely see off the Captain on his Southampton departures. After bidding them goodbye Captain Smith finds his Chief Officer to get the sailing report. Henry Wilde had only been assigned Chief Officer the previous day and reported for duty at 6:00 a.m. that morning but he reports what he has learned about the condition of equipment, stores, and the readiness of public areas and staterooms. Later that morning Captain Smith musters the crew for a brief lifeboat drill to satisfy a Board of Trade requirement for their representative Captain Maurice Clarke. The crew lowers starboard lifeboats 11 and 15 into the water, briefly maneuvers them in the water, then returns them to their davits.

In issuing the certificate to permit sailing Captain Clarke signs off that he has witnessed a lifeboat drill and also that *Titanic* has enough coal to reach New York. Due to the recent coal strike *Titanic* will depart with less than half the coal she was designed to carry, barely enough to make New York, and some of that coal is already burning.

> **British Wreck Commissioner's Inquiry** – Testimony of Captain Maurice Clarke, examined by Mr. Clement Edwards.
> 24119. Was there any report made to you about a fire having taken place in the bunker in Section 5?
> Clarke – No.
> 24120. In the ordinary case ought such a report to have been made to you if there was a serious fire before the ship sailed?
> Clarke – Yes, if it was a serious fire it ought to have been reported to me.
> 24121. If it was sufficiently serious for it to be reported—if it was regarded as so serious by the Officer that it ought to be reported to the makers, would it, in your view, be sufficiently serious for a report to be made to you?
> Clarke – Hardly, it is not an uncommon thing to have these small fires

in the bunkers.

After signing off on the Board of Trade paperwork Captain Smith states in the *Master's Report to the Company*:

> "I herewith report this ship loaded and ready for sea. The engines and boilers are in good order for the voyage, and all charts and sailing directions up-to-date.—Your obedient servant, Edward J. Smith"

A total of 2215 passengers, White Star crew, and non-White Star staff will be aboard the *Titanic* when she heads across the North Atlantic for New York after stops in Cherbourg, France and Queenstown, Ireland. Of that total, 1800 crew, staff, and passengers from all classes board *Titanic* at her point of embarkation, Southampton, England. *Titanic* was built to carry passengers to and from America and while the rich travel well, the poor travel with all they own–often in a single suitcase.

Third Class Steerage

Titanic was especially designed to take advantage of the large numbers of immigrants that travel Third Class in steerage. The lower decks of a ship where the steering mechanisms are located is the origin of the term steerage but it eventually came to mean the isolated portion of the ship that carried Third Class immigrants. The steerage section is isolated from the other passenger decks because U.S. immigration law requires it to prevent the spread of lice and communicable diseases to other passenger classes.

While docked for provisioning in Southampton, *Titanic's* mooring cables provide the means for rats, attracted by the food stores, to find their way on board and take up residence in the cargo holds and steerage cabins. Rat guards are eventually placed on the mooring cables to prevent further infestation but steerage passengers will travel with unwelcome company.

Third Class passengers board on the Well Deck near the bow or further aft on C Deck. Prior to boarding they must have their identification cards reviewed and they are checked by a health inspector to ensure they will be allowed into the United States. Many of the immigrants do not speak English and the Third Class Bedroom Stewards are still learning the ship and their duties. With the ensuing chaos and confusion the stewards help their people find the right steerage cabin but finding anything else is left to the steerage passengers.

Single men are shown to their steerage accommodations in the bow end of the ship while single women and families are assigned berths closer to the stern. This arrangement is to discourage mingling of single men and women. The bow and stern steerage berths will be the roughest riding positions during the Atlantic crossing.

The Third Class cabins contain bunk beds to house four or six people many of whom will be complete strangers and may speak different languages. Third Class passengers will share communal bathrooms. Two bathtubs are also available, one for men, the other for women. Mattresses, pillows, electricity, and running water are among the comforts and luxuries the *Titanic* offers steerage passengers during their voyage to America. White Star Line also offers another perk to attract the immigrant trade: At a time when most other lines require steerage passengers to carry their own food, White Star provides three meals a day for Third Class passengers aboard the *Titanic*. Many find their *Titanic* accommodations to be better than what they are leaving, and they are likely better than what they will endure in their first experience in America.

Third Class passengers pay $15 to $40 (about $350 to $900 today) to start their American dream aboard the *Titanic*.

Third Class passengers traveling from Southampton, total 494, including:

Mr. Olaus Jørgensen Abelseth – Abelseth, who had already emigrated to America from Norway in 1902, is returning to Minnesota after an extended visit with his relatives in Norway. Five other Norwegians are travelling with him, Adolf Humblen, Anna Salkjelsvik, his cousin Peter Søholt, Sigurd Hansen Moen (married to Olaus' sister) and Karen Marie Abelseth (not related). Karen is the daughter of one of Olaus' neighbors from the time he lived in Norway. She is only 16 and Olaus is looking after her on the trip to America.

Olaus and Adolf will share cabin G-63, near the bow on F-Deck, with other Third Class male passengers. Søholt and Moen will be in cabin G-73. Karen and Anna will share accommodations with other single women near the stern.

Second Class

With little of the chaos being experienced by the steerage class, Second Class passengers board at their entrance on C Deck. Second Class consists of businessmen, vacationers, middle-class families, and others with a reason to go, or return, to America. Unlike Third Class where the price of a ticket to America may be a person's life savings, Second Class passengers have the means to travel but choose not to pay, or can't afford, the additional cost of First Class luxuries. A Second Class ticket costs about $60 ($1375 in today's dollars). This provides a cabin that sleeps two or four with built in berths, each with their own privacy curtain. Each cabin has a washbasin and chamber pot for the seasick. Second Class passengers also share communal bathrooms but, compared with Third Class, significantly fewer passengers share a bathroom.

A total of 241 Second Class passengers board in Southampton including:

Mr. Lawrence Beesley – Beesley, 34, was born in Wirksworth, Derbyshire on December 31, 1877. Beesley was educated at Derby School and at Caius College in Cambridge. After teaching Grammar School for two years he moved to Dulwich College as a science master. He resigned his position to go for a holiday in the States, and visit his brother in Toronto. Beesley, a widower, leaves his young son behind when he boards the *Titanic* with a Second Class ticket. He will occupy cabin D-56.

Mr. Charles Eugene Williams – Williams, 23, from Harrow, England, isn't notable for his wealth or class stature. He is bound for New York where he will defend his squash racquet world title against American champion G. Standing for a $5,000 purse.

Mr. Masabumi Hosono – Hosono, 41, a Civil Servant for the Japanese Ministry of Transport, is returning to his home in Tokyo after a two year assignment in Siberia studying the Russian state railway system. He has a wife and four children and his family is from a long line of Samurai Warriors. Hosono stopped over in London to visit a friend who had happened to book Second Class passage on the *Titanic*. When his friend had to cancel at the last minute Hosono bought his ticket, making him the only person of Japanese descent that will sail aboard the *Titanic*.

Mr. Edgar Samuel Andrew – Andrew, 17, is returning to New York to attend his brother's wedding. He was initially booked to travel aboard the *Oceanic* but due to the coal strike he was forced to change his plans. His frustration is apparent in a letter he sent to his friend, Josey Cowan, on April 8, 1912.

> You figure Josey I had to leave on the 17th this (month) aboard the 'Oceanic', but due to the coal strike that steamer cannot depart, so I have to go one week earlier on board the 'Titanic'. It really seems unbelievable that I have to leave a few days before your arrival, but there's no help for it, I've got to go. You figure, Josey, I am boarding the greatest steamship in the world, but I don't really feel proud of it at all, right now I wish the 'Titanic' were lying at the bottom of the ocean.

First Class

The rich, the famous, captains of industry and politics, well known authors, artists, and entertainers booked passage aboard *Titanic* for her maiden voyage. They paid from $150 ($3500 in today's dollars) for a cabin on a lower deck, up to $2500 ($58,000 today) for a larger suite in a more desirable location. All First Class accommodations are equipped with heaters, telephones, and call bells for summoning their steward. One of the two luxury Parlor Suites with wardrobe rooms, private baths, and a private promenade was reserved for J.P. Morgan, owner of White Star's parent company International Mercantile Marine. The other was booked for $4,350 (about $100,000 in today's dollars). When they purchased their First Class tickets passengers received a White Star Line map of the *Titanic* prepared exclusively for First Class. The 5 X 10 inch folded map's cover includes these details:

Southampton – Cherbourg – New York Service
(Via Queenstown Westbound, and via Plymouth Eastbound)
R.M.S. "TITANIC"
(Combination of Turbine and Reciprocating Engines)
TRIPLE SCREW . . 45,000 Tons
Length 882.6 – Breadth 92.6
ONE OF TWO LARGEST STEAMERS IN THE WORLD
Plan of First Class Accommodations

The unfolded map measures 40 X 30 inches and reveals the location of all First Class accommodations on decks A, B, C, D, and E along with the location of amenities including First Class Smoking Room, Lounge, Gymnasium, Restaurant, and Staircases. It also details many of *Titanic's* First Class facilities:

> Restaurant. – In addition to the regular Dining Saloon there is a large modern à la carte restaurant, on Deck B, where meals may be obtained at any time between 8:00 a.m. and 11:00 p.m. at fixed charges… The Restaurant is under the management of the Company, who have appointed Mr. L. Gatti, late of Oddenino's Imperial Restaurant, London as manager.
>
> Turkish, Electric, and Swimming Baths. – A fully-equipped Turkish Bath is situated on Deck F, consisting of the usual steam, hot temperature, shampooing, and cooling room…
>
> A Gymnasium, fully supplied with modern appliances, is situated on the Boat Deck, and is open for exercise by Ladies and Gentlemen during the same hours as the Baths…
>
> A Squash Racket Court is provided on Deck F, and is in charge of a professional player.
>
> A Verandah Cafe and Palm Court are situated on Deck A, where light refreshments are served.

First Class passengers board the *Titanic* at the First Class main entrance on B Deck and are immediately treated to *Titanic's* Grand Staircase with its massive overhead dome and chandelier. They are met by First Class Stewards with a flower for each man's buttonhole. Some carry their First Class maps aboard but they aren't immediately needed as First Class passengers are escorted by Stewards to their cabins. All the First Class accommodations are located on five decks amidship where the ship's motion and resulting seasickness are less likely to be a concern. Notable among the 178 First Class passengers embarking from Southampton are:

Mr. Joseph Bruce Ismay – J. Bruce Ismay is the President and Managing Director of International Mercantile Marine, the company that owns White Star Line and the *Titanic*. He usually accompanies his ships on their maiden voyages and the *Titanic* is no exception. Traveling as a First Class passenger Ismay boards at 9:30 a.m. with his wife and three children who are not accompanying him on the voyage but enjoy a tour of the magnificent vessel. Ismay's valet, Richard Fry and his secretary, William Henry Harrison accompany him and also travel First Class. Ismay will occupy luxury Parlor Suite B-52. The suite, with its own private promenade, is available due to J.P. Morgan canceling his plans to return to New York on *Titanic's* maiden voyage. Fry and Harrison will occupy the adjoining cabins B-54 and B-56.

The Countess of Rothes – Lucy Noël Martha Dyer-Edwards is Scotland's Countess of Rothes. She was born in Kensington, London on Christmas day 1878. She married the 19th Earl of Rothes, Norman Evelyn Leslie on April 19,

1900. The Earl and Countess have two sons.

The Countess is traveling to Vancouver, BC, Canada with her cousin Gladys Cherry, and her maid Roberta Maioni. The Countess and Miss Cherry will occupy cabin B-77 and Miss Maioni B-79.

Colonel Archibald Gracie – Archibald Gracie IV, 54, was born January 17, 1859, in Mobile, Alabama. His father, Brigadier General Archibald Gracie Jr. served with the Confederate forces and fought through the Battle of Chickamauga, one of the bloodiest battles of the American Civil War. On December 2, 1864, General Gracie was killed while observing Union Army movements at the siege of Petersburg, Virginia.

Archibald Gracie IV, although only five years old when his father died, spent seven years writing the book, "The Truth About Chickamauga." Following the book's publication in 1912, Colonel Gracie took a trip to Europe to relax, leaving his wife and daughter at home. He travelled to Europe on the *Oceanic* and made friends with one of the ship's officers, Herbert Pitman, who will serve as *Titanic's* Third Officer. Gracie booked return passage on the *Titanic* and will occupy cabin C-51.

Major Archibald Willingham Butt – Archibald "Archie" Butt, 46, was born on September 26, 1865 to a prominent Georgia family. He graduated from Tennessee's University of the South in 1888 and began a career in journalism. He later became secretary of the Mexican Embassy but left Mexico in 1898 to join the army during the Spanish-American War. Butt decided to stay in the military and served in the Philippines, then Cuba, before becoming military aide to President Theodore Roosevelt in 1908. Currently a trusted military aide to President William Howard Taft, Butt's health began to deteriorate in 1912. Needing rest, he took leave from the White House and sailed for Europe with his close friend artist Francis Millet, who was en-route to Rome on business. Millet and Major Butt stayed in the seventeenth century villa that went with Millet's job as director of the new American Academy of Art. After Millet's wife Lily arrived, the Major left to visit the German and French embassies and then traveled to England to visit his brother. Both Millet and the Major are returning to Washington on the *Titanic* although Millet will board in Cherbourg, France. Major Butt is in full uniform to begin the maiden voyage. He will occupy cabin B-38.

Mr. Clarence Bloomfield Moore – Moore, 47, lives in Washington D.C. with his wife Mabelle and their five children. Moore is a member of the brokerage firm of W. B. Hibbs and Company of Washington. He also owns a farm in Montgomery County, Maryland, where he raises cattle and horses, and has real estate investments near Leesburg, Virginia. Moore is returning from England after purchasing 50 pairs of hounds for the newly formed Rock Creek Hunt Club. He is looking forward to sharing time with friends and fellow travelers, Major Butt and Frank Millet, also heading home to Washington. The fox hounds are not returning with Moore on the *Titanic* when he boards at Southampton. Moore's manservant Charles Harrington does accompany him.

Major Arthur Godfrey Peuchen – Peuchen, 52, was born in Montreal, Quebec, on April 18, 1859. He moved to Toronto in 1871 where he enlisted in the Queen's Own Rifles and attained the ranks of Lieutenant in 1888, Captain in 1894, and Major in 1904. In 1893 Arthur Peuchen married Margaret Thompson and together they had a son and a daughter. Peuchen was, for a time, Vice-Commodore of the Royal Canadian Yacht Club in Toronto. Peuchen is the president of the Standard Chemical Company and, with company refineries in England, France, and Germany, he is often abroad. This crossing on the *Titanic* is his fortieth transatlantic voyage. The only misgiving he has about sailing on the *Titanic* is Captain Smith— "Surely not that man!" Peuchen complains upon learning Smith is the captain. He believes Smith is too old for the job and is also aware of Smith's recent experience as master of the *Olympic*. Major Peuchen will occupy cabin C-104.

Mr. and Mrs. Isidor Straus – Isidor Straus, 67, was born in Rhenish Bavaria on February 6, 1845. He emigrated with his family to the United States in 1854, settling in the town of Talbotton, Georgia. In 1871, Isidor Straus married Rosalie Ida Blun. They are parents to seven children. He served as a U.S. Congressman for New York State between 1895 and 1897 as a Democrat. In 1896 the Straus brothers gained full ownership of R. H. Macy & Co. Mr. and Mrs. Straus are inseparable, writing to each other every day when they are apart.

Early in April 1912 Isidor and his wife Ida along with their daughter Beatrice travelled to Europe on the German Liner *Amerika*. They prefer to travel by German steamer wherever possible but for their return passage Mr. and Mrs. Straus, minus Beatrice, choose the *Titanic*. They will travel First Class and board at Southampton. Travelling with them are Isidor's manservant John Farthing and Ida's newly employed maid Ms. Ellen Bird. Their party will occupy cabins C-55-57.

Mr. William Thomas Stead – Stead, 62, of Cambridge House, Wimbledon Park, London SW is a well known journalist, author, spiritualist, psychic researcher, and peace activist. He and his wife Lucy have six children. Controversial and influential Stead, through a series of articles entitled *The Truth about the Navy*, in 1885, forced the government to supply an extra £3,500,000 to bolster weakening naval defenses. Stead also published the controversial *The Maiden Tribute of Modern Babylon* in 1885 to expose criminal vice and child prostitution resulting in the resurrection of the dormant *Criminal Law Amendment Act* which raised the age of consent from twelve to sixteen. In 1886 Stead published an article that unfortunately did not move the government to act. In the fictional story entitled *How the Mail Steamer Went Down in Mid-Atlantic, by a Survivor* an unnamed steamer collides with another ship and there is a large loss of life due to a shortage of lifeboats. Stead wrote, "This is exactly what might take place and will take place if liners are sent to sea short of boats." In 1892 Stead published another fictional story entitled *From the Old World to the New*. In this story the White Star Line's *Majestic* carries a clairvoyant who senses a disaster when another ship collides with an iceberg. Stead's story has a happy ending when the *Majestic*, mastered by Captain Edward J. Smith, manages to avoid the ice and rescue the survivors. Stead created and edited a periodical called *Borderland* between 1893 and 1897. The quarterly was devoted to spiritualism and Stead's interest in psychic research.

Stead's reputation began to suffer to some extent due to his increasing pacifism at a time when the government was trying to rally support for the war in South Africa. After visiting the Tsar of Russia in 1898 Stead founded the weekly *War against War*. In opposition to the war in the Transvaal he wrote "Shall I Slay my Brother the Boer" and preached "peace through arbitration." Stead's outspoken devotion and journalistic crusade for world peace resulted in his nomination for the 1903 Nobel Peace Prize.

William Stead is convinced that communication with the other side, the so-called dead in the spirit world, is possible and that he indeed receives messages and is able to produce automatic writing. Stead claims to be in contact with Julia Ames, an American journalist who died in December 1891. He founded *Julia's Bureau* in 1909, at the request of Julia and others that had passed over, in order to facilitate communication between our world and theirs. His outspoken belief, work and publications, including *How I Know That the Dead Return* published in 1911, no doubt also tarnish his reputation among those unwilling to consider his theories and evidence.

William Stead is traveling to America to participate in a peace congress at Carnegie Hall at the request of President William Howard Taft. In the days leading up to *Titanic's* maiden voyage Stead writes this letter to the editor of *The American Review of Reviews*:

> The general feeling of unrest which is surging over the world just now is profoundly disquieting many minds, although it is raising high hopes in others. Mrs. Besant, with whom I am lunching to-day, is very confident that the signs of the times foreshadow the second coming of the Divine incarnation; while in the other camp there is a general conviction that the end of all things is near at hand. It is a mighty interesting time to live in, although somewhat trying to one's nerves. We have got enough coal in our house to last another ten days, and then we are done. If things settle down into something like decent order here, I think I shall start for New York on the *Titanic*, which sails, if it can get coal enough, on April 10. It will be her first voyage, and the sea trip will do me good, and I shall have a chance of seeing you all for a few days. I should not remain more than a week in America.

Stead will travel First Class on the *Titanic* and occupy cabin C-87.

Mr. and Mrs. William Ernest Carter – William Carter along with his wife Lucile, both 36, and their children Lucile and William are residents of Bryn Mawr, Pennsylvania. William Carter is from the well-known family that made their wealth in Pennsylvania coal. Lucile (Polk) Carter of Baltimore is a direct descendant of President James K. Polk. The Carters are returning home after several months in England's Melton Mowbray district where William joined hunts and played polo. They board the *Titanic* as First Class passengers and will occupy cabins B-96 and 98.

Travelling with the Carters are Mrs. Carter's maid Auguste Serreplan, Mr. Carter's manservant Alexander Cairns, and their two dogs. Carter's 25 horsepower Renault automobile will be stowed in the cargo hold and his chauffeur, Charles Aldworthand, will travel Second Class.

Mr. and Mrs. Charles M. Hays – Charles Hays, 55, was born in Rock Island, Illinois, on May 16, 1856. He was educated at the Rock Island public schools then, at age 17, went to work for the Atlantic and Pacific Railway. He was appointed general manager of the Wabash Railway network in 1889 and moved to Montreal to become general manager of the Grand Trunk Pacific Railway in 1896. Hayes and his wife Clara (Gregg) have four daughters.

The Grand Trunk railroad is 100-million in debt when Hays arrives in England for a directors meeting. His proposals include upgrading rolling stock, double tracking, and building a chain of luxury hotels across Canada. While in England Hayes receives news that his daughter, Louise, is having a difficult pregnancy and might have to deliver by cesarean section.

Hays' business dealings included discussions with White Star Line about a European line to the Orient using White Star ships and his transcontinental railroad. This led Bruce Ismay to invite Hays and his party to travel for their return trip, as his guests, aboard the *Titanic*. The Hays party will occupy four cabins with Mr. and Mrs. Hays in B-69, daughter and son-in-law Orian and Thornton Davidson in B-71, their maid Miss Perreault in B-73, and Hays secretary, Vivian Payne, in B-24.

Mr. and Mrs. Jacques H. Futrelle – Jacques Futrelle, 37, was born April 9, 1875 in Pike County, Georgia. He attended the Pike County public schools and was also mentored by his father in basic academics and French.

Futrelle began his career at the age of 18 when he took a job with the *Atlanta Journal*. He would also work for the *Boston Post*, the *New York Herald*, and the *Boston American*. He began a series of stories centered around a detective character he created who would eventually appear in over forty stories. Jacques became a well known novelist by the early 20th century – his best known works being: *The Thinking Machine*, *The Thinking Machine On The Case*, *The Diamond Master*, and *The High Hand*.

Jacques and his wife May (Peel) have two children, John and Virginia. May has also authored several novels and magazine articles. The couple were in Europe while Jacques worked a series of magazine articles. Jacques Futrelle celebrated his 37th birthday the previous night. The Futrells will occupy cabin C-123.

Southampton Departure Near-Miss

The *Titanic* departs from Southampton at Noon but not without a near-miss with the docked passenger ship *New York*. The water surge from *Titanic's* propeller causes the laid-up *New York* to bob up and down, breaking her mooring lines. The *New York's* stern swings out and is drawn toward the passing *Titanic*. Captain Smith quickly orders, "Full Astern!" to stop *Titanic's* forward motion. The resulting backwash forces the *New York* away from the *Titanic*. At the same time the tug *Vulcan* is able to attach ropes on the stern of the *New York* to help hold her in place. A collision is avoided by only about four feet. This ominous beginning to the maiden voyage delays *Titanic* by a little more than an hour. Shortly after she is again underway *Titanic* passes the spot where the *Hawke* collided with the *Olympic* in 1911, under similar circumstances, while the *Olympic* was under the command of Captain Smith.

Chief Engineer Joseph Bell described their near-miss in a letter to his son Frank. Written on board the *Titanic* the letter is posted at Queenstown on Thursday April 11, 1912.

> Dear Frank,
> I hope that you got to Belfast all right and started work on time, I got your wire from Liverpool.
> We have made a good run from Southampton everything working A1, we nearly had a collision with the *New York* and *Oceanic* when leaving Soton, the wash of our propellers made the two ships range about when we were passing them, this made their mooring ropes break and the *New York* set off across the river until the tugs got hold of her again, no damage was done but it looked like trouble at the time. Keep well and be a good lad.
> Regards to Mrs. Johnston, Your loving father. J. Bell.

Cherbourg, France

After leaving Southampton with 929 passengers and 897 staff and crew, the *Titanic* sails to Cherbourg, France and anchors in Cherbourg harbor. The Cherbourg docks aren't large enough to accommodate the massive liner so the passengers are ferried out to the *Titanic*. A total of 142 First Class and 30 Second Class passengers are transported on the tender *Nomadic* while 102 Third Class steerage passengers ride with the mail on the *Traffic*.

First Class

Notable among First Class passengers embarking from Cherbourg are:

Sir Cosmo Edmund Duff-Gordon and Lady Lucile Wallace Sutherland Duff-Gordon – Sir Cosmo Edmund Duff-Gordon, 49, was born on July 22, 1862 the son of Cosmo Lewis Duff-Gordon. Cosmo Duff-Gordon was educated at Eton and in 1896 he became the fifth Baron of his family estate. Cosmo Duff-Gordon is a proficient fencer and represented Great Britain at the 1908 Olympics.

Lady Duff-Gordon (Lucy Christiana Sutherland), 48, was born on June 13, 1863 the daughter of Douglas Sutherland, a Toronto engineer. She married at age 18 and had a child but divorced in 1888. To support herself she started a dressmaking business that grew to become one of the great couture houses of London under the name "The Maison Lucile." Lucy took on Sir Cosmo Duff-Gordon as a business partner and in 1900 they were married.

Accompanying the Duff-Gordons is Lady Duff-Gordon's maid, Laura Mabel Francatelli. Lady Duff-Gordon will occupy cabin A-20 and Ms Francatelli cabin E-36. Sir Cosmo will occupy cabin A-16. The Duff-Gordons choose to travel incognito and register as Mr. and Mrs. Morgan.

Colonel and Mrs. John Jacob Astor IV – John Jacob Astor IV was born in Rhinebeck, New York on July 13, 1864, the son of William Astor and great-grandson of fur-trader John Jacob Astor. Colonel Astor is Harvard educated and after spending a few years abroad, returned to manage the family's fortune. In 1897 Astor built the Astoria Hotel adjoining the Waldorf, built by his cousin, in New York City. The new complex became known as the Waldorf-Astoria. Astor later added two other hotels to his real-estate holdings, the Hotel St. Regis in 1905 and the Knickerbocker in 1906.

Astor was a Colonel, staffed to General Levi P. Morton and later, during the Spanish-American War in 1898, was commissioned as a lieutenant colonel in the U.S. volunteers. In 1909, after a nineteen-year marriage that produced a son and daughter, Astor divorced his wife, Ava. Two years later he married eighteen-year-old Madeleine Force who was a year younger than his son. To get out of the public spotlight and let the gossip die down the newlyweds decided to winter overseas. They travelled to Egypt and Paris before deciding to return to America as First Class passengers on *Titanic's* maiden voyage.

Also boarding at Cherbourg with Colonel and Mrs. Astor are Colonel Astor's manservant Mr. Victor Robbins, Mrs. Astor's maid Miss Rosalie Bidois, and her private nurse Miss Caroline Louise Endres, and their pet Airedale Kitty. The Astor party will occupy cabins C-62-64.

Mrs. Charlotte Drake Cardeza – Charlotte Drake, 58, was born to Thomas and Matilda Drake on April 10, 1854. Thomas Drake was a British textile manufacturer. She married James Warburton Martinez Cardeza in 1874 and divorced him in 1900. The couple had one child, Thomas Drake Martinez Cardeza, in 1876. Charlotte and her son are returning to their home in Germantown, Pennsylvania after a safari in Africa and a visit to Thomas' hunting reserve in Hungary. The Cardeza's baggage includes fourteen trunks, four suitcases and three crates of clothes and other valuables.

Accompanying Charlotte Cardeza and her son Thomas are her maid Anna Ward and his manservant Gustave Lesueur. The Cardeza party boards at Cherbourg and will occupy suite B-51-53-55, one of the two expensive and luxurious Parlor Suites on the *Titanic* (Bruce Ismay has the other).

Mrs. Margaret Brown – Margaret (Tobin) Brown was born in Hannibal, Missouri on July 18, 1867 to parents that were Irish immigrants. She grew up near the Mississippi River and worked stripping tobacco leaves as a teenager. She married James Joseph "J.J." Brown, a miner whose parents had also immigrated from Ireland, in 1886. The Browns had two children, Catherine Ellen (Helen) and Lawrence. J.J. Brown made his fortune in mining after devising a way to mine previously unreachable gold. He would go on to become one of the most successful mining men in the country. After 23 years of marriage, Margaret and J.J. separated in 1909. That same year Margaret Brown ran for the Colorado State Senate eight years before women had the right to vote. Margaret's cash settlement and monthly allowance following her separation from J.J. allows her to maintain her travels and lifestyle. Margaret and her daughter Helen, who is a student at the Sorbonne, had been traveling throughout Europe and had joined Colonel Astor's party touring North Africa and Egypt. When Margaret receives word that her first grandchild is ill she immediately books passage home on the *Titanic*, the first available ship, while Helen decides to stay behind in London. Because of her quick decision to return home most of her family and friends have no idea Margaret Brown is traveling aboard the *Titanic*.

Mr. James Clinch Smith – Smith, 56, is a descendant of the legendary Richard "Bull Rider" Smith, founder of Smithtown, Long Island, New York. Born on April 3, 1856, Clinch Smith, one of eleven children, grew up in Smithtown. He graduated from Columbia University Law School in 1878 and practiced in New York City. Smith, a popular figure in New York society, is a member of many of New York's most elite clubs. In 1895 he married Bertha Ludington Barnes of Chicago, an accomplished musician and composer. In 1904 they moved to Paris, where Bertha pursued her musical career and received much attention for organizing an orchestra consisting of only women. Although he spends most of his time in Paris, Smith returns to America at least once every year. Bertha had planned to travel home with her husband on this trip but at the last minute it was decided that he would go back alone to prepare the homestead for her return in a few months. One of Smith's oldest friends, Colonel Archibald Gracie, is also on the voyage having boarded in Southampton. Clinch Smith is traveling First Class and will occupy cabin A-7.

Mr. Francis Davis Millet – Millet, 65, was born in Mattapoisett, Massachusetts on November 3, 1846. Following a Harvard education he became a reporter, then city editor, of the *Boston Courier*. He then turned his lithography hobby into his life's work. Winning instant acclaim at the Royal Academy of Fine Arts at Antwerp, Belgium. Millet represented several American and English newspapers during the Russian-Turkish War and later published accounts of his travels. His work as a decorative artist can be seen at the Baltimore Customs House, Trinity Church of Boston, and the Capitol Buildings of Wisconsin and Minnesota. His paintings are located in New York City's Metropolitan Museum and the Tate Gallery in London. In 1893 Millet, serving as superintendent of decoration, created the White City for the World's Columbian Exhibition in Chicago.

Frank Millet is returning to Washington after spending a month in Rome carrying out his duties as director of the new American Academy of Art. Millet and his wife Lily spent two days in Paris before she left for the family home in the village of Broadway in Worcestershire and he left for Cherbourg to board the *Titanic*. Millet is joining friend and traveling companion Major Archibald Butt who boarded in Southampton. Frank Millet will occupy First Class cabin E-38.

After boarding Millet fondly describes *Titanic's* size and luxurious appointments in a letter to an old friend, but isn't flattering in his description of fellow travelers.

On board R.M.S. Titanic April 11, 1912.

Dear Alfred

I got yours this morning and was glad to hear from you. I thought I told you my ship was the Titanic. She has everything but taxicabs and theatres. Table d' hote, restaurant à la carte, gymnasium, Turkish baths, squash court, palm gardens, smoking rooms for "Ladies and Gents," intended I fancy to keep the women out of the men's smoking room which they infest in the German and French steamers. The fittings are in the order of Haddon Hall and are exceedingly agreeable in design and color. As for the rooms they are larger than the ordinary hotel room and much more luxurious with wooden bedsteads, dressing tables, hot and cold water, etc., etc., electric fans, electric heater and all. The suites with their damask hangings and mahogany oak furniture are really very sumptuous and tasteful. I have the best room I have ever had in a ship and it isn't one of the best either, a great long corridor in which to hang my clothes and a square window as big as the one in the studio alongside the large light. No end of furniture, cupboards, wardrobe, dressing table, couch, etc., etc. Not a bit like going to sea. You can have no idea of the spaciousness of this ship and the extent and size of the decks. The boat deck has an uninterrupted space as long as our tennis court almost, and the chair decks are nearly as wide as our large courtyard, or quite. 500 people don't make a show on the decks.

Queer lot of people on the ship. Looking over the list I only find three or four people I know but there are a good many of "our people" I think and a number of obnoxious ostentatious American women, the scourge of any place they infest and worse on shipboard than anywhere. Many of them carry tiny dogs and lead husbands around like pet lambs. I tell you the American woman is a buster. She should be put in a harem and kept there…

Miss Dorothy Gibson – Dorothy Gibson, 22, was born Dorothy Winifred Brown in Hoboken, New Jersey. Her father died when Dorothy was a child and her mother married John Leonard Gibson. Dorothy married in 1910 but separated a short time later and eventually divorced.

Gibson sang and danced in a number of Broadway musicals between 1907 and 1911 and in 1909 started modeling for illustrator Harrison Fisher. She soon became one of his favorite models with her image appearing on magazine covers, postcards, and various other merchandise.

Dorothy Gibson got her break in motion pictures when she was hired as a leading lady for the American branch of the French company Éclair. She portrayed Revolutionary War heroine Molly Pitcher in the historical pageant, *Hands Across the Sea* in 1911. Other films followed including a romantic comedy titled, *The Easter Bonnet*.

In March 1912 Dorothy decided it was time for a vacation and sailed for Europe with her mother. A few weeks later Dorothy's producer, Jules Brulatour, sent a wire asking her to return to start work on a new film. Dorothy, who is having an affair with Brulatour, booked First Class passage back to New York for herself and her mother.

Miss Edith Russell – Edith Louise Rosenbaum, 33, is a journalist better known as Edith Russell. She is returning to the states after covering French fashion at Paris' Easter Sunday races. Edith attempts to purchase insurance on her luggage and belongings but is told insurance is not necessary for an unsinkable ship. She boards the *Titanic* as a First Class passenger at Cherbourg.

Edith writes this letter, posted from Queenstown, to her secretary back in Paris.

> My Dear Mr Shaw:
>
> This is the most wonderful boat you can think of. In length it would reach from the corner of the Rue de la Paix to about the Rue de Rivoli.
>
> Everything imaginable: swimming pool, Turkish bath, gymnasium, squash courts, cafes, tea gardens, smoking rooms, a lounge bigger than the Grand Hotel Lounge; huge drawing rooms, and bed rooms larger than in the average Paris hotel. It is a monster, and I can't say I like it, as I feel as if I were in a big hotel, instead of on a cozy ship; everyone is so stiff and formal. There are hundreds of help, bell boys, stewards, stewardesses and lifts. To say that it is wonderful, is unquestionable, but not the cozy ship-board feeling of former years. We are now off Queenstown. I just hate to leave Paris and will be jolly glad to get back again. Am going to take my very much needed rest on this trip, but I cannot get over my feeling of depression and premonition of trouble. How I wish it were over!
>
> Yours sincerely, Edith

Mr. Karl Howell Behr – Karl Behr, 26, was born May 30, 1885, in Brooklyn, New York. A Yale educated lawyer, Behr is also a well known lawn tennis star who played on the United States Davis Cup team in 1907. Behr and partner Beals C. Wright took runner up honors in the 1907 Wimbledon men's doubles championship.

Behr is pursuing a courtship of Miss Helen Monypeny Newsom, 19, who has been touring Europe with her mother and stepfather, Mr. and Mrs. Beckwith. The trip to Europe was Mrs. Beckwith's idea to separate the couple and discourage Mr. Behr's pursuit. In response Behr invented the need for a business trip to Europe. He then booked return passage on the same ship as the object of his desire, hoping a romance is in store for the maiden's voyage.

Karl Behr will occupy First Class cabin C-148. Helen Monypeny Newsom is booked in cabin D-47. Mr. and Mrs. Beckwith will occupy cabin D-35.

Mr. Charles D. Williams and Richard Norris Williams II – R. Norris Williams, 21, was born in Geneva, Switzerland on January 29, 1891. He is travelling First Class with his father, Charles, from Geneva to the family's home in Radnor, PA. The elder Williams, a great-great-grandson of Benjamin Franklin, had practiced law in Philadelphia before moving to Geneva with his wife in 1888. The younger Williams is an accomplished tennis player winning championships in France and Switzerland and plans to take part in American tournaments before going on to study at Harvard.

Mr. Benjamin Guggenheim – Benjamin Guggenheim, 46, lives in New York, NY with his wife Floretta (Seligman) and their three daughters. He acquired his wealth by adding the smelting business to the Guggenheim family mining interests in the latter half of the 1880s. Currently president of the International Steam Pump Company with offices in London and Paris, Guggenheim is returning home from a three month business trip. Guggenheim and his valet, Mr. Victor Giglio, board the *Titanic* at Cherbourg, France and will occupy First Class cabin B-84. His chauffeur, Mr. René Pernot, will travel Second Class.

Also boarding from the French port is Guggenheim's French mistress.

Mme. Léontine Pauline Aubart – Madame Aubart, 24, is known as "Ninette" and is a singer from Paris, France. She is also the mistress of millionaire Benjamin Guggenheim who is traveling home to New York. She boards *Titanic* with her maid Emma Sägesser and is ticketed to occupy First Class cabin B-35.

Mr. and Mrs. George Dunton Widener – George Widener, 50, is from Elkins Park, Pennsylvania. He is the son of P.A.B. Widener who is a member of the board of the Fidelity Trust Company of Philadelphia, the bank that controls International Mercantile Marine–owners of White Star Line. George Widener is heir to the largest fortune in Philadelphia but he is also wealthy in his own right running a successful Philadelphia streetcar business.

Widener, his wife Eleanor, and son Harry Elkins Widener had been vacationing in Paris and staying at the Paris Ritz Hotel. They are returning to Philadelphia with their two servants Edwin Keeping and Emily Geiger and board the *Titanic* as First Class passengers. The Widener party will occupy cabins C-80-82.

Mr. and Mrs. John Borland Thayer – John Thayer, 49, Second Vice-President of the Pennsylvania Railroad, lives with his wife Marian and their four children in Haverford, Pennsylvania. Mr. and Mrs. Thayer, accompanied by their son Jack, had recently been in Berlin as guests of the American Consul. They are returning home along with Mrs. Thayer's maid Margaret Fleming. Their party boards the *Titanic* as First Class passengers and will occupy cabin C-68.

Mr. and Mrs. Lucian P. Smith – Lucian Smith, 24, and his wife, eighteen-year-old Eloise (Hughes) Smith, are returning to their West Virginia home following their world-tour honeymoon which started aboard the *Olympic*. Lucian is from a Pennsylvania family with large coal interests while Eloise is the daughter of West Virginia Congressman James A. Hughes and Belle Vinson Hughes of the Vinson family that is well-known in politics. The newlyweds are returning early from their honeymoon and board the *Titanic* in Cherbourg with First Class ticket 13695. The Smiths will occupy cabin C-31.

Mr. and Mrs. Dickinson H. Bishop – Dickinson Bishop was born on March 24, 1887 in Dowagiac, Michigan the son of George Bishop and Virginia (Jennie) Dickinson. Dick Bishop was a wealthy young widower whose first wife had willed him a major share in the Round Oak Stove Company in Dowagiac. He married 19 year old Helen Walton, of a well-to-do family from Sturgis, Michigan, on November 7, 1911. The Bishops are returning from a four-month honeymoon to Egypt, Italy, France, and Algiers, delaying their departure so they could return on the *Titanic's* maiden voyage. The Bishops will occupy First Class cabin B-49.

Third Class

Mrs. Hanna Youssef Touma (née Razi) – Although not notable among those boarding at Cherbourg, Mrs. Touma, 29, is also destined for Dowagiac, Michigan, the same small town that Dickinson and Helen Bishop call home. Hanna and her children, nine year old Maria and George, eight, are leaving their home in Tibinin, Lebanon to reunite with her husband, Darwis Touma. Darwis bought a farm near Dowagiac after emigrating to the United States in 1911. He saved and sent Hanna enough money to bring the rest of the family to America to join him. Hanna and the children traveled by camel caravan to Beirut, then by ship to Marseilles, France, followed by a train trip to Cherbourg before boarding the *Titanic* as Third Class passengers. Darwis does not know his wife and the children are traveling aboard the *Titanic*.

Queenstown, Ireland

The *Titanic* departs Cherbourg, France for Queenstown, Ireland at 8:10 p.m.. Arriving 14 hours later on April 11th, the *Titanic* anchors two miles off shore and waits for her last set of passengers.

The tender *Ireland* delivers three First Class and seven Second Class passengers and 1385 sacks of mail. The tender *America* transports 113 steerage passengers bringing the Third Class total to 709 with at least that many First Class dreams of a new life in America. While taking on the Queenstown passengers, a stoker, his face black from working his shift with the coal below deck, climbs up *Titanic's* unused fourth funnel to take a look outside. As he looks about, several passengers are startled when they notice the strange black face peering from the gigantic funnel. Like the near-miss leaving Southampton, some take this sighting as another bad omen and warning sign.

Typical among the Third Class passengers boarding at Queenstown is:

Mr. Daniel Buckley – Buckley, 21, is a farm laborer from Kingwilliamstown, Co Cork, Ireland and is among those dreamers boarding the *Titanic* with a Third Class ticket at Queenstown. He has everything he owns in an old suitcase tied shut with a piece of twine but his shoes are good and his spirits are high. Buckley is joined by his friends Miss Bridget Bradley, 22, Miss Nora O'Leary,16, and Miss Hannah Riordan,18, whose sister had arranged a domestic service job for her. Their party also includes Patrick Denis O'Connell,17, Hannah's cousin Patrick O'Connor, 23, and Michael Linehan, 21. All are looking for adventure and a better life in America.

While *Titanic* is anchored in Queenstown harbor, seven First Class passengers disembark having completed their planned cross-channel voyage. Also disembarking in accordance with his own plan is a Fireman/Stoker who apparently joined the crew to get a free ride across the channel to his Queenstown home. The Postal Clerks send off sacks of outgoing mail including letters and postcards from passengers and crew. Many of the recipients will learn of *Titanic's* fate before receiving the last correspondence ever sent by their family member or friend.

J. Bruce Ismay, President and Managing
Director of International Mercantile Marine

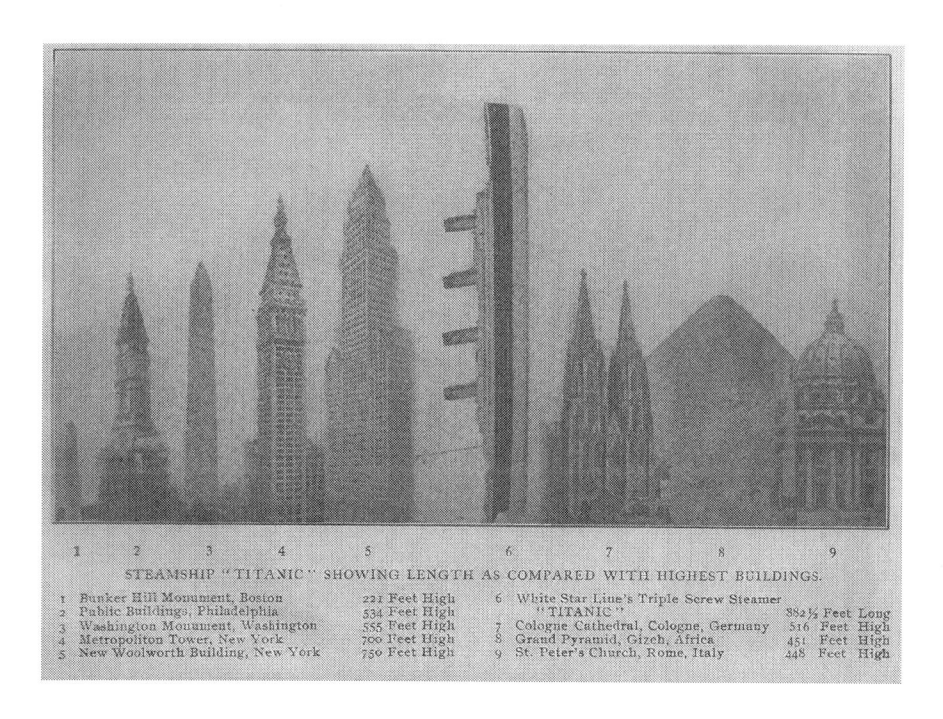

STEAMSHIP "TITANIC" SHOWING LENGTH AS COMPARED WITH HIGHEST BUILDINGS.

1	Bunker Hill Monument, Boston	221 Feet High	6	White Star Line's Triple Screw Steamer
2	Public Buildings, Philadelphia	534 Feet High		"TITANIC" 882½ Feet Long
3	Washington Monument, Washington	555 Feet High	7	Cologne Cathedral, Cologne, Germany 516 Feet High
4	Metropoliton Tower, New York	700 Feet High	8	Grand Pyramid, Gizeh, Africa 451 Feet High
5	New Woolworth Building, New York	750 Feet High	9	St. Peter's Church, Rome, Italy 448 Feet High

Titanic under construction at Harland & Wolff in Belfast

Titanic's propellers

The Triple Screw Steamer *Titanic*

Titanic's Gymnasium

Titanic's First Class Smoking Room

The First Class Promenade Deck

The Upper Boat Deck with *Titanic's* Lifeboats

Titanic's Grand Staircase

RMS Olympic damage that resulted from the collision with British war vessel *HMS Hawke*

Captain Edward J. Smith

Major Archibald Butt

Isidor Straus

Mrs. Lucien P. Smith

William T. Stead

Colonel and Mrs. John Jacob Astor

Mrs. George D. Widener | George D. Widener

Mrs. John B. Thayer | John B. Thayer

Ms. Margaret Brown

Chapter 6

THE ATLANTIC VOYAGE

"Capt. Smith knew the sea and his clear eye and steady hand had often guided his ship through dangerous paths. For 40 years storms sought in vain to vex him or menace his craft. But once before in all his honorable career was his pride humbled or his vessel maimed. Each new advancing type of ship built by his company was handed over to him as a reward for faithful services and as an evidence of confidence in his skill. Strong of limb, intent of purpose, pure in character, dauntless as a sailor should be, he walked the deck of his majestic structure as master of her keel."
~ Excerpt from the Speech of Senator William Alden Smith - IN THE SENATE OF THE UNITED STATES, Tuesday, May 28, 1912.

The *RMS Titanic*

The RMS (Royal Mail Ship) designation has been in use since 1840 and in 1850 contracts to carry the mail were awarded to private companies. Having the RMS distinction was seen as a mark of quality and a competitive advantage because the mail had to be on time.

> **British Wreck Commissioner's Inquiry** – Testimony of J. Bruce Ismay, examined by the Attorney General.
> 18295. She carried mails as well as passengers?
> Ismay – Yes.
> 18296. That was under contract which you had with the British Government?
> Ismay – Yes.
> ...18300. I only want to ask you one question with reference to it. Under that contract are you bound to keep up a certain rate of speed?
> Ismay – No.
> 18301. What I wanted to know was whether there was any such condition in the contract that your vessels must be constructed to steam at 20 knots or anything of that kind?
> Ismay – That I am not quite clear about. There is some reference in the contract. I think we are allowed to run a ship with mails even at 18 knots.

18302. I think you said in America 16, but we will look at the contract and see how that is?
Ismay – It is down in writing.
18303. But the substance of it is that you are not bound to proceed at any rate at anything like the speed at which your vessels can go?
Ismay – No, there is no penalty for not making a certain speed; in other words, we get paid a lump sum.

The mail, including 200 bags of registered mail, is entrusted to two British and three American postal clerks.

- **Mr. John Richard Jago Smith** resides in Cornwall, England. Smith, 35, is a member of the British Sea Post Department and joined *Titanic* in Southampton with colleague James Williamson.

- **Mr. James B. Williamson** resides in Dublin, Ireland. Williamson is 35 years old and single.

- **Mr. William Logan Gwinn** resides in Asbury Park, New Jersey, USA. Gwinn was scheduled to work the *Philadelphia*, but requested an earlier voyage after learning his wife was ill. He was transferred to the *Titanic* and joined in Southampton.

- **Mr. John Starr March** resides in Newark, New Jersey, USA. March, 50, is the oldest postal clerk aboard. His eight-year marine postal career includes service on the *Olympic* and the *Kaiser Wilhelm der Grosse*.

- **Mr. Oscar Scott Woody** resides in Clifton, Virginia, USA. Oscar Woody will be celebrating his 44th birthday aboard the *Titanic* on April 15th.

With passengers and mail securely on board the *Titanic*, the American flag is raised to signify her next port of call. The *Titanic* departs Queenstown for New York at 1:30 p.m. on April 11th, 1912. She carries 2215 passengers and crew and over 3400 sacks of the British Royal Mail on her maiden voyage.

Smooth Sailing

After leaving Queenstown the *Titanic*, averaging 21 knots in clear and calm weather, covers 464 miles by noon on Friday. Captain Smith receives various Marconigrams along the way. The messages are received by the Marconi Operators and passed on to Captain Smith or an officer on the bridge. Messages offering congratulations and good luck make their way to Captain Smith including this Marconigram from *Empress of Britain* on Friday:

> *Commr. Titanic. Officers and self send greetings and best of luck to the Titanic her Officers and Commander. Murray.*

The Captain sends this response:

Many thanks for your kind message from all here. Smith.

Some of the Marconigrams also contain ice warnings, a common occurrence for transatlantic crossings in April, including this from the Captain of the *Le Touraine* on Friday evening:

From Touraine to Captain Titanic. My position 7pm GMT Lat 49.28 long 26.28 W dense fog since this night crossed thick icefield lat 44.58 long 50.40 Paris saw another icefield and two icebergs lat 45.20 Long 50.09 Paris saw a derelict lat 40.56 long 68.38 Paris please give me your position. Best regards and Bon Voyage.

Most aboard are having a bon voyage as the fine weather continues and the *Titanic* covers an additional 519 miles by noon on Saturday. While passengers and crew have the pleasant weather in common, life aboard ship offers vastly different experiences for each passenger class, crew rank, and staff status.

While *Titanic* lists a total 2215 passengers and crew, the reality is that she carries very distinct subsets of that total. Each group literally has their own place aboard ship with restrictions on where they eat and sleep, and where on the ship they are allowed to visit and congregate.

Third Class Steerage

The first days of the voyage find the over 700 Third Class passengers well fed and looking forward to a new life in America. After the hectic boarding process in Southampton the steerage passengers settle in and find the bathrooms they will share and dining saloons where they will eat. They also discover their limits as they encounter the locked doors separating Third Class steerage from the First and Second Class sections of the ship. On D Deck near the bow there is a large room for Third Class gatherings. Access to this room is from the decks above and below with a solid wall separating the room from the First Class space that follows aft. Another wall with a single locked door separates the Third Class cabins in the stern end of the ship. Along the port side of E Deck is a 12 foot wide corridor that runs nearly the entire length of the ship. It serves as the primary crew corridor and is the only bow to stern route available to Third Class passengers to visit family and friends with berths in the opposite end of the ship. The corridor is called "Scotland Road" after the busy working class street in Liverpool.

Many steerage passengers take full advantage of the open-air promenade on the forward and aft Well Decks, gladly sharing the limited space with cargo cranes.

They take meals in one of the Third Class dining saloons, one in Section 8, the other in Section 9, on F Deck. The stark furnishings consist of long tables and wooden benches. With a capacity of 473 they quickly learn which of the two meal shifts to attend. Very few miss any of the hearty and delicious meals during the voyage.

The upcoming Third Class menu for April 14th:

Breakfast – Oatmeal porridge with milk; vegetable stew; fried tripe with onions; bread, butter and marmalade; Swedish bread; coffee and tea.

Lunch – Bouillon Soup; roast beef and gravy; green beans; boiled potatoes; cabin biscuits; bread; prunes and rice.

Dinner – Rabbit pie; baked potatoes; bread and butter; rhubarb and ginger jam; Swedish bread; tea.

After a meal many enjoy a smoke or chew in the Third Class Smoking Room while others pass the time reading or playing cards in one of the Third Class common areas.

At night the Third Class General Room on C Deck near the stern is busy with spontaneous celebrations. Dancing and singing follow the lively music from the upright piano and bagpipes. Anyone owning a musical instrument, or anyone who can bang out a tune, joins in. The ample flow of beer helps convince many others that their own musical talent is worthy of being heard. The rollicking festivities continue until the stewart turns out the lights at 10:00 p.m.

Second Class

Titanic carries 284 Second Class passengers on her maiden voyage across the Atlantic. The fine but cool weather finds Second Class passengers strolling along their outdoor promenade on the aft portion of the Boat Deck, admiring the splendid, unending ocean view.

Second Class passenger Lawrence Beesley described his experience in his book – *The Loss of the SS. Titanic*:

> "Each morning the sun rose behind us in a sky of circular clouds, stretching round the horizon in long, narrow streaks and rising tier upon tier above the sky-line, red and pink and fading from pink to white, as the sun rose higher in the sky. It was a beautiful sight to one who had not crossed the ocean before (or indeed been out of sight of the shores of England) to stand on the top deck and watch the swell of the sea extending outwards from the ship in an unbroken circle until it met the sky-line with its hint of infinity: behind, the wake of the vessel white with foam where, fancy suggested, the propeller blades had cut up the long Atlantic rollers and with them made a level white road bounded on either side by banks of green, blue, and blue-green waves that would presently sweep away the white road, though as yet it stretched back to the horizon and dipped over the edge of the world back to Ireland and the gulls, while along it the morning sun glittered and sparkled. And each night the sun sank right in our eyes along the sea, making an undulating glittering path way, a golden track charted on the surface of the ocean which our ship followed unswervingly until

the sun dipped below the edge of the horizon, and the pathway ran ahead of us faster than we could steam and slipped over the edge of the skyline,--as if the sun had been a golden ball and had wound up its thread of gold too quickly for us to follow."

When the evening turns cold an indoor promenade with floor-to-ceiling windows is available on C Deck and surrounds the Second Class entrance and library. Locked doors keep this section separate from the forward First Class areas and from the neighboring Third Class promenade aft.

Second Class passengers take their meals in the Second Class Dining Saloon located on the Saloon Deck near the stern. Their dining saloon has a capacity of 394 and is furnished with large tables with white tablecloths and linen napkins. The chairs surrounding the rectangular tables are bolted to the floor and swivel to offset the ship's rocking motion.

The Second Class three-course dinner planned for April 14th is:

1st Course – Consomme with tapioca

2nd Course – Baked haddock with sharp sauce; curried chicken and rice; spring lamb with mint sauce; roast turkey with cranberry sauce; green peas; puree turnips; rice; boiled and roast potatoes

Dessert Course – Plum pudding; wine jelly; coconut sandwich; Ice Cream; assorted nuts; fresh fruit; cheese; biscuits

First Class

E Deck, also called the Upper Deck, is the lowest deck level with First Class accommodations. Access to the E Deck First Class cabins from the upper decks is by way of the elevators or the Grand Staircase. On the starboard side of E Deck a narrow corridor connects these First Class cabins. The counterpart to the "Scotland Road" corridor for the crew and Third Class passengers, this passage is aptly named "Park Lane" after a fashionable London street. The connecting doors between other classes and crew accommodations on E Deck are closed and locked.

With smooth sailing through the first days of the voyage, First Class passengers take full advantage of the amenities offered by the new liner including the squash racquet court and salt water swimming pool. At the Enquiry Office on the Shelter (C) Deck they pay the three dollar fee to send ten word wireless Marconigrams or pay the one dollar fee to use the Turkish bath.

The Promenade (A) Deck is exclusively for the enjoyment of First Class passengers and includes a Promenade facing the bow overlooking the Well Deck two decks below. This Promenade extends back along each side of the ship to the aft end where it overlooks the aft Well Deck. The forward half of both side Promenades are enclosed with large windows to keep out water spray from the bow. The Verandah Cafe and Palm Court Cafe are located on the Promenade Deck and are often frequented by the well-to-do in First Class who are entertained by the orchestra's violin, cello and piano trio. This deck also includes the First Class Lounge, Reading and Writing Room, Library, and Smoking Room. The Smoking Room is where the men congregate to play cards and to discuss business, politics, or nothing in particular. When Archie Butt is present the Smoking Room conversation inevitably turns to Roosevelt and Taft's battle for the Republican nomination. Major Butt currently works in Taft's administration and had previously worked in Roosevelt's so his is a sought after opinion even as he tries to avoid the topic. When the cards are dealt it's time for the professional cardsharps to go to work fleecing those who choose to partake in what they believe to be a fair game of chance. Crossing the Atlantic back and forth has proven lucrative for these unscrupulous professionals and at least three of these *gamblers* are said to be traveling aboard the *Titanic*.

The First Class À la Carte Restaurant is located just aft of the Grand Staircase on the B Deck. This First Class only restaurant is open from 6:00 a.m. to 10:00 p.m. and is frequented by many of the elite and well-to-do passengers. The restaurant is a private concession managed by Italian businessman A.P. Luigi Gatti.

Sig. Gaspare Antonino Pietro (Luigi) Gatti – Luigi Gatti, 37, was born in Montalto Pavese, Italy in January 1875. One of eleven children, Luigi was the only one to move away from Italy. Gatti married a British subject and they live on Harborough Road, Southampton along with their son, Vittorio. Gatti runs two Ritz restaurants in London, the "Gatti's Adelphi" and the "Gatti's Strand." He also runs the À la Carte Restaurant on the *Olympic*.

Gatti's À la Carte Restaurant aboard *Titanic* is self-sufficient with its own cooks, waiters, clean up crew and other mostly French and Italian staff drawn from his two London restaurants.

First Class passengers pay to dine at Gatti's restaurant with its choice cuisine, fine wine, and orchestra entertainment but when they choose to dine in their First Class Dining Saloon, they find comfortable armchairs at beautifully set tables that seat parties of two, four, or six. They experience magnificent meals served on fine White Star china.

From the upcoming First Class menu:

Consomme fermier; cockie leekie; fillets of brill; egg a L'Argenteuil; chicken ala Maryland; corned beef; vegetables; dumplings.

From the Grill – Grilled mutton chops; mashed, fried, and baked jacket potatoes; custard pudding; apple meringue; pastry.

Buffet – Salmon mayonnaise; potted shrimps; Norwegian anchovies; soused herrings; plain and smoked sardines; roast beef; round or spiced beef; veal and ham pie; Virginian and Cumberland ham; Bologna sausage; brawn; galantine of chicken; corned ox tongue; lettuce; beetroot; tomatoes.

Cheeses – Cheshire, Stilton, Gorgonzola, Edam, Camembert, Roquefort, St. Ivel, Cheddar.

This fine meal is the upcoming First Class *lunch* for April 14th.

After a fine dining experience, many First Class passengers enjoy a stroll along their open promenade on the Boat Deck that runs along both port and starboard sides from the forward Officer's Promenade to the Second Class Promenade aft. The Boat Deck is also the destination for First Class passengers seeking a more vigorous workout in the gymnasium where there are specific hours set aside for men and other times scheduled for women. Both First and Second Class passengers share their Boat Deck promenades with *Titanic's* 16 wooden lifeboats. Any more than those sixteen would take up too much of the precious promenade real estate.

The Orchestra

Members of the orchestra are employed by C.W. and F.N. Black the firm which contracts with all of the steamship companies to provide musicians. In 1911 Black paid their musicians 6 pounds, 10 shillings a month plus a monthly uniform allowance but this year their salary was cut to 4 pounds a month with no uniform allowance. The eight member orchestra is primarily for the enjoyment of First Class but they share Second Class accommodations in cabin E.

The *Titanic's* orchestra is:

- **Mr. Wallace Henry Hartley**, 33, Violinist, of Dewsbury, England is the Bandmaster. Hartley played on the Cunard Liner *Mauretania* prior to joining the *Titanic*.
- **Mr. W. Theodore Ronald Brailey**, 24, Pianist, of London had previously served on the Cunard's *Carpathia* before joining the *Titanic*.
- **Mr. Roger Marie Bricoux**, 20, Cellist, of Lille, France also played on the *Carpathia* with Theodore Brailey.
- **Mr. John Frederick Preston Clarke**, Bass Violist, 30, is from Liverpool, England.
- **Mr. John "Jock" Law Hume**, 21, Violinist, is from Dumfries, England.
- **Mr. Georges Alexandre Krins**, 23, Violinist, was born in Paris but currently resides in London and is the Bandmaster of the String Trio.
- **Mr. Percy Cornelius Taylor**, 32, Cellist, resides in London.
- **Mr. John Wesley Woodward**, 32, Cellist, of Oxfordshire, England was on board the *Olympic* when she collided with *HMS Hawke*.

The violin, cello and piano trio play at Gatti's À la Carte Restaurant and the Café Parisien.

The quintet entertains passengers at teatime and during after-dinner concerts. They will also perform during the Sunday morning service that is open to all passenger classes.

First Class Passengers

At the start of the voyage Colonel Archibald Gracie, always a gentleman, formally offers his services to four "unprotected" ladies. A gentleman's offer of protection is a customary practice for ladies that are travelling unaccompanied. The ladies Gracie extends this offer to are three sisters and their friend returning to America after attending a family funeral in England. The sisters are Mrs. E. D. Appleton, Mrs. R. C. Cornell and Mrs. John Murray Brown. Their friend is Miss Edith Evans. Gracie knows the sisters well. His wife and the sisters are friends, and the Colonel knew Mrs. Appleton's husband at St. Paul's Academy.

No offer of services is necessary for several recently married First Class couples returning from months-long honeymoons that included tours of Europe, Egypt, or other exotic locations. The richest and most celebrated of these couples are Colonel and Mrs. John Jacob Astor IV. Colonel Astor, 47, had recently married eighteen-year-old Madeleine Force and the couple decided to travel Europe while the gossip ran its course in the States. Aboard ship their wedding is old news but speculation among the women of First Class is brewing as the gossip turns to Madeleine's condition and the reason for her morning *seasickness*. Madeleine Astor isn't the only young bride aboard the *Titanic* nor is she the only one suspected of being in a family way after a long honeymoon. Could it be that Dick Bishop's nineteen-year-old wife Helen, or perhaps Lucian Smith's bride Eloise, is expecting? What about John and Nellie Snyder, or George and Dorothy Harder or that young, apparently rich, couple from Spain?

Another First Class newlywed couple, Albert Dick, 31, and his wife Vera, are also a topic of conversation. Much to Bert's chagrin, a young steward has taken an interest in his seventeen-year-old bride. Vera isn't discouraging the attention and she is seen flirting with the steward, a man named Jones.

Dorothy Gibson, the 22 year old starlet, is traveling under the watchful eye of her mother. She is nonetheless enjoying her celebrity aboard the *Titanic*, easily socializing with other famous and rich First Class passengers.

"Pardon me," Major Butt says in his unmistakable Georgian drawl, "Oh, Miss Gibson," he continues, recognizing the woman who nearly bumped into him. The Major is walking on the Boat Deck with Frank Millet. They are enjoying the fine weather and discussing the possibility of the *Titanic* reaching New York early.

"How clumsy of me, Major. I was looking for mother instead of looking where I was going," replies the young Miss Gibson. She smiles at the Major, then her glance moves to Frank Millet.

"No, Miss Gibson, I would be the clumsy one," Archie Butt starts, then notices her interest in Millet. "How rude of me, Miss Gibson; may I introduce Mr. Frank Millet."

"The artist?" she asks Millet.

"Yes, I have been called that." Millet replies.

"So very pleased to meet you," she says, offering Millet her white gloved hand.

"The pleasure is mine, I'm sure," Millet accepts her hand briefly with a slight bow.

"I'm an artist too," Dorothy tells him, "currently on stage and in motion pictures. You've heard of 'The Lucky Holdup' haven't you, Mr. Millet?"

"I'm afraid I have not."

"I'm in that picture. It premiered in New York the day we sailed. I'm also a model for Mr. Harrison Fisher, the artist. I'm his favorite. He has had me pose on several occasions. Certainly you've heard of him?"

"I don't believe I know the man but I'm certain he did wonderful work when he had you, Miss Gibson." Millet, not intending the remark quite like it sounded, quickly adds, "My line of work is decoration painting and landscape."

"Oh, and aren't the decorations and appointments on this magnificent ship simply wonderful? Oh, and the pool—have you been for a swim? I've never seen such a splendid ship."

"Yes, it is practically indescribable," says Millet, "As a matter of fact I posted a letter in Queenstown and I could hardly put into words the luxury and beauty of the *Titanic*," leaning in slightly Millet confides, "but I had no problem describing the ladies that adorn the decks of First Class."

"How very kind of you, Mr. Millet. Oh, there's mother now. So very nice to make your acquaintance, but I really must be on my way." Dorothy Gibson smiles again at Major Butt and Frank Millet before she makes her way toward her mother.

Millet returns to his conversation with the Major, curious how his friend knew the young American starlet.

"I made it a point to meet her," he says, "The lady makes quite an entrance."

"And a lovely departure too," adds Millet discreetly admiring Miss Gibson as she walks away.

Captain Smith, as is his routine, strolls the Boat Deck Promenade and interacts with the First Class passengers, many of whom he knows well from previous voyages. Rumors of his retirement following *Titanic's* maiden voyage have been circulating on board and are the topic of discussion when George Widener, wealthy Pennsylvanian and heir to the largest fortune in Philadelphia, approaches the Captain.

"Captain Smith, I understand this is it, your final voyage as White Star Line's Commodore?" George Widener questions the Captain around a hardy handshake.

"By George, you must be listening to the same rumor that's been circulating on every voyage for a year now," the Captain replies.

"Oh, but it must be true this time. You will see the grandest ship ever built through her maiden voyage, retire to much fanfare, and then turn her over to the Chief Officer for the return trip. That is why you brought on the new Chief Officer, Wilde is it?"

"Chief Officer Wilde is with us because of his experience on the *Olympic*.

There is no more to it than that," Captain Smith says, then adds with a grin, "and there's nothing to these retirement rumors."

"But Captain we have already planned a party in your honor. Gatti will certainly put together something special. You will join us on Sunday night?" asks Widener.

"Of course George. You're a hard man to turn down."

"Let's make it 7:30 then," Widener says before the Captain moves on to greet other acquaintances.

Karl Behr and Helen Newsom take advantage of the fair weather and calm seas to meet on the boat deck when Helen can get out from under her mother's scrutiny. Karl is succeeding in his quest to win Helen's heart, but they both know they must convince Helen's mother to support their future union if there is to be one.

During the next 24 hours, from Saturday noon to Sunday noon, *Titanic* makes 22 knots and covers another 546 miles. The passengers begin to speculate that they may arrive in New York on Tuesday night instead of Wednesday morning.

The Deck Crew

The deck crew carries out the day-to-day, on deck operation of the ship. They are trained to manage the deck lines, deck cranes, winches, and lifeboat davits.

Titanic's deck crew includes six Lookouts who are Able Bodied Seamen who work two to a shift in the crow's nest. The Lookouts climb a 50 foot ladder inside the forward mast to reach the exposed crow's nest where their shifts are only two hours long because of the extremely cold winds they tolerate while on duty.

The lookouts are normally supplied with glasses (binoculars) to aid them in seeing over long distances, but the glasses are locked up and unavailable. After accompanying the *Titanic* from Belfast, Second Officer David Blair was bumped off the ship in Southampton by Chief Officer Wilde's appointment. Blair forgot to leave the only key to the locker containing the lookout's binoculars.

After departing Queenstown the Lookouts ask for glasses but none are forthcoming.

> **British Wreck Commissioner's Inquiry** – Testimony of Lookout Reginald R. Lee, examined by Mr. Harbinson.
> 2639. You say you asked for glasses. Who did you ask?
> Lee – I did not ask.
> 2640. Did you know that anybody asked for glasses?
> Lee – Yes, I think Simmons asked.
> 2641. Who did he ask?
> Lee – He was supposed to ask one of the Officers on the bridge, but I do not know whether he asked. I am only just saying what I was told.
> ...2646. (The Commissioner.) Who was the one that asked?
> Lee – I think it was Simmons.

2647. What makes you think so?

Lee – Because I can remember the conversation about it. We all spoke about it together.

2648. Who was there at this conversation?

Lee – Fleet, Hogg, Evans, Simmons, and myself were all there.

2649. And were you all talking about binoculars?

Lee – They were asking why they could not have them, because they had been in use from Belfast to Southampton, and they wanted to know what had become of the glasses that we had used in that time.

Below Deck

The weather doesn't matter too much below deck as the Engineering Crew works to keep up the necessary steam and the Victualling Department works to feed and meet the needs of the passengers. Many of the crew members get to and from their dormitories and work assignments by way of the Scotland Road corridor they share with Third Class passengers on the port side of E Deck.

The Engineers work in the turbine and reciprocating engine rooms to keep *Titanic's* engines, generators, and other mechanical equipment running while the Greasers work to keep it lubricated.

In order for *Titanic* to average better than 21 knots over the first three days of her transatlantic maiden voyage, the Coal Trimmers must keep the coal moving from the coal bunkers to the Stokers (firemen). The trimmers are also responsible for moving coal around their bunker to keep the pile level. If too much coal builds up on one side of a coal bunker, the ship could list to that side. Coal trimming is the lowest paid job and has the worst working conditions aboard ship. The coal bunkers are poorly lit, full of coal dust, and extremely hot with the residual heat from the boilers.

The Stokers keep the coal flowing into the 159 furnaces that fire the ship's 29 boilers. Next to each boiler is a chute from the coal bunkers located between the boiler rooms. The Coal Trimmers, working inside these bunkers, shovel the coal down the coal chute to a Stoker who constantly shovels it into one of *Titanic's* hungry furnaces. Shifts for all the Stokers is a very demanding four hours on, followed by eight hours off. The heat in the boiler rooms often exceeds 120 °F, so most of the stokers work wearing only their undershirts and shorts.

While the passengers enjoy their promenade decks and the accommodating weather, *Titanic's* firemen, including Lead Fireman Charles Hendrickson, work night and day to control the coal fire that has plagued the ship since departure.

British Wreck Commissioner's Inquiry – Testimony of Charles Hendrickson, examined by Mr. Lewis.

5239. Did you hear when the fire commenced?

Hendrickson – Yes, I heard it commenced at Belfast.

5240. When did you start getting the coal out?

Hendrickson – The first watch we did from Southampton we started to get it out.

5241. How many days would that be after you left Belfast?

Hendrickson – I do not know when she left Belfast to the day.

5242. It would be two or three days, I suppose?

Hendrickson – I should say so.

The Victualling Crew

Members of *Titanic's* Victualling Department see to the needs of all passenger classes and are supervised by two Pursers who are also the direct link between passengers and the ship's officers.

Bath Stewards maintain supplies in the communal bathrooms. Glory-Hole Stewards clean and maintain the common toilets in First, Second, and Third Class, and the crew areas. Linen Stewards provide all the bed sheets and other linens. Bedroom Stewards are assigned to each class. The First Class Bedroom Stewards not only clean the rooms and make beds, but also serve food in the rooms and assist the passengers in getting dressed. Each First Class Bedroom Steward is responsible for three to five rooms. Second Class Stewards are responsible for up to 10 rooms and Third Class Stewards for as many as 25 rooms. The Stewards rely on tips for a significant portion of their income. The 20 female Stewardesses on board serve the women passengers.

The Victualling crew also includes the Galley and Kitchen staff, the chefs, cooks, butchers, and bakers who work in the kitchens to cook the meals for each passenger class.

Charles Joughin, 32, is a Chief Baker in charge of a staff of 13 bakers. Joughin transferred from the *Olympic* and was on board the *Titanic* for her delivery trip from Belfast. He signed-on again in Southampton. As Joughin prepared for the voyage, he considered it necessary to pack his favorite spirit of inebriation to keep him warm during the cold April crossing—a decision that would prove to be most advantageous.

Chapter 7

Icebergs and Warnings

High Tides and Icebergs

The large icebergs being encountered in the shipping lanes of the North Atlantic in the spring of 1912 were created when huge chunks of fresh water ice broke away from Greenland's Jakobshavn Polar Glacier. These massive, floating icebergs drifted in the currents of Baffin Bay west of Greenland, until the current took them southwest, through the Davis Strait. The Labrador Current then carried the icebergs south until the larger ones ran aground along the Labrador coast.

On January 3, 1912 the earth was at its closest point to the sun during its annual orbit. On January 4th the moon was at its closest point to the earth, and on the opposite side of earth than the sun. This rare combination of the earth's closeness to the sun and moon created higher than normal tides. These tides re-floated many of the larger, grounded icebergs. The Labrador Current carried these re-floated icebergs south of Newfoundland and into the North Atlantic shipping lanes.

Excerpt from the British Wreck Commissioner's Inquiry Report:

> It may be useful here to give some definitions of the various forms of ice to be met with in these latitudes, although there is frequently some confusion in their use.
>
> An **Iceberg** may be defined as a detached portion of a Polar glacier carried out to sea. The ice of an iceberg formed from a glacier is of quite fresh water, only about an eighth of its mass floats above the surface of sea water.
>
> A "**Growler**" is a colloquial term applied to icebergs of small mass, which therefore only show a small portion above the surface. It is not infrequently a berg which has turned over, and is therefore showing what has been termed "black ice," or more correctly, dark blue ice.
>
> **Pack Ice** is the floating ice which covers wide areas of the polar seas, broken into large pieces, which are driven ("packed") together by wind and current, so as to form a practically continuous sheet. Such ice is generally frozen from seawater, and not derived from glaciers.
>
> **Field Ice** is a term usually applied to frozen sea water floating in much

looser form than pack ice.

An **Icefloe** is the term generally applied to the same ice (i.e., field ice) in a smaller quantity.

A **Floe Berg** is a stratified mass of floe ice (i.e., sea-water ice).

The Marconi Wireless

Guglielmo Marconi, born April 25, 1874, in Bologna, Italy, was the second son born to an Italian country gentleman's family. He took an early interest in physical and electrical science and in 1895 conducted experiments at his father's country estate where he successfully sent wireless signals over a distance of a mile and a half.

In England in 1896 Marconi was granted the world's first patent for a system of wireless telegraphy and in July 1897 formed The Wireless Telegraph & Signal Company Limited. He renamed his company the Marconi's Wireless Telegraph Company Limited in 1900, the same year he patented, "tuned or syntonic telegraphy." In December 1901, Marconi, determined to prove that wireless waves were not affected by the curvature of the Earth, used his system for transmitting the first wireless signals across the Atlantic, a distance of 2100 miles.

Between 1902 and 1912 Marconi patented several other related inventions including the magnetic detector which became the standard for wireless receivers. In 1907 he opened the first transatlantic commercial service between Glace Bay, Nova Scotia, Canada, and Clifden, Ireland. Guglielmo Marconi was awarded the Nobel Prize for physics in 1909. Marconi Wireless Radio was quickly recognized as essential for communication with and between ocean going ships.

The International Marconi Wireless Telegraph Company licenses shipboard applications from the Postmaster-General of the country whose flag the ship sails under. The *Titanic* installation is the property of the Marconi Company under contract with White Star Line. The 5 kilowatt installation is the best available and is guaranteed to transmit and receive over a distance of 350 miles but in reality is capable of far greater reach. The system draws power from the ships dynamos or from the emergency dynamos or, if those fail, from a back up battery in the wireless cabin. To meet any emergency White Star Line also required the essential parts of the wireless apparatus be installed on the *Titanic* in duplicate. As long as the Marconi cabin remains above water it will be possible to transmit wireless messages.

The Marconi Company employs the two wireless operators assigned to the *Titanic*, Senior Wireless Operator Jack Phillips and Junior Wireless Operator Harold Bride. Between them the wireless station is manned around the clock.

Mr. John 'Jack' George Phillips – Phillips, 25, graduated from the Marconi Company's Wireless Telegraphy Training School in August 1906 and received his first post aboard the White Star Liner *Teutonic*. For the next two years he sailed on various liners until he was given an operating post at the Marconi station just outside of Clifden on the West Coast of Ireland in 1908. Phillips returned to sea on the *Adriatic* in 1911 and in 1912 joined his favorite ship, the *Oceanic* sailing from Southampton to New York. After returning to England in March 1912 Phillips was appointed by the Marconi Company to serve on the *Titanic*. He joined the ship in Belfast. Phillips tested the Marconi equipment during sea trials and the voyage from Belfast to Southampton and found it to be in perfect working order.

Mr. Harold Sydney Bride – Bride, 22, obtained his certificate of proficiency in radio-telegraphy from the Postmaster-General in June, 1911. Bride's first ship was the *Haverford*, and he also served on the *Lusitania*, *La France* and the *Anselm*, before being appointed to the *Titanic* by the Marconi Company. Bride also joined in Belfast and assisted Phillips in testing the Marconi equipment.

Phillips and Bride report to, and are accountable to, The International Marconi Wireless Telegraph Company. They are required to inform the crew, usually an officer, of emergency messages and messages that pertain to the navigation of the ship. The Operators also relay messages picked up from other ships, essentially networking to extend the reach of wireless communication, but their main concern is sending and receiving paid messages for the passengers who tip for this service.

In the three days since departing Phillips and Bride receive and send over 250 passenger Marconigrams but the Marconi Wireless isn't working Saturday. Passenger messages accumulate while Phillips and Bride work to diagnose and fix the problem. It takes seven hours get the Wireless back up and running. By Sunday morning there is a large backlog of messages to send and the messages continue to come in, as passengers anticipate the ship being in wireless transmission range of the Cape Race, Newfoundland station. Sunday will be a very busy day for *Titanic's* Marconi men.

Sunday's Ice Warnings

At 9:00 a.m. on Sunday morning, April 14th, an iceberg warning is sent from the *Caronia* to *Titanic*.

> *West-bound steamers report bergs, growlers and field ice in 42 N. from 49 to 51 W.*

Titanic replies at 9:44 a.m..

> *Thanks for message and information. Have had variable weather throughout—Smith*

At 12:30 p.m. on Sunday Second Officer Charles Lightoller relieves First Officer William Murdoch on the bridge in order for Murdoch to have his lunch. A short time later Captain Smith makes his way to the bridge and shares the *Caronia* Marconigram indicating "bergs, growlers and field ice" with Lightoller.

British Wreck Commissioner's Inquiry – Testimony of Charles Lightoller, examined by Solicitor General John Simon.

13481. Do you recollect, or can you help us at all, did that indication 42 N. indicate to you that it was near where you were likely to go?

Lightoller – It would, had I taken particular notice of the latitude, though as a matter of fact, latitude with regard to ice conveys so very little.

13482. Is that because it tends to set north or south?

Lightoller – North and south, yes.

13483. (The Commissioner.) I do not follow that?

Lightoller – We take very little notice of the latitude because it conveys very little. You cannot rely on latitude.

13484. (The Solicitor-General.) For ice?

Lightoller – Yes.

13485. (The Solicitor-General.) He answered that "because the ice tends to set north and south." (To the witness.) Then do you attach more importance to the longitude?

Lightoller – Far more.

13486. I notice your recollection of the message is you recollect 49 and 51 W.?

Lightoller – Distinctly.

13487. That is longitude. Did you form any sort of impression at that time as to what time of day or night you were likely to reach the area indicated?

Lightoller – Not at that time.

13488. I know you worked it out, or helped to work it out later?

Lightoller – It was worked out.

At 1:42 p.m. on Sunday afternoon a wireless message from the *Baltic* reports icebergs 250 miles ahead but within five miles of *Titanic's* current course. It also warns of the position of the *Deutschland* and that she is not under control.

Captain Smith, 'Titanic.' – Have had moderate, variable winds and clear, fine weather since leaving. Greek steamer 'Athenai' reports passing icebergs and large quantities of field ice to-day in lat. 41° 51' N., long. 49° 52' W. Last night we spoke German oiltank steamer 'Deutschland,' Stettin to Philadelphia, not under control, short of coal, lat. 40° 42' N., long. 55° 11' W. Wishes to be reported to New York and other steamers. Wish you and 'Titanic' all success. – Commander.

Captain Smith shares the *Baltic* message with Bruce Ismay.

British Wreck Commissioner's Inquiry – Testimony of J. Bruce Ismay, examined by the Attorney General.

18323. ...Now on this day, on the 14th, did you get information from

the Captain of ice reports?
Ismay – The Captain handed me a Marconi message which he had received from the "Baltic" on the Sunday.
18324. He handed you the actual message as it was delivered to him from the "Baltic"?
Ismay – Yes.
18325. Do you remember at what time it was?
Ismay – I think it was just before lunch.
18326. On the Sunday?
Ismay – Yes, on the Sunday.
…18351. Very well. Now let us take it that you received it immediately before lunch. You said nothing about it then, as I understand you?
Ismay – No, I did not.
18352. But having read it, you put it in your pocket?
Ismay – Yes.
…18356. Then you spoke about it in the afternoon to two lady passengers?
Ismay – Yes.
18357. Will you tell me to whom you spoke?
Ismay – I spoke to Mrs. Thayer and Mrs. Ryerson.

Mrs. Emily Ryerson along with her husband Arthur and three of their children are traveling back to their home in Cooperstown, NY. after learning of the death of their son Arthur Jr. in a motor car accident. Emily, mourning the loss of her son, had not yet appeared on deck in public but on Sunday afternoon she agrees to join her friend Marian Thayer for a stroll. After the ladies walk for nearly an hour, they decide to rest in the deck chairs outside the aft staircase on A-Deck and enjoy the sunset. Shortly after settling into their chairs they are approached by Bruce Ismay who inquires if they are enjoying the voyage and then shows them the ice warning from the *Baltic*. Ismay explains that it means there is a possibility of meeting icebergs in the area.

British Wreck Commissioner's Inquiry – Testimony of J. Bruce Ismay, examined by the Attorney General.
18424. Did [the *Baltic* message] not convey to you that it was possible to ascertain whether the latitude and longitude designated in that Marconigram would be a track that you would have to cross?
Ismay – For me to ascertain that?
18325. Yes?
Ismay – No. That is for the Captain of the ship. He was responsible for the navigation of the ship. I had nothing to do with the navigation.
18426. Yet you were the managing Director and he thought it of sufficient importance to bring you the first Marconigram which he had shown to you on this voyage and give it to you, and then you put it in

your pocket?
Ismay – Yes.
18427. And you, of course, appreciated that that report meant to you that you were approaching ice, as you told us?
Ismay – Yes.
18428. And you knew also that you would be approaching ice that night?
Ismay – I expected so, yes.
18429. And that you therefore would be crossing the particular region which was indicated in that Marconigram that night?
Ismay – I could not tell that.
18430. About that region?
Ismay – Yes, I presume so.
18431. And therefore that it behoved those responsible for the navigation of the ship to be very careful?
Ismay – Naturally.

Excerpt from the British Wreck Commissioner's Inquiry Report:
Mr. Ismay, the Managing Director of the White Star Line, was on board the 'Titanic,' and it appears that the Master handed the 'Baltic's' message to Mr. Ismay almost immediately after it was received. This no doubt was in order that Mr. Ismay might know that ice was to be expected. Mr. Ismay states that he understood from the message that they would get up to the ice "that night." Mr. Ismay showed this message to two ladies, and it is therefore probable that many persons on board became aware of its contents.

Captain Smith sends this reply to the *Baltic*:

Commander Baltic. Thanks for your message and good wishes. Had fine weather since leaving. Smith.

At 1:45 p.m., just after receiving the *Baltic's* message, the German liner *Amerika* sends a message through *Titanic's* wireless via Cape Race to the US Hydrographic Office in Washington.

'Amerika' passed two large icebergs in 41° 27'N., 50° 8'W., on the 14th of April.

Amerika's message is overheard by the Marconi Operator but isn't passed on to the Captain or any other officer.
This message from the *Caronia* is passed on to Captain Smith:

Commander Titanic. All best wishes, success, much love. George and Katie Riggs – Caronia.

At 5:50 p.m. Captain Smith alters course slightly to the south and west of the normal track. This "turning the corner" course alteration to bring the ship from a southwesterly to a westerly course was delayed by 30 minutes taking *Titanic* eight miles south of the original course. This may have been done to avoid the ice reported by the *Baltic* while staying north of the drifting *Deutschland*. This minor alteration keeps the *Titanic* on the customary course for an April crossing.

At 6:52 p.m. the Captain sends a response to the earlier Marconigram:

Riggs Caronia. Many thanks, love to both.—Smith.

Shortly after 7:00 p.m. Captain Smith retrieves the *Baltic* message from Bruce Ismay and posts it in the chart room. He then prepares for the dinner party being hosted in his honor by Mr. and Mrs. George Widener.

Second Officer Charles Lightoller presented testimony before the British Wreck Commissioner's Inquiry concerning his watch, the ship's speed, and the expectation the *Titanic* would reach the reported icefields that night.

British Wreck Commissioner's Inquiry – Testimony of Charles Lightoller, examined by the Solicitor General.
13502. Did you learn whether while you had been off duty during the afternoon any further information had reached the "Titanic" about ice?
Lightoller – Not that I remember.
...13505. Now what did you notice about the speed of your vessel?
Lightoller – As far as I could tell, her speed was normal.
13506. Were they telegraphed at full speed ahead?
Lightoller – At full speed.
13507. (The Commissioner.) What do you mean by normal?
Lightoller – Full speed.
13508. What is full speed; can you give me how many knots?
Lightoller – We were steaming, as near as I can tell from what I remember of the revolutions—I believe they were 75—and I think that works out at about 21 1/2 knots the ship was steaming.
...13515. And during your watch which extended from 6 till 10, did she maintain the same speed, as far as you know?
Lightoller – As far as I know.
13516. Then who would be on the bridge—is it one or two of the Junior Officers would be on the bridge with you?
Lightoller – Two Junior Officers on watch at all times.
13517. There would be a Quartermaster at the wheel?
Lightoller – And a stand-by Quartermaster.
13518. Another Quartermaster standing by?
Lightoller – Exactly.
13519. And there would be two look-out men in the crow's-nest?

Lightoller – At all times.

13520. What was the practice in the "Titanic" as far as this voyage is concerned about having a look-out man anywhere else?

Lightoller – In anything but clear weather we carry extra look-outs.

13521. But where do you put them?

Lightoller – If the weather is fine, that is to say if the sea allows it, we place them near the stem head; when the weather does not allow us placing them at the stem head, then probably on the bridge.

13522. And as far as your watch was concerned, 6 to 10 on the evening of April 14th, was there any look-out except the two men in the crow's-nest?

Lightoller – No.

13523. What was the weather?

Lightoller – Perfectly clear and fine.

…13527. Of course the sea was calm?

Lightoller – Comparatively smooth.

13528. Could you see the stars?

Lightoller – Perfectly clear. There was not a cloud in the sky.

13529. There was no moon, I think?

Lightoller – No moon.

13530. During your watch was any change made in the course?

Lightoller – Not to my recollection.

13531. Then when you had taken the ship over from Mr. Wilde and gathered this information, I think you gave some directions to one of the Junior Officers?

Lightoller – I directed the sixth Officer to let me know at what time we should reach the vicinity of the ice. The Junior Officer reported to me, "About 11 o'clock."

13532. Do you recollect which of the Junior Officers it was?

Lightoller – Yes, Mr. Moody, the sixth.

13533. That would involve his making some calculations, of course?

Lightoller – Yes.

13534. Had this Marconigram about the ice with the meridians on it been put up; was it on any notice board, or anything of the sort?

Lightoller – That I could not say with any degree of certainty. Most probably, in fact very probably, almost certainly, it would be placed on the notice board for that purpose in the chart room.

13535. At any rate when you gave Mr. Moody those directions he had the material to work on?

Lightoller – Exactly.

13536. And he calculated and told you about 11 o'clock you would be near the ice?

Lightoller – Yes.

13537. That is to say an hour after your watch finished?

Lightoller – Yes. I might say as a matter of fact I have come to the conclusion that Mr. Moody did not take the same Marconigram which Captain Smith had shown me on the bridge because on running it up just mentally, I came to the conclusion that we should be to the ice before 11 o'clock, by the Marconigram that I saw.

13538. (The Commissioner.) In your opinion when in point of fact would you have reached the vicinity of the ice?

Lightoller – I roughly figured out about half-past nine.

…13558. And being on the bridge, and in charge, would it be your responsibility to determine any question about reduction of speed?

Lightoller – If I thought it necessary I should advise the Commander.

13559. But you thought the weather was clear enough and you could see?

Lightoller – Perfectly clear.

…13566. Now when you were in the vicinity of the ice, as you believed you were at 9:30 entering the dangerous field, did not it occur to you that you might run foul of a growler?

Lightoller – No, My Lord, I judged I should see it with sufficient distinctness to define it—any ice that was large enough to damage the ship.

13567. 21 knots is about 700 yards a minute. Is your view that you could see a growler at a safe distance at night time going at that pace?

Lightoller – I judged that I could see a growler at a mile and a half, More probably two miles.

At 7:30 p.m. a message from the *Californian* to the *Antillian* is picked up by the *Titanic*. The message gives *Californian's* position as 42.3 N, 49.9 W and warns of three large bergs five miles to the south. The message is delivered to the bridge by Harold Bride but does not get to Captain Smith who is attending the Widener dinner party. Captain Smith's delayed, "turning the corner" course alteration now has the *Titanic* steaming directly toward the reported ice – only 50 miles away.

Chapter 8

Into the Perfect Calm - Prelude to Collision

On Sunday evening the women of First Class dress in their finest gowns for dinner and most add a wrap for warmth against the noticeably dropping temperature. Also noticeable to many of the passengers is a change in the feel of the engines when an extra boiler is lit. Talk of an early arrival continues and anticipation rises for the next day's noon mileage total.

The Widener Dinner Party

At 7:30 p.m. that Sunday evening Captain Smith arrives at the dinner party in Luigi Gatti's À la Carte restaurant. The event, in honor of Captain Smith's rumored retirement, is hosted by George and Eleanor Widener and their son Harry. The Wideners are a wealthy family from Pennsylvania and have included other well-to-do Pennsylvanians that are traveling on the *Titanic* including John Thayer, Second Vice-President of the Pennsylvania Railroad, and his wife Marian as well as Mr. and Mrs. William Carter from the well known Philadelphia family that made their wealth in Pennsylvanian coal. The Wideners also invited Major Archibald Butt, President Taft's trusted military aide. The Major is known to be an engaging dinner guest with his entertaining stories and Washington gossip. Exquisite food and wine are served to the Widener party amidst the sound of the nearby string trio. Captain Smith, following White Star regulations, does not try the wine or consume any alcoholic beverage.

William Stead, Benjamin Guggenheim, Colonel and Mrs. Astor, Sir Cosmo and Lady Duff-Gordon, and Mr. and Mrs. Isidor Straus also dine in the À la Carte restaurant at various times that night as do Broadway producer Henry Harris and his wife Rene, novelist Jacques Futrelle and his wife May, and newlyweds Lucian and Eloise Smith. Dorothy Gibson also makes a glamorous appearance while Captain Smith enjoys his dinner and converses with the wealthy elite.

Following dinner Captain Smith makes his way to the bridge to confer with his second officer. The ladies retire to the library or their cabins while the gentlemen gravitate to the Smoking Room for cards and conversation, and perhaps a brandy with their cigar. Between hands of Bridge Whist, Harry Widener, John Thayer, Major Butt, and William Carter again toast the absent Captain Smith, his retirement, real or rumored, being the reason for the dinner party.

Clarence Moore and Frank Millet, who chose to dine in the First Class Dining

Room, also retire to the Smoking Room. Moore joins Archie Butt, Harry Widener, and William Carter to play Bridge Whist using his new deck from the Kalamazoo Playing Card Co. Millet starts a game of cards with New York stockbroker Frederick Hoyt while Lucian Smith attempts to communicate his way through a bridge game with three Frenchmen. The men are joined there by William Stead, Frederick Seward, and later by Norris Williams and his father, Charles.

The men share stories of their adventures and escapades including a story Charles Williams tells about his trip to Liverpool in November 1879 aboard the *Arizona*. On that cold November night the *Arizona* collided with an iceberg that crushed her bow, but she was able to make it to St. John's and didn't sink.

Meanwhile, unbeknownst to the Captain, crew or passengers, the *Titanic* steams toward her own iceberg at 21.5 knots.

The Curse of the Princess of Amen-Ra

William Stead, the renowned British journalist, medium, and psychic researcher, entertains the men in the First Class Smoking Room with stories of his experiences and spiritualist beliefs. With the attention of all near him, he tells the story of the curse of the Princess of Amen-Ra.

"The Princess of Amen-Ra lived 1500 years before Christ. Upon her death she was laid to eternal rest in an ornately carved wooden coffin and then buried in a vault at Luxor, on the banks of the Nile," Stead tells his curious audience. "Four rich, young English gentlemen were visiting the Luxor excavations in 1898 and were fascinated by the mummy case containing the remains of the Princess. After drawing lots to see which of them would offer to buy her, the winner was successful in securing the coffin for several thousand pounds. He escorted his prize purchase back to his hotel room and an hour later was seen walking back towards the desert. This man was never seen again. His companions too were victims of the Princess of Amen-Ra curse. One was accidently shot and lost his arm, another lost his entire wealth, and the last became seriously ill."

"What became of the coffin?" an impatient listener asks.

"The coffin with the remains of this evil princess was sent to England where it was purchased by a London businessman. After a series of accidents to his family and a fire in his house, he donated it to the British Museum. The cursed coffin continued to claim victims with those who moved, touched, or even laid eyes on the coffin, suffering injuries or untimely death.

"From the Egyptian Room, where the coffin was displayed, night watchmen heard strange and unexplained noises in the night and other exhibits in the room were found out of place the next day. One watchman died, another quit, and the cleaning crew simply refused to enter the room. The museum authorities ultimately decided the coffin with the remains of the Princess of Amen-Ra should not be displayed and moved it to the basement. Once again those making this decision and handling the coffin suffered severe illness and sudden death."

"How is it you know of this?" asks one of Stead's enthralled listeners.

"Oh, by now the newspapers had it," replied Stead, "and they were not immune to the curse. It seems that a photographer took a picture of the mummy case for one of the papers planning a story. When he developed the picture a horrible image of a human face was clearly visible on the coffin and after viewing this image the photographer shot himself. Terrible calamities have also befallen all who have dared write of the curse and while I will freely share the story with you here tonight, I will never put pen to paper to write it down."

"Is it still in the basement of the museum?" asks Frederick Seward, a New York lawyer, intently listening to Stead's tale.

"No, unfortunately it's not," says Stead. "It was sold to a private collector who, of course, experienced similar misfortune and attempted, without success, to have the evil princess exorcised."

"Just now you said it was 'unfortunate' that this wretched mummy was not in the museum's basement. In what way is it unfortunate other than to the poor fellow who now owns her?" Lucian Smith asks the storyteller.

This is followed by a few chuckles before Stead replies, "By this time the story was known and more importantly believed. No British museum would take the mummy, but she was eventually sold to an American archaeologist," Stead said, then after a pause, "in New York."

"But how will it get to New York? Captains and crews are notorious for their superstitions. No sailing ship would invite catastrophe, real or imagined." said a disbelieving Charles Williams.

"Perhaps not. But perhaps—"

"Excuse me, Mr. Stead," a concerned Frederick Hoyt cuts him off, "where is the coffin of the Princess of Amen-Ra right now? What ship would even consider transporting her?"

"Perhaps an unsinkable one," replies Stead ignoring the first question. With his audience in stunned silence, William Stead sips his brandy for the first time since starting the story.

The Perfect Calm

The night air is cold with the temperature dropping 10°F over the past two hours. The night sky is moonless but beautifully starlit and exceptionally clear. The North Atlantic ocean is unusually calm and the surface is absolutely flat with no swell. This uncharacteristically flat sea provides an apparently comfortable visibility but denies the lookouts of a key visual distinction of an upcoming iceberg.

> **British Wreck Commissioner's Inquiry**: Testimony of Second Officer Charles Lightoller, examined by the Solicitor General.
> Lightoller – In the event of meeting ice there are many things we look for. In the first place a slight breeze. Of course, the stronger the

breeze the more visible will the ice be, or rather the breakers on the ice. Therefore at any time when there is a slight breeze you will always see at nighttime a phosphorescent line round a berg, growler, or whatever it may be; the slight swell which we invariably look for in the North Atlantic causes the same effect, the break on the base of the berg, so showing a phosphorescent glow. All bergs – all ice more or less have a crystallised side.

13570. It is white?

Lightoller – Yes; it has been crystallised through exposure and that in all cases will reflect a certain amount of light, what is termed ice-blink, and that ice-blink from a fairly large berg you will frequently see before the berg comes above the horizon.

13571. Now let me follow. Was there any breeze on this night?

Lightoller – When I left the deck at 10 o'clock there was a slight breeze – Oh, pardon me, no. I take that back. No it was calm, perfectly calm.

13572. And there was no breeze. Was there any?

Lightoller – As far as we could see from the bridge the sea was comparatively smooth. Not that we expected it to be smooth, because looking from the ship's bridge very frequently with quite a swell on the sea will appear just as smooth as a billiard table, perfectly smooth; you cannot detect the swell. The higher you are the more difficult it is to detect a slight swell.

13573. That means, then, does it not, that if you are on the bridge and you are relying on the fact that there may be a slight swell you really cannot tell from the bridge whether there is a swell or not – a slight swell?

Lightoller – We look at it rather the other way – that, though the sea may appear smooth, we pretty well know that there is a swell, though it may not be visible to the eye, nor yet have any effect on the ship. It is a most rare occurrence

13574. You mean there nearly always is a swell in the North Atlantic?

Lightoller – This is the first time in my experience in the Atlantic in 24 years, and I have been going across the Atlantic nearly all the time, of seeing an absolutely flat sea.

13575. Do you agree from that experience that this was an occasion when it was an absolutely flat sea?

Lightoller – Absolutely flat.

13576. (The Commissioner.) Not in fact, but to all appearance?

Lightoller – In fact, My Lord.

Just before 9:00 p.m. the Captain excuses himself from his dinner companions and heads for the bridge. The possibility of meeting ice along with the current weather and resulting calm, flat ocean, is the subject of this exchange on the

The Perfect Calm

bridge of the *Titanic*.

"There is not much wind," Captain Smith comments to his Second Officer, Charles Lightoller.

"No wind, quite flat, a flat calm. Pity the breeze had not kept up through the ice region," replies Lightoller.

The reason isn't stated but was obvious to both men as it would be to any experienced seaman; without any breeze there would be no water ripples breaking on the base of an iceberg giving early warning of its presence.

"In any case," Lightoller adds, "there will be a certain amount of reflected light from the bergs."

"Oh yes, there will be reflected light. Even with the blue side of the berg toward us, the outline, the white outline will probably give us sufficient warning," agrees Captain Smith, adding, "but if there was even a slight degree of haze, no doubt we would have to slow down."

"In this weather we should be able to see it at a good distance, as far as we can see, we should be able to see it," says Lightoller.

"If it becomes at all doubtful let me know at once, I will be just inside," Captain Smith says, ending the conversation. Captain Smith then retires to his quarters.

> **British Wreck Commissioner's Inquiry**: Testimony of Second Officer Charles Lightoller, examined by the Solicitor General.
> 13636. (The Commissioner.) If what becomes doubtful?
> Lightoller – The general conditions, My Lord, I suppose he would mean – if it were at all doubtful about the distance I could see, principally.
> 13637. You were relying at this time exclusively upon the look-out; you were not taking any measures to reduce the speed?
> Lightoller – None, My Lord.
> 13638. And therefore you were relying for safety entirely on the look-out?
> Lightoller – Yes.
> ...13656. What was the very first thing you did after the Captain went in about half-past nine? Did not you send a message to the crow's-nest?
> Lightoller – Yes, I did.
> 13657. What was it?
> Lightoller – To keep a sharp look out for ice, particularly small ice and growlers.
> 13658. That was half-past nine?
> Lightoller – And I think I told them to pass that word on until daylight – to keep a sharp look out till daylight.
> ...13661. Now did you send that message in consequence of your conversation with the Captain?
> Lightoller – No, I thought it was a necessary precaution. That is a message I always send along when approaching the vicinity of ice or a

derelict, as the case may be. If I know we are approaching the vicinity of a derelict, I send the word along to let them know what to look out for. It is just the same with regard to a Lightship, say the Nantucket Lightship; I tell them to keep a sharp look out for the Nantucket Lightship to give them an idea what they are looking for.

…13667. Very well, I think you caused that message to be sent to the crow's-nest by one of the Junior Officers who was with you on the bridge?

Lightoller – Yes, Mr. Moody.

At 9:40 p.m. Senior Wireless Operator Jack Phillips receives this message from the steamship *Mesaba*:

> From 'Mesaba' to 'Titanic' and all east-bound ships. Ice report in lat. 42° N. to 41° 25' N., long. 49° to long. 50° 30' W. Saw much heavy pack ice and great number large icebergs. Also field ice. Weather good, clear.

Phillips is still working on the pressing task of clearing passenger messages from the backlog that built up while the wireless was out of service the day before. He puts the *Mesaba* message aside intending to deliver it to the bridge when he's finished but the message reporting heavy pack ice and icebergs in the immediate area never makes it to the Captain, the bridge, or any officer.

Keep a Sharp Lookout for Ice

After having Sixth Officer James Moody send word to the crow's nest to keep a sharp lookout for ice, Second Officer Charles Lightoller is near the end of his watch on the bridge of the *Titanic*. He is keeping his own lookout for ice, weather, and conditions in general.

> **British Wreck Commissioner's Inquiry** – Testimony of Second Officer Charles Lightoller, examined by the Solicitor General.
>
> 13695. And on this occasion, during this half hour, you were, in fact, using sometimes your eyes and sometimes your glasses?
>
> Lightoller – Yes, exactly.
>
> 13696. That brought you up to the end of your watch at 10 o'clock. Was the speed of the ship maintained up to that time?
>
> Lightoller – As far as I know.
>
> 13697. I mean you gave no orders to stop it?
>
> Lightoller – None whatever.
>
> 13698. Did the night continue clear and calm?
>
> Lightoller – Perfectly calm, up to 10 o'clock, and clear.
>
> 13699. And so far as those conditions are concerned, was there any change up to the time you handed over the ship?
>
> Lightoller – None whatever. If I might say one fact I have just remembered?

13700. Do.
Lightoller – Speaking about the Commander, with reference to ice, of course, there was a footnote on the night order book with regard to ice. The actual wording I cannot remember, but it is always customary. Naturally, every commander, in the night order book, issues his orders for the night, and the footnote had reference to keeping a sharp look out for ice. That is initialed by every Officer.
13701. Who was it that took the ship over from you at 10 o'clock?
Lightoller – Mr. Murdoch.

Murdoch's Watch

At 10:00 p.m. First Officer William Murdoch takes over the bridge watch. The night is still perfectly clear and the air temperature has dropped to 32°F. The cloudless, moonless night sky, brilliant with stars, meets the flat, calm sea to form a distant horizon.

"We're up around the reported ice about now," Second Officer Lightoller tells Murdoch.

"Certainly so," replies Murdoch, well aware of the dangers of meeting ice, "I had a lamp trimmer see to closing the forescuttle hatch to keep everything dark before the bridge."

Lightoller and Murdoch converse about the cold weather and other aspects of an ordinary watch handover between bridge officers as the *Titanic* continues steaming along at almost 22 knots.

> **British Wreck Commissioner's Inquiry** – Testimony of Second Officer Charles Lightoller, examined by the Solicitor General.
> 13707. When you handed over the ship at the end of your watch to Mr. Murdoch, just tell us, as carefully and fully as you can, what was the report you made to Mr. Murdoch? What was it you passed along to him?
> Lightoller – I should give him the course the ship was steering by standard compass. I mentioned the temperature – I think he mentioned the temperature first; he came on deck in his overcoat, and said, "It is pretty cold." I said, "Yes it is freezing." I said something about we might be up around the ice any time now, as far as I remember. I cannot remember the exact words, but suggested that we should be naturally round the ice. I passed the word on to him. Of course, I knew we were up to the 49 degrees by, roughly, half-past 9; that ice had been reported. He would know what I meant by that, you know—the Marconigram.
> 13708. I will tell you what I want to know. Did you say anything to him at 10 o'clock about a calculation having been made by the Junior Officer or anything of that sort?
> Lightoller – I may have done; I really cannot recollect it now, I may

have told him that Moody worked it out 11, or I may have told him half-past 9.

The Commissioner:
You yourself knew the boat was already in the ice region at this time?
Lightoller – Yes.

...13714. You are handing the ship over at 10 o'clock to Mr. Murdoch who was on the bridge at the time of the accident. Now what I want to know is what was it you told him, as fully as you can, about ice?
Lightoller – I am very sorry, but my memory will not help; I cannot recollect word for word, merely that I gave Mr. Murdoch to understand that we were in the ice region; as to the actual words I said to him, I may have put it many ways – I cannot remember how I did.

13715. I follow you cannot give us the actual words, and your memory does not serve you to say whether you told him anything about your view that you had passed the meridian or Mr. Moody's view that you would not reach the position until 11 o'clock?
Lightoller – No, I really could not say.

13716. Did you say anything to him about your conversation with the Captain and the order the Captain had given?
Lightoller – Oh! Undoubtedly.

13717. You did?
Lightoller – Oh, undoubtedly.

13718. You would report to him that the Captain had been on the bridge?
Lightoller – Yes.

13719. As far as you remember did you report anything about orders as to speed?
Lightoller – No orders. No orders were passed on about speed.

13720. (The Commissioner.) Did you tell him what message you had sent to the crow's-nest?
Lightoller – Yes, I did.

13721. You told Mr. Murdoch that?
Lightoller – Yes, I told Mr. Murdoch I had already sent to the crow's-nest, the carpenter, and the engine room as to the temperature, and such things as that – naturally, in the ordinary course in handing over the ship everything I could think of.

Properly relieved, Lightoller leaves for his deck go-round while Murdoch reviews the night order book.

10:00 p.m. is also the time Quartermaster Robert Hichens relieves his counterpart Alfred Oliver as helmsman at the ship's wheel.

Robert Hichens – Hichens, 29, served as Quartermaster on many vessels prior to signing on with the *Titanic* on April 6th in Southampton. Hichens had worked aboard mail boats and liners, and the troop ship *Dongola* just prior to joining *Titanic* but this is Hitchens first trip across the North Atlantic.

British Wreck Commissioner's Inquiry – Testimony of Robert Hichens, examined by the Attorney General.
935. Did you relieve Quartermaster Oliver?
Hichens – I did.
936. At what time?
Hichens – Ten o'clock.
937. What was the course given to you?
Hichens – N. 71º W.
938. Do you know what was the course which was given to Quartermaster Oliver?
Hichens – That was the same course.
939. Was there a course-board in the wheelhouse?
Hichens – Yes.
940. Was there anything on the course-board to indicate the course you were to steer?
Hichens – Yes, N. 71º.
941. That was on the course-board?
Hichens – That was on the course-board, the steering compass.
942. Was she a good steering ship?
Hichens – Fairly well, yes.

Archie Jewell is one of six lookouts aboard the *Titanic*. On this Sunday he is on the 8 to 10 p.m. watch with George Symons. With the weather clear no additional lookouts are deployed and the ship's speed is maintained at 21.5 knots.

British Wreck Commissioner's Inquiry: Testimony of Lookout Archie Jewell, examined by the Solicitor General.
13. Let us just get it clear. There was you and there was Symons in the crow's-nest. Were there no other look-out men on duty?
Jewell – No, not so long as the weather was clear.
14. Then on this night, during your watch from 8 to 10, was the weather clear?
Jewell – Yes.
15. Was there any moon?
Jewell – No, I never see no moon.
16. Was it starry?
Jewell – Yes.
17. Now do you remember when you were on your watch, from 8 to 10, any message coming to you about ice?
Jewell – Yes, about 9.30.
18. What was the message?
Jewell – To keep a sharp look-out for all ice, big and small.

19. How did the message come to you?
Jewell – On the telephone; we have a telephone in the crow's-nest.
20. That was telephoned up to the crow's-nest, and where was the telephone from?
Jewell – From the bridge.
21. Then it would be the Officer on the bridge who would telephone to you?
Jewell – Yes.
22. Do you happen to know who it was – which Officer it was?
Jewell – I could not say. I think the Second Officer was on watch at the time.
23. Up to that time, up to the time you got that message, had you seen any ice?
Jewell – No.
24. And after you got that message until you went off duty, did you keep a sharp look-out?
Jewell – Yes, and passed the word along.
25. And did you see any ice?
Jewell – No.
26. (The Commissioner.) What do you mean by "passed the word along" – to keep a sharp look-out for ice?
Jewell – To the other look-out.
27. How far does the other look-out stand from you?
Jewell – They relieve me from the nest.
28. (The Solicitor-General.) The two of you were together in the crow's-nest, and you would be relieved at 10 o'clock?
Jewell – Yes, that is right.
29. And when you were relieved at 10 o'clock did you hand on this message?
Jewell – Yes.
30. Who were the look-out men who relieved you at 10 o'clock?
Jewell – Fleet and Lee.

Mr. Frederick Fleet – Lookout, Age 24, joined the crew in Belfast. He had sailed for four years as lookout on the *Oceanic* before joining the *Titanic*.

Mr. Reginald Lee – Lookout, Age 41, transferred from the *Olympic* and signed on *Titanic* in Southampton on April 6th.

Archie Jewell and George Symons pass on Lightoller's message when they are relieved in the crow's nest at 10:00 p.m. by Fred Fleet and Reg Lee.

"Sharp lookout for ice, sure, anybody come up with our glasses?" Fleet asks Lee as they settle in.

"They haven't been seen since Southampton. I heard Blair left with the locker key so our glasses are locked up tight," Lee replies.

"And we're not expectin' an officer to offer up a pair now are we?" offers

Fleet.

"No, but they won't help much anyway what with the flat sea and no moon. Besides we'll spot any ice large enough to be a problem in good time without 'em."

"Well; I'd rather have glasses," says Fleet, then jokingly adds, "but I'll keep a sharp lookout …for ice was it?" The lookout men see their breath as they laugh in the clear, cold North Atlantic air.

> **British Wreck Commissioner's Inquiry** – Testimony of Lookout Frederick Fleet, examined by the Attorney General.
> 17235. When you relieved Jewell and Symons on Sunday, 14th April, at 10 o'clock you went to the crow's-nest?
> Fleet – Yes.
> 17236. Was any word passed to you when you relieved them?
> Fleet – Yes.
> 17237. Tell us what it was.
> Fleet – They told us to keep a sharp look out for small ice and growlers.
> …17244. Up to that time had you heard anything at all about ice?
> Fleet – No.
> 17245. Now at the time you went into the crow's-nest, which would be at 10 o'clock on that night, was the sky clear?
> Fleet – Yes.
> 17246. The sea we know was very calm?
> Fleet – The sea calm.
> 17247. The stars shining?
> Fleet – Yes.

Just north of the *Titanic* the *Californian* is stopped for the night in an ice field and attempts to send out another ice warning. At 10:55 p.m. the *Californian's* wireless operator calls up the *Titanic*. Senior Wireless Operator Jack Phillips is on duty and the strong signal from the nearby *Californian* is too loud in his ears. He abruptly interrupts the intended ice warning with, "Keep out! Shut up! You're jamming my signal. I'm working Cape Race." The *Californian's* only wireless operator listens to *Titanic's* wireless traffic until 11:30 p.m. then turns off his set and retires for the night.

Captain Smith and the Officers of the *Titanic* understand they are in the area of previously reported ice, but some of the ice reports did not reach the Captain or the bridge. In total, the reported ice positions tell a story of upcoming hazards that are immediate but, without all the ice warnings, the magnitude of the approaching peril is not fully grasped by the Captain or Officers. Without a clear picture, but with a clear night and flat sea, the *Titanic* steams full-speed-ahead into the perfect calm.

Chapter 9

ICEBERG RIGHT AHEAD

The Iceberg's Journey

The iceberg, a child of Mother Nature, was born when she broke away from her polar glacier and was set adrift in the currents west of Greenland. When the pack ice melted enough to free her, the current carried her south with the southwest wind. Accompanied by sister bergs and brother growlers she traveled through the Davis Strait into the Labrador Sea leaving her Greenland origins to the north. Large, even as icebergs go, she drifted south until she found and gouged the seabed of the shallower waters of the Labrador coast. While men build their unsinkable ship with open-top watertight compartments and precious few lifeboats, the iceberg waited with the patience of Father Time until the Earth, Moon, and Sun aligned to provide the high tides of January 1912. A tidal bulge, the size of which has not been known for a 1000 years, freed the iceberg from the ocean floor to continue her journey. The Labrador current carried the iceberg south of Newfoundland toward her destined appointment with man, his machine, and history.

In the spring of 1912 the iceberg and her sister bergs show off the tip of their magnificence, the portion present above the surface of the North Atlantic. Passing ships snap photographs while their Captains use wireless signals to alert other Captains of the presence and location of the icebergs. On the night of April 14, 1912 the iceberg is lying in silent witness to the majestic starlit sky in the perfect calm of the North Atlantic. She is undetected on the horizon, where it's hard to tell where the stars end and the dark calm sea begins, until she is suddenly discovered by a man riding high aboard man's unsinkable folly. But this man and the ones he warns see only the tip of the magnificent iceberg with the larger and more serious threat invisible beneath the sea. With the bow proudly displaying "TITANIC" in the cold night air, the ship desperately tries to avoid the giant iceberg but touches her just below the surface. With that touch *Titanic*, man's small and fragile creation, cracks like an eggshell and her watertight compartments, lifeboat capacity, and unsinkable myth will soon be cruelly exposed. The iceberg sheds specks of ice, her tiny tears, on the deck of the passing ship, knowing *Titanic's* maiden voyage will soon come to an early end on the bottom of the sea.

A Slight Haze but Nothing to Report

On Sunday night April 14, 1912 the sea temperature is slowly dropping and by 10:30 p.m. is down to 31°F. As is his habit when off duty and with little else to do, Chief Baker Charles Joughin enjoys a bit of his drink to lift his spirit and warm him against the cold April night. It won't be the last time he visits his bottle this night.

That Sunday night Fourth Officer Joseph Boxhall is working the 8:00 p.m. to Midnight watch on the bridge of the *Titanic*. Much of his shift is spent in the chart room, just off the bridge, working up stellar observations. No additional ice messages reach the bridge during his watch, but Boxhall expects that *Titanic* will come up on the reported ice during his shift.

The officers and crew of the *Titanic* tend to their duties in the freezing cold night air. Those duties include looking after the fresh water so it won't freeze and keeping a sharp lookout for ice.

Lookouts Fred Fleet and Reg Lee shiver trying to stay warm against the cold night as they keep watch in the crow's nest of the *Titanic*. As their watch wears on, the contrast between the sea and sky on the horizon begins to diminish with the appearance of a slight distant haze.

British Wreck Commissioner's Inquiry – Testimony of Lookout Frederick Fleet, examined by the Attorney General.
17248. Could you clearly see the horizon?
Fleet – The first part of the watch we could.
17250. After the first part of the watch what was the change if any?
Fleet – A sort of slight haze.
17252. Was the haze on the waterline?
Fleet – Yes.
17253. It prevented you from seeing the horizon clearly?
Fleet – It was nothing to talk about.
17254. It was nothing much, apparently?
Fleet – No.
17255. Was this haze ahead of you?
Fleet – Yes.
17256. Was it only ahead, did you notice?
Fleet – Well, it was only about 2 points on each side.

British Wreck Commissioner's Inquiry – Testimony of Lookout Reginald Lee, examined by the Attorney General.
2401. What sort of a night was it?
Lee – A clear, starry night overhead, but at the time of the accident there was a haze right ahead.
2402. At the time of the accident a haze right ahead?
Lee – A haze right ahead – in fact it was extending more or less round the horizon. There was no moon.

2403. And no wind?
Lee – And no wind whatever, barring what the ship made herself.
2404. Quite a calm sea?
Lee – Quite a calm sea.
2405. Was it cold?
Lee – Very, freezing.
…2419. Before half-past eleven on that watch—that is, seven bells—had you reported anything at all, do you remember?
Lee – There was nothing to be reported.

Examined by Mr. Harbinson.
2662. You knew that ice was about?
Lee – You could smell it.

"Iceberg Right Ahead!"

By 11:30 p.m., an hour and a half into their watch, the slight haze noticed by lookouts Fleet and Lee is directly ahead of the *Titanic*.

At 11:40 p.m., with the *Titanic* steaming ahead at 21.5 knots, Fleet sees an absence of stars in the haze on the horizon quickly take the form of a more distinct black mass and he suddenly realizes it's an iceberg, dead ahead, only 500 yards away.

British Wreck Commissioner's Inquiry – Testimony of Lookout Frederick Fleet, examined by the Attorney General.
17274. Who was it first saw the berg? Was it you or Lee?
Fleet – Well, I do not know.
17275. Well, which of you gave the signal?
Fleet – I did.
17276. …Now describe to my Lord what it was you saw?
Fleet – Well a black object.
17277. A black object. Was it high above the water or low?
Fleet – High above the water.
17278. What did you do?
Fleet – I struck three bells.
17279. Was it right ahead of you, or on the port or starboard bow?
Fleet – Right ahead.
17280. You struck three bells immediately, I suppose?
Fleet – Yes, as soon as I saw it.
17281. What did you do next?
Fleet – I went to the telephone.
17282. Was that on the starboard side of the crow's-nest?
Fleet – Yes.
17283. You went to the telephone, and ?
Fleet – Rang them up on the bridge.

After Fleet strikes three bells he immediately telephones the bridge. Sixth Officer James Moody picks up just as an anxious Fleet asks "Are you there?"

"Yes. What do you see?" asks Moody.

"Iceberg right ahead!"

"Thank you," Moody replies.

"Iceberg right ahead," Moody immediately tells First Officer William Murdoch who had already heard the warning bells.

"Hard-a-starboard," Murdoch instinctively shouts to Quartermaster Robert Hichens, who swings the wheel counter clockwise as far as it will go.

This command, a holdover from the days when the ship's rudder was controlled in an opposing manner by the ship's tiller, is to steer the bow to port or to the left. Murdoch immediately signals the engine room to stop the engines and then reverse them to full astern. With Hichens holding tight against the wheel the bow of the ship slowly moves to port, left of the fast approaching iceberg. Murdoch sounds the warning alarm to notify the firemen the watertight doors are about to close. The men on the bridge can now only watch, wait, and silently pray they have done enough. Their wait is a short one.

> **British Wreck Commissioner's Inquiry** – Testimony of Quartermaster Robert Hichens, examined by the Attorney General.
>
> 950. You got the order, "Hard-a-starboard"?
>
> Hichens – Yes.
>
> …956. You proceeded at once to put the wheel hard-a-starboard?
>
> Hichens – Immediately, yes.
>
> 957. Before the vessel struck had you had time to get the wheel right over?
>
> Hichens – The wheel was over then, hard over.
>
> …959. Who gave the order "hard-a-starboard"?
>
> Hichens – Mr. Murdoch, the First Officer.

> **British Wreck Commissioner's Inquiry** – Testimony of Lookout Frederick Fleet, examined by the Attorney General.
>
> 17288. What did you do next?
>
> Fleet – I kept the look-out again.
>
> 17289. You were approaching the berg meanwhile?
>
> Fleet – Yes.
>
> …17292. …Did you notice any change in the heading of your vessel after you gave this report?
>
> Fleet – After I rang them up on the phone and looked over the nest she was going to port.
>
> …17296. You saw her head turn to port, I think I understood you to say?
>
> Fleet – Yes.

From the crow's nest Fleet and Lee anxiously watch as the iceberg, towering 60 feet above the water, closes on the *Titanic*. Each is wordlessly trying to will the ship's bow away from the fast approaching peril and after several agonizingly long seconds, *Titanic* begins to veer to port. It appears she may clear the berg but the maneuver is too late—*Titanic's* bow strikes the iceberg below the waterline on the starboard side.

> **British Wreck Commissioner's Inquiry** – Testimony of Lookout Frederick Fleet, examined by the Attorney General.
> 17323. Did you have any conversation with your mate, Lee, after you struck?
> Fleet – Well, I told him I thought it was a narrow shave – after we had hit it, after we had hit the ice.
> 17324. (The Commissioner.) It was a little more than a shave?
> Fleet – That was only my idea.
> 17325. (The Attorney General.) You thought it was not anything very serious?
> Fleet – No, it was such a slight noise; that is why I said it.

Hard-a-Port

After being relieved at the wheel by Robert Hichens at 10:00 p.m. Quartermaster Alfred Olliver is running messages for the officers and is just returning to the bridge when the collision occurs. He hears First Officer Murdoch's hard-a-port order completing the port-around attempt that, as it turned out, was too little, too late. The hard-a-port maneuver did cause the stern of the *Titanic* to swing away and disengage from the underwater contact with the iceberg.

> **United States Senate Inquiry** – Testimony of Quartermaster Alfred Olliver, questioned by Senator Burton.
> Senator Burton – Just state what happened.
> Mr. Olliver – When I was doing this bit of duty I heard three bells rung up in the crow's nest, which I knew that it was something ahead; so I looked, but I did not see anything. I happened to be looking at the lights in the standing compass at the time. That was my duty, to look at the lights in the standing compass, and I was trimming them so that they would burn properly. When I heard the report, I looked, but could not see anything, and I left that and came and was just entering on the bridge just as the shock came. I knew we had touched something.
> Senator Burton – Just describe what that shock was.
> Mr. Olliver – I found out we had struck an iceberg.
> Senator Burton – Did you see that iceberg?
> Mr. Olliver – Yes; I did, sir.
> Senator Burton – Describe it.
> Mr. Olliver – The iceberg was about the height of the boat deck; if

anything, just a little higher. It was almost alongside of the boat, sir. The top did not touch the side of the boat, but it was almost alongside of the boat.
Senator Burton – What kind of a sound was there?
Mr. Olliver – The sound was like she touched something; a long grinding sound, like.
Senator Burton – How long did that sound last?
Mr. Olliver – It did not last many seconds.
Senator Burton – How far aft did the grinding sound go?
Mr. Olliver – The grinding sound was before I saw the iceberg. The grinding sound was not when I saw the iceberg.
Senator Burton – Where was the iceberg when you saw it, abeam or abaft?
Mr. Olliver – Just abaft the bridge when I saw it.
…Senator Burton – Do you know whether the wheel was hard-a-port then?
Mr. Olliver – What I know about the wheel—I was stand-by to run messages, but what I knew about the helm is, hard-a-port.
Senator Burton – Do you mean hard-a-port or hard astarboard?
Mr. Olliver – I know the orders I heard when I was on the bridge was after we had struck the iceberg. I heard hard-a-port, and there was the man at the wheel and the officer. The officer was seeing it was carried out right.
Senator Burton – What officer was it?
Mr. Olliver – Mr. Moody, the sixth officer, was stationed in the wheelhouse.
Senator Burton – Who was the man at the wheel?
Mr. Olliver – Hichens, quartermaster.
…Senator Burton – Did you see the iceberg?
Mr. Olliver – I tell you, sir. I saw the tip top of it.
Senator Burton – What color was it?
Mr. Olliver – It was not white, as I expected to see an iceberg. It was a kind of a dark-blue. It was not white.

"She Hit Us"

British Wreck Commissioner's Inquiry – Testimony of Lookout Reginald Lee, examined by the Attorney General.
2433. Where did you get the iceberg—on what side of you?
Lee – On the starboard hand as she was veering to port.
…2437. You were watching the berg. You had got the berg on the starboard side as the vessel's head veered to port?
Lee – Yes.

2438. And you watched it?

Lee – I watched it.

2439. Now could you give us any idea of what height there was of ice out of the water? I only want to have some idea of it.

Lee – It was higher than the forecastle; but I could not say what height was clear of the water.

…2441. …What did it look like? It was something which was above the forecastle?

Lee – It was a dark mass that came through that haze and there was no white appearing until it was just close alongside the ship, and that was just a fringe at the top.

2442. It was a dark mass that appeared, you say?

Lee – Through this haze, and as she moved away from it, there was just a white fringe along the top. That was the only white about it, until she passed by, and then you could see she was white; one side of it seemed to be black, and the other side seemed to be white. When I had a look at it going astern it appeared to be white.

2443. At that time the ship would be throwing some light upon it; there were lights on your own ship?

Lee – It might have been that.

2444. Can you give us an idea to the best of your ability how far off she was when you passed her to starboard?

Lee – She hit us.

…2759. I think there is one other thing you may still be able to tell us. When she struck, did the blow continue? Did she seem to be ripping along?

Lee – There was a rending of metal.

2760. Did you notice that?

Lee – Yes. You could hear that from where we were.

2761. You could hear a rending of metal?

Lee – Yes, you could hear a rending of metal right away. It seemed to be running right along the starboard side.

"Shut All Dampers"

Lead Fireman Frederick Barrett is on duty in Boiler-Room 6 in stokehold No. 10, located in *Titanic's* fifth compartment back from the bow, 26 feet below the waterline. He is in charge of eight firemen and four coal trimmers. They are busy keeping the furnaces fired for boiler six, the forward most boiler. Barrett is conversing with the Second Engineer on the starboard side of the hold when he sees the red-light signal to stop and shouts out to his firemen, "Shut all dampers," in order to deny air to the burning coal.

British Wreck Commissioner's Inquiry – Testimony of Frederick Barrett, examined by the Solicitor General.
1866. What was the next thing that happened?
Barrett – The crash came before we had them all shut.
1867. They were shutting them when the crash came?
Barrett – Yes.
1868. Where was the crash – what was it you felt or heard or saw?
Barrett – Water came pouring in two feet above the stokehold plate; the ship's side was torn from the third stokehold to the foreward end.
…1873. …Where did the water come from?
Barrett – Well, out of the sea, I expect.
1874. …I wanted to know where it came from—underneath or from the side or from the port side or from the starboard side?
Barrett – The starboard side.
1875. Can you tell us at all compared with where you were standing whether it came from above or below?
Barrett – About two feet from where I was standing.
…1901. …The water came into No. 6 section, where you were at work?
Barrett – Yes.
1902. Just after you had given the order to close the dampers, and while they were being closed; is that right?
Barrett – Yes.
1903. Did it come in fast?
Barrett – Yes.
1904. Did it come in fast enough to begin to flood the place?
Barrett – Yes.
1905. Then what was it that you did?
Barrett – Me and Mr. Hesketh jumped into this section, and the watertight compartment closed up.
…1915. Can you tell me whether that is one of the watertight doors that is worked from the bridge?
Barrett – It is.

Fireman George Beauchamp is among the firemen that stay behind in Boiler-Room 6.

British Wreck Commissioner's Inquiry – Testimony of George W. Beauchamp, examined by Mr. Raymond Asquith.
661a. Did you notice the shock when the ship struck?
Beauchamp – Yes, Sir, I noticed the shock.
662. Was it a severe shock?
Beauchamp – Just like thunder, the roar of thunder.
663. And immediately after the shock was any order given?

Beauchamp – Yes.
664. What order?
Beauchamp – To stand by, to stop. The telegraph went "Stop."
664a. (*The Commissioner.*) You got that order from the bridge, "Stop"?
Beauchamp – Yes.
664b. (*Mr. Raymond Asquith.*) And were the engines stopped at once or not?
Beauchamp – The telegraph rung off "Stop," so I suppose they were.
665. Did the engineer in your section give you any order?
Beauchamp – Yes; the engineer and the leading stoker shouted together – they said, "Shut the dampers."
666. Did you shut the dampers?
Beauchamp – Yes, immediately; "shut everything up."
667. Was anything done to the watertight doors after that time?
Beauchamp – Yes, immediately the telegraph rang "off" and the order was given to shut up everything, the watertight doors dropped.

"Just a Trembling of the Ship"

Less than 30 seconds elapse from the iceberg sighting to the collision. The impact jars and jostles the crew in the forward area but is barely noticed by most of the crew and passengers.

British Wreck Commissioner's Inquiry – Testimony of Saloon Steward James Johnson, examined by Mr. Rowlatt.
3358. Where were you when the accident happened?
Johnson – About the amidships saloon, I should think. We were all talking a few chairs up. It would be about the third or fourth table up.
…3360. Did you feel the shock?
Johnson – I did not feel much because we thought she had lost her wheel or something, and somebody passed the remark, "Another Belfast trip."
3361. Another what?
Johnson – To go back to Belfast it meant.
3362. Do you belong to Belfast?
Johnson – I belong to Scotland.

British Wreck Commissioner's Inquiry – Testimony of Seaman John Poingdestre, examined by Mr. Butler Aspinall.
2792. Did you feel the shock from the ship striking the iceberg?
Poingdestre – Yes.
2793. Where were you?
Poingdestre – Underneath the forecastle, outside the mess room, on the port side.

2795. Can you tell me this; at the time you felt the shock do you think your engines were working astern or working ahead?
Poingdestre – I felt the vibration, but I could not say whether the engine was going ahead or astern.
…2799. Having felt the shock, what did you do?
Poingdestre – Came out on the forewell deck.
2801. What did you see?
Poingdestre – I knew we had struck an iceberg.
2802. Why did you know you had struck an iceberg?
Poingdestre – I saw the ice on the deck.

British Wreck Commissioner's Inquiry – Testimony of Seamen Joseph Scarrott, examined by Mr. Butler Aspinall.
339. What did you feel?
Scarrott – Well, I did not feel any direct impact, but it seemed as if the ship shook in the same manner as if the engines had been suddenly reversed to full speed astern, just the same sort of vibration, enough to wake anybody up if they were asleep.
340. Did you feel anything besides that?
Scarrott – No.
341. Did you feel the ship strike anything?
Scarrott – No, not directly.
342. "Not directly," you say?
Scarrott – Not as if she hit anything straight on – just a trembling of the ship.

The same trembling of the ship is felt by Captain Smith who immediately rushes to the bridge and inquires of his First Officer, "What is it, what's happened?"
"We hit an iceberg, Sir," First Officer Murdoch tells his Captain. "I put her hard-a-starboard and reversed the engines but she was too close and we struck before I could port around. I could not do any more,"
"Close the watertight doors," Smith tells Murdoch.
"Sir, they are already closed," replies Murdoch.

Chapter 10

Immediate Aftermath

Half Speed Ahead

At 11:40 p.m. Fourth Officer Joseph Boxhall is on his way to the bridge when he is surprised by three bells. He reaches the bridge as the *Titanic's* bow strikes the iceberg and just as First Officer Murdoch pulls the lever closing the watertight doors. Murdoch then orders, "Hard-a-port" to complete the port-around and draw the ship's stern away from the iceberg preventing further damage.

Captain Smith arrives on the bridge just after the collision and quickly confers with First Officer Murdoch before sending Boxhall to inspect the forward part of the ship. Captain Smith then commands that the ship steam forward at half-speed ahead. Quartermaster Alfred Olliver is the stand-by quartermaster on the bridge.

> **United States Senate Inquiry** – Testimony of Quartermaster Alfred Olliver, questioned by Senator Burton.
> Senator Burton – Were the engines reversed; was she backed?
> Mr. Olliver – Not whilst I was on the bridge; but whilst on the bridge she went ahead, after she struck; she went half speed ahead.
> Senator Burton – The engines went half speed ahead, or the ship?
> Mr. Olliver – Half speed ahead, after she hit the ice.
> Senator Burton – Who gave the order?
> Mr. Olliver – The captain telegraphed half speed ahead.
> Senator Burton – Had the engines been backing before he did that?
> Mr. Olliver – That I could not say, sir.
> Senator Burton – Did she have much way on?
> Mr. Olliver – When?
> Senator Burton – When he put the engines half speed ahead?
> Mr. Olliver – No, sir. I reckon the ship was almost stopped.
> Senator Burton – He must have backed the engines, then.
> Mr. Olliver – He must have done so, unless it was hitting the iceberg stopped the way of the ship.

The half speed ahead order is possibly given to calm and reassure passengers or to make some progress toward Halifax, the closest port, but the order is also given before the full extent of the damage is realized.

Boiler Room 6

The Tank Top is the top of the ship's double bottom hull and serves as the foundation for the boilers, coal bunkers, engines, and other equipment. This is the only level with watertight doors that can be closed electronically from the bridge.

While the cold sea rushes in, Fireman George Beauchamp and the other firemen in Boiler-Room 6 rake the fires until the flooding causes them to bolt up the escape ladder to safety.

> **British Wreck Commissioner's Inquiry** – Testimony of George W. Beauchamp, examined by Mr. Raymond Asquith.
> 668e. After the watertight doors were closed, was any order given to you with regard to the fires?
> Beauchamp – Yes, I could not say when – it was a few minutes afterwards; the order was given to draw fires.
> 669. A few minutes after what?
> Beauchamp – After the order was given to shut up, an order was given to draw fires. I could not say how many minutes, but the order was given to draw fires.
> 670. And did you obey that order?
> Beauchamp – Yes.
> 671. Did you see any water?
> Beauchamp – Water was coming in on the plates when we were drawing the fires.
> 672. What do you mean by "the plates"?
> Beauchamp – The plates of the stokehold where you stand.
> 672a. (*The Commissioner.*) You mean where the stokers were standing?
> Beauchamp – Yes.
> 673. What happened then?
> Beauchamp – The water was just coming above the plates then.
> 673a. (*Mr. Raymond Asquith.*) You mean it was coming through the floor?
> Beauchamp – Yes, coming through the bunker door and over the plates.
> 674. Through the bunker door?
> Beauchamp – Yes, coming through the bunker like.
> 675. When you had drawn the fires what did you do next?
> Beauchamp – Waited till everything was shut down and an order was given. Someone shouted "that will do," when everything was safe, when everything was shut down.
> 676. What did you do?
> Beauchamp – When the order was given someone shouted "that will do," and so I went to the escape ladder.
> 677. Is that the ladder by which you get out of your stokehold when

the watertight doors are closed?
Beauchamp – Yes, the escape ladder.

Boiler Room 5

Lead Fireman Frederick Barrett and Engineer John Hesketh are in Boiler-Room No. 6, located in *Titanic's* fifth compartment back from the bow when the hull plates split open and the sea rushes in. Both scramble through the bulkhead doorway into Boiler-Room 5 in *Titanic's* sixth compartment as the watertight door closes behind them.

> **British Wreck Commissioner's Inquiry** – Testimony of Frederick Barrett, examined by the Solicitor General.
>
> 1916. At the time the accident happened it (watertight door) was open. You and Mr. Hesketh got through it just in time and it shut down behind you?
> Barrett – Yes.
> 1917. Then when you got into the next section, No. 5, did you find water there?
> Barrett – I went through this bunker here – it is a coal bunker – and then the water was rushing in.
> 1918. You say you went through the coal bunker, which is immediately abaft of the watertight door which you had passed through?
> Barrett – Yes.
> 1919. And did you find water coming in in that bunker?
> Barrett – Yes, pouring in the bunker.
> 1920. Was it coming in rapidly?
> Barrett – Yes.
> 1921. Could you tell us from what level it was coming in? The same as the other?
> Barrett – Two feet above the plates.
> …1924. And water was coming into the stokehold?
> Barrett – No, only into the bunker.
> 1925. And that is as far aft as the rent seemed to go?
> Barrett – Yes.
> 1926. Then what did you do when you got into No. 5?
> Barrett – Mr. Hesketh shouted out "all hands stand by your stations." That is for the men to stand by the fires. My station was in the next boiler room, and Mr. Shepherd and I went up an escape and down to the boiler room, but we could not get in. There were 8 feet of water in it.
> …1952. When you found there were eight feet of water there, what did you do then?
> Barrett – We came back to No. 5.

1953. Again using these emergency ladders?
Barrett – Yes.
1954. That really means, does it not, passing over the top of the bulkhead?
Barrett – Yes; you come out into the alleyway where the passengers would be.
…1964. And when you got back to No. 5, how much water was there in No. 5?
Barrett – None.
1965. Let us understand it. You said that the bunker in No. 5 had got some water coming into it?
Barrett – Yes; but the hole was not so big in that section as it was in No. 6 section. By the time the water had got there she had stopped.
1966. So that the water was not coming into No. 5 fast enough to flood it?
Barrett – No.
1967. Were the pumps working in No. 5?
Barrett – I could not tell you.

First Class Passengers

After 11:00 p.m. the First and Second Class lounges and smoking rooms are the only public rooms open. The men are still enjoying their evening when *Titanic* strikes the iceberg. Some of the men feel the vibration through the floor as the ship scrapes along the iceberg and leave to investigate. After learning they had struck an iceberg, and being reassured there was no reason to worry, most of the men return to their card games. William Carter chooses to check on his wife and children and Lucian Smith leaves to find Eloise, his bride of two months.

J. Bruce Ismay, President and Managing Director of International Mercantile Marine the parent company of White Star Line, is awakened by the impact.

> **British Wreck Commissioner's Inquiry** – Testimony of J. Bruce Ismay, examined by the Attorney General.
> 18502. …At the time of the impact you were in bed and asleep?
> Ismay – I was.
> 18503. You were awakened by the impact?
> Ismay – Yes.
> 18504. Did you realise what had happened?
> Ismay – I did not.
> 18505. Did you then get up?
> Ismay – I stayed in bed a little time, and then I got up. I really thought what had happened was we had lost a blade off the propeller.
> 18506. You got up, and where did you go?
> Ismay – I went along the passageway out of my room and I met a

steward.
18507. Did you ask him what had happened?
Ismay – I asked him what had happened.
18508. What did he say?
Ismay – He told me he did not know.
18509. Then what did you do?
Ismay – I went back to my room and I put a coat on, and I went up onto the bridge.

Dorothy Gibson and her mother Pauline settle into a late Bridge game with William T. Sloper, a stockbroker, and Frederick K. Seward, a New York lawyer Dorothy knows from church. They are still enjoying their game at 11:30 p.m. when a Library Steward asks them to finish up so he can close the library and retire. The group plays a few more minutes before concluding their game. Dorothy announces that she would enjoy a stroll on the promenade deck prior to retiring, and William Sloper agrees to accompany her but suggests they both put on warmer clothes. Sloper returns after retrieving his hat and coat and waits for Dorothy on the A Deck grand staircase landing.

He describes what happened next in his book – *Ship to Shore:*

> "Suddenly the ship gave a lurch and seemed to slightly keel over to the left. At the same moment Dorothy came hastily up the stairs and we ran together onto the promenade deck on the starboard side. Peering off into the starlit night, we could both of us see something white looming up out of the water and rapidly disappearing off the stern."

Lady Rothes and her cousin Gladys Cherry retire early on this cold Sunday night. She later told the *New York Herald* what happened next.

Excerpt from the *NY Herald* article published Sunday April 21, 1912:

> "I went to bed at half-past seven," she said, "and my cousin, Miss Gladys Cherry, who shared my room—No. 77 on deck B—also retired. It was bitterly cold. I was awakened by a slight jar and then a grating noise. I turned on the light and saw that it was 11:46, and I wondered at the sudden quiet. Gladys had not been awakened and I called her and asked did she not think it strange that the engines had stopped. As I opened our cabin door I saw a steward. He said we had struck some ice. Our fur coats over our night gowns were all the clothes we had. My cousin asked the chief steward if there was any danger and he answered, 'Oh no, we have just grazed some ice and it does not amount to anything.'
> "As we hurried along Lambert Williams came up and explained that the water-tight compartments must surely hold. Just then an officer hurried by, 'Will you all get your lifebelts on! Dress warmly and come up to A deck!' Quite stunned by the order, we all went. As I was going in to our stateroom my maid said water was pouring into the racquet court. I gave her some brandy, tied on her lifebelt and told her to go

straight up on deck. We had to ask a steward where our lifebelts could be found. The man said he was sure they were unnecessary until we told him we had been ordered to do so. We dressed as warmly as we could and went up to A deck. Mr. Brown, the purser, touched his hat as we passed, saying:—'It is quite all right; don't hurry!' What a lovely night it was!"

The Bishops are in their stateroom when *Titanic* strikes the iceberg. Dick Bishop is reading and feels a slight shudder during impact. His wife Helen had already retired and isn't disturbed by the collision but she is awakened by her husband a short time later.

> **United States Senate Inquiry** – Testimony of Helen Bishop, questioned by Senator Smith.
> Senator Smith – I wish you would tell the committee what you did after learning of this accident.
> Mrs. Bishop – My husband awakened me at about a quarter of 12 and told me that the boat had struck something. We both dressed and went up on the deck, looked around, and could find nothing. We noticed the intense cold; in fact, we had noticed that about 11 o'clock that night. It was uncomfortably cold in the lounge. We looked all over the deck; walked up and down a couple of times, and one of the stewards met us and laughed at us. He said, "You go back downstairs. There is nothing to be afraid of. We have only struck a little piece of ice and passed it." So we returned to our stateroom and retired. About 15 minutes later we were awakened by a man who had a stateroom near us. We were on B deck, No. 47. He told us to come upstairs. So we dressed again thoroughly and looked over all our belongings in our room and went upstairs. After being there about 5 or 10 minutes one of the men we were with ran up and spoke to the captain, who was just then coming down the stairs.
> Senator Smith – Who was the man?
> Mrs. Bishop – Mr. Astor.
> Senator Smith – Col. Astor?
> Mrs. Bishop – Yes. The captain told him something in an undertone. He came back and told six of us, who were standing with his wife, that we had better put on our lifebelts. I had gotten down two flights of stairs to tell my husband, who had returned to the stateroom for a moment, before I heard the captain announce that the lifebelts should be put on. That was about three or four minutes later that the captain announced the lifebelts should be put on. We came back upstairs and found very few people up.

Just after midnight the Squash Racket Court in section four on the lower (G) deck, 32 feet above the keel, begins to flood. The boilers shut down and the relief pipes begin to blow off huge noisy steam clouds. Colonel Archibald Gracie is asleep in his stateroom when the collision occurs but wakes when he hears steam escaping and realizes there's no machinery running.

> **United States Senate Inquiry** – Testimony of Colonel Archibald Gracie as told to Senator Smith.
>
> Col. Gracie – I was awakened in my stateroom at 12 o'clock. The time, 12 o'clock, was noted on my watch, which was on my dresser, which I looked at promptly when I got up. At the same time, almost instantly, I heard the blowing off of steam, and the ship's machinery seemed to stop.
>
> It was so slight I could not be positive of it. All through the voyage the machinery did not manifest itself at all from my position in my stateroom, so perfect was the boat. I looked out of the door of my stateroom, glanced up and down the passageway to see if there was any commotion, and I did not see anybody nor hear anybody moving at all; but I did not like the sound of it, so I thought I would partially dress myself, which I did, and went on deck.
>
> I went on what they call the A deck. Presently some passengers gathered around. We looked over the sides of the ship to see whether there was any indication of what had caused this noise. I soon learned from friends around that an iceberg had struck us.
>
> Presently along came a gentleman, described by Mr. Stengel here, who had ice in his hands. Some of this ice was handed to us with the statement that we had better take this home for souvenirs. Nobody had any fear at that time at all. I looked on deck outside to see if there was any indication of a list. I could not distinguish any. At that time I joined my friend, Mr. Clint Smith, and he and I in the cabin did notice a list, but thought it best not to say anything about it for fear of creating some commotion. Then we agreed to stick by each other through thick and thin if anything occurred, and to meet later on. He went to his cabin and I went to mine. In my cabin I packed my three bags very hurriedly. I thought if we were going to be removed to some other ship it would be easy for the steward to get my luggage out.
>
> As I went up on deck the next time I saw Mr. Ismay with one of the officers. He looked very self-contained, as though he was not fearful of anything, and that gave encouragement to my thought that perhaps the disaster was not anything particularly serious.

When Colonel Gracie comes across the squash racket coach in the stairway of C-Deck, he jokingly cancels his morning lesson. The noisy steam clouds continue from the boiler relief pipes while *Titanic's* orchestra plays ragtime in the First Class Lounge.

"She is making water in the forepeak tank…"

> **United States Senate Inquiry** – Testimony of Lamp Trimmer Samuel Hemming, questioned by Senator Smith.
> Senator Smith – What was your position on the Titanic?
> Mr. Hemming – Lamp trimmer.
> Senator Smith – What were your duties?
> Mr. Hemming – To mix the paint, and all that kind of thing for the ship, and to look after all the decks, trim all the lamps, and get them in proper order. That is all, I think. To put the lights in at nighttime and take them off at daybreak.
> Senator Smith – Where were you the night of this accident?
> Mr. Hemming – I was in my bunk.
> Senator Smith – Were you asleep?
> Mr. Hemming – Yes, sir.
> Senator Smith – Were you awakened by anybody?
> Mr. Hemming – I was awakened by the impact, sir.
> Senator Smith – What did you do when you were awakened?
> Mr. Hemming – I went out and put my head through the porthole to see what we hit. I made the remark to the storekeeper. "It must have been ice." I said, "I do not see anything."
> …Senator Smith – What did you do then?
> Mr. Hemming – I went up under the forecastle head to see where the hissing noise came from.
> Senator Smith – What did you find?
> Mr. Hemming – Nothing.
> Senator Smith – Go right along and tell what you did.
> Mr. Hemming – I did not see anything. I opened the forepeak storeroom; me and the storekeeper went down as far as the top of the tank and found everything dry.
> I came up to ascertain where the hissing noise was still coming from. I found it was the air escaping out of the exhaust of the tank.
> At that time the chief officer, Mr. Wilde, put his head around the hawse pipe and says: "What is that, Hemming?" I said: "The air is escaping from the forepeak tank. She is making water in the forepeak tank, but the storeroom is quite dry." He said, "All right," and went away.

Second Class Passengers

Lawrence Beesley is bound for a holiday in the States, and to visit his brother in Toronto. He is reading in his bunk in cabin 56 on the Saloon Deck. Like many passengers still awake he noticed, "what seemed to me nothing more than an extra heave of the engines and a more than usually obvious dancing motion of the mattress on which I sat."

He describes what happened next in his book – *The Loss of the SS. Titanic*.

"And so, with no thought of anything serious having happened to the ship, I continued my reading; and still the murmur from the stewards and from adjoining cabins, and no other sound: no cry in the night; no alarm given; no one afraid—there was then nothing which could cause fear to the most timid person. But in a few moments I felt the engines slow and stop; the dancing motion and the vibration ceased suddenly after being part of our very existence for four days, and that was the first hint that anything out of the ordinary had happened. We have all 'heard' a loud-ticking clock stop suddenly in a quiet room, and then have noticed the clock and the ticking noise, of which we seemed until then quite unconscious. So in the same way the fact was suddenly brought home to all in the ship that the engines—that part of the ship that drove us through the sea—had stopped dead. But the stopping of the engines gave us no information: we had to make our own calculations as to why we had stopped. Like a flash it came to me: 'We have dropped a propeller blade: when this happens the engines always race away until they are controlled, and this accounts for the extra heave they gave'; not a very logical conclusion when considered now, for the engines should have continued to heave all the time until we stopped, but it was at the time a sufficiently tenable hypothesis to hold. Acting on it, I jumped out of bed, slipped on a dressing-gown over pyjamas, put on shoes, and went out of my cabin into the hall near the saloon. Here was a steward leaning against the staircase, probably waiting until those in the smoke-room above had gone to bed and he could put out the lights. I said, 'Why have we stopped?' 'I don't know, sir,' he replied, 'but I don't suppose it is anything much.' 'Well,' I said, 'I am going on deck to see what it is,' and started towards the stairs. He smiled indulgently at me as I passed him, and said, 'All right, sir, but it is mighty cold up there.' I am sure at that time he thought I was rather foolish to go up with so little reason, and I must confess I felt rather absurd for not remaining in the cabin: it seemed like making a needless fuss to walk about the ship in a dressing-gown. But it was my first trip across the sea; I had enjoyed every minute of it and was keenly alive to note every new experience; and certainly to stop in the middle of the sea with a propeller dropped seemed sufficient reason for going on deck."

Charles E. Williams is on his way to New York to defend his squash title. After practicing Sunday night he leaves the squash racquet court about 10:30 p.m. and stops by the Second Class Smoking Room where several gentlemen are playing cards. Williams and others observing the card game are still there when they hear and feel the impact with the iceberg. Williams rushes out in time to see the towering berg on the starboard side as the *Titanic* passes by. After admiring the size of the passing iceberg, the card players return to their game.

Lawrence Beesley finds nothing but the freezing cold when he reaches the deck in his dressing gown but learns of the iceberg from Williams and the others in the Smoking Room. With this information Beesley decides to return to the warmth of his cabin and continue reading.

From his book – *The Loss of the SS. Titanic*:

> "Presently, hearing people walking about the corridors, I looked out and saw several standing in the hall talking to a steward—most of them ladies in dressing-gowns; other people were going upstairs, and I decided to go on deck again, but as it was too cold to do so in a dressing-gown, I dressed in a Norfolk jacket and trousers and walked up. There were now more people looking over the side and walking about, questioning each other as to why we had stopped, but without obtaining any definite information. I stayed on deck some minutes, walking about vigorously to keep warm and occasionally looking downwards to the sea as if something there would indicate the reason for delay. The ship had now resumed her course, moving very slowly through the water with a little white line of foam on each side. I think we were all glad to see this: it seemed better than standing still. I soon decided to go down again, and as I crossed from the starboard to the port side to go down by the vestibule door, I saw an officer climb on the last lifeboat on the port side—number 16—and begin to throw off the cover, but I do not remember that any one paid any particular attention to him. Certainly no one thought they were preparing to man the lifeboats and embark from the ship. All this time there was no apprehension of any danger in the minds of passengers, and no one was in any condition of panic or hysteria; after all, it would have been strange if they had been, without any definite evidence of danger."

A Rush of Water

Following the collision, Lead Fireman Frederick Barrett is working under the direction of Senior Assistant 2nd Engineer Bertie Wilson and Junior Assistant 2nd Engineers Herbert Harvey and Jonathan Shepherd. The bulkhead between the rapidly flooding Boiler-Room 6 and Boiler-Room 5 where Barrett and the Engineers are working is one side of the coal bunker that had been on fire throughout the voyage until the coal was finally cleared on Saturday.

> **British Wreck Commissioner's Inquiry** – Testimony of Frederick Barrett, examined by the Solicitor General.
> 1982. Then you were given an order by Mr. Harvey to remain there, and I suppose you did. What did the other hands there do?
> Barrett – I sent them up.
> 1984. Then you and Mr. Harvey were left alone in No. 5?

Barrett – And Mr. Wilson and Mr. Shepherd.
1985. The three engineers and you. Was it still clear of water?
Barrett – Yes.
1986. So the bulkhead in front of No. 5 was holding the water back?
Barrett – Yes.
…2012. …what was the next order you got from Mr. Harvey?
Barrett – To fetch some men down to keep the fires pulled.
2013. Would that be in all the sections?
Barrett – No; only in No. 5 section.
2014. How many men were wanted for that?
Barrett – I got between 15 and 20 down. There were 30 furnaces to pull.
…2019. How long do you think it would take them to draw the fires?
Barrett – It would take them 20 minutes.
2020. And after they had drawn the fires what happened to them?
Barrett – I sent them up again.
…2024. Then what was the next order?
Barrett – He (Mr. Harvey) asked me to lift the manhole plate off.
…2027. Is it in the floor?
Barrett – Yes.
…2030. And what happened then?
Barrett – Mr. Shepherd was walking across in a hurry to do something and then fell down the hole and broke his leg.
…2033. What did you do with him?
Barrett – We lifted him up and carried him into the pump room, me and Mr. Harvey.
2035. At this time, in this No. 5, was it easy to see?
Barrett – No, all the water which had been thrown on the furnaces when they were pulled out was making the stokehold thick with steam.
2036. And then you attended to Mr. Shepherd as best you could. Did you stay there after that?
Barrett – Just about a quarter of an hour after that.
2037. And during that quarter of an hour did No. 5 keep free from water?
Barrett – Yes.
2038. Then tell us what happened at the end of a quarter of an hour.
Barrett – A rush of water came through the pass – the forward end.
2039. You say the forward end of the pass. What is the pass?
Barrett – It is a space between the boilers where we walk through.
…2044. Supposing that the bulkhead which is the fore-end of No. 5 had given way, would water come through it and through this pass?
Barrett – Yes.
…2060. (The Commissioner.) Something that had been holding the

water back gave way?
Barrett – That is my idea, my Lord.
2061. (The Solicitor-General.) So it came with a rush? How fast did it fall?
Barrett – I never stopped to look. I went up the ladder. Mr. Harvey told me to go up.

Third Class Passengers

Daniel Buckley, traveling in steerage, is roused by the collision and finds the floor to his quarters wet as he leaves his bed to investigate.

> **United States Senate Inquiry** – Testimony of Daniel Buckley as told to Senator Smith.
> Mr. Buckley – …This night of the wreck I was sleeping in my room on the "Titanic", in the steerage. There were three other boys from the same place sleeping in the same room with me.
> I heard some terrible noise and I jumped out on the floor, and the first thing I knew my feet were getting wet; the water was just coming in slightly. I told the other fellows to get up, that there was something wrong and, that the water was coming in. They only laughed at me. One of them says: "Get back into bed. You are not in Ireland now."
> I got on my clothes as quick as I could, and the three other fellows got out. The room was very small, so I got out, to give them room to dress themselves.
> Two sailors came along, and they were shouting: "All up on deck, unless you want to get drowned."
> When I heard this, I went for the deck as quick as I could. When I got up on the deck I saw everyone having those lifebelts on only myself; so I got sorry, and said I would go back again where I was sleeping and get one of those life preservers; because there was one there for each person.
> I went back again, and just as I was going down the last flight of stairs the water was up four steps, and dashing up. I did not go back into the room, because I could not. When I went back toward the room the water was coming up three steps up the stairs, or four steps; so I did not go any farther. I got back on the deck again, and just as I got back there, I was looking around to see if I could get any of those lifebelts, and I met a First Class passenger, and he had two. He gave me one, and fixed it on me.
> …Senator Smith – You had two or three boys with you?
> Mr. Buckley – Yes; three boys that came from the same place in Ireland.
> Senator Smith – What became of those other three boys?

Mr. Buckley – I can not say. I did not see them any more after leaving the room where I parted from them.

Third Class passenger Miss Amy Stanley is traveling to America to become a children's maid in New Haven, Connecticut. She described her experience in a letter to her parents.

Partial content of Amy Stanley's letter:

> "I was writing a postcard the night that the boat struck the iceberg. It was about 11:30 p.m. I got out of bed and put my coat on and went out on deck and asked the steward what was the matter. He told me it was only the engines stopped, and ordered all the women back to bed. But I did not go. I shared a cabin with an American lady and child. I assisted them to dress, and then we went up on deck."

From his berth on F Deck in the bow of the ship, Norwegian Olaus Abelseth is jostled awake by the impact. After dressing, he goes up and discovers ice on deck on the starboard side. Abelseth makes his way to E Deck and heads aft along the "Scotland Road" alleyway in search of Karen, the 16 year old daughter of his friend, whom he had promised to look after. He finally finds her near the main Third Class staircase near the stern. Abelseth and Karen then meet up with the rest of their group and make their way to the aft Well Deck to wait for instructions.

Assessing the Damage

After impact the Mail Sorting Room in compartment 4 of the Orlap Deck is flooding. All five Postal Clerks work against the quickly rising water to move 200 bags of registered mail, weighing nearly 100 lbs each, up one deck to the G Deck Mailroom. Postal Clerk Jago Smith then leaves to find Captain Smith. Soon the G Deck Mailroom also starts to flood and the Postal Clerks start carrying mail to D deck believing the mail bags would eventually be off-loaded through the First Class entrance.

Shortly after Captain Smith issued the half-ahead order Chief Officer Henry Wilde arrives on the bridge with news that the forepeak ballast tank is taking in seawater. With the news of this breach Captain Smith orders the engines stopped. Captain Smith then goes to the Marconi room and tells Senior Wireless Operator Jack Phillips that the ship struck an iceberg and to be ready to send out the distress call if it becomes necessary.

Fourth Officer Boxhall makes his way down to F deck to look for damage and finds none, but he does find small chunks of ice on the Well Deck on his way back to the bridge.

About 11:55 p.m. Boxhall returns to the bridge and reports to Captain Smith that he found no damage on the decks he inspected. The Captain then sends him to find the Carpenter to sound the ship (check for damage). After leaving the bridge Boxhall meets Carpenter John Hutchinson and later Mail Clerk

Jago Smith both on their way to find the Captain with news that the forward compartments are flooding. Boxhall tells them to report to the Captain then he proceeds to the Mail Sorting Room to determine the extent of the flooding.

About this time Bruce Ismay arrives on the bridge in his slippers with his overcoat over his pajamas.

> **British Wreck Commissioner's Inquiry** – Testimony of J. Bruce Ismay, examined by the Attorney General.
> 18510. Was Captain Smith there?
> Ismay – He was.
> 18511. Then did you ask him what had happened?
> Ismay – I did.
> 18512. And what did he tell you?
> Ismay – He told me we had struck ice.
> 18513. Did you ask him anything further?
> Ismay – I asked him whether he thought the damage was serious, and he said he thought it was.
> 18514. What did you do then?
> Ismay – I then went downstairs again; down below.
> 18515. Did you meet Mr. Bell, the Chief Engineer?
> Ismay – I met the Chief Engineer at the top of the staircase.
> 18516. Did you have some conversation with him – will you tell us what it was?
> Ismay – I asked him whether he thought the ship was seriously damaged, and he said he thought she was, but, as far as I remember, he thought the pumps would control the water.
> …18519. Did you hear any order given by Captain Smith?
> Ismay – I went up after that on to the bridge, and I heard Captain Smith give an order; I am not quite certain whether it was to lower the boats or to get the boats out; it was in connection with the boats.

Just before Midnight Captain Smith issues orders to uncover the lifeboats. Chief Officer Wilde takes charge of the even numbered lifeboats on the port side while First Officer Murdoch oversees starboard preparations. Wilde sends Quartermaster Oliver to find the boatswain and tell him to uncover the lifeboats and make them ready for lowering. Smith also orders the manual watertight bulkhead doors be closed. Unlike the automatic doors that had been closed from the bridge, the remaining watertight doors at the other deck levels have to be closed manually by the crew using a special key.

> **United States Senate Inquiry** – Testimony of Bedroom Steward Henry S. Etches, questioned by Senator Smith.
> Senator Smith – Where were you when the collision came?
> Mr. Etches – Asleep, sir.
> Senator Smith – In what part of the ship?

Mr. Etches – In our apartments, which were about the middle of the E Deck, in what we call the working alleyway.

Senator Smith – How many people slept in the same room with you?

Mr. Etches – Nineteen of us, sir.

Senator Smith – What time did you retire that night?

Mr. Etches – At half-past 9, sir. I was due again at 12 o'clock.

Senator Smith – Due on watch or on duty at 12 o'clock midnight?

Mr. Etches – Yes, sir.

Senator Smith – How were you awakened?

Mr. Etches – I was awakened by something, but I did not know what it was, and I called to my mate and I said "What time is it that they are going to call us next?" It was then between 25 minutes and 20 minutes to 12. He said, "I don't know." I turned over to go to sleep again. At that minute I heard a loud shout, "Close watertight bulkheads." I recognized it as our boatswain's voice; it was extra loud. I looked out and he was running from fore to aft.

Senator Smith – What was he saying?

Mr. Etches – The one shout, "Close watertight bulkhead doors."

Captain Smith then leaves the bridge to make his own inspection tour with Thomas Andrews. Together they make their way to the lower decks to inspect the damage and flooding. Captain Smith asks Andrews for his initial assessment. "Three compartments already gone," replies Andrews, referring to three watertight compartments. At this point Smith and Andrews separate with Andrews continuing his inspection while Captain Smith returns to the bridge.

The Captain then gives the order for passengers and crew to get ready with life belts on deck. He then sends Fourth Officer Boxhall to rouse Officers Lightoller and Pitman and to work out the ship's position.

Thomas Andrews soon discovers that five, not three, watertight compartments are rapidly flooding and realizes the *Titanic* is doomed. He races back up to the bridge, arriving about 12:25 a.m. Andrews finds Captain Smith and Bruce Ismay on the bridge and together they move to the chart room where Andrews quickly reports *Titanic's* unavoidable fate, "Five compartments are flooding and the pumps can't keep up. Captain she will founder."

"But the *Titanic* can't sink," replies Bruce Ismay in a tone of unbelieving surprise. "She…"

"She certainly can and will," Andrews says, cutting off Ismay, then adds,"It is a mathematical certainty that if more than four forward holds flood, the water will spill into the next compartment, then the next, and continue to do so. Gentlemen the *Titanic* is doomed."

"How long can she last?" asks Captain Smith.

"An hour, two at most," replies Andrews.

Chapter 11

Keep the Bad News Quiet

Thomas Andrews, while on his way to inspect for damage and before realizing the *Titanic* will founder, reassures some of the First Class passengers.

British Wreck Commissioner's Inquiry – Testimony of Saloon Steward James Johnson, examined by Mr. Rowlatt.
3400. Had you seen Mr. Andrews in the reception room?
Johnson – I saw him speaking to some ladies, and they were all in a bunch and he said he thought it would be all right. He said, "Be easy, it will be all right." I asked him, and he said; "All right."
3401. Were those First Class passengers?
Johnson – Yes, all First Class passengers just at the corner of the reception room, down the companion stairs.

Sam Hemming went back to bed after reporting the forepeak ballast tank was making water but is roused a short time later.

United States Senate Inquiry – Testimony of Lamp Trimmer Samuel Hemming, questioned by Senator Smith.
Senator Smith – What did you do then?
Mr. Hemming – I went back and turned in.
Senator Smith – Do you mean that you went back to your bunk and went to sleep?
Mr. Hemming – Me and the storekeeper went back and turned into our bunks.
Senator Smith – How long did you stay in your bunks?
Mr. Hemming – We went back in our bunks a few minutes. Then the joiner came in and he said: "If I were you, I would turn out, you fellows. She is making water, one-two-three, and the racket court is getting filled up."
Just as he went, the boatswain came, and he says, "Turn out, you fellows," he says; "you haven't half an hour to live." He said: "That is from Mr. Andrews." He said: "Keep it to yourselves, and let no one know."

After reporting *Titanic's* fate to Captain Smith, Thomas Andrews happens upon Stewardess Mary Sloan and he gently advises her, "It is very serious, but keep the bad news quiet, for fear of panic."

Mary Sloan does keep the seriousness of the situation to herself as do others who learn the truth early on. This initial attempt to avert panic appears to be working. Many passengers, not yet fully aware of the severity and urgency of the situation, are in no particular hurry to leave their warm cabins let alone get off an unsinkable ship on a freezing cold April night.

Lawrence Beesley describes the sensibilities of those on deck this way in his book – *The Loss of the SS. Titanic:*

> "Now, before we consider any further the events that followed, the state of mind of passengers at this juncture, and the motives which led each one to act as he or she did in the circumstances, it is important to keep in thought the amount of information at our disposal…a perfectly still atmosphere; a brilliantly beautiful starlight night, but no moon, and so with little light that was of any use; a ship that had come quietly to rest without any indication of disaster—no iceberg visible, no hole in the ship's side through which water was pouring in, nothing broken or out of place, no sound of alarm, no panic, no movement of any one except at a walking pace; the absence of any knowledge of the nature of the accident, of the extent of damage, of the danger of the ship sinking in a few hours, of the numbers of boats, rafts, and other lifesaving appliances available, their capacity, what other ships were near or coming to help—in fact, an almost complete absence of any positive knowledge on any point. I think this was the result of deliberate judgment on the part of the officers, and perhaps, it was the best thing that could be done."

Bread for the Boats

Chief Baker Charles Joughin and his men are tasked with supplying the lifeboats with bread and other provisions.

> **British Wreck Commissioner's Inquiry** – Testimony of Chief Baker Charles Joughin, examined by the Solicitor General.
> 5919. Did not you hear any orders given about provisions for the boats?
> Joughin – Not directly from any Officer. Word was passed down from the top deck and I received it eventually through other channels.
> 5920. What was it?
> Joughin – "Provision boats," or put any spare provisions you have in the boats, that was it.
> 5921. As I understand, the biscuits, the hard bread, would be in the boats already, or ought to be?
> Joughin – Yes.

The Perfect Calm

5922. And it would only be the soft bread you had to think about?
Joughin – Any surplus stuff we had around that was handy we would put into the boats.
5923. You heard that order passed along. Did you take steps to send up some provisions to the boats?
Joughin – Yes.
5924. What was it you did, you and your men?
Joughin – I sent thirteen men up with four loaves apiece, 40 pounds of bread each as near as I could guess.
…5978. …Could you tell us at all what time you think that was? – You say it was half-past twelve when you got on to the boat deck yourself?
Joughin – That was just after I had passed the first lot of bread up, and I went down to my room for a drink, as a matter of fact, and as I was coming back I followed up my men on to the deck.

Warm Clothing and Lifebelts

Orders pass down to the Bedroom Stewards to make the rounds of their rooms and have the passengers proceed to the Boat Deck in warm clothing with lifebelts on. The Bedroom Stewards, many unaware the *Titanic* is sinking, rouse their passengers while reassuring them the situation is under control. The word passes quickly amongst First Class passengers.

The First Class Bedroom Stewards are responsible for three to five rooms and in most cases know by name the passengers who occupy those rooms. Many of those rooms are close to the Boat Deck where skeptical First Class passengers are the first to arrive.

United States Senate Inquiry – Testimony of Alfred Crawford, questioned by Senator Smith
Senator Smith: What is your business or occupation?
Mr. Crawford – Bedroom Steward.
…Senator Smith: What are your duties?
Mr. Crawford – Attending to all the passengers requirements, cleaning their rooms and everything, sir.
Senator Smith: In any particular part of the ship?
Mr. Crawford – Yes, sir; in one certain part. I was on B deck, right forward.
Senator Smith: That is where?
Mr. Crawford – In the fore part of the ship; in the bow part.
Senator Smith: That is on the second from the Boat Deck?
Mr. Crawford – The second from the Boat Deck; yes, sir.
Senator Smith: Do you know any of the passenger's in your part of this ship?
Mr. Crawford – I know three ladies: Mrs. Rogers, Miss Rogers, and her

niece; also Mr. Stewart, that I had in my section, and there was a Mr. and Mrs. Bishop.
Senator Smith: Mr. and Mrs. Bishop?
Mr. Crawford – They were a newly married couple.
Senator Smith: I would like you to state what you did just after the impact on the night of the accident.
Mr. Crawford – After we struck I went out and saw the iceberg passing along the starboard side. Then I went back and went around to all the staterooms to see that all the passengers were up and called all those; and as I was going around Mr. and Mrs. Bishop came out and asked me what was the matter. I said we had run into a piece of ice. I told them to go back to their rooms and dress; to put on as much of their clothes as they could; that I did not think there was any immediate danger. Afterwards a gentleman—a Mr. Stewart—came down and asked me to help dress him, and to tie his shoes, and I did so. He went on deck and came back again and told me that it was serious; that they had told passengers to put on lifebelts. I got the lifebelts down and tied one on him, and also one on others. I gave them to other ladies and gentlemen on the deck. After that, during that time, I saw Mr. Ismay come out of his room, and a bedroom steward named Clark, and went on deck.

First Class passengers begin to congregate on the Boat Deck. Dick and Helen Bishop are among the first but still not believing it would be necessary to board a lifeboat, leave their newly acquired dog, Freu Freu, in their stateroom. Finding only a few passengers on the starboard side they go to the port side to investigate but find only two passengers and return to the starboard side. This would prove to be a fortunate decision for Mr. Bishop.

Other First Class passengers, along with their personal maids and valets, make their way on deck with their lifebelts on. Among them Margaret Brown, Mr. and Mrs. Isidor Straus, and Sir Cosmo and Lady Duff Gordon. The First Class passengers, with lifebelts on, converse and enjoy *Titanic's* orchestra as they comply with what many believe is a temporary inconvenience. Benjamin Guggenheim makes a brief appearance on the Boat Deck with Madame Aubart and her maid, Miss Emma Sägesser, before deciding to return to his cabin to change into more appropriate dress. Just before leaving the deck Guggenheim tries to comfort Emma, telling her in German, "We will soon see each other again! It's just a repair. Tomorrow the *Titanic* will go on again."

While many First Class passengers, families, and servants make their way to the Boat Deck, the Wideners, Carters, Thayers, Ryersons, and the ladies' personal maids congregate on the enclosed First Class promenade on A Deck to await further instructions. Colonel and Mrs. Astor choose to wait in the gymnasium where it is warmer and Madeleine will be more comfortable. Sitting on mechanical horses with his lifebelt on and dressed in his Blue serge suit and brown flannel shirt with diamond cufflinks, Colonel Astor checks the time on his gold pocket watch. He still isn't convinced all the fuss is necessary. To pass the time he finds a spare lifebelt and cuts the lining with his knife to show Madaleine what makes it float. Joining the Astors in the gymnasium for a time are Mr. Henry Sleeper Harper, whose occupation is listed as "Of Independent Means," and his wife Myra (Haxtun). Accompanying the Harpers is their dragoman (interpreter/guide) Hammad Hassab who was employed by Harper in Cairo, Egypt. Harper's reason for bringing this mysterious and handsome servant with him on the voyage home has been a topic of speculation and gossip among the First Class passengers the entire trip. The Harper's Pekinese dog, Sun Yat-Sen, is also on hand.

Some choose not to comply with the Steward's urging and for the time being remain steadfastly in the place of their choosing. In the First Class Smoking Room Major Butt, Frank Millet, and Clarence Moore continue their card game while journalist and spiritualist William Stead is content reading a book.

Second Class Bedroom Stewards covering up to 10 rooms, and Third Class Stewards covering as many as 25 rooms, also make the rounds knocking on doors to wake unsuspecting passengers.

> **British Wreck Commissioner's Inquiry** – Testimony of Third Class Steward John E. Hart, examined by the Solicitor General.
> 9833. Is your name Hart or Stewart?
> Hart – Hart.
> 9834. Were you a Third Class steward on the "Titanic"?
> Hart – Yes.
> 9835. And at the time when the collision occurred were you off duty and in your bunk?
> Hart – Yes.
> …9847. You heard there had been an accident?
> Hart – Yes, they said there had been an accident.
> 9848. I think at first you did not think it was serious, and did not take much notice of it?
> Hart – Yes, and went to sleep.
> 9849. Who was it who came afterwards and gave instructions?
> Hart – The Chief Third Class Steward, Mr. Kieran.
> 9851. What were the orders to pass along?
> Hart – He passed several orders. To me he said, "Go along to your rooms and get your people about."
> 9852. Would your rooms be the Third Class passengers' rooms?
> Hart – Yes.
> 9853. Which part of the Third Class accommodation is it that you were responsible for?
> Hart – Section K and part of M, the adjoining section, on E deck.
> …9865. How many Third Class passengers had you in your sections altogether?

Hart – Somewhere about 58.

…9879. When you got those instructions just tell us what you did.

Hart – The Chief Third Class Steward was there, and he said "Get your people roused up and get lifebelts placed upon them; see that they have lifebelts on them." I did so.

…9883. (The Commissioner.) Were most of them up or were they asleep?

Hart – The majority were up. They had been aroused before I got there.

9884. (The Solicitor General.) They are not single cabins, these Third Class compartments, are they; not single berths?

Hart – They consisted of four berth-rooms and two berth-rooms, and two six berth-rooms.

9885. And what did you do about the lifebelts?

Hart – I saw the lifebelts placed on them that were willing to have them put on them.

9886. (The Commissioner.) Some would not put them on?

Hart – Some refused to put them on.

9887. (The Solicitor General.) Did they say why?

Hart – Yes, they said they saw no occasion for putting them on; they did not believe the ship was hurt in any way.

9888. Up to this time were any instructions given for your people to go to any other part of the ship?

Hart – Not to my knowledge.

9889. Just tell us next what the next instructions were, or the next thing that you did. I will put the question in another way. You have told us that the instructions you got from Mr. Kieran, that you were to rouse up your people and get lifebelts on them. Did he say anything about future instructions that would be given?

Hart – He said there would be further instructions; that I was to stand by my own people.

…9915. You would have colleagues, other of the Third Class Stewards, of course; do you know whether they were doing what you were doing?

Hart – All the men that had rooms were.

…9918. You mean to say they roused the passengers and tried to get them to put on lifebelts?

Hart – Yes.

9919. How many Third Class Stewards would there be who would have charge of rooms in the afterend of the ship?

Hart – Eight.

Latitude 41.46 N, Longitude 50.14 W

While *Titanic's* bow is filling with the cold North Atlantic sea, Fourth Officer Boxhall calculates *Titanic's* position based on the speed they had maintained throughout the night. Boxhall works out their position to be Latitude 41.46 N, Longitude 50.14 W and writes this down on a piece of paper for Captain Smith.

> **British Wreck Commissioner's Inquiry** – Testimony of Joseph G. Boxhall, examined by the Solicitor General.
>
> 15635. …When the "Titanic" struck, of course it was necessary to ascertain her position in order that the distress messages might be sent out?
>
> Boxhall – Just so.
>
> 15639. So that what you had to do after the disaster had occurred would be to take the position on the chart at 7:30, take your course, take your speed and calculate where you would be?
>
> Boxhall – Yes, from the 7:30 position I allowed a course and distance which gave the position. I worked it out for 11:46 as a matter of fact.
>
> 15642. And that is the position, 41º 46' N., 50º 14' W.?
>
> Boxhall – Yes.
>
> 15643. Can you tell me what speed you assumed as between the 7:30 position and the time you struck?
>
> Boxhall – Twenty-two knots.
>
> 15653. You thought 22 knots was the proper average speed during that time?
>
> Boxhall – Yes, I allowed 22 knots, and I thought that was about correct.

While *Titanic's* orchestra entertains unsuspecting and reassured passengers, Captain Smith takes *Titanic's* estimated position to the Marconi room and instructs Senior Operator Jack Phillips to commence with the *CQD* distress call.

Chapter 12

Distress Calls and Rockets

"It is plain to see that the need, which nothing but wireless telegraphy can fill, is that of communication with vessels at sea. Our government, with its usual enterprise, is alive to this. Wireless telegraphy undoubtedly came into the navy to stay, and has grown in usefulness and importance. Its commercial application over the seas is already vast. We have been accustomed to feel that when loved ones went out upon the great deep they passed, for the time being, beyond our knowledge and beyond reach of our sympathy, and became imprisoned in a realm of danger from which no cry for help or assurance of safety could reach us. Now, through this wonderful invention, we may learn their progress from day to day, even from hour to hour. They can tell us of their daily health; they can transact matters of daily business; they can assure us that they are speeding over sunny seas; or they can ask, when in distress, that a vessel be sent to their relief."

~ 1912, Book of Wonders and Curious Things

CQD and SOS

The *SOS* distress signal was first proposed at the international Conference on Wireless Communication at Sea, in Berlin, in 1906 and was ratified by the international community in 1908. British wireless operators prefer the older *CQD* code, however, and rarely use the *SOS* signal.

> **British Wreck Commissioner's Inquiry** – Testimony of Guglielmo Marconi, examined by the Attorney General.
> 24850. Mr. Marconi, you are the inventor of your system of wireless telegraphy?
> Marconi – Yes.
> ...24854. ...Has there been a form of agreement between your Company and shipowners which was arrived at in the early stages of your system of wireless telegraphy, and which is practically still adhered to?
> Marconi – Yes.
> 24856. ... CQ, as I understand it – you will correct me if it is wrong

in summarising the effect of this document—is a call which means "all stations"?
Marconi – Yes.
24857. And then the signal CQD is, or was, at any rate, the distress signal that is to be used?
Marconi – Yes, the distress signal.
24858. On and after the 1st February, 1904, was the call to be given by ships in distress or requiring assistance, CQD?
Marconi – Yes, CQD.
24859. And, according to the Regulations, that signal must not be given except by order of the Captain of the ship in distress – is that right?
Marconi – Yes, that is right.
24860. Or by other vessels retransmitting the signals which they have received on account of the ship in distress?
Marconi – Exactly.
24861. According to your regulations I see all stations must recognise the urgency of this call and make every effort to establish satisfactory communication with the least possible delay?
Marconi – Yes.
…24865. In 1906 the International Radio-Telegraph Convention laid down some principles and regulations which were to govern wireless telegraphic communications at sea?
Marconi – Yes.
24866. Which came into force in July, 1908?
Marconi – July, 1908.
24867. And those are substantially, with certain additions of your own, the regulations which are still in force?
Marconi – They are substantially the regulations still in force.
…24870. At that time was the distress call altered from CQD to SOS?
Marconi – It was, but I might say that CQD, being so well known amongst the operators on the ships, has been used as well as the SOS as an additional sign.
24871. That means that a number of operators were in the habit of using the CQD, or knew of it as a distress signal, and that sometimes that is used and sometimes the SOS?
Marconi – I should say the SOS is always used, but also the CQD.
24872. Is the SOS a very simple signal to give or receive?
Marconi – Yes, it is simple.
24873. Can you tell us why the SOS was adopted?
Marconi – I really cannot say. I think CQD is just as good, but they wanted to make a change.
24874. (The Commissioner.) Who made the change?
Marconi – The International Convention on Wireless telegraphy held

at Berlin in 1906.

...24877. What does SOS stand for, anything, or is it simply three letters?

Marconi – Simply three letters, My Lord.

24878. I understand that CQD stood for "Come quick, danger"?

Marconi – It can be interpreted that way.

24879. (The Attorney General.) It really is an easy way to remember it, and SOS is, I am told, "Save our souls." It is simply an easy way to remember it?

Marconi – That is so.

Come at Once – Have Struck Berg

On the night of April 14, 1912 Senior Wireless Operator Jack Phillips had just finished clearing a backlog of passenger messages to and from Cape Race when he feels the collision. A few minutes later Junior Wireless Operator Harold Bride enters from the adjoining cabin to start his shift.

"Did that business that shook the ship rouse you?" Phillips asks Bride as he enters the Marconi Room.

"What business would that be?"

"It felt as though we struck something just a few minutes ago."

"Well, I slept right through whatever it was," said Bride before inquiring about the status of the message backlog.

> **British Wreck Commissioner's Inquiry** – Testimony of Harold Bride, examined by the Attorney General.
>
> 16495. ... Tell us in your own way; how did you know first of all there had been a collision?
>
> Bride – Mr. Phillips intimated that he thought we had struck something from the fact of feeling the shock.
>
> 16496. You yourself had not felt it?
>
> Bride – No.
>
> 16497. Had you been asleep?
>
> Bride – Yes.
>
> 16498. Did you remain in the room with Mr. Phillips at 12 o'clock?
>
> Bride – Yes.
>
> 16499. At that time were you sending any messages?
>
> Bride – No.
>
> 16500. Did the Captain come in to you?
>
> Bride – He did shortly afterwards.
>
> 16501. Between the time of your coming up, and the Captain coming in to you, had you sent any messages?
>
> Bride – No.
>
> 16502. Or received any?

Bride – No.
16503. Then what did the Captain say?
Bride – The Captain told us he wanted assistance.
16504. I am not quite sure that I understand what you mean by that: assistance where?
Bride – He gave us to understand he wanted us to call CQD
16505. That is to say that what the Captain wanted you to do was to call for assistance from other vessels?
Bride – Yes.

Captain Smith delivers *Titanic's* position to Senior Wireless Operator Jack Phillips.

At 12:27 a.m. Phillips sends out the first *CQD* distress call for *MGY* (*Titanic's* call letters) over the ship's wireless. The message is picked up by the *La Provence* and by the Cape Race station.

The *Mount Temple* also receives *Titanic's* distress call and then sends:

> Titanic sending CQD Answer him, but he replies: "Can not read you, old man, but here my position, 41.44 N 50.24 W. Come at once. Have struck berg." Informed captain.

At 12:36 a.m. Phillips realizes the position he is sending is slightly different than what Fourth Officer Boxhall had written on the paper delivered by Captain Smith. He immediately starts sending the correct position, a difference of about 5 miles.

12:37 a.m. – Cape Race reports that *Titanic* gives corrected position as 41.46 N 50.14 W. He says "have struck iceberg".

12:37 a.m. – From *Carpathia*: *CQD* call received from *Titanic* by *Carpathia*. *Titanic* said "Come at once. We have struck a berg. It's a CQD OM (old man). Position 41.46 N. 50.14 W."

Distress Rockets

Report excerpt from the United States Senate Inquiry – Titanic;

> The committee deems it important to emphasize the meaning of signals of distress and includes in its report the international code, which is as follows:
>
> **SIGNALS OF DISTRESS**
> When a vessel is in distress and requires assistance from other vessels or from the shore, the following shall be the signals to be used or displayed by her, either together or separately:
> **AT NIGHT**
> 1. A gun or other explosive signal fired at intervals of about a minute.
> 2. Flames on the vessel (as from a burning tar barrel, oil barrel, etc.).

3. Rockets or shells, throwing stars of any color or description, fired one at a time at short intervals.
4. A continuous sounding with any fog-signal apparatus.

After working out the ship's position Fourth Officer Joseph Boxhall is assisting with the work of preparing the lifeboats when a light is spotted on the horizon.

"There's a light. I see a light," someone calls out.

"I see it too," another seaman yells.

"I'll check it with glasses," Boxhall responds then hurries to the bridge to get a better look. Boxhall can't see the light until he uses a pair of binoculars but then determines he is seeing the two masthead lights of a vessel, about half a point on the port bow. Boxhall sends for some rockets then finds Captain Smith and reports the vessel sighting.

"How far off?" the Captain asks.

"Can't say for sure but I've sent for rockets to signal her."

"Carry on with the rockets and let me know when she responds."

At 12:38 a.m. Fourth Officer Joseph Boxhall, Quartermaster George Rowe and Quartermaster Arthur J. Bright, begin firing rockets from an angled rail attached to the bridge. While Rowe and Bright continue firing rockets, Boxhall attempts to contact the vessel with a Morse lamp.

British Wreck Commissioner's Inquiry – Testimony of Fourth Officer Joseph Boxhall, examined by Mr. Raymond Asquith.

15395. How many rockets did you send up about?

Boxhall – I could not say, between half a dozen and a dozen, I should say, as near as I could tell.

15396. What sort of rockets were they?

Boxhall – The rocket distress signal.

15397. Can you describe what the effect of those rockets is in the sky; what do they do?

Boxhall – You see a luminous tail behind them and then they explode in the air and burst into stars.

15398. Did you send them up at intervals one at a time?

Boxhall – One at a time, yes.

15399. At about what kind of intervals?

Boxhall – Well, probably five minutes; I did not take any times.

15400. Did you watch the lights of this steamer while you were sending the rockets up?

Boxhall – Yes.

15401. Did they seem to be stationary?

Boxhall – I was paying most of my attention to this steamer then, and she was approaching us; and then I saw her sidelights. I saw her green light and the red. She was end-on to us. Later I saw her red light. This is all with the aid of a pair of glasses up to now. Afterwards I saw the ship's red light with my naked eye, and the two masthead lights. The only description of the ship that I could give is that she was, or I judged her to be, a four-masted steamer.

15402. Why did you judge that?

Boxhall – By the position of her masthead lights; they were close together.

15403. Did the ship make any sort of answer, as far as you could see, to your rockets?

Boxhall – I did not see it. Some people say she did, and others say she did not. There were a lot of men on the bridge. I had a Quartermaster with me, and the Captain was standing by, at different times, watching this steamer.

15404. Do you mean you heard someone say she was answering your signals?

Boxhall – Yes, I did, and then she got close enough, and I Morsed to her – used our Morse lamp.

15405. You began Morsing to her?

Boxhall – Yes.

15406. When people said to you that your signals were being answered, did they say how they were being answered?

Boxhall – I think I heard somebody say that she showed a light.

15407. Do you mean that she would be using a Morse lamp?

Boxhall – Quite probably.

15408. Then you thought she was near enough to Morse her from the "Titanic"?

Boxhall – Yes, I do think so; I think so yet.

15409. (The Commissioner.) What distance did you suppose her to be away?

Boxhall – I judged her to be between 5 and 6 miles when I Morsed to her, and then she turned round—she was turning very, very slowly until at last I only saw her stern light, and that was just before I went away in the boat.

Fourth Officer Joseph Boxhall is ordered to leave for his lifeboat station while Quartermasters George Rowe and Arthur Bright fire additional rockets. Rowe and Bright fire the last rocket at 1:50 a.m. just before Captain Smith orders them to help launch the collapsible lifeboats.

Altogether the men fire a total of eight rockets from the sinking *Titanic*.

Answering the Call

That night *Titanic's* sister ship, *Olympic*, is heading east toward Europe with 500 miles between her and the westbound *Titanic*. Architect Daniel Burnham is sailing on the *Olympic*, and for no apparent reason thinks about his old friend

Frank Millet who is traveling aboard the *Titanic*. Burnham and Millet are among the last living designers and builders of the World's Columbian Exposition of 1893, better known as the Chicago World's Fair. The exposition was built to commemorate one of the first trans-Atlantic voyages, Columbus's discovery of America, 400 years earlier. Burnham decides to send his friend a mid-ocean wireless greeting but the steward returns with his message still in hand; no greetings will be sent to *Titanic* that night as she is sending a distress signal and at that very moment the *Olympic* is rushing to her aid. Soon enough memories of their World's Fair accomplishments will be Burnham's alone.

Numerous other, closer ships also hear *Titanic's* distress signals:

12:42 a.m. – *Mount Temple* reports *MGY* still calling *CQD* Our captain reverses ship and steams for *MGY*. We are about 50 miles off.

12:50 a.m. – *Mount Temple* reports that *Frankfurt* answers *MGY*. *MGY* gives him his position and asks "Are you coming to our assistance?" *DFT* asks: "What is the matter with you?" *MGY* replies: "We have struck iceberg and sinking; please tell captain to come." "OK; will tell the bridge right away." "OK; yes; quick."

12:52 a.m. – From *Olympic*: Hear *Titanic* signaling to some ship about striking an iceberg. Am not sure it is the *Titanic* who has struck an iceberg. Am interfered by atmospherics and many stations working.

Phillips continues transmitting the *CQD* distress call until Harold Bride suggests, "Send the other call, *SOS*"

"I don't know why they ever changed it," replies Phillips as he sends out the *CQD* call.

"This may be your last chance to send it," Bride jokes.

"I'll use both calls and see who we get."

At 12:57 a.m. Phillips begins to intersperse *SOS* with the traditional *CQD* call. *Mount Temple* reports *MGY* calling *SOS*

The *Mount Temple* (49 miles away), *Frankfort* (153 miles), *Birma* (70 miles), *Baltic* (253 miles), and *Virginian* (170 miles) prepare at various times to come to the assistance of the *Titanic*. The closest ship the *Californian*, less than 10 miles away, doesn't grasp the meaning of the distress rockets and, with her wireless off, doesn't hear the distress calls.

The *Carpathia*, 58 miles southeast, receives the distress call and immediately heads full speed to the rescue.

> **British Wreck Commissioner's Inquiry** – Testimony of Harold Bride, examined by the Attorney General.
>
> 16532. Do you remember the Captain coming in and telling you about the vessel?
>
> Bride – The Captain kept in communication with us; we either went to him or he came to us.
>
> 16533. What about?
>
> Bride – He came in and told us at one time she would not last very

long, and he informed us when the engine room was flooded.

16534. Was that before or after you had had the message from the "Carpathia;" do you recollect?

Bride – After.

16535. If I follow you correctly, you have got the message from the "Frankfurt," and you have got the message from the "Carpathia" that she was coming to your assistance, and then you got the message or messages from the "Olympic"?

Bride – Yes.

16536. And other vessels?

Bride – The messages from the "Olympic" spread over to the time when we left the cabin; from the time we first established communication, Captain Haddock was sending us communications until the time we left the cabin for good.

16537. He was communicating with you, sending you messages throughout?

Bride – Yes.

16538. Now, I want you to tell me after that, and before you left for good, as you have told us, did you have any discussion or conversation with Mr. Phillips about the relative strength of the signals of the "Frankfurt," and the "Carpathia"?

Bride – Yes.

16539. What did he say?

Bride – Mr. Phillips was of the opinion that the "Frankfurt" was the nearer of the two vessels as the strength of the "Frankfurt's" signals was greater than those of the "Carpathia."

16540. Did you establish communication with the "Baltic" at all?

Bride – Yes.

16541. Did you send her a message?

Bride – I myself informed the "Baltic" of the condition of things.

16542. When you say the condition of things, would you tell us as well as you can to the best of your recollection—I know it is rather hard for you at this moment, but so far as you can?

Bride – I explained to the "Baltic" that we had had a collision, and we were sinking fast.

16543. When you sent that message was Mr. Phillips there?

Bride – No.

16544. Where had he gone?

Bride – He had gone outside to have a look round.

16545. When he came back did you tell him?

Bride – Yes.

…16548. Did he tell you what he had found out?

Bride – Yes.

16549. What did he say?
Bride – He told me the forward well deck was awash.
16550. Did he tell you anything else?
Bride – He told me, as far as I remember, that they were putting the women and children in the boats and clearing off.
16551. Was anything said about a list, do you remember?
Bride – There was a heavy list to port.
16552. Did you notice that?
Bride – Yes.
16553. (The Commissioner.) You noticed that yourself?
Bride – Yes.
16554. After he came back and told you that, do you remember the Captain coming in?
Bride – Yes.
16555. What did he tell you?
Bride – He told us to clear out.
16556. (The Commissioner.) To clear out of the room?
Bride – Yes.
16557. (The Attorney General.) To clear out—why?
Bride – It was very evident the ship was sinking.
16558. That you were to shift for yourselves—to do the best you could?
Bride – Yes; words to that effect.
16559. Do you remember whether at that time you were called up?
Bride – Yes; Mr. Phillips took the phones when the Captain had gone away and he started in to work again.
16560. That was after the Captain had come in and told you to shift for yourselves?
Bride – Yes.
…16564. Did he then communicate with the "Carpathia"?
Bride – Yes.
16565. To the best of your recollection, what was it he said?
Bride – To the best of my recollection he told the "Carpathia" the way we were abandoning the ship, or words to that effect.

Rather than clearing out and shifting for themselves both Jack Phillips and Harold Bride remain in the radio room and continue sending distress calls. At 1:50 am Jack Phillips sends the last wireless distress message the *Carpathia* will hear from the *Titanic*, – "…Engine room full up to boilers."

Chapter 13

Aboard the Carpathia

On Sunday night April 14, 1912 the *Carpathia*, under the command of 40 year-old Captain Arthur Henry Rostron, is en route to Fiume, Austria-Hungary after departing from New York City on April 11th. Captain Rostron later testified before the Senate inquiry to his experience and recent appointment to Captain of the *Carpathia*.

United States Senate Inquiry – Testimony of Arthur H. Rostron, questioned by Senator Smith.
Senator Smith – Please give your full name and address.
Mr. Rostron – Arthur Henry Rostron, Woodville, Victoria Road, Crosby, Liverpool.
Senator Smith – What is your business, Captain?
Mr. Rostron – Seaman.
Senator Smith – How long have you been engaged in this business?
Mr. Rostron – Twenty-seven years.
Senator Smith – What positions have you filled?
Mr. Rostron – Every rank in the merchant service up to captain.
Senator Smith – In what companies or on what lines?
Mr. Rostron – First of all I was two years as a cadet on the training ship *Conway* in the Mersey, Liverpool, after which I went under sail as an apprentice with Williams & Milligan's ships. I was an apprentice for three years, after which I was second mate, after passing my examinations. Then, after getting my mates certificate, I went as mate on another sailing ship. Then I passed for extra master and joined the Cunard Steamship Co. in 1895.
Senator Smith – You are now captain of the *Carpathia*?
Mr. Rostron – I am now captain of the *Carpathia*, Cunard Line.
Senator Smith – How long have you been captain of the *Carpathia*?
Mr. Rostron – My appointment on the *Carpathia* dates from the 18th of January.
Senator Smith – Of this year?
Mr. Rostron – Of this year; yes sir.
Senator Smith – Were you captain of any other vessel?

Mr. Rostron – The whole of last year, from the 1st of January of last year, I was captain of the *Pannonia*.
Senator Smith – Of the same line?
Mr. Rostron – Of the same line. Previous to that I was captain of several other smaller cargo boats running between Liverpool and the Mediterranean.

Charles H. Marshall is among the passengers making the Atlantic crossing on the *Carpathia*. Marshall knows his three nieces are travelling the opposite direction aboard the new unsinkable *Titanic* and wonders what stories of their Atlantic crossing adventure they will have to share. He will find out much sooner than he could ever have imagined.

Harold Cottam, 21, is *Carpathia's* only Marconi wireless operator. After reporting the evenings messages to the bridge, Cottam decides to monitor the Cape Race, Newfoundland station before retiring for the night. Cottam described what followed in testimony before the Senate inquiry.

> **United States Senate Inquiry** – Testimony of Harold T. Cottam, questioned by Senator Smith.
> Senator Smith – What were you doing last Sunday evening about 10 o'clock?
> Mr. Cottam – Receiving the news from Cape Cod, the long-distance station.
> ...Senator Smith – What kind of news?
> Mr. Cottam – General news.
> Senator Smith – General news for the accommodation for passengers on ship?
> Mr. Cottam – Yes, sir.
> ...Senator Smith – After you finished the Cape Cod business, what did you do then?
> Mr. Cottam – At the latter end of the news from Cape Cod, he was sending a lot of messages for the *Titanic*.
> Senator Smith – What time was that?
> Mr. Cottam – About 11 o'clock.
> Senator Smith – What had you been doing just preceding the message from the *Titanic*?
> Mr. Cottam – Reporting the day's communications to the bridge.
> Senator Smith – Had you closed your station for the night?
> Mr. Cottam – No.
> ...Senator Smith – And then did you sit down to your instrument?
> Mr. Cottam – Yes, sir.
> Senator Smith – And received this message?
> Mr. Cottam – I received about four.
> Senator Smith – In how many minutes?

Mr. Cottam – About seven or eight minutes.

...Senator Smith – Simply this Cape Cod relay service?

Mr. Cottam – Yes, sir; sending messages for the *Titanic*. I was taking the messages down with the hope of re-transmitting them the following morning.

...Senator Smith – After you got through with this regular business, then what did you do?

Mr. Cottam – I called the *Titanic*.

Senator Smith – You called the *Titanic* yourself?

Mr. Cottam – Yes, sir.

Senator Smith – Who told you to do it?

Mr. Cottam – I did it of my own free will.

Senator Smith – You did it of your own accord?

Mr. Cottam – Yes, sir.

Senator Smith – What did you say?

Mr. Cottam – I asked him if he was aware that Cape Cod was sending a batch of messages for him.

Senator Smith – And did they reply?

Mr. Cottam – Yes, sir.

Senator Smith – What did they say?

Mr. Cottam – "Come at once."

Senator Smith – Did you gather from that that they had received your communication?

Mr. Cottam – Yes, sir.

Senator Smith – And this was the reply?

Mr. Cottam – He said, "Come at once. It is a distress message; CQD."

Senator Smith – Only the three words were used?

Mr. Cottam – No, sir, all the lot. The whole message was for me.

Senator Smith – When you received that message, what did you do?

Mr. Cottam – I confirmed it by asking him if I was to report it to the captain.

Senator Smith – Before you reported to the captain you asked him if you were to report it to the captain?

Mr. Cottam – Yes, sir.

Senator Smith – Did you get an answer?

Mr. Cottam – Yes, sir.

Senator Smith – What did it say?

Mr. Cottam – It said, "Yes."

Senator Smith – How did you happen to confirm it?

Mr. Cottam – By asking him if –

Senator Smith (interrupting) – I know, but what prompted you to confirm it before you delivered it to the captain?

Mr. Cottam – Because it is always wise to confirm a message of that description.

...Senator Smith – How much time elapsed between the time when you received that distress call and the time you communicated it to the captain?

Mr. Cottam – A matter of a couple of minutes.

Senator Smith – Only a couple of minutes?

Mr. Cottam – Yes, sir.

Senator Smith – Did you send any messages after that to the *Titanic*?

Mr. Cottam – Yes, sir.

...Senator Smith – At the instance of the captain?

Mr. Cottam – Yes, sir.

Senator Smith – What messages?

Mr. Cottam – Our position.

...Senator Smith – Did you get any reply to that?

Mr. Cottam – Yes, sir.

Senator Smith – How long afterwards?

Mr. Cottam – Immediately, sir.

Senator Smith – Signed by anyone?

Mr. Cottam – No, sir.

Senator Smith – What did it say?

Mr. Cottam – It simply gave me "Received."

...Senator Smith – When did you next hear from the *Titanic*, or communicate with her?

Mr. Cottam – About four minutes afterwards.

Senator Smith – Did you communicate with her, or she with you?

Mr. Cottam – We communicated with each other.

Senator Smith – Who sent the first message?

Mr. Cottam – I did.

...Senator Smith – What did you say in that?

Mr. Cottam – Confirmed both positions, that of the *Titanic* and ours.

Senator Smith – Did you get anything back from that?

Mr. Cottam – No, sir; only an acknowledgment.

United States Senate Inquiry – Testimony of Arthur H. Rostron, questioned by Senator Smith.

Senator Smith – What time in the day did you leave New York?

Mr. Rostron – At noon on Thursday.

Senator Smith – I wish you would tell the committee what occurred after that day, as nearly as you can, up to the present time.

Mr. Rostron – We backed out from the dock at noon on Thursday. We proceeded down the river, the weather being fine and clear, and we left the pilot at the pilot boat and passed the Ambrose Channel Lightship about 2 o'clock p.m. I can not give you the exact time, now, because, as a matter of fact, I have not looked at a single date or time of any kind. I have not had the time to do so.

Senator Smith – I mean approximately?

Mr. Rostron – From that up to Sunday midnight we had fine, clear weather, and everything was going on without any trouble of any kind.

At 12:35 a.m. on Monday I was informed of the urgent distress signal from the *Titanic*.

Senator Smith – By whom?

Mr. Rostron – By our wireless operator, and also by the first officer. The wireless operator had taken the message and run with it up to the bridge, and gave it to the first officer who was in charge, with a junior officer with him, and both ran down the ladder to my door and called me. I had only just turned in. It was an urgent distress signal from the *Titanic*, requiring immediate assistance and giving me his position.

The position of the *Titanic* at the time was 41° 46' north, 50° 14' west. I can not give you our correct position, but we were then–

Senator Smith – Did you give the hour?

Mr. Rostron – Yes, 12:35; that was our apparent time. I can give you the New York time, if you would rather have it?

Senator Smith – Yes; please do so.

Mr. Rostron – The New York time at 12:35 was 10:45 p.m. Sunday night. Immediately on getting the message, I gave the order to turn the ship around, and immediately after I had given that order I asked the operator if he was absolutely sure it was a distress signal from the *Titanic*. I asked him twice.

Senator Smith – Just what was that signal?

Mr. Rostron – I did not ask him. He simply told me that he had received a distress signal from the *Titanic*, requiring immediate assistance, and gave me his position; and he assured me he was absolutely certain of the message.

In the meantime I was dressing, and I picked up our position on my chart, and set a course to pick up the *Titanic*. The course was north 52 degrees west true 58 miles from my position.

I then sent for the chief engineer. In the meantime I was dressing and seeing the ship put on her course. The chief engineer came up. I told him to call another watch of stokers and make all possible speed to the *Titanic*, as she was in trouble.

He ran down immediately and told me my orders would be carried out at once.

After that I gave the first officer, who was in charge of the bridge, orders to knock off all work which the men were doing on deck, the watch on deck, and prepare all our lifeboats, take out the spare gear, and have them all ready for turning outboard.

Immediately after I had done that I sent for the heads of the different departments, the English doctor, the purser, and the chief steward, and they came to my cabin, and then I issued my orders.

I do not know whether you care to hear what my orders were exactly.

Senator Smith – Yes, sir; we would like to hear them.

Mr. Rostron – As a matter of fact, I have them all written down here. We carry an English doctor, an Italian doctor, and a Hungarian doctor. My orders were these:

- English doctor, with assistants, to remain in First Class dining room.

- Italian doctor, with assistants, to remain in Second Class dining room.

- Hungarian doctor, with assistants, to remain in Third Class dining room.

- Each doctor to have supplies of restoratives, stimulants, and everything to hand for immediate needs of probable wounded or sick.

- Purser, with assistant purser and chief steward, to receive the passengers, etc., at different gangways, controlling our own stewards in assisting *Titanic* passengers to the dining rooms, etc.; also to get Christian and surnames of all survivors as soon as possible to send by wireless.

- Inspector, steerage stewards, and master at arms to control our own steerage passengers and keep them out of the Third Class dining hall, and also to keep them out of the way and off the deck to prevent confusion.

- Chief steward: That all hands would be called and to have coffee, etc., ready to serve out to all our crew.

- Have coffee, tea, soup, etc., in each saloon, blankets in saloons, at the gangways, and some for the boats.

- To see all rescued cared for and immediate wants attended to.

- My cabin and all officials' cabins to be given up. Smoke rooms, library, etc., dining rooms, would be utilized to accommodate the survivors.

- All spare berths in steerage to be utilized for *Titanic's* passengers, and get all our own steerage passengers grouped together.

- Stewards to be placed in each alleyway to reassure our own passengers, should they inquire about noise in getting our boats out, etc., or the working of engines.

- To all I strictly enjoined the necessity for order, discipline and quietness and to avoid all confusion.
- Chief and first officers: All the hands to be called; get coffee, etc. Prepare and swing out all boats.
- All gangway doors to be opened.
- Electric sprays in each gangway and over side.
- A block with line rove hooked in each gangway.
- A chair sling at each gangway, for getting up sick or wounded.
- Boatswains' chairs. Pilot ladders and canvas ash bags to be at each gangway, the canvas ash bags for children. I may state the canvas ash bags were of great assistance in getting the infants and children aboard.
- Cargo falls with both ends clear; bowlines in the ends, and bights secured along ship's sides, for boat ropes or to help the people up.
- Heaving lines distributed along the ship's side, and gaskets handy near gangways for lashing people in chairs, etc.
- Forward derricks, topped and rigged, and steam on winches; also told off officers for different stations and for certain eventualities.
- Ordered company's rockets to be fired at 2:45 a.m. and every quarter of an hour after to reassure *Titanic*.

This is a copy of what I am sending to our own company.
Senator Smith – We would like to have you leave a copy of that with the committee, if you can.
Mr. Rostron – Yes, sir; I shall do it with pleasure. One more thing: As each official saw everything in readiness, he reported to me personally on the bridge that all my orders were carried out, enumerating the same, and that everything was in readiness.
This was at 3:45. That was a quarter of an hour before we got up to the scene of the disaster. The details of all this work I left to the several officials, and I am glad to say that they were most efficiently carried out.
Senator Smith – I should judge from what you say that you made 19 1/4 knots from the time you got the signal of distress from the *Titanic*, until you reached the scene of the wreck or loss?
Mr. Rostron – No, it was 58 miles, and it took us three and a half hours.
...Senator Smith – What was the last message you had from the ship?
Mr. Rostron – "Engine room nearly full."
...Senator Smith – At what hour was that?
Mr. Rostron – That would have been about 1 o'clock. That would be

25 minutes after.
Senator Smith – Was that all?
Mr. Rostron – That was the last message we got. It was either "Engine room nearly full," or "Engine room full," or "Engine room-filling." The exact words I could not give you. The impression was quite enough for me, as to the condition the ship was in.

Carpathia's normal speed is 14.5 knots but Captain Rostron and his crew have her racing to the *Titanic's* rescue at 17.5 knots using all the steam and speed they can find. Rostron adds an additional lookout to the crow's nest, places two lookouts in the bow, adds lookouts on each bridge wing, and adds an officer to the bridge. He does not intend to meet the same fate as the *Titanic* while speeding to her rescue.

After reporting *Carpathia's* position and confirming the position of the *Titanic* the *Carpathia's* Marconi wireless operator, Harold Cottam, continues to monitor and communicate with the *Titanic* as they race to the rescue.

United States Senate Inquiry – Testimony of Harold T. Cottam, questioned by Senator Smith
Senator Smith – When did you next communicate or receive a communication?
Mr. Cottam – A few minutes afterwards.
Senator Smith – How many minutes?
Mr. Cottam – I could not say, sir, because there was another ship calling the *Titanic*.
Senator Smith – How do you know?
Mr. Cottam – Because I heard it.
Senator Smith – What did you hear?
Mr. Cottam – I heard him calling the *Titanic*.
Senator Smith – I understand, but what was said?
Mr. Cottam – There was nothing but the call, sir.
Senator Smith – A distress call?
Mr. Cottam – No, sir.
Senator Smith – Do you know what boat it was?
Mr. Cottam – The *Frankfurt*.
…Senator Smith – The German boat was calling the *Titanic*?
Mr. Cottam – Yes, sir.
Senator Smith – And did that disarrange your signals?
Mr. Cottam – No, sir.
Senator Smith – But after that call was finished, then what did you get, if anything?
Mr. Cottam – I heard the *Olympic* calling the *Titanic*.
Senator Smith – Did you hear the *Titanic* calling the *Olympic*?
Mr. Cottam – No, sir; not at first.

Senator Smith – But you heard the *Olympic* calling the *Titanic*?
Mr. Cottam – Yes, sir.
Senator Smith – What did the *Olympic* say?
Mr. Cottam – He was calling him and offering a service message.
...Senator Smith – Then what followed?
Mr. Cottam – Nothing, for about a half a minute. Everything was quiet.
...Senator Smith – After this minute, then what?
Mr. Cottam – I asked the *Titanic* if he was aware that the *Olympic* was calling him, sir.
Senator Smith – What was the reply?
Mr. Cottam – He said he was not.
...Senator Smith – Then what followed?
Mr. Cottam – He told me he could not read him because the rush of air and the escape of steam;
...Senator Smith – Well, go right ahead and tell us just what occurred as long as you were aboard that ship doing work to the time of the rescue of these people.
Mr. Cottam – I was in communication at regular intervals the whole of the time until the last communication gained with the *Titanic*.
Senator Smith – You heard that?
Mr. Cottam – Yes, sir.
Senator Smith – What was said in that message?
Mr. Cottam – He told him to come at once; that he was head down. And he sent his position.
Senator Smith – And do you know whether he got any reply to that message?
Mr. Cottam – Yes, sir.
Senator Smith – What was it?
Mr. Cottam – "Received." He told him the message was received.
...Senator Smith – You were in regular communication?
Mr. Cottam – Yes, sir.
Senator Smith – With the *Titanic?*
Mr. Cottam – Yes, sir.
Senator Smith – Until the last communication was heard?
Mr. Cottam – Yes; until the last communication was heard.
Senator Smith – What was the last one?
Mr. Cottam – The last one was, "Come quick; our engine room is filling up to the boilers."
...Senator Smith – I thought I understood the captain to say that one of the last messages told the sinking ship that they were within a certain distance and coming hard, or coming fast.
Mr. Cottam – I called him with that message, but I got no

acknowledgment.

Senator Smith – Just tell us what that message was. You called him with that message?

Mr. Cottam – Yes, sir.

Senator Smith – We would like to know about that; just tell what it was.

Mr. Cottam – The captain told me to tell the *Titanic* that all our boats were ready and we were coming as hard as we could come, with a double watch on in the engine room, and to be prepared, when we got there, with lifeboats. I got no acknowledgment of that message.

Chapter 14

Loading and Launching the Lifeboats

The *Titanic* carries 16 wooden lifeboats, 14 with a design capacity of 65 people each, and two emergency clippers designed to hold 40 people each. The lifeboats are located on the Boat Deck—the uppermost deck of the ship. To make use of these boats the crew needs to strip off the boat covers and put the plugs in place. The crew can then swing the boats out on their davits over the edge of the ship and above the water 70 feet below. A crank is used to lower each boat to the edge of the deck railing for loading. The boats can also be lowered and loaded from one of the lower decks with open access.

Captain Smith has already ordered the lifeboats prepared. Chief Officer Henry Wilde passed on the order to strip the boat covers but, not wanting to start undue panic, is averse to seeking the Captain's order to start loading the lifeboats. Second Officer Charles Lightoller, having already survived one shipwreck during his career, grasps the urgency of the situation and approaches Captain Smith for orders. At 12:30 a.m., fifty minutes after the collision and right after learning the full extent of the damage, Smith gives the order to start loading the lifeboats—women and children first. If every lifeboat is filled to capacity there is enough room for 1178 of the estimated 2215 on board. *Titanic's* fate has company.

> **British Wreck Commissioner's Inquiry** – Testimony of Second Officer Charles H. Lightoller, examined by the Solicitor General.
> 13818. What length of time would this operation of uncovering all these boats take?
> Lightoller – You mean, given the crew?
> 13819. You were engaged on this work. I want to realise how long you were engaged on it?
> Lightoller – Well, I really could not say what time the after boats were finished uncovering. Knowing that the Third Officer was there in charge I did not bother so much about that as the forward ones, and about the time I had finished seeing the men distributed round the deck, and the boat covers well under way and everything going smoothly, I then enquired of the Chief Officer whether we should carry on and swing out.

Loading and Launching the Lifeboats

13820. And what did Mr. Wilde say about that – what were the orders?

Lightoller – I am under the impression that Mr. Wilde said "No," or "Wait," something to that effect, and meeting the Commander, I asked him, and he said, "Yes, swing out."

13821. And did you get that done?

Lightoller – Yes, on the port side. I did not go to the starboard side again.

13822. Up to the time of swinging out the boats which had been stripped, at any rate, on the port side, what about the passengers?

Lightoller – I had met a few passengers on deck, not many.

13823. Had you heard any general orders given about getting them?

Lightoller – No, I could not hear any.

13824. Was the steam still blowing off all this time?

Lightoller – Still blowing off, yes.

Lightoller's testimony continues. Concerning the order to load women and children…

13871. Who gave it, and when was it given?

Lightoller – The Captain gave it to me.

13872. What was the order?

Lightoller – After I had swung out No. 4 boat I asked the Chief Officer should we put the women and children in, and he said "No." I left the men to go ahead with their work and found the Commander, or I met him and I asked him should we put the women and children in, and the Commander said "Yes, put the women and children in and lower away." That was the last order I received on the ship.

13873. Was that, as you understood it, a general order for the boats?

Lightoller – Yes, a general order.

With the Captain's order Second Officer Charles Lightoller takes charge of loading the even-numbered port side boats intending to strictly enforce the "women and children" general order. Meanwhile, some of the richest men in the world gather with their families in the relative comfort of the enclosed A Deck promenade or in the nearby gymnasium.

Lightoller still can't be heard due to the noise from steam being released through the safety valves and starts using hand signals to direct the work. After having lifeboat 4 lowered to the A Deck he finds the windows needed for access locked and sends a seaman to find the key.

First Officer William Murdoch sees to loading the starboard boats with women and children *first* but then allows men aboard.

The first lifeboats to depart carry First Class passengers and crew and aren't filled to capacity. Seaman William Lucas later tells the British inquiry why.

British Wreck Commissioner's Inquiry – Testimony of William Lucas, examined by Mr. Rowlatt.

1479. Had you received the order that women were to be put in the boats?
Lucas – Yes.
1480. Whom did you receive that from?
Lucas – Mr. Moody, the Sixth Officer.
1481. Was he there or was he by the falls?
Lucas – He was near me when I was lowering.
1482. And you called out for women and there were no more?
Lucas – That is right, Sir.
1483. That was right at the afterend was it?
Lucas – Yes, the afterend of all.
1484. Do you know where the access from the Third Class accommodation comes up?
Lucas – Well, I never knew my way up myself and I was a sailor on the ship.
1485. I daresay you had never been that way before?
Lucas – No. I do not think those people had time to go there without directions from somebody; I hardly knew my way there myself.
1486. When you say the way, what do you mean – the way where to?
Lucas – The Boat Deck.
…1499. Did you know what the passengers were on the Boat Deck – First Class, Second Class, or Third Class?
Lucas – The majority First Class.
1500. Along where you were?
Lucas – Yes.
1501. How many boats did you see filled. How many boats did you take notice of as they were being filled?
Lucas – About nine.
1502. Could you see whether they were all filled to the full capacity?
Lucas – They were not all filled.
1503. Why was that?
Lucas – Because there were no women knocking about.

Starboard No. 7

First Officer Murdoch orders Lookout George Hogg into lifeboat 7 to check the plugs. After ensuring they're in place, Hogg jumps out but Murdoch orders him back in to help load passengers. Murdoch and Fifth Officer Harold Lowe begin to usher reluctant passengers toward the boat when a crewman calls out "Put in the brides and grooms first!"

Newlyweds Mr. and Mrs. John Snyder come forward and are helped into Boat 7 but Albert Dick and his young bride Vera choose not to get in.

Newlyweds Dick and Helen Bishop are also among the first to be ushered into the boat.

United States Senate Inquiry – Testimony of Helen Bishop, questioned by Senator Smith.

Mrs. Bishop – We were on B deck, and we came back up to A deck. There was very little confusion; only the older women were a little frightened. They were up, partially dressed. So I sent a number of them back and saw that they were thoroughly dressed before they came up again. Then we went up onto the Boat Deck on the starboard side. We looked around, and there were so very few people up there that my husband and I went to the port side to see if there was anyone there. There were only two people, a young French bride and groom, on that side of the boat, and they followed us immediately to the starboard side. By that time an old man had come upstairs and found Mr. and Mrs. Harder, of New York. He brought us all together and told us to be sure and stay together; that he would be back in a moment. We never saw him again. About five minutes later the boats were lowered, and we were pushed in. At the time our lifeboat was lowered I had no idea that it was time to get off.

Senator Smith – Tell me which lifeboat you refer to?

Mrs. Bishop – The first lifeboat that was taken off the *Titanic* on the starboard side. I think it was No. 7. Officer Lowe told us that.

Senator Smith – All right. Proceed.

Mrs. Bishop – We had no idea that it was time to get off, but the officer took my arm and told me to be very quiet and get in immediately. They put the families in the first two boats. My husband was pushed in with me, and we were lowered away with 28 people in the boat.

Senator Smith – Was that a large lifeboat?

Mrs. Bishop – Yes; it was a wooden lifeboat.

Senator Smith – And there were 28 people in it?

Mrs. Bishop – Yes. We counted off after we reached the water.

Senator Smith – How many women were there?

Mrs. Bishop – There were only about 12 women.

Senator Smith – And the rest were

Mrs. Bishop. (interposing) Were men.

Senator Smith – Yes; but I want to divide the rest into two classes, the crew and the passengers.

Mrs. Bishop – There were three of the crew. The rest of them were passengers. We had no officer in our boat.

After feeling and hearing the collision with the iceberg, Dorothy Gibson finds her mother and they rejoin their bridge partners William Sloper and Frederick Seward on the Boat Deck.

William T. Sloper described what happened next in his book – *Ship to Shore*.

"Dorothy Gibson was the only one who seemed to realize the desperate situation we were in because she had become quite hysterical and kept repeating over and over so that people standing near us could hear, 'I'll never ride in my little grey car again.' There was no doubt in Dorothy's mind in what she wanted to do and her mother was satisfied to go along with Dorothy. So with the help of the first officer, I handed Dorothy down into the bow of the lifeboat. Mr. Seward and the junior officer handed Mrs. Gibson down after her daughter. Luckily for both Seward and me, Dorothy held onto my hand and demanded that we get into the boat with them, 'We won't go unless you do' she said. 'What do you say?' I asked Seward. 'What's the difference we may as well go along with them.' Finding seats for ourselves we sat in the lifeboat designed for 65 persons for about ten minutes looking up into the rim of the faces of the passengers looking down at us trying to make up their minds to get in with us. After 19 people had finally made up their minds and had been lowered into the boat the first officer asked for the last time through his megaphone, 'Are there anymore who would like to get into this boat before we lower away.?' When no one else made the move toward him, he gave the signal to lower us away. Then began a jerky descent to the surface of the ocean 60 feet below. Fortunately for us the three sailors knew their business, for in a few minutes they skillfully launched our boat on the surface of the ocean without accident."

At 12:40 a.m., with Lookout men Archie Jewell and George Hogg aboard and Hogg in command, boat 7, with a capacity of 65 people, lowers away with only 28 aboard. Once in the water Hogg asks a lady if she can steer and she says she can. Hogg tells her, "You may sit here and do this for me and I will take the stroke oar."

With help from his passengers including Helen Bishop, pregnant at the time, Hogg rows lifeboat 7 away from the *Titanic*.

Starboard No. 5

Murdoch, Lowe, and Third Officer Pitman, with Bruce Ismay's help, load lifeboat 5. Karl Behr finds Helen Newsom on the starboard Boat Deck with her mother Sallie and step-father Richard Beckwith. Behr followed Helen to Europe and is following her home to continue their courtship. Behr joins the group on deck that includes Helen, her parents, and their friends from Boston, Edwin and Gertrude Kimball. They wait with their lifebelts on while the Third Officer and Bruce Ismay continue to urge women and children into the boat. Newlyweds George and Dorothy Harder of New York are allowed to get in the lifeboat as are several other First Class couples, including Samuel Goldenberg and his wife Nella, and Norman and Bertha Chambers. Dr. Washington Dodge sees his wife, Ruth, and son, Washington Jr. into the boat but doesn't join them.

Benjamin Guggenheim and his valet, Mr. Victor Giglio, return to the Boat Deck dressed in their finest evening wear. Guggenheim states, "We've dressed up in our best and are prepared to go down like gentlemen," but his bravado is displayed after only one lifeboat has been launched and there is still doubt about the need to board one.

With many reluctant passengers seemingly more worried about the 70 foot distance the lifeboat will be lowered to reach the water than they are about the larger boat sinking, Mrs. Kimball asks Mr. Ismay if it would be possible that her group all go together. Ismay replies, "Of course, madam, every one of you," and ushers the Kimballs, the Beckwiths, their daughter Helen, and Karl Behr into the boat. An additional 11 men also board before Murdoch sends the boat off at 12:45 a.m. with Third Officer Pitman in charge. Murdoch tells Pitman, "Good-bye and good luck," as the boat lowers away. Starboard lifeboat No. 5 leaves with 2 deck crew, a Bedroom Steward, and 33 First Class passengers aboard but room for 29 more.

> **British Wreck Commissioner's Inquiry** – Testimony of Harold G. Lowe, examined by Mr. Cotter.
> 15975. Do you remember being at No. 5 boat with Mr. Murdoch?
> Lowe – Yes.
> 15976. Do you remember meeting a gentleman there who was interfering with the work?
> Lowe – Yes.
> 15977. Who was it?
> Lowe – I afterwards learned it was Mr. Bruce Ismay.
> 15978. What did he say to you or say to anybody; was he giving orders?
> Lowe – No, he was trying all in his power to help the work, and he was getting a little bit excited.
> 15979. What was he doing to help the work?
> Lowe – He was going like this, "Lower away, lower away" (Showing.)
> 15980. What did you say to Mr. Ismay?
> Lowe – I think you know.
> 15981. Did you see Mr. Ismay go into any boat?
> Lowe – No. I told him what I said, and I told the men to go ahead clearing No. 3 boat, and Mr. Ismay went there and helped them.
>
> Examined by Sir Robert Finlay.
> 15983. Did Mr. Ismay do all he could to help?
> Lowe – He did everything in his power to help.

Starboard No. 3

Murdoch and Lowe turn their attention to lifeboat 3. Murdoch orders Seaman George A. Moore into the boat to help the women board. After passing on boarding boats 7 and 5, honeymooners Albert and Vera Dick decide to go in lifeboat 3. Charles Hays sees his wife Clara and daughter Orian (Hays) Davidson into the boat, and assures his wife that the *Titanic* will stay afloat long enough for all to be rescued. Hays and his son-in-law Thorton do not join their wives in the lifeboat. Thomas Cardeza does join his mother, Charlotte, in the boat as does her maid, Anna Ward, and his manservant, Gustave Lesueur. Mr. Henry Sleeper Harper and his wife Myra are also among those that board boat 3, as is Hammad Hassab, their Egyptian manservant. Harper also carries their Pekinese dog aboard. With men being allowed in the Starboard boats, Robert Daniel, a Philadelphia banker, takes a spot but doesn't bring his champion bulldog, still housed in *Titanic's* kennel. The lifeboat, with a capacity of 65, is lowered away at 12:55 a.m. with 26 First Class passengers, including 12 men, and a crew of six. Seaman George Moore takes charge and mans the tiller when the boat reaches the sea.

> **United States Senate Inquiry** – Testimony of Seaman George Moore, questioned by Senator Newlands.
> Senator Newlands – …Go on and tell what happened.
> Mr. Moore – I went on the starboard side of the Boat Deck and helped clear the boats; swung three of the boats out; helped to lower No. 5 and No. 7. When we swung No. 3 out, I was told to jump in the boat and pass the ladies in. I was told that by the first officer. After we got so many ladies in, and there were no more about, we took in men passengers. We had 32 in the boat, all told, and then we lowered away.
> Senator Newlands – Why did you not take more than 32 in that boat?
> Mr. Moore – That is not up to me, sir; that was for the officer on top.
> Senator Newlands – Did you not think at the time that it ought to have been more heavily loaded?
> Mr. Moore – It seemed pretty full, but I dare say we could have jammed more in. The passengers were not anxious to get in the boats; they were not anxious to get in the first lot of boats.
> Senator Newlands – What was your feeling at the time?
> Mr. Moore – I thought, myself, that there was nothing serious the matter until we got away from the ship and she started settling down.
> Senator Newlands – You would have been as well pleased to have stayed on the ship as to get on the lifeboat?
> Mr. Moore – I would at that time, sir.

Colonel Astor, still unperturbed even as the boats are being loaded, ridicules the suggestion of leaving the unsinkable *Titanic* for a small lifeboat and tells Mrs. Astor, "We are much safer here than in that little boat."

Portside No. 8

Unable to load lifeboat 4 until the A Deck windows are unlocked, Second Officer Charles Lightoller moves to help load lifeboat 8 instead. Lightoller helps Chief Officer Henry Wilde, and Captain Smith load boat 8 with women and children. Sixth Officer James Moody establishes a boundary line allowing only women and children past to board the port side lifeboats.

> **United States Senate Inquiry** – Testimony of Colonel Archibald Gracie as told to Senator Smith.
> Col. Gracie – Moody was his name. He said, "No man beyond this line." Then the women went beyond that line. I saw that these four ladies, with whose safety I considered myself entrusted, went beyond that line to get amidships on this deck, which was A deck. Then I saw Mr. Straus and Mrs. Straus, of whom I had seen a great deal during the voyage. I had heard them discussing that if they were going to die they would die together.

After seeing her maid, Ellen Bird, into the lifeboat Mrs. Isidor "Ida" Straus begins to enter the boat but turns back to rejoin her husband. Friends Colonel Archibald Gracie and Clinch Smith try to persuade her to get into the boat but she refuses. Bedroom Steward Alfred Crawford does get into boat 8 to man an oar. He gave this testimony at the Senate inquiry.

> **United States Senate Inquiry** – Testimony of Alfred Crawford, questioned by Senator Smith.
> Senator Smith – Did you know Mr. and Mrs. Straus?
> Mr. Crawford – I stood at the boat where they refused to get in.
> Senator Smith – Did Mrs. Straus get into the boat?
> Mr. Crawford – She attempted to get into the boat first and she got back again. Her maid got into the boat.
> Senator Smith – What do you mean by "she attempted" to get in?
> Mr. Crawford – She went to get over from the deck to the boat, but then went back to her husband.
> Senator Smith – Did she step on the boat?
> Mr. Crawford – She stepped onto the boat, on to the gunwales sir; then she went back.
> Senator Smith – What followed?
> Mr. Crawford – She said, "We have been living together for many years, and where you go I go."
> Senator Smith – To whom did she speak?
> Mr. Crawford – To her husband.
> Senator Smith – Was he beside her?
> Mr. Crawford – Yes; he was standing away back when she went from the boat.
> Senator Smith – You say there was a maid there also?

Mr. Crawford – A maid got in the boat and was saved; yes, sir.
Senator Smith – Did the maid precede Mrs. Straus into the boat?
Mr. Crawford – Mrs. Straus told the maid to get into the boat and she would follow her; then she altered her mind and went back to her husband.
Senator Smith – Which one of the boats was that?
Mr. Crawford – No. 8, on the port side.

Lucy Noël Martha, the Countess of Rothes, along with her cousin, Miss Gladys Cherry, and maid, Roberta Maioni, are among the 22 women from First Class that do get into boat 8. Mrs. Maria Castellana, the bride from Madrid, Spain, also boards the boat but her husband Victor can only watch while the boat lowers away at 1:00 a.m. carrying only 25. Lightoller puts Seaman Thomas W. Jones is in command.

United States Senate Inquiry – Testimony of Thomas Jones, questioned by Senator Newlands.
Senator Newlands – Did you think at that time it would be as safe to stay on the ship as to go in the boat?
Mr. Jones – I thought they were only sending us away for an hour or so, until they got squared up again.
Senator Newlands – Until they got what?
Mr. Jones – Until they got her pumped out.
Senator Newlands – Can you give me the names of any passengers on your boat?
Mr. Jones – One lady. She had a lot to say, and I put her to steering my boat.
Senator Newlands – What was her name?
Mr. Jones – Lady Rothe. She was a countess or something.

Lady Rothes later shared her experience with the *New York Herald*. Excerpt from the *New York Herald* article published Sunday April 21, 1912.

"Captain Smith stood shoulder to shoulder with me as I got into the life boat, and the last words were to the able seaman–Tom Jones–'Row straight for those ship lights over there; leave your passengers on board of her and return as soon as you can.' Captain Smith's whole attitude was one of great calmness and courage, and I am sure he thought that the ship—whose lights we could plainly see—would pick us up and that our life boats would be able to do double duty in ferrying passengers to the help that gleamed so near.

"There were two stewards in boat No. 8 with us and thirty-one women. The name of the steward was Crawford. We were lowered quietly to the water, and when we had pushed off from the *Titanic's* side I asked the seaman if he would care to have me take the tiller, as I knew something about boats. He said, 'Certainly, lady.' I climbed aft into the stern sheets and asked my cousin to help me.

"The first impression I had as we left the ship was that above all things we must not lose our self-control. We had no officer to take command of our boat, and the little seaman had to assume all the responsibility. He did it nobly, alternately cheering us with words of encouragement, then rowing doggedly."

ABS Thomas Jones, with Lady Rothes steering, has lifeboat 8 row toward the still visible lights of a ship that has yet to respond to *Titanic's* rockets or distress calls.

Emergency Clipper 1

On the starboard side First Officer William Murdoch is approached by Sir Cosmo and Lady Duff-Gordon as he prepares to load the starboard emergency clipper. Sir Cosmo inquires if he and his wife can get in the boat and Murdoch agrees to let them board.

> **British Wreck Commissioner's Inquiry** – Testimony of Lady Duff-Gordon, examined by the Attorney General.
> 12874. Just tell us quite shortly – I do not want to go into it in any detail – but quite shortly, how it was you went into that boat. Do you remember?
> Lady Duff-Gordon – Oh, quite well.
> 12875. Well, would you tell my Lord?
> Lady Duff-Gordon – After the three boats had gone down, my husband, Miss Franks and myself were left standing on the deck. There were no other people on the deck at all visible and I had quite made up my mind that I was going to be drowned, and then suddenly we saw this little boat in front of us – this little thing (pointing on the model.) – and we saw some sailors, and an Officer apparently giving them orders and I said to my husband "Ought we not to be doing something?" He said, "Oh, we must wait for orders" and we stood there for quite some time while these men were fixing up things, and then my husband went forward and said, "Might we get into this boat?" and the Officer said in a very polite way indeed "Oh certainly; do; I will be very pleased." Then somebody hitched me up from the deck and pitched me into the boat and then I think Miss Franks [Miss Laura Francatelli] was pitched in. It was not a case of getting in at all. We could not have got in, it was quite high. They pitched us up in the sort of way (Indicating.) into the boat and after we had been in a little while the boat was started to be lowered and one American gentleman got pitched in, and one American gentleman was pitched in while the boat was being lowered down.

At 1:05 a.m., with Lookout George Symons in command, Emergency Clipper 1 is lowered away with First Class passengers Mr. Abraham Lincoln Salomon, Mr. Charles Emil Henry Stengel, Sir Cosmo and Lady Duff-Gordon, and her secretary, Miss Laura Mabel Francatelli. Seven crew members brought the total to 12 on a boat that could hold 40.

Portside No. 6

After the safety valves releasing excess steam pressure close Second Officer Lightoller can be heard and gives orders to the deck crew to load lifeboat 6 with women and children. Lucian Smith convinces his pregnant wife, Eloise, to board the boat while he stays behind.

Eloise (Hughes) Smith described her experience in an affidavit for the U.S. Senate Inquiry.

> **United States Senate Inquiry** – Statement of Mrs. Lucian P. Smith (partial content):
> ...There was no commotion, no panic, and no one seemed to be particularly frightened; in fact, most of the people seemed interested in the unusual occurrence, many having crossed 50 and 60 times. However, I noticed my husband was busy talking to any officer he came in contact with; still I had not the least suspicion of the scarcity of lifeboats, or I never should have left my husband.
> When the first boat was lowered from the left-hand side I refused to get in, and they did not urge me particularly; in the second boat they kept calling for one more lady to fill it, and my husband insisted that I get in it, my friend having gotten in. I refused unless he would go with me. In the meantime Capt. Smith was standing with a megaphone on deck. I approached him and told him I was alone, and asked if my husband might be allowed to go in the boat with me. He ignored me personally, but shouted again through his megaphone, "Women and children first." My husband said, "Never mind, captain, about that; I will see that she gets in the boat." He then said, "I never expected to ask you to obey, but this is one time you must; it is only a matter of form to have women and children first. The boat is thoroughly equipped, and everyone on her will be saved." I asked him if that was absolutely honest, and he said, "Yes." I felt some better then, because I had absolute confidence in what he said. He kissed me good-by and placed me in the lifeboat with the assistance of an officer. As the boat was being lowered he yelled from the deck, "Keep your hands in your pockets it is very cold weather."

Margaret (Tobin) Brown, later known as "Molly," helps load lifeboat 6 until Lightoller, with no other women and children waiting, insists she also go aboard. Lightoller then orders Quartermaster Robert Hichens to command the boat. At 1:10 a.m., while the boat is being lowered, Hichens alerts Lightoller that only one seaman (Lookout Frederick Fleet) is on board. To remedy this, Major Arthur Godfrey Peuchen, Vice Commodore of the Royal Canadian Yacht Club, volunteers to join the lifeboat. Lightoller agrees as long as Peuchen is sailor enough to shimmy down a rope into the boat. The 52 year old Major takes up the challenge and is the only adult male passenger Lightoller allows into a lifeboat that night. Boat 6, with a capacity of 65, leaves with the 2 crew, Major Peuchen, 1 stowaway, and 20 First Class women including Mrs. Elizabeth Rothschild, and her Pomeranian dog.

> **British Wreck Commissioner's Inquiry** – Testimony of Quartermaster Robert Hichens, examined by the Attorney General.
> 1118. Who gave orders for her to be pushed off?
> Hichens – The Second Officer, Mr. Lightoller, ordered the boat to be lowered away.
> …1124. Were there any other passengers on the deck so far as you could see when you got the order to lower away – when the order was given to lower away?
> Hichens – Yes, there were some passengers there.
> 1125. Women?
> Hichens – I think there were one or two women, Sir, besides gentlemen as well. They felt half inclined – they did not care about getting into the boat.
> 1126. Who felt half inclined?
> Hichens – Why, the passengers, Sir.
> …1164. Then you got the order from Mr. Lightoller, the Second Officer, to steer for a vessel which was two points on the port bow, or, rather, I said for a vessel, you said for a light; it is the same thing?
> Hichens – Yes.
> 1167. When had you first seen that light two points on the port bow?
> Hichens – While we were in the boat, Sir, taking the passengers on board. That was the order then, to steer for that light.
> 1169. When you looked and saw this light, could you tell what it was at all?
> Hichens – No. We surmised it to be a steamboat.

About 1:15 a.m. water reaches *Titanic*'s name on the bow as she lists to port and the tilt of the deck grows steeper. A few minutes later the bow pitches as water floods through the port anchor-chain holes. With the gravity of the situation no longer in doubt, more lifeboats fill and launch closer to capacity. The first six lifeboats have been launched with only one Third Class passenger aboard. Both the Senate and British inquiries explore why.

United States Senate Inquiry – Testimony of Third Class passenger Daniel Buckley, questioned by Senator Smith.
Senator Smith – Was there any effort made on the part of the officers or crew to hold the steerage passengers in the steerage?
Mr. Buckley – I do not think so.
Senator Smith – Were you permitted to go on up to the top deck without any interference?
Mr. Buckley – Yes, sir. They tried to keep us down at first on our steerage deck. They did not want us to go up to the First Class place at all.
Senator Smith – Who tried to do that?
Mr. Buckley – I can not say who they were. I think they were sailors.
Senator Smith – What happened then? Did the steerage passengers try to get out?
Mr. Buckley – Yes; they did. There was one steerage passenger there, and he was getting up the steps, and just as he was going in a little gate a fellow came along and chucked him down; threw him down into the steerage place. This fellow got excited, and he ran after him, and he could not find him. He got up over the little gate. He did not find him.
Senator Smith – What gate do you mean?
Mr. Buckley – A little gate just at the top of the stairs going up into the First Class deck.
Senator Smith – There was a gate between the steerage and the First Class deck?
Mr. Buckley – Yes. The First Class deck was higher up than the steerage deck, and there were some steps leading up to it; 9 or 10 steps, and a gate just at the top of the steps.
Senator Smith – Was the gate locked?
Mr. Buckley – It was not locked at the time we made the attempt to get up there, but the sailor, or whoever he was, locked it. So that this fellow that went up after him broke the lock on it, and he went after the fellow that threw him down. He said if he could get hold of him he would throw him into the ocean.
Senator Smith – Did these passengers in the steerage have any opportunity at all of getting out?
Mr. Buckley – Yes; they had.
Senator Smith – What opportunity did they have?
Mr. Buckley – I think they had as much chance as the First and Second Class passengers.

British Wreck Commissioner's Inquiry – Testimony of Third Class Steward John E. Hart, examined by the Solicitor General.
...9921. Now just tell us about the next thing.
Hart – I was standing by waiting for further instructions. After some

little while the word came down, "Pass your women up on the Boat Deck." This was done.

9922. That means the Third Class?

Hart – Yes, the Third Class.

9923. Anything about children?

Hart – Yes. "Pass the women and children."

9924. "Pass the women and children up to the Boat Deck"?

Hart – Yes, those that were willing to go to the Boat Deck were shown the way. Some were not willing to go to the Boat Deck, and stayed behind. Some of them went to the Boat Deck, and found it rather cold, and saw the boats being lowered away, and thought themselves more secure on the ship, and consequently returned to their cabin.

9925. You say they thought themselves more secure on the ship? Did you hear any of them say so?

Hart – Yes, I heard two or three say they preferred to remain on the ship than be tossed about on the water like a cockle shell.

9926. Can you in any way help us to fix the time, or about the time, when the order was given to pass the Third Class women and children up to the Boat Deck? Could you tell us how long it was after you were first roused, or how long it was before the ship went down?

Hart – Well, as near as I can. The vessel struck, I believe, at 11:40. That would be 20 minutes to 12. It must have been three parts of an hour before the word was passed down to me to pass the women and children up to the Boat Deck.

9927. (The Commissioner.) This would be about 12:30?

Hart – Yes, My Lord, as near as can be.

9928. (The Solicitor General.) You say the word was passed down and you heard it?

Hart – Yes.

9929. And you had your other colleagues there, other Third Class Stewards. Was the word passed along?

Hart – Yes, we were in a bunch. The whole sections are in a bunch. The word was passed right round, "Women and children to the Boat Deck," at somewhere about 12:30.

9931. In order that your Third Class women and children should get from those quarters up to the Boat Deck, they would have to mount a number of decks and go up a number of stairs?

Hart – I did not take them that way.

9932. How did you take them?

Hart – I took them along to the next deck, the C Deck, the first saloon deck.

9933. You are making it very clear. There is a Third Class stairway going up?

Hart – Yes.

9934. Did you take them by the Third Class stairway up to C Deck?

Hart – I took them up into the after-Well Deck, that would be the Third Class deck up one companion to C Deck.

9935. Do you see the plan (Pointing on the plan.)?

Hart – There is no occasion; I know the ship.

9936. It is to help us, not you. You say there are a series of stairways indicated. It is the Third Class stairway going up, is it not?

Hart – Yes.

…9942. Is it a wide stairway with rails dividing the stairs into sections?

Hart – Yes, it is very wide.

9943. So that 20 or 30 people could walk up abreast?

Hart – Well, hardly that.

9944. Well, 15 people?

Hart – I should imagine six aside could go up easily.

9945. That would bring them up then, as I follow you, to the C Deck, to the after-well deck; and how would you get them from there to the Boat Deck?

Hart – I took them along to the First Class main companion from there.

…9948. That would mean on C Deck going forward. Would it mean passing the Second Class library, and all that?

Hart – Yes. The beginning of that deck is the Second Class, and further along, the saloon.

9949. Then did you guide them up that First Class stairway to the Boat Deck?

Hart – Right to the Boat Deck.

9950. At that time, when you took up your people by that route, was there any barrier that had to be opened, or was it open to pass?

Hart – There were barriers that at ordinary times are closed, but they were open.

9952. How many people of your lot did you take up the first time you went up this course to the Boat Deck?

Hart – Somewhere about 30.

9953. All women and children of the Third Class?

Hart – Yes, on that occasion, on the first occasion.

About this time Chief Officer Henry Wilde approaches Second Officer Lightoller and asks where the firearms are kept. The guns were Lightoller's responsibility when he was First Officer in Belfast. Lightoller leads Wilde, Captain Smith, First Officer Murdoch, and Fifth Officer Lowe to the locker holding the guns and ammunition. The officers arm themselves in case it becomes necessary. It soon would.

Portside No. 16

When Third Class passengers are allowed onto the Boat Deck Olaus Abelseth and his companions make sure 16 year-old Karen Abelseth gets into boat 16. Bruce Ismay and Thomas Andrews continue helping the crew load and launch the portside boats. Stewardess Mary Sloan is also busy helping people board the boats when her glance catches that of Thomas Andrews.

"Miss Sloan, you must board a boat now," Andrews calls out upon recognizing her.

"But there are so many others; all my friends are staying behind. It would be mean to go," she protests, but is cut off by Andrews as he reaches her.

"It would be mean not to go. Now please Miss Sloan, there's no time. You must go now!"

Sixth Officer James Moody is supervising the loading of lifeboat 16 as Thomas Andrews follows up his urgent plea by guiding Mary Sloan into the boat just ahead of a rush of panicking passengers. Sloan is the last person to board lifeboat 16 before she is lowered at 1:20 a.m. with 52 aboard. The passengers are mostly Second and Third Class women. There are also two crewmembers aboard including Seaman Ernest Archer who gave this testimony at the U.S. Senate inquiry.

> **United States Senate Inquiry** – Testimony of Ernest Archer, questioned by Senator Bourne.
> Senator Bourne – Then what?
> Mr. Archer – Then when I got to No. 16 boat the officer told me to get into the boat and see that the plug was in; so I got in the boat. I seen that the plug was in tight; then they started to put passengers in, and I assisted to get them in.
> Senator Bourne – Were you still remaining in No. 16?
> Mr. Archer – Still remaining in the boat and assisting the passengers, children and ladies, to the boat.
> Senator Bourne – Did any men get in?
> Mr. Archer – No, sir; I never saw any men get in, sir; only my mate.
> Senator Bourne – You were directed by the officer to get into the boat, and your mate was directed by the officer to get into the boat?
> Mr. Archer – So far as I know, he was, sir. I never heard the order for him to get in. I was busy with the children. I was busy. I did not know who was speaking.
> Senator Bourne – Then what?
> Mr. Archer – I heard him give orders to lower the boat. The last order I received after I heard that was from the officer, to allow nobody in the boat, and there was no one else to get into the boat. That was just prior to starting the lowering.
> Senator Bourne – You and your mate were in the boat?
> Mr. Archer – Yes, sir.

The Perfect Calm

Senator Bourne – Was the officer in the boat?
Mr. Archer – No; no officer in the boat.
Senator Bourne – Then you lowered the boat?
Mr. Archer – We lowered the boat, and my mate pulled at the releasing bar for both falls, and that cleared the boat, and we started to pull away.
Senator Bourne – Having about 50 passengers in the boat and only your mate and yourself?
Mr. Archer – Yes, sir; the master-at-arms [Joseph Bailey] came down after us. He was the coxswain.
Senator Bourne – He came down one of the ropes?
Mr. Archer – Yes, sir; came down the fall.
Senator Bourne – He was sent by an officer?
Mr. Archer – I presume he was sent by an officer.
Senator Bourne – To help fill up your complement?
Mr. Archer – He said he was sent down to be the coxswain of the boat.

Portside No. 14

Chief Officer Wilde and Fifth Officer Lowe fill lifeboat 14 with women and children but a few men also make it aboard including squash racquet world champion, Englishman Charles Williams. Most are Second Class passengers with a few passengers from First Class and Third Class.

> **United States Senate Inquiry** – Testimony of Fifth Officer Harold Lowe, questioned by Senator Smith.
> Senator Smith – Who had charge of the loading of lifeboat No. 14?
> Mr. Lowe – I had.
> Senator Smith – And how many people did you put into it?
> Mr. Lowe – Fifty-eight.
> Senator Smith – How many women; do you know?
> Mr. Lowe – They were all women and children, bar one passenger, who was an Italian, and he sneaked in, and he was dressed like a woman.
> Senator Smith – Had woman's clothing on?
> Mr. Lowe – He had a shawl over his head, and everything else; and I only found out at the last moment. And there was another passenger that I took for rowing.
> Senator Smith – Who was that?
> …Mr. Lowe (referring to book) – "C. Williams, racket champion of the world,"…

Boat 14 lowers away at 1:25 a.m. with 40 people, including Fifth Officer Harold Lowe and Seaman Joseph Scarrott, aboard.

British Wreck Commissioner's Inquiry – Testimony of Joseph Scarrott, examined by Mr. Butler Aspinall.

383. ...Now having got to boat 14, which was your boat, what was done about that?

Scarrott – Directly I got to my boat I jumped in, saw the plug in, and saw my dropping ladder was ready to be worked at a moment's notice; and then Mr. Wilde, the Chief Officer, came along and said, "All right; take the women and children," and we started taking the women and children. There would be 20 women got into the boat, I should say, when some men tried to rush the boats, foreigners they were, because they could not understand the order which I gave them, and I had to use a bit of persuasion. The only thing I could use was the boat's tiller.

...386. Did you get these men out of your boat, or prevent them getting in?

Scarrott – Yes, I prevented five getting in. One man jumped in twice and I had to throw him out the third time.

387. Did you succeed in getting all the women and children that were about into your boat?

Scarrott – Yes, when Mr. Lowe came and took charge he asked me how many were in the boat; I told him as far as I could count there were 54 women and four children, one of those children being a baby in arms. It was a very small baby which came under my notice more than anything, because of the way the mother was looking after it, being a very small child.

...393. Was Mr. Lowe, the Fifth Officer, also in the boat?

Scarrott – We were practically full up. I was taking the women in when Mr. Lowe came. There was another Officer with him on the Boat Deck, but I do not know which one that was, and he said to this other Officer: "All right, you go in that boat and I will go in this." That would mean No. 16 boat; she was abaft us, the next boat. Mr. Lowe came in our boat. I told him that I had had a bit of trouble through the rushing business, and he said, "All right." He pulled out his revolver and he fired two shots between the ship and the boat's side, and issued a warning to the remainder of the men that were about there. He told them that if there was any more rushing he would use it. When he fired the two shots he fired them into the water. He asked me, "How many got into the boat?" I told him as near as I could count that that was the number, and he said to me, "Do you think the boat will stand it?" I said, "Yes, she is hanging all right." "All right," he said, "Lower away 14."

Testimony of Fifth Officer Harold G. Lowe, examined by Mr. Rowlatt.

15855. ...Did you use a revolver at all?

Lowe – I did.

15856. How was that?

Lowe – It was because while I was on the Boat Deck just as they had started to lower, two men jumped into my boat. I chased one out and to avoid another occurrence of that sort I fired my revolver as I was going down each deck, because the boat would not stand a sudden jerk. She was loaded already I suppose with about 64 people on her, and she would not stand any more.
15857. You were afraid of the effect of any person jumping in the boat through the air?
Lowe – Certainly, I was.
15858. In your judgment had she enough in her to lower safely?
Lowe – She had too many in her as far as that goes. I was taking risks.

Fifth Officer Lowe succeeds in keeping more passengers from leaping into boat 14 as she lowers away but as the boat approaches the water the after-fall twists and hangs up while the forward fall continues lowering. This leaves the boat precariously hovering at a 45 degree angle with the aft end of the boat 10 feet in the air. Lowe and Scarrott worry that the boats plug may give way but decide to drop her to the sea by the releasing gear. Scarrott quickly checks the plug and finding that it held, mans an oar as boat 14 rows away from the sinking ship.

Portside No. 12

Chief Officer Wilde and Second Officer Lightoller then move to lifeboat 12. At 1:30 a.m., with a capacity of 65 people, she is lowered with 42 women and children and two seamen on board. Seaman John Thomas Poingdestre is in command.

> **British Wreck Commissioner's Inquiry** – Testimony of John Poingdestre, examined by Mr. Butler Aspinall.
> 2925. Now what happened with regard to your boat, No. 12?
> Poingdestre – We filled her up with women and children – me and Mr. Lightoller, the Second Officer.
> …2928. How many would it hold?
> Poingdestre – The full carrying capacity of the big lifeboats is 65.
> …2958. Do you know how it comes that there were not more than 42 put into this boat?
> Poingdestre – Yes.
> 2959. Why?
> Poingdestre – Well the reason is that the falls would not carry any more.
> 2960. You mean somebody was frightened of the falls?
> Poingdestre – Yes, the Second Officer, Mr. Lightoller.
> 2962. What orders did he give you?
> Poingdestre – To lay off and stand by close to the ship.

...2965. How did the passengers behave – well?
Poingdestre – Well, they did not where I was.
2966. (The Commissioner.) What were they doing?
Poingdestre – They were trying to rush No. 12 and No. 14 boats.
2968. (Mr. Butler Aspinall.) Did you have to keep them back?
Poingdestre – Yes, to the best of my ability.
2969. Who did that?
Poingdestre – Myself and Mr. Lightoller and the other two sailors who were standing by to lower. They could not lower the boat as it should have been lowered because of the passengers. Men were on the boat falls; they could not get them clear.
2970. Could you tell the Court who those were who were trying to rush the boat?
Poingdestre – Passengers.
2971. What sort of passengers?
Poingdestre – Second and Third.
2972. (The Commissioner.) Men passengers?
Poingdestre – Yes, my Lord.

Examined by Mr. Holmes.
3192. The number of 40 that you have given us of passengers that got into your boat was only a rough estimate on your part. You did not count them?
Poingdestre – That is correct.
3194. Did the boat appear to you to be sufficiently full when it was lowered?
Poingdestre – Yes, because people with lifebelts on take up room for two.

The wireless distress calls are now nearing desperation as the sea is quickly claiming its titanic prize, "We are sinking fast; Women and children in boats; Cannot last much longer."

Starboard No. 9

On the starboard side First Officer William Murdoch is now assisted by Sixth Officer James Moody. Murdoch and Moody load a few First Class passengers and some crew, but mostly women, children and men from Second and Third class fill lifeboat 9. Benjamin Guggenheim's French mistress Madame Aubart and her maid, Miss Emma Sägesser, are among those helped into boat 9. The boat leaves in command of Boatswain Albert M. Haines with 40 aboard at 1:30 a.m..

United States Senate Inquiry – Testimony of Albert Haines, questioned by Senator Smith.
Mr. Haines – We had the boat crew there, and Mr. Murdoch came

along with a crowd of passengers, and we filled the boat with ladies, and lowered the boat, and he told me to lay off and keep clear of the ship. I got the boat clear, sir, and laid out near the ship. I did not think the ship would sink, of course, sir. When I saw her going down by the head, I pulled farther away, for the safety of the people in the boat.
Senator Smith – How far away?
Mr. Haines – About 100 yards away at first, sir.

Starboard No. 11

At 1:35 a.m. First Officer Murdoch launches lifeboat No. 11 with 50 people aboard and Quartermaster Sidney James Humphries in command. Passengers are mostly women and children from Second and Third class but also include some First Class passengers including Edith Russell (Rosenbaum) and Emma Schabert. Emma's brother, Mr. Philip Edmund Mock, takes his chance when he jumps into the lowering lifeboat.

Edith's account of her experience was reported in the April 23, 1912 edition of the *New York Times* (partial content):

"Out of all the criticism of J. Bruce Ismay, Managing Director of the White Star Line, because of his conduct following the *Titanic* disaster, there has come praise from a woman who declares that she owes her life to the White Satr [sic; should be "Star"] official. This woman is Miss Edith L. Rosenbaum of 45 Merrill Road, Far Rockaway.

"Miss Rosenbaum told a reporter for THE TIMES yesterday that she was among the last who, preferring her chances on the sinking vessel to the risk of the lifeboats in an open sea, departed from the doomed liner. She was forced to take to the lifeboat only by the physical force of Mr. Ismay, who, she declares, caught her by the arm on the Boat Deck and thrust her down a narrow stairway to A deck, where she was heaved over safely into the life craft.

"'I believe,' said Miss Rosenbaum, 'that Mr. Ismay must have entered his lifeboat at the very last moment, judging by the fact that I myself was among the last to leave the *Titanic*. I last saw him calling out, "Any more women? If so, all off now."'

"'I think that Mr. Ismay should not be censured, as he took his chances after all the women in that part of the ship had been saved.'

"...'Women were being placed in the lifeboats,' continued Miss Rosenbaum, 'as I stood perplexed on the Boat Deck. Just then I happened to turn around and I caught sight of a man standing in one of the doors. He was calling out and asking if all the women were being cared for. As he caught sight of me he motioned to me and I approached him. As I have said, this man was Mr. Ismay, who seized my arm and cried, "Woman, what are you doing here? All women should be off the boat!" He thrust me down the passageway to A deck, where I found myself between two lines of men. I was picked up by two of them, carried to the side of the lifeboat, and thrust over into it head first.'

"'I screamed as I lurched into the craft, and at the same time lost both my slippers. I remonstrated against going out in the lifeboat, and some of the men assisted me back to the deck again, where I recovered my slippers.'

"'I had scarcely recovered from this frightful experience when one of the men hastened to my side. It happened that he was an acquaintance I had made in Cherbourg, Mr. Mork, [sic; should be "Mock"] a miniature painter. He persuaded me to enter the lifeboat, and facilitated matters by allowing me to step upon his knee, gaining the lifeboat with less difficulty than the first time. The boat was not filled, and there were no other women in sight. As it swung out on the davits and lowered to the water Mr. Mork jumped in after me.'"

The À la Carte Restaurant Staff

The First Class À la Carte Restaurant located on B Deck is a private concession owned and operated by Italian businessman A.P. Luigi Gatti. His 68 employees are primarily Italian and French. They speak little or no English. They are not part of the White Star crew nor are they passengers—leaving them with no assistance and little chance of escaping the sinking ship.

> **British Wreck Commissioner's Inquiry** – Testimony of Saloon Steward James Johnson, examined by Mr. Cotter.
> 3620. Now I want to ask you a very vital question. How many men were in the steward department of the "Titanic"?
> Johnson – I think something like 470 altogether – there must have been.
> 3621. Were they all Englishmen?
> Johnson – I do not know whether the restaurant were included in it or not.
> 3622. There is a restaurant there?
> Johnson – Yes.
> 3623. What is that staff constituted of?
> Johnson – Mostly Italians and French. I do not know. I never mix with them, so I cannot tell you; but there were none of them Englishmen as a rule.
> 3624. How many Italians and Frenchmen would there be in the crew?
> Johnson – Do you mean my average?
> 3625. Yes?
> Johnson – Well, I should say 50 to 60.
> 3626. Can you tell us whose jurisdiction they were under outside the captain – the chief steward or somebody else?
> Johnson – Mr. Gatti.

3627. Who was Mr. Gatti?
Johnson – A nice little man.
3628. What was Mr. Gatti's position on board the "Titanic"?
Johnson – He was like chief steward in his own department.
3629. Do you know if any of Mr. Gatti's men took part in any drill at all; had they a boat station?
Johnson – I do not know.
3630. Did you see any of those men after, shall I say, the alarm had been given?
Johnson – Well, I saw them all bunched together, but everyone was bunched together at first; but after that I only saw one, and he saved himself.

British Wreck Commissioner's Inquiry – Testimony of Paul Mauge, examined by the Attorney General.
20074. Were you Secretary to the Chef of the Restaurant À la Carte on the "Titanic"?
Mauge – Yes, I was.
20075. You have never been on a ship before?
Mauge – No, it was the first time.
…20125. What became of all the other persons who were employed in the restaurant; did they remain on the deck or did they go up with you?
Mauge – Well, I go down again, and I said to the chef, "There is some danger happening; we must get up." He lost his temper – he lost himself.
…20128. And lost his head – is that what you mean?
Mauge – Yes. I said to the other cooks to wait for us. After that we had been by the Third Class deck just at the back, and we have been trying to go on the Second Class passenger deck. Two or three stewards were there, and would not let us go. I was dressed and the chef was too. He was not in his working dress; he was just like me. I asked the stewards to pass. I said I was the secretary to the chef, and the stewards said, "Pass along, get away." So the other cooks were obliged to stay on the deck there; they could not go up. That is where they die.
…20132. You say they would not let them pass. You were allowed to pass?
Mauge – They let me pass, me and the chef, because I was dressed like a passenger. I think that was why they let me pass.
…20139. (The Commissioner.) Why were they not allowed to get up on the Boat Deck? Why was it they were kept from getting to the Boat Deck?
Mauge – Well, I cannot say; I do not know.
20140. (The Attorney General.) How many of them were there?

Mauge – I think all the members of the restaurant were there.
20141. How many would that be?
Mauge – Perhaps 60.
20142. You mean "soixante"?
Mauge – Ah! You understand French. Yes, 20 cooks and 40 waiters.
20143. They were all men, I suppose?
Mauge – Yes.

Examined by Mr. Scanlan.

20184. …This did not apply to passengers, did it; there were no passengers prevented from going up?
Mauge – No, there were not.

Starboard No. 13

Murdoch next oversees loading and lowering lifeboat 13. Third Class passenger Daniel Buckley along with some other male passengers jump into the boat as it is being loaded. Buckley, covered in a ladies shawl, is undetected and left on board as the other men are forced out.

United States Senate Inquiry – testimony of Daniel Buckley as told to Senator Smith.
Mr. Buckley – …Then the lifeboats were preparing. There were five lifeboats sent out. I was in the sixth. I was holding the ropes all the time, helping to let down the five lifeboats that went down first, as well as I could.
When the sixth lifeboat was prepared, there was a big crowd of men standing on the deck. And they all jumped in. So I said I would take my chance with them.
Senator Smith – Who were they?
Mr. Buckley – Passengers and sailors and firemen mixed. There were no ladies there at the same time. When they jumped, I said I would go too. I went into the boat. Then two officers came along and said all of the men could come out. And they brought a lot of steerage passengers with them; and they were mixed, every way, ladies and gentlemen. And they said all the men could get out and let the ladies in. But six men were left in the boat. I think they were firemen and sailors.
I was crying. There was a woman in the boat, and she had thrown her shawl over me, and she told me to stay in there. I believe she was Mrs. Astor [Buckley was in boat 13 while Mrs. Astor went in boat 4]. Then they did not see me, and the boat was lowered down into the water, and we rowed away out from the steamer. The men that were in the boat at first fought, and would not get out, but the officers drew their revolvers, and fired shots over our heads, and then the men got out.

À la Carte Restaurant Chef Mr. Pierre Rousseau, 49, and Paul Mauge, secretary to the chef, make their way to the Boat Deck after they are allowed to pass by the Stewards who at the time are not allowing any of the other restaurant staff to leave their deck.

> **British Wreck Commissioner's Inquiry** – Testimony of Paul Mauge, examined by the Attorney General.
> 20151. Then after you got up to the Boat Deck they were still putting the women and children into the boats?
> Mauge – Yes.
> 20152. Did you see any boats lowered whilst you were on the Boat Deck?
> Mauge – I do not follow you exactly.
> 20153. (The Commissioner.) Did you see any boats put into the water?
> Mauge – Yes, I saw some; just the last one.
> 20154. (The Attorney-General.) On which side do you mean?
> Mauge – On this side.
> 20155. The starboard side?
> Mauge – Yes.
> 20156. Do you mean the last one of the last four?
> Mauge – It was the second or third, I cannot say which of the two.
> 20157. Do you mean you saw the second or third of the last four boats on the starboard side let down into the water?
> Mauge – Yes.
> 20158. And filled with women and children, were they?
> Mauge – No, because some of the women stayed with their husbands and would not like to go.
> 20159. You got into one of the boats, did you not?
> Mauge – Oh, no; the second or third lifeboat was between two decks and I jumped directly from the top deck to this lifeboat. About six or ten persons were jumping in it.
> …20162. But it was stopped between the two decks?
> Mauge – Yes, was stopped between the two decks.
> 20163. And then you jumped into it?
> Mauge – Yes.
> …20167. …You got into the boat, and eventually were saved?
> Mauge – Yes, but before that I did ask the chef to jump many times, but the chef was too fat I must say – too big, you know. He could not jump.

From his book – *The Loss of the SS. Titanic*, Second Class passenger Lawrence Beesley relates how he was able to survive.

> "I heard a cry from below of, 'Any more ladies?' and looking over the edge of the deck, saw boat 13 swinging level with the rail of B deck, with the crew, some stokers, a few men passengers and the rest ladies,– the latter being about half the total number; the boat was almost full and just about to be lowered. The call for ladies was repeated twice again, but apparently there were none to be found. Just then one of the crew looked up and saw me looking over. 'Any ladies on your deck?' he said. 'No,' I replied. 'Then you had better jump.' I sat on the edge of the deck with my feet over, threw the dressing-gown (which I had carried on my arm all of the time) into the boat, dropped, and fell in the boat near the stern.
>
> "As I picked myself up, I heard a shout: 'Wait a moment, here are two more ladies,' and they were pushed hurriedly over the side and tumbled into the boat, one into the middle and one next to me in the stern.
>
> "…As they tumbled in, the crew shouted, 'Lower away'; but before the order was obeyed, a man with his wife and a baby came quickly to the side: the baby was handed to the lady in the stern, the mother got in near the middle and the father at the last moment dropped in as the boat began its journey down to the sea many feet below."

Lifeboat 13 leaves at 1:40 a.m. with 55 people, mostly Second and Third Class women and children, aboard. First Class passenger Dr. Washington Dodge also finds room in the boat after helping the women and children board. Also leaving in boat 13 are Lookout Reginald Lee, several Firemen, and two Seamen. The boat is in command of Lead Fireman Frederick Barrett.

> **British Wreck Commissioner's Inquiry** – Testimony of Frederick Barrett, examined by the Solicitor General.
>
> 2168. …as it was being lowered down the side the main discharge from the engine room threatened to swamp the boat?
>
> Barrett – Yes.
>
> 2169. It was somewhere opposite the rear funnel, was it not?
>
> Barrett – Yes.
>
> 2170. Then there was one other boat on the starboard side still, No. 15; what was happening to that at this time?
>
> Barrett – It was getting lowered about 30 seconds after us. It was coming on top of us.
>
> 2171. It was coming on top of you. Just tell us about that shortly?
>
> Barrett – Yes. When we found the discharge was coming out we stopped lowering and all the hose was tied up in the boat. I had a knife and I cut the hose adrift and shoved two oars over the forward end to shove the lifeboat off the ship's side. We got into the water and there was a bit of a current and it drifted us under No. 15 boat, and I sung out "Let go the

after fall." Nobody seemed to realise what I was doing. I walked across the women to cut the fall, and the other fall touched my shoulder.

2172. Supposing the ship was going down by the head and No. 15 boat was being lowered, after No. 13 boat was in the water No. 15 boat would tend to get on the top of No. 13?

Barrett – Yes.

2173. Then whatever the cause, you say No. 15 was coming on top of you?

Barrett – Yes.

2174. Did you get clear?

Barrett – We just got clear.

2175. Then what happened to No. 13, the boat you were in?

Barrett – We got the oars out. I did not see anybody that was going to take charge of the boat. The rudder was lying in the stern at the bottom, and I shipped the rudder and took charge of the boat till after the "Titanic" sank.

Starboard No. 15

While Murdoch was loading lifeboat 13 Sixth Officer Moody is simultaneously loading lifeboat 15 and she lowers a mere 30 seconds later with 68, mostly Third Class passengers, aboard.

> **British Wreck Commissioner's Inquiry** – Testimony of Third Class Steward John E. Hart, examined by the Solicitor General.
>
> 9965. Did you bring up any more?
>
> Hart – Yes, about 25. I had some little trouble in getting back owing to the males wanting to get to the Boat Deck.
>
> 9966. The men?
>
> Hart – Yes. After the word was passed round for women and children, I was delayed a little time in getting a little band together that were willing to go to the boats.
>
> 9967. A band of women and children?
>
> Hart – Yes.
>
> 9968. How many did you gather?
>
> Hart – Somewhere about 25.
>
> 9969. Were those all people from the rooms you were responsible for?
>
> Hart – No, also from other sections.
>
> 9970. Were they all Third Class passengers?
>
> Hart – Yes.
>
> 9971. Did you guide them by the same route?
>
> Hart – Yes.
>
> 9972. Where did you take them to?
>
> Hart – I took them to the only boat that was left then, boat No. 15.
>
> 9973. This is an important thing. You say the only boat that was left?

Hart – That I could see.

…9988. When you got with these people to No. 15 was there room for them in it?

Hart – Yes, they were placed in it.

9989. Now this is on the Boat Deck?

Hart – Yes.

…9997. I daresay you can tell us a bit further about it. When you got to boat 15 with these 25 people, were there any people in boat No. 15 already?

Hart – Yes.

9998. About how many, or who?

Hart – Well, I can give you a rough estimate.

9999. Yes, of course?

Hart – The last 25 were passed in from the Boat Deck.

10000. Your 25?

Hart – Yes.

10001. (The Commissioner.) Were they mixed, women and children, or were they women?

Hart – There were three children with them, My Lord.

10002. Twenty-two women and three children?

Hart – The boat was then lowered to A deck. We there took in about five women, three children, and one man. He had a baby in his arms.

10005. You were in her, as I understand?

Hart – Yes.

10006. Did you get in her from the Boat Deck?

Hart – Yes.

10008. How many people do you think were in boat No. 15 after she got into the water, and when she was saved?

Hart – I would not like to vouch for its accuracy, but I can give you an estimate.

10009. What is your estimate?

Hart – I should say somewhere about 70 after we left A deck.

10010. Another Witness has told us he thinks 68?

Hart – Well, it is a rough estimate; it is pretty near it.

The full lifeboat is nearly lowered on top of lifeboat 13 but a collision is barely avoided as boat 13 pulls away just in time. In the water Fireman Frank Dymond commands boat 15.

With most of the forward boats now away passengers begin to move to the stern area. Chief Officer Wilde and First Officer Murdoch continue loading passengers in the Portside boats. Charles Joughin is also helping passengers into the lifeboats. Then, after refusing to take a spot in a lifeboat, returns to his cabin to await his fate with the rest of his bottle.

Emergency Clipper 2

Wilde oversees loading of the portside emergency clipper. Passengers include seven First Class women, six Third Class women, children and one man, two crew from the Victualling department, and two deck crew including Fourth Officer Joseph Boxhall. The boat lowers only 15 feet before reaching the water. In normal circumstances it would have been 70 feet.

> **British Wreck Commissioner's Inquiry** – Testimony of Joseph Boxhall, examined by Mr. Raymond Asquith.
> 15424. Who was superintending the filling of that boat?
> Boxhall – Mr. Wilde, or, I presume, Mr. Wilde was superintending the filling. The order was given to lower away when I was told to go in it and the boat was full; they had started the tackles when I got in.
> 15426. Did you notice what other boats there were on the port side at the time?
> Boxhall – There was only one boat hanging there in the davits, No. 4.
> 15427. That was the boat next to yours?
> Boxhall – Yes.
> 15428. Can you say how many people were in that boat No. 2?
> Boxhall – I endeavoured to count them, but I did not succeed very well. I judge between 25 and 30 were in her.
> 15429. Were they mostly women, or were they mixed men and women?
> Boxhall – The majority were women. I know there were 3 crew, 1 male passenger, and myself.
> 15430. And you think the rest were women?
> Boxhall – They were. There were several children in the boat.

With a capacity of 40, Emergency Clipper 2 is lowered and leaves at 1:45 a.m. with only 17 aboard.

Portside No. 10

Second Class passenger Masabumi Hosono makes his way to the upper deck. He is the only Japanese passenger aboard and the only of oriental heritage that is not traveling in Third Class. He is stopped in his initial attempt to reach the Boat Deck by a Steward believing he is a steerage passenger trying to go up before Third Class is allowed on deck.

Murdoch loads lifeboat 10 and puts Seaman Edward John Buley in charge. When she begins lowering at 1:50 a.m. with 55 aboard someone shouts, "Room for two more."

Masabumi Hosono sees a man jump in and, following his example, jumps undetected into the lowering boat.

From Hosono's diary:

"I tried to prepare myself for the last moment with no agitation, making up my mind not to leave anything disgraceful as a Japanese. But still I found myself looking for and waiting for any possible chance for survival.

"I myself was deep in desolate thought that I would no more be able to see my beloved wife and children, since there was no alternative for me than to share the same destiny as the Titanic. But the example of the first man making a jump led me to take this last chance.

"Fortunately the men in charge were taken up with something else and did not pay much attention. Besides, it was dark, and so they would not have seen who was a man and who a woman."

United States Senate Inquiry – Testimony of Seaman Edward John Buley, questioned by Senator Fletcher.
Senator Fletcher – Were any ladies on the deck when you left?
Mr. Buley – No, sir. Ours was the last boat up there, and they went around and called to see if there were any, and they threw them in the boat at the finish, because they didn't like the idea of coming in.
Senator Fletcher – Pushed them in, you mean?
Mr. Buley – Threw them in. One young lady slipped, and they caught her by the foot on the deck below, and she came up then and jumped in.

Portside No. 4

By now, the A Deck windows have been opened and lifeboat 4 can be loaded. With the help of Colonel Gracie and Clint Smith, Second Officer Lightoller loads women and children into boat 4. He spots and tries to remove 13 year old John Borie Ryerson, but Arthur Ryerson, the boy's father, persuades Lightoller to let him to stay in the boat with the rest of his family. At that point Lightoller orders that no more boys will be allowed in the boat. William Carter also sees his family safely aboard but not until after his wife Lucile places a large ladies hat on 11 year old William Jr.

John Thayer helps his wife Marian aboard while George Widener and his son Harry help Mrs. Widener into the lifeboat. William Carter then suggests that it is time for the men to find a spot on a boat for themselves. They decline, preferring to take their chances with the other men staying aboard the *Titanic*.

Colonel Astor, by now having changed his mind about their situation, helps his wife climb through the window of the enclosed promenade into the lifeboat. The Colonel then asks Lightoller if, due to her delicate condition, he could join her. Lightoller tells him that no men can enter until all the women are loaded. Astor accepts this and inquires about the boat number. Just before 1:50 a.m. Colonel John Jacob Astor IV bids his 18 year old pregnant wife goodbye.

Lightoller orders lifeboat 4 lowered with Madeleine Astor, Marian Thayer, Eleanor Widener, the Carter and Ryerson families along with other First and Second Class women and children on board. Colonel Astor, George and Harry

Widener, John Thayer, William Carter, and Arthur Ryerson then watch as Quartermaster Walter John Perkis helps lower the lifeboat to the sea with 36 empty places.

> **United States Senate Inquiry** – Testimony of Walter J. Perkis, questioned by Senator Perkins.
> Mr. Perkis – …The boat was lowered. I lowered No. 4 into the water, and left that boat, and walked aft; and I came back, and a man that was in the boat, one of the seamen that was in the boat at the time, sung out to me, "We need another hand down here." So I slid down the lifeline there from the davit into the boat.
> Senator Perkins – How far is the distance from the upper deck down to the water?
> Mr. Perkis – About seventy-odd feet.
> Senator Perkins – And you went hand over hand down?
> Mr. Perkis – Down the lifeline; yes, sir.
> Senator Perkins – It is quite a distance to go down in that way. You were a quartermaster?
> Mr. Perkis – Yes, sir.
> Senator Perkins – You had charge of the boat, did you not?
> Mr. Perkis – I took charge of the boat after I got in.

Shortly after being launched boat 4 rescues eight swimming crew members from the water near the ship. Two die shortly after being pulled aboard. Lamp Trimmer Samuel Hemming is one of the swimmers who survives.

> **United States Senate Inquiry** – Testimony of Samuel Hemming, questioned by Senator Smith
> Mr. Hemming – …I went and looked over the starboard side, and everything was black. I went over to the port side and saw a boat off the port quarter, and I went along the port side and got up the after boat davits and slid down the fall and swam to the boat and got it.
> Senator Smith – You swam out to this boat that you saw?
> Mr. Hemming – Yes, sir.
> Senator Smith – How far was it from the side of the Titanic?
> Mr. Hemming – About 200 yards.
> Senator Smith – Did you have a lifebelt on?
> Mr. Hemming – No, sir.
> Senator Smith – When you reached the boat, what did you find?
> Mr. Hemming – I tried to get hold of the grab line on the bows, and it was too high for me, so I swam along and got hold of one of the grab lines amidships.
> Senator Smith – What did you do then?
> Mr. Hemming – I pulled my head above the gunwale, and I said, "Give us a hand in, Jack." Foley was in the boat. I saw him standing up in

the boat. He said, "Is that you, Sam?" I said, "Yes;" and him and the women and children pulled me in the boat.

Collapsible C

Murdoch and Wilde turn their attention to Collapsible C which had been placed in the lifeboat 1 davits near the bridge. Bruce Ismay helps them load Third Class women and children in the boat including Assyrian Hanna Touma and her children, and 21 year-old Miss Anna Kristine Salkjelsvik, a member of the group of Norwegians traveling to Minnesota. Miss Amy Stanley is also amongst those finding a place in the boat. She later relates her experience in a letter to her parents.

Partial content of Amy Stanley's letter:

> "We tried to reach the boats. Then I saw two fellows (whom we met at meals, the only men we made real friends of) coming towards us, who assisted us over the railings into the lifeboat. As we were being lowered a man about 16 stone jumped into the boat almost on top of me. I heard a pistol fired–I believe it was done to frighten the men from rushing the boat. This man's excuse was that he came because of his baby. When we rowed off the child must have died had I not attended to it."

At 2:00 a.m., with Collapsible C almost full, Wilde calls for more women and children but with none immediately available he orders the boat lowered away with Quartermaster George Rowe in charge. There are six available spaces. First Class passenger William Carter of Pennsylvania, who had just seen his family safely into lifeboat 4, jumps in as the boat is lowered. He is joined by Bruce Ismay.

> **British Wreck Commissioner's Inquiry** – Testimony of J. Bruce Ismay, examined by the Attorney General.
> 18557. Did you see how many passengers were put into this collapsible?
> Ismay – No, I did not see at the time.
> 18558. Did she appear to be full?
> Ismay – She was very fairly full.
> 18559. Would you tell us what happened after you got the women and children in?
> Ismay – After all the women and children were in and after all the people that were on deck had got in, I got into the boat as she was being lowered away.
> 18560. There was no order to you to get in?
> Ismay – No, none.
> 18561. Did any other passenger get in?
> Ismay – One.
> 18562. That is a Mr. Carter?

Ismay – Mr. Carter.
18563. Am I right, then, in this, that there were women and children and some members of the crew to man the boat and two passengers, yourself and Mr. Carter?
Ismay – Yes, and four Chinamen were in the boat.
18564. Four Chinamen who, we have heard, were discovered after the boat was lowered?
Ismay – Yes.
18566. Before you got into the boat was any attempt made to call up other passengers to come up onto the Boat Deck?
Ismay – That I do not know; I was never off the Boat Deck.
…18571. Did you think then when you left the vessel that she was rapidly going down?
Ismay – I did.

With the forward Well Deck flooded, Collapsible C is the last starboard-side lifeboat launched by the crew.

Collapsible D

Only one more lifeboat would launch from the port side. Collapsible boat D is already hooked to the davit tackles where lifeboat 2 had been by the time Chief Officer Wilde joins Second Officer Lightoller to assist with the loading. With a capacity of 47, Collapsible D is one of the last boats left.

As the desperate crowd begins to descend upon the boat Lightoller draws his pistol and calls for the crew to surround it and allow only women and children aboard. Jacques Futrelle manages to convince his wife May to get into the collapsible after she had previously refused to board other boats without him. Colonel Archibald Gracie and Clint Smith find Mrs. Caroline Brown and Miss Edith Evans, two of the four unescorted ladies Gracie had promised to protect, on the Boat Deck. They had become separated from Brown's sisters Mrs. Malvina Cornell and Mrs. Charlotte Appleton; Malvina had already left in boat 2 and Charlotte was already in Collapsible D. Gracie and Smith quickly usher the ladies to where Wilde and Lightoller are loading women and children into the boat. Miss Evans, believing the boat is nearly full, hesitates then tells Mrs. Brown, "You go first, you have children waiting at home."

Wilde, certain the ship is nearing the end, orders Lightoller to stay aboard Collapsible D but, still intending to get Collapsible B off, he refuses and jumps out of the boat leaving Quartermaster Arthur Bright in charge.

As Collapsible D, with only 17 aboard, is lowered the short distance to the rising water two men jump aboard as it passes the rapidly flooding A deck. Seaman William Lucas spots Miss Evans and calls up, "There's another boat going to be put down for you." But there is no boat for Edith Evans as she is left to contemplate the words of the fortune teller who had recently warned her to beware of water.

British Wreck Commissioner's Inquiry – Testimony of William Lucas, examined by Mr. Rowlatt.

1531. You were telling us about this collapsible boat; you assisted to get her out?

Lucas – Yes.

…1538. Who got into her?

Lucas – About forty women.

1539. And what men?

Lucas – Well, I found three men in the boat afterwards, but I never saw them in the boat when she went away.

1541. Who were the other men? Were they seamen?

Lucas – One-quartermaster and two foreigners in the boat.

1543. Two foreign passengers?

Lucas – Yes.

1544. Do you know what class they were?

Lucas – Well, I should think they were Third Class.

At 2:05 a.m. Collapsible D is the last lifeboat launched by the crew. Almost 1,500 people are still aboard the *Titanic*.

Chapter 15

Aboard the Californian

Captain Stanley Lord, 34, is Master of the liner *Californian* of the Leyland Line, part of J.P. Morgan's IMM shipping conglomerate that also owns White Star Line. On the night of Sunday April 14, 1912 the *Californian* is on a voyage carrying cargo, but no passengers, from London to Boston. Captain Lord stops her at the edge of the icefield which other ships had warned about for days. This is Lord's first experience with field ice and he elects to maintain minimum steam and stop for the night.

That night and during the early morning hours of April 15th Captain Stanley Lord and several officers see the lights of a nearby steamer. They attempt, but fail, to make contact with the ship with their Morse lamp. The officers of the bridge continue to monitor the unidentified ship and take her fading light as an indication the distance between them is increasing. In an unimaginable way, it is.

British Wreck Commissioner's Inquiry – Testimony of Stanley Lord, examined by the Attorney General.
6755. Did you see your Third Officer attempt to communicate with him?
Lord – I did.
6756. How?
Lord – By a Morse lamp.
6758. Did he get any reply?
Lord – No.
6759. By this time had you been able to detect her sidelights at all?
Lord – I could see her green light then.
6760. How far do you judge she was when you could see her green light?
Lord – Well, I saw it some time between 11 and half-past; I do not know exactly.
6761. What distance do you think she was from you when you could see the lights?
Lord – About five miles.
6762. As much as that?

Lord – About that, I should think.
…6767. Then at 12 o'clock the Second Officer relieved the Third Officer?
Lord – Ten minutes past 12.
6768. You were still on deck?
Lord – Yes.
6769. And did you tell him anything with regard to this vessel?
Lord – I told him to watch that steamer – that she was stopped.
6770. She was stopped?
Lord – The other steamer was stopped.
6771. When did you notice the other steamer was stopped?
Lord – About half-past 11.
6772. And he was to let you know if she did what?
Lord – If she altered her bearings or got any closer to us – drifted towards us.
…6805. Can you tell us whether you saw one or two masthead lights?
Lord – I only saw one.
6806. You only saw one?
Lord – The Third Officer said he saw two.
…6812. Is the Third Officer still in the ship?
Lord – Yes.
6813. Will you tell me his name?
Lord – Mr. Groves.

The Only Passenger Steamer Near Us is the 'Titanic'

Charles Victor Groves, 24, preferred sailing with cargo rather than passengers. He had a Second Mate's certificate but was serving as Third Officer on the *Californian*. Interested in signalling, Groves was teaching himself wireless telegraphy and made regular visits to the *Californian's* wireless cabin but on this Sunday night Groves is on the 8:00 p.m. to Midnight watch. The night is starlit and the North Atlantic is clear, calm, and absolutely flat.

Aboard the approaching *Titanic* the Marconi wireless operator is catching up on a backlog of passenger messages while the lookouts are keeping a sharp lookout for ice.

British Wreck Commissioner's Inquiry – Testimony of Charles Groves, examined by Mr. Rowlatt
8135. Now, what did you see, and when?
Groves – As I said before, the stars were showing right down to the horizon. It was very difficult at first to distinguish between the stars and a light, they were so low down. About 11:10, ship's time, I made out a steamer coming up a little bit abaft our starboard beam.
…8150. How were you heading?

Groves – At that time we would be heading N.E. when I saw that steamer first, but we were swinging all the time because when we stopped the order was given for the helm to be put hard-a-port, and we were swinging, but very, very slowly.

…8160. Could you form any judgment how far off she was?

Groves – When I saw her first light I should think she would be about 10 or 12 miles.

…8163. (Mr. Rowlatt) Did she appear to get nearer?

Groves – Yes.

8164. The lights clearer?

Groves – Yes, all the time.

8165. Was she changing her bearing?

Groves – Slowly.

8166. Coming round more to the south and west?

Groves – More on our beam, yes, more to the south and west, but very little.

8167. Did you report that to the captain?

Groves – Yes, because, as I said before, he left orders to let him know if I saw any steamers approaching.

…8172. Did you say what sort of a steamer you thought she was?

Groves – Captain Lord said to me, "Can you make anything out of her lights?" I said, "Yes, she is evidently a passenger steamer coming up on us."

…8176. Did you say why you thought she was a passenger steamer?

Groves – Yes. I told him that I could see her deck lights and that made me pass the remark that she was evidently a passenger steamer.

8178. How many deck lights had she? Had she much light?

Groves – Yes, a lot of light. There was absolutely no doubt her being a passenger steamer, at least in my mind.

…8207. You went on the bridge after he had told you to signal with the Morse light?

Groves – Yes.

8208. And you did signal and then, as I understand, the Captain came on to the bridge?

Groves – Not until after I was Morsing. I was actually Morsing when he came up.

8209. Very well, he came up and he remarked to you, "She does not look like a passenger steamer"?

Groves – That is so.

8210. And you said, "It is"?

Groves – Yes.

8211. Now you said something about the lights going out; what was it?

Groves – Well he said to me, "It does not look like a passenger steamer."

I said, "Well, she put her lights out at 11:40"—a few minutes ago that was.
8212. Then had she put her lights out before the captain came on the bridge?
Groves – Yes, my Lord.
8214. And you told the captain this, did you?
Groves – Yes.
8215. What did he say to that; did he say anything?
Groves – When I remarked about the passenger steamer he said: "The only passenger steamer near us is the 'Titanic.'"

White Rockets Bursting in the Sky

On the morning of April 15th at 12:10 a.m., thirty minutes after the *Titanic* struck the iceberg, Third Officer Groves is relieved by Herbert Stone the *Californian's* 24 year old Second Officer.

Aboard the *Titanic* the crew is busy readying the lifeboats while Captain Smith and Thomas Andrews are just beginning to realize the full extent of the damage. Soon Fourth Officer Boxhall would be sending up distress rockets hoping to alert the nearby unknown vessel that the *Titanic* is in trouble.

> **British Wreck Commissioner's Inquiry** – Testimony of Herbert Stone, examined by Mr. Aspinall.
> 7823. Did the Third Officer make any communication to you about this steamer when you relieved him?
> Stone – He told me the steamer had stopped about one bell and that he had called her up on the Morse lamp and got no answer.
> 7824. Did you continue to keep this vessel under observation?
> Stone – The whole time.
> 7825. Was there any reason for that?
> Stone – None whatever except that it was another ship, stopped in ice the same as ourselves.
> 7827. After a time did you make any communication to the captain?
> Stone – Yes.
> 7828. How?
> Stone – By means of the speaking tube.
> 7829. What did you communicate to him?
> Stone – I communicated that I had seen white lights in the sky in the direction of this other steamer, which I took to be white rockets.
> 7830. What time was it you gave him that information?
> Stone – Just about 1:10.
> 7832. Now, will you tell me what you had seen?
> Stone – First of all, I was walking up and down the bridge and I saw one white flash in the sky, immediately above this other steamer. I did not know what it was; I thought it might be a shooting star.

...7837. Was it like a distress signal?
Stone – It was just a white flash in the sky; it might have been anything.
7838. I know, but what did it suggest to your mind? What did you say to yourself? What did you think it was?
Stone – I thought nothing until I brought the ship under observation with the binoculars and saw the others.
7839. Then you took up your glasses, apparently, and looked?
Stone – Yes.
7840. And how many more did you see?
Stone – I saw four more then.
7841. What were they, rockets?
Stone – They had the appearance of white rockets bursting in the sky.
7842. Did they come in quick succession?
Stone – At intervals of about three or four minutes.

Shortly after the 12:10 a.m. watch came on, Captain Lord leaves the bridge to lie down and rest in the chart room.

British Wreck Commissioner's Inquiry – Testimony of Stanley Lord, examined by the Attorney General.
6787. Then you went to lie down in the chart room?
Lord – Yes, I told him I was going to lie down in the chart room then.
6788. A little later did he whistle down the tube and tell you she was altering her bearings?
Lord – A quarter-past 1:00.
6789. Did he say how she was altering her bearings?
Lord – Towards the S.W.
6790. Did he tell you whether he had seen any signal?
Lord – He said he saw a white rocket.
6791. From her?
Lord – From her.

British Wreck Commissioner's Inquiry – Testimony of Herbert Stone, examined by Mr. Butler Aspinall.
7878. Did the Master, when you had this communication through the tube, tell you to go on Morsing this vessel?
Stone – Yes.
7879. And did he tell you that you were to send him any news and give him any information that you had got?
Stone – When I received any information to send the Apprentice down to him with it.
7880. That is Gibson?
Stone – Yes.

She Looks Very Queer Out of the Water

James Gibson, 20, is an apprentice aboard the *Californian* and is on the Midnight to 4:00 a.m. watch with Second Officer Stone on the morning of April 15, 1912. They are aware of a ship that has stopped within sight of their position but unaware that the desperate Officers and crew of the *Titanic* are racing against time to load and launch their lifeboats as the sea spills into her fatally wounded hull.

British Wreck Commissioner's Inquiry – Testimony of James Gibson, examined by the Solicitor General.
7424. When was it that you saw any ship's light round you first?
Gibson – About twenty minutes past twelve.
7425. What was the light that you saw?
Gibson – A white masthead light and a red sidelight.
7426. Could you see both those lights clearly?
Gibson – I could see the red light with the glasses.
7427. You used glasses to see the red light, the port light, but you could see the white light, could you, with your naked eyes?
Gibson – Yes.
7328. Could you see more than one white light?
Gibson – I saw a glare of lights on her after deck.
7429. You mean the port-hole lights?
Gibson – A glare of white lights on her after deck.
7430. I do not think you quite answered the question I was putting to you. Did you or did you not see any second white steamer lights?
Gibson – Not distinctly, sir.
…7440. Did you form any view as to how far away the ship was?
Gibson – From four to seven miles.
7441. Did you notice anything about her masthead light, her white light?
Gibson – Yes.
7442. What was it?
Gibson – It was flickering.
7443. Did you form an opinion about it; what did you think she was doing?
Gibson – I thought it was a Morse light calling us up.
7444. That would be using her masthead light to send Morse signals?
Gibson – I did not know it was the masthead light then.
7445. Using a light to send Morse signals?
Gibson – Yes.
7446. Did you report this?
Gibson – I went to the keyboard and called it up. I went to our keyboard and called her up.
…7451. When you tried to call up this steamer with your Morse

signals, could you get into communication with her?
Gibson – No, Sir; the lights were still flickering.
...7455. Could you read it if it was clear?
Gibson – I could have done if it was a Morse light, but I looked at her through the glasses afterwards, and found it was a masthead light.
...7459. And did you come to the conclusion that she was not sending any Morse messages at all?
Gibson – Yes.
7460. You have told us, I think, that the Officer of the watch was Mr. Stone, the Second Officer?
Gibson – Yes.
7461. Did you report to him; did you call his attention to the lights you had seen?
Gibson – Yes.
...7476. Now, I just want to get what happened after that. You have told me that the Second Officer said to you that the ship had fired five rockets?
Gibson – Yes.
7477. Did he tell you anything else about what he had been doing while you had not been there?
Gibson – He told me that he had reported it to the Captain.
7478. Did he tell you what the Captain had instructed him to do?
Gibson – Yes.
7479. What was it?
Gibson – To call her up on the Morse light.
...7482. What had been the result?
Gibson – She had not answered him, but fired more rockets.
7483. Did you see her fire these further rockets?
Gibson – I saw three rockets.
...7501. What color rockets were they?
Gibson – White ones.
7502. When you got your glasses on the vessel and saw the first rocket going up through them, could you make out the vessel at all?
Gibson – No, Sir, just her lights.
7503. (The Commissioner.) Still this glare of light?
Gibson – Yes.
7504. Did that indicate, that glare of light, that this was a passenger steamer?
Gibson – No, Sir.
7505. (The Solicitor General.) When you saw the first of these three rockets through your glasses did you report what you saw to the Officer?
Gibson – Yes.
7506. Did he tell you whether he saw the second or the third rocket?

Gibson – Yes, Sir.
7507. Did he?
Gibson – Yes, Sir.
…7511. What happened after that?
Gibson – About twenty minutes past one the Second Officer remarked to me that she was slowly steaming away towards the south-west.
7512. Had you remained on the bridge from the time that you saw these three rockets until then?
Gibson – Yes.
7513. Had you been keeping her under observation?
Gibson – Yes.
7514. Looking at her with your glasses from time to time?
Gibson – Yes.
7515. What had you noticed between one o'clock and twenty minutes past one, looking at her through your glasses?
Gibson – The Second Officer remarked to me, "Look at her now; she looks very queer out of the water; her lights look queer."
7516. You are sure that is what he said – "She looks very queer out of the water"?
Gibson – Yes.
7517. Did he say what he meant?
Gibson – I looked at her through the glasses after that, and her lights did not seem to be natural.
7518. (The Commissioner.) What do you mean by that?
Gibson – When a vessel rolls at sea her lights do not look the same.
7519. But there was no water to cause her to roll, was there; you were not rolling?
Gibson – No.
…7527. You have told us what the Officer said to you. Did you think yourself when you looked at her through the glasses that something was wrong?
Gibson – We had been talking about it together.
7528. (The Commissioner.) I should very much like you to tell me what you had been saying to the Officer.
Gibson – He remarked to me –
7529. I should like you to tell me what were you saying to each other.
Gibson – He remarked to me that a ship was not going to fire rockets at sea for nothing.
… 7533. What took place after that between you and him?
Gibson – We were talking about it all the time, Sir, till five minutes past two, when she disappeared.

The Ship has Disappeared

The curious Officers of the *Californian* see a total of eight rockets launched from the nearby unidentified steamer. The Second Officer and Apprentice, observing the ship from the bridge, notice, "…she looks very queer out of the water; her lights look queer," and later see, "that the ship has disappeared in the S.W." They are content with reporting their observations to the Captain but, without orders, do no more.

> **British Wreck Commissioner's Inquiry** – Testimony of Stanley Lord, examined by the Attorney General.
>
> 7321. If the Marconi operator had been called up then, and he had put the receiver on he would have heard the "Titanic's" messages?
> Lord – Yes.
> 7322. Do you understand Marconi telegraphy at all?
> Lord – I know the idea of it. I cannot use it.
> 7323. Do you know the CQD. signal?
> Lord – I know it.
> 7324. And the SOS.?
> Lord – Yes.
> 7325. Can you receive that signal?
> Lord – They go too quickly for me.
> 7326. So that anybody on your ship who had put the receiver to his ears would have then heard the "Titanic's" message, the CQD. or the SOS.?
> Lord – They would have heard the buzzing, yes.
> 7327. They would have been able to distinguish the signal as long as she was giving it?
> Lord – The operator would. I do not think anyone else on the ship would.
> 7328. The operator would if you had called him?
> Lord – Yes.

Other than their earlier attempts to contact the ship by Morse light the Captain and Officers of the *Californian* take no action. No one calls for the wireless operator and *Titanic's CQD* and *SOS* signals are not heard by anyone aboard the *Californian*.

Just after 2:15 a.m. on the morning of April 15, 1912 Captain Stanley Lord is half asleep in the chart room aboard the *Californian* and doesn't grasp the details or significance of the information he has received from the bridge. Meanwhile Captain John Smith is wide awake on the bridge of the *Titanic* and in a momentary flash vividly recalls all of his 62 years as he accompanies his ship to the bottom of the North Atlantic.

Chapter 16

TITANIC'S LAST MINUTES

"As the ship was sinking the strains of music were wafted over the deck. It was not the note of any martial anthem that had, in days gone by, led embattled legions on to victory. It was a more inspiring stanza than this. It was a loftier and holier melody amid the anguish and the sublime pathos of that awful hour that swept through the compartments of the sinking ship. It was a rallying cry for the living and the dying – to rally them not for life, but to rally them for their awaiting death. Almost face to face with their Creator, amid the chaos of this supreme and solemn moment, in inspiring notes the unison resounded through the ship. It told the victims of the wreck that there was another world beyond the seas, free from the agony of pain, and, though with somber tones, it cheered them on to their untimely fate. As the sea closed upon the heroic dead, let us feel that the heavens opened to the lives that were prepared to enter.

"Father of the Universe, what an admonition to the Nation! The sounds of that awe-inspiring requiem that vibrated o'er the ocean have been drowned in the waters of the deep, the instruments that gave them birth are silenced as the harps were silenced on the willow tree, but if the melody that was rehearsed could only reverberate through this land 'Nearer, My God, to Thee,' and its echoes could be heard in these halls of legislation, and at every place where our rulers and representatives pass judgment and enact and administer laws, and at every home and fireside, from the mansions of the rich to the huts and hovels of the poor, and if we could be made to feel that there is a divine law of obedience and of adjustment, and of compensation that should demand our allegiance, far above the laws that we formulate in this presence, then, from the gloom of these fearful hours we shall pass into the dawn of a higher service and of a better day, and then, Mr. President, the lives that went down upon this fated night did not go down in vain."

~ Excerpt from the Speech of Senator Isidor Raynor – IN THE SENATE OF THE UNITED STATES, Tuesday, May 28, 1912.

Every Man for Himself

As *Titanic's* forecastle head sinks under water and the tilt of her decks continue to grow steeper, Thomas Andrews, the ship's builder, waits for the end alone in the First Class Smoking Room. Captain Smith, having done all he can, tells his crew, "It's every man for himself," and to "be British!" He chooses to wait on the bridge. The wait won't be long.

After the last lifeboat leaves the sinking ship, Major Butt, Clarence Moore, and Frank Millet struggle together to maintain their place on the steep incline of the deck, while William Stead meditates alone after suggesting a final number to Bandmaster Hartley. Soon they will be taking their chances and their last breath in the North Atlantic.

After seeing their women and children safely into a lifeboat, John Thayer sticks with his friends George and Harry Widener. As the bow continues to dip into the ocean the men make their way to the stern to postpone their fate just a little longer. They aren't alone as hundreds move to claim a spot on the rising stern, holding on to anything and to each other to avoid for as long as possible the frigid, deadly water that is taking the *Titanic*. Isidor and Ida Straus quietly wait for the end, tightly clutching each other on a pair of deck chairs. When Colonel John Jacob Astor realizes all hope is gone he releases his Airedale, Kitty, Robert Daniel's prize bulldog, Gamon de Pycombe, and all the other dogs from the *Titanic's* kennel.

The Postal Clerks continue their attempts to save the mail until after the last lifeboat leaves and they too realize the futility of their effort. Wallace Hartley leads the orchestra in, "Nearer, My God, To Thee" while Father Thomas Byles hears confession and gives absolution to over one hundred Second and Third Class passengers huddling together on the ever steepening Boat Deck. As the bow continues to submerge, the stern and propellers lift out of the water. The North Atlantic ocean is now only ten feet below the Promenade Deck.

Both Jack Phillips and Harold Bride remain on duty until water begins flooding the wireless room. Philips sends *Titanic's* last wireless message at 2:12 a.m., just minutes before her bow plunges under the sea.

Collapsible boat B floats free but upside down. Panicking passengers and crew jump overboard in an effort to reach it. A few minutes later Collapsible A is launched by the sea from the starboard side. The last boat floats off upright but is swamped and without the sides raised.

Second Officer Charles Lightoller and Chief Officer Henry Wilde

As the water rises on the Boat Deck, Second Officer Charles Lightoller and Chief Officer Henry Wilde desperately try to free Collapsible B from the roof of the officers' quarters. Lightoller climbs on the roof and, using a pen knife borrowed from Colonel Gracie, strips the covers and cuts the ropes away from the Collapsible.

They are joined by the wireless operators, Jack Phillips and Harold Bride, as they escape the flooding Marconi room. The men are able to send the boat down to the flooded Boat Deck just before *Titanic's* bow plunges under. As the bow goes out from under them Lightoller turns, faces the sea, and dives in. Chief Officer Henry T. Wilde is swept off the ship with Collapsible B and is never seen again.

British Wreck Commissioner's Inquiry – Testimony of Charles Lightoller, examined by the Solicitor General.

14054. You had better just tell us what your own experiences were. What happened to you?

Lightoller – Well, I was swimming out towards the head of the ship, the crow's nest. I could see the crow's nest. The water was intensely cold, and one's natural instinct was to try to get out of the water. I do not know whether I swam to the foremast with that idea, but of course I soon realized it was rather foolish, so I turned to swim across clear of the ship to starboard. The next thing I knew I was up against that blower on the fore part of the funnel. There is a grating.

…14057. You found yourself against that?

Lightoller – Yes, the water rushing down held me there a little while. The water was rushing down this blower.

14058. Did it drag you against it?

Lightoller – It held me against the blower.

14059. Against the mouth of it?

Lightoller – Yes. After a while there seemed to be a rush of air from down below, and I was blown away from it.

14060. Air coming out of the ship, as it were?

Lightoller – Yes.

14061. Had you been dragged below the surface?

Lightoller – Yes.

14062. Have you any idea, were you dragged a long way down?

Lightoller – It seemed a good long while; I do not suppose it was many moments, though.

14063. Then you came up to the surface?

Lightoller – Yes.

…14068. When you came up where did you find yourself?

Lightoller – I found myself alongside of the collapsible boat, which I had previously launched on the port side, the one I had thrown on to the Boat Deck.

14069. The one still shut up?

Lightoller – Yes, still shut up, bottom up.

14070. Were you able to make use of it to clamber on to it?

Lightoller – Not at that time. I just held on to something, a piece of rope or something, and was there for a little while, and then the forward funnel fell down. It fell within 3 or 4 inches of the boat. It lifted the boat bodily and threw her about 20 feet clear of the ship as near as I could judge.

14071. Did you notice when you came up to the surface and found this collapsible boat near you whether the whole of the ship had disappeared?

Lightoller – Oh, no.

14072. She had not?

Lightoller – No. The forward funnel was still there – all the funnels were above water.

14073. (The Commissioner.) When you first came up?

Lightoller – When I first came up.

Wireless Operators Harold Bride and Jack Phillips

After abandoning the Marconi cabin Wireless Operators Jack Phillips and Harold Bride join the men trying to free the Collapsible B lifeboat. Just after freeing the boat, the *Titanic's* bow plunges under. Phillips and Bride are swept off the ship with the Collapsible lifeboat.

British Wreck Commissioner's Inquiry – Testimony of Harold Bride, examined by the Attorney General.

16613. ... I have looked up your evidence in America. Did you find yourself at the under-side of the collapsible boat?

Bride – I was on the under-side of the boat, yes.

16614. I want you to tell us about it.

Bride – I was on the underside of the boat. After I had been there two or three seconds I cleared myself and swam away from it.

16615. The collapsible boat is a flat kind of thing like a raft?

Bride – Yes.

16616. You mean, you found yourself on the underside of that?

Bride – Yes.

16617. (*The Commissioner.*) In the water?

Bride – Yes.

16618. Knocking your head against the bottom of it?

Bride – I was upside down myself. I was lying on my back.

16619. (*The Solicitor General.*) You were lying on your back, and found yourself on the underside of this raft?

Bride – Yes.

16620. Was there an air space between the underside of that and the top of the water?

Bride – I could not find it.

16621. Then you were in the water?

Bride – Yes.

16622. (*The Commissioner.*) You cannot have been very long there?

Bride – Oh, no.
16623. You must have got out of that position?
Bride – Yes, I did.
The Commissioner – What is this material to?
16624. (*The Solicitor General.*) It is not very material except that one likes to be satisfied we have got hold of the same gentleman who gave evidence in America. I read here: "You remained under the boat how long?" and you are recorded as giving an answer: "I should say about three-quarters of an hour or half." Is that right?
Bride – No. Senator Smith pressed that question, and I could not give him any idea, he said: "How long did it seem"? and I said: "It seemed a lifetime."

Colonel Archibald Gracie and James Clint Smith

Colonel Gracie and Clint Smith attempt to head for the stern but can't get through the crowd of passengers still coming up from steerage. As the *Titanic* founders and the water rushes towards them, Gracie jumps with the wave, catches hold of a railing, and pulls himself up. Clinch Smith disappears beneath the waves.

> **United States Senate Inquiry** – Testimony of Archibald Gracie, questioned by Senators Burton, Fletcher, and Smith.
> Col. Gracie – Mr. Smith jumped to try to reach the deck. I jumped also. We were unsuccessful. Then the wave came and struck us, the water came and struck us, and then I rose as I would rise in bathing in the surf, and I gave a jump with the water, which took me right on the hurricane deck, and around that was an iron railing, and I grabbed that iron railing and held tight to it; and I looked around, and the same wave which saved me engulfed everybody around me. I turned to the right and to the left and looked. Mr. Smith was not there, and I could not see any of this vast mass of humanity. They had all disappeared. Officer Lightoller tells me that at the same time he was on the bridge deck, where I have marked it "L," and that the first officer, Murdoch, was about 15 feet away, where you see that boat near the davits there. That boat, I understand, was thrown overboard.
> Senator Burton – What do you say became of that boat?
> Col. Gracie – It was thrown overboard.
> Senator Fletcher – It was never launched?
> Col. Gracie – It was never launched; no, sir.
> Senator Smith – That is not the boat that was taken from the top of the officers' quarters, the collapsible?
> Col. Gracie – There were two; one on the port side and this one on the starboard side. This knife which was called for may have been wanted

for the boat on the other side, on the bridge deck there. I heard that they called for two knives. There is where the officers' quarters were, possibly.

Senator Smith – So far as you know, was this boat to which you have referred put to any use that night?

Col. Gracie – Yes.

Senator Smith – Describe it.

Col. Gracie – That is the boat that I came to when I came up from below. I was taken down with the ship, and hanging on to that railing, but I soon let go. I felt myself whirled around, swam under water, fearful that the hot water that came up from the boilers might boil me up – and the Second Officer told me that he had the same feeling – swam it seemed to me with unusual strength, and succeeded finally in reaching the surface and in getting a good distance away from the ship.

Senator Smith – How far away?

Col. Gracie – I could not say, because I could not see the ship. When I came up to the surface there was no ship there. The ship would then have been behind me, and all around me was wreckage. I saw what seemed to be bodies all around. Do you want me to go through the harrowing details?

Senator Smith – No; I am not particular about that. I would like to know specifically whether, while this ship was sinking, and you were in close proximity to it, you noticed any special suction?

Col. Gracie – No; I noticed no suction, and I did not go down so far as that it would affect my nose or my ears. My great concern was to keep my breath, which I was able to do, and being able to do that was what I think saved me.

Senator Smith – Was the water cold?

Col. Gracie – I did not notice any coldness of the water at that time. I was too much preoccupied in getting away.

Senator Smith – Did it have any bad effect on you?

Col. Gracie – No, not then, but afterwards, on the raft. I was on the raft, which I will speak of, all night; and I did not notice how cold the water was until I got on the raft. There was a sort of gulp, as if something had occurred, behind me, and I suppose that was where the water was closing up, where the ship had gone down; but the surface of the water was perfectly still, and there were, I say, this wreckage, and these bodies, and there were the horrible sounds of drowning people and people gasping for breath.

While collecting the wreckage together I got on a big wooden crate, some sort of wooden crate, or wood of that sort. I saw an upturned boat, and I struck out for that boat, and there I saw what I supposed were members of the crew on this upset boat. I grabbed the arm of one of them and pulled myself up on this boat.

Senator Smith – Did anybody resist you at all?

Col. Gracie – What is that?

Senator Smith – Was there any resistance offered?

Col. Gracie – Oh, no; none whatever. I was among the first. I suppose the boat was then about half full.

Senator Smith – How many were on it?

Col. Gracie – I suppose there must have been between 15 and 20.

Senator Smith – Was Officer Lightoller on it?

Col. Gracie – Yes; Officer Lightoller was on that same boat.

Senator Smith – At that time?

Col. Gracie – At that same time. Then I came up to the surface and was told by Lightoller what had occurred. One of the funnels fell from the steamer, and was falling toward him, but when it was going to strike him, young Mr. Thayer, who was also on the same boat, said that it splashed near him, within 15 yards, he said, and it splashed him toward this raft. We climbed on this raft. There was one man who was in front, with an oar, and another man in the stern with what I think was a piece of a board, propelling the boat along. Then we loaded the raft, as we now call it, with as many as it would contain, until she became under water, until we could take no more, because the water was up to our waists.

Senator Smith – Just one moment. That was while you were on the bottom of the overturned boat?

Col. Gracie – Of the overturned boat; yes, sir.

Senator Smith – Was that a collapsible?

Col. Gracie – That was a collapsible canvas boat.

Thirty one men climb on or cling to the overturned Collapsible B including Second Officer Lightoller, Colonel Gracie, two other First Class passengers, and the two Marconi Operators Jack Phillips and Harold Bride. The rest are all crew, mainly firemen. Second Officer Lightoller assumes command of the lifeboat. They paddle away from the remaining swimmers, fearing that they will be swamped.

Mr. Charles D. Williams and R. Norris Williams II

As the *Titanic* founders R. Norris Williams II, 21, and his father Charles find themselves swimming for their lives in the cold water. Norris is astonished as he comes face to face with a bulldog doing the same. Just then *Titanic's* forward funnel collapses narrowly missing Norris Williams but crushing to death his father and many other swimming passengers including Colonel John Jacob Astor. The resulting wave pushes Norris toward Collapsible A. He grabs the side and holds on until he is hauled aboard.

Mr. Olaus Jørgensen Abelseth

United States Senate Inquiry – Testimony of Olaus Abelseth, taken separately before Senator Smith.
Senator Smith – Go ahead and tell us just what happened.
Mr. Abelseth – ...I was standing there, and I asked my brother-in-law if he could swim and he said no. I asked my cousin if he could swim and he said no. So we could see the water coming up, the bow of the ship was going down, and there was a kind of an explosion. We could hear the popping and cracking, and the deck raised up and got so steep that the people could not stand on their feet on the deck. So they fell down and slid on the deck into the water right on the ship. Then we hung onto a rope in one of the davits. We were pretty far back at the top deck.
My brother-in-law said to me, "We had better jump off or the suction will take us down." I said, "No. We won't jump yet. We ain't got much show anyhow, so we might as well stay as long as we can." So he stated again, "We must jump off." But I said, "No; not yet." So, then, it was only about 5 feet down to the water when we jumped off. It was not much of a jump. Before that we could see the people were jumping over. There was water coming onto the deck, and they were jumping over, then, out in the water.
My brother-in-law took my hand just as we jumped off; and my cousin jumped at the same time. When we came into the water, I think it was from the suction – or anyway we went under, and I swallowed some water. I got a rope tangled around me, and I let loose of my brother-in-law's hand to get away from the rope. I thought then, "I am a goner." That is what I thought when I got tangled up in this rope. But I came on top again, and I was trying to swim, and there was a man – lots of them were floating around – and he got me on the neck like that (illustrating) and pressed me under, trying to get on top of me. I said to him, "Let go." Of course, he did not pay any attention to that, but I got away from him. Then there was another man, and he hung on to me for a while, but he let go. Then I swam; I could not say, but it must have been about 15 or 20 minutes. It could not have been over that. Then I saw something dark ahead of me. I did not know what it was, but I swam toward that, and it was one of those collapsible boats. When we jumped off of the ship, we had life preservers on. There was no suction from the ship at all. I was lying still, and I thought "I will try to see if I can float on the lifebelt without help from swimming," and I floated easily on the lifebelt.
When I got on this raft or collapsible boat, they did not try to push me off and they did not do anything for me to get on. All they said when I got on there was, "Don't capsize the boat." So I hung onto the raft for

a little while before I got on.

Some of them were trying to get up on their feet. They were sitting down or lying down on the raft. Some of them fell into the water again. Some of them were frozen; and there were two dead, that they threw overboard.

Senator Smith – Were the three relatives of yours from Norway lost?

Mr. Abelseth – Yes; they were lost.

Senator Smith – You never saw them after you parted from them at the time you spoke of?

Mr. Abelseth – No, sir.

About 30 people manage to get aboard or cling to the still floating but swamped Collapsible A; only 12 will manage to survive.

Coal Trimmer Thomas P. Dillon

Coal Trimmer Thomas Dillon is on duty the night of the accident and makes his way on deck with other crewmembers from his watch but the lifeboats are gone.

> **British Wreck Commissioner's Inquiry** – Testimony of Thomas Dillon, examined by Mr. Asquith.
>
> 3856. How did you get off the ship?
>
> Dillon – I left her in the water.
>
> 3857. (The Commissioner.) Am I to understand that you were actually on board the "Titanic" when she went down?
>
> Dillon – Yes, my Lord.
>
> …3871. How did you get off the ship into the water?
>
> Dillon – I went down with the ship, and shoved myself away from her into the water.
>
> 3872. Were you sucked down at all?
>
> Dillon – About two fathoms.
>
> 3873. And did you then come up again to the surface?
>
> Dillon – I seemed to get lifted up to the surface.
>
> 3875. Were you picked up by one of the boats?
>
> Dillon – Yes.
>
> 3876. Do you know which one?
>
> Dillon – Afterwards I found out; it was No. 4 boat.
>
> 3877. Did you have to swim far? Were you swimming long in the water before you were picked up?
>
> Dillon – I suppose about twenty minutes.
>
> 3878. Did you see any of the other passengers in the water – any other people in the water of any sort?
>
> Dillon – Yes.
>
> 3879. Many?

Dillon – About a thousand.
3880. Were there any others near the boat when you were picked up?
Dillon – I do not know.
3881. (The Commissioner.) Did you say "I saw about one thousand people in the water"?
Dillon – From my estimation, my Lord.

Chief Baker Charles Joughin

Chief Baker Charles Joughin emerges from his room after having what he thought would be his last taste of liqueur.

> **British Wreck Commissioner's Inquiry** – Testimony of Charles Joughin, examined by the Solicitor General.
> 6020. Now we just want to finish your experience. You say you went below after No. 10 had gone. Did you stay below or did you go up again?
> Joughin – I went down to my room and had a drop of liqueur that I had down there, and then while I was there I saw the old doctor and spoke to him and then I came upstairs again.
> 6022. Just tell us shortly what you did?
> Joughin – I saw that all the boats had gone – I saw that all the boats were away.
> …6026. Yes, what next?
> Joughin – I went down on to "B" deck. The deck chairs were lying right along, and I started throwing deck chairs through the large ports.
> …6030. I think one sees why. Just to make it clear, why did you do that?
> Joughin – It was an idea of my own.
> 6031. Tell us why; was it to give something to cling to?
> Joughin – I was looking out for something for myself, Sir.
> 6032. Quite so. Did you throw a whole lot of them overboard?
> Joughin – I should say about 50.
> …6039. Then, after having thrown these deckchairs overboard, did you go up to the Boat Deck again?
> Joughin – I went to the deck pantry.
> 6040. Tell us what happened?
> Joughin – I went to the deck pantry, and while I was in there I thought I would take a drink of water, and while I was getting the drink of water I heard a kind of a crash as if something had buckled, as if part of the ship had buckled, and then I heard a rush overhead.
> 6041. Do you mean a rush of people?
> Joughin – Yes, a rush of people overhead on the deck.
> …6049. You say that you heard this sound of buckling or crackling.

Was it loud; could anybody in the ship hear it?
Joughin – You could have heard it, but you did not really know what it was. It was not an explosion or anything like that. It was like as if the iron was parting.

The stern rises out of the water as the bow continues to sink. A huge roar is heard as moveable objects inside the *Titanic* crash toward the submerged bow. With the angle of the rising stern growing steeper, the pressure between the suspended stern and submerged bow increases. When *Titanic's* tilt exceeds 45 degrees, the structure's steel begins to rip apart. Many of those in the lifeboats mistake the crashing and ripping metal sounds for explosions as the *Titanic*, with her stern well out of the water, begins breaking in two. The ship's lights blink once, then go out before *Titanic's* bow breaks away just forward of the third funnel. The sinking bow takes 5 minutes to find the ocean floor.

Accounts from the Lifeboats

Seaman George Symons watches from lifeboat 1 about 200 yards away.

British Wreck Commissioner's Inquiry – Testimony of George Symons, examined by the Attorney General.
11515. Did you see her head going well down?
Symons – Her head was going well down.
11516. And you saw her stern out of the water like that? (Describing.)
Symons – Yes, her stern was well out of the water.
11517. I understand you to say that at one period you saw her stern right itself?
Symons – It righted itself without the bow; in my estimation she must have broken in half.

Seaman John T. Poingdestre provided this account from lifeboat 12.

British Wreck Commissioner's Inquiry – Testimony of John Poingdestre, examined by Mr. Aspinall.
3106. You said you saw the "Titanic" sink?
Poingdestre – Yes.
3107. How far away were you when she sank?
Poingdestre – About 150 yards.
3108. Now will you describe to us what you saw happen when she sank?
Poingdestre – Well, I thought when I looked that the ship broke at the foremost funnel.
3109. What led you to that conclusion?
Poingdestre – Because I had seen that part disappear.
3110. If she sank by the head you would see that part disappear, would you not?

Poingdestre – Yes.

3111. What was there about the disappearance that led you to think she broke?

Poingdestre – Because she was short; the afterpart righted itself after the foremost part had disappeared.

3112. (The Commissioner.) Do you mean to say that the fore part of the vessel went down to the bottom, and that then the remainder came on an even keel?

Poingdestre – Yes.

3113. (Mr. Butler Aspinall.) Before the ship sank just tell me this, what was the position of the vessel? I have a pen in my hand.

Poingdestre – Well, the water was up to the Officers' house.

3114. Assume, for a moment, that is the Officers' house. Now could you see under the keel of the ship abaft the Officers' house?

Poingdestre – Yes, the propeller and everything was quite clear.

3115. Underneath?

Poingdestre – Yes.

3116. Then the water comes up to the Officers' house. Was it then that the forward part disappeared?

Poingdestre – Yes.

3117. And then what happened to the afterpart?

Poingdestre – It uprighted itself, as if nothing had happened.

3118. You mean it came back like that, so to speak?

Poingdestre – Yes, straight on the water again.

3119. Did it float on the water for any appreciable time?

Poingdestre – Not above a couple of minutes.

Seaman Edward Buley is in lifeboat 10 about 200 yards away.

United States Senate Inquiry – Testimony of Edward Buley, questioned by Senator Fletcher.

Senator Fletcher – After you left her, her bow continued to go under?

Mr. Buley – Settled down; yes, sir. She went down as far as the afterfunnel, and then there was a little roar, as though the engines had rushed forward, and she snapped in two, and the bow part went down and the afterpart came up and stayed up five minutes before it went down.

Senator Fletcher – Was that perpendicular?

Mr. Buley – It was horizontal at first, and then went down.

Senator Fletcher – What do you mean by saying she snapped in two?

Mr. Buley – She parted in two.

Senator Fletcher – How do you know that?

Mr. Buley – Because we could see the afterpart afloat, and there was no forepart to it. I think she must have parted where the bunkers were. She parted at the last, because the afterpart of her settled out of the water horizontally after the other part went down. First of all you could see her propellers and everything. Her rudder was clear out of the water. You could hear the rush of the machinery, and she parted in two, and the afterpart settled down again, and we thought the afterpart would float altogether.

Senator Fletcher – The afterpart kind of righted up horizontally?

Mr. Buley – She uprighted herself for about five minutes, and then tipped over and disappeared.

Senator Fletcher – Did it go on the side?

Mr. Buley – No, sir; went down headforemost.

Senator Fletcher – That makes you believe the boat went in two?

Mr. Buley – Yes, sir. You could see she went in two, because we were quite near to her and could see her quite plainly.

British Wreck Commissioner's Inquiry – Testimony of Charles H. Lightoller, examined by the Solicitor General.

14074. I do not know whether you can help us at all in describing what happened to the ship. You were engaged and had other things to think about; but what did happen to the ship? Can you tell us at all?

Lightoller – Are you referring to the reports of the ship breaking in two?

14075. Yes?

Lightoller – It is utterly untrue. The ship did not and could not have broken in two.

Everyone Else

After the bow tears away, the stern portion of the *Titanic* settles back into the water and, righting itself, offers a sliver of short-lived hope to those still clinging to the remaining portion of the ship. As this last piece of the foundering ship quickly fills with water, the stern again tilts high into the air, almost perpendicular with the flat calm sea, then slowly disappears into the North Atlantic. It is 2:20 a.m. The *Carpathia*, rushing to the rescue, is still an hour and a half away while the crew of the nearby *Californian* ponders, but doesn't realize, what they have just witnessed.

Nearly 1500 people now struggle against the frigid, 28º F water. Screams and agonizing cries fill the cold night air as panicking men, women, and children desperately wage their own personal battles to survive, grasping for anything or anyone that might help them escape the painfully freezing water. Some with lifebelts, some without, attempt to swim toward one of the collapsible boats that have been washed off the deck. When these boats, one overturned, the other swamped, can't take on any more people, the unlucky ones are warned or pushed away while the collapsibles row away from the ensuing bedlam.

Others accept their fate and some actively practice their faith. The Reverend John Harper, struggling in the ice cold water without a lifebelt, encourages those near him to, "Believe on the Lord Jesus Christ and thou shalt be saved." He continues his final quest to save souls until, for the last time, he slips beneath the surface and into the warm embrace of his Maker.

For those now struggling in freezing cold water in their final agonizing minutes of life, their class status or mariner's rank has no bearing on their shared fate. Their desperate cries are to no avail as they individually and collectively begin to succumb to hypothermia. First their body and then their will desert each according to personal fortitude as the ability to move, to scream, to fight for life is painfully lost. As they slowly freeze to death, with all hope of earthly survival gone, each welcomes in their last living moment—the ship sent to them by the guardian of their soul.

The bodies without lifebelts slip into the depths of their watery grave while the dead with lifebelts float frozen on the flat calm surface of the salt-water sea.

Believers in communication with the spirit world would later learn what came next from a message reportedly received through a medium from the spirit of *Titanic* victim William T. Stead. Stead's message was published in the 1913 book – *Has W.T. Stead Returned?, A SYMPOSIUM Edited by JAMES COATES, Ph.D., F.A.S.*

> "It was at my request the band played 'Nearer, my God, to Thee.' Never was it played with more thrilling effect; never were the messages of life, death, and immortality, so fervently given to the world.
>
> "When I became conscious, I saw her from whose heart was wrung, by affliction, the inspired words of this hymn. She was surrounded by a bright band of risen spirits, singing the hymn and illuminating the surroundings by the radiance of their presence. I saw ministering spirits, glorified spirits, helping the feeble ones whose bodies went down with the vessel or perished in the numbing waters. They were arousing those, brave or terror-stricken, who had faced the reality. Many soon realised the great change had come, but the majority are as blind as bats. They cannot help themselves. Pray for them."

Chapter 17

ONE LIFEBOAT RETURNS

After leaving the *Titanic* some of the lifeboats row toward the light of a ship that appeared to be about 5 miles away but never seems to get any closer. They give up the pursuit when the *Carpathia* is spotted. Other lifeboats, some less than half full, are near enough to see the *Titanic* go under. Many are also close enough to hear the collective screams, desperate cries, and final moans from the mass of humanity pleading for help and dying in the freezing cold water.

Emergency Clipper 1

After the *Titanic* sinks, Lead Fireman Charles Hendrickson tells the others in the lifeboat they should go back to rescue the people swimming in the water but Lady Duff-Gordon warns they might be swamped. Sir Duff-Gordon agrees with his wife that it would be dangerous to go back.

> **British Wreck Commissioner's Inquiry** – Testimony of Charles Hendrickson, examined by Mr. Rowlatt.
> 5056. You said, and it is to your credit, that you suggested that you should go back to the help of those people?
> Hendrickson – Yes; I proposed going back and they would not hear of it.
> 5057. In the presence of those cries for help from the drowning, were you the only one in the boat to propose to go back to the rescue?
> Hendrickson – I never heard anyone else.
> …5131. It is the duty of the crew to exhaust every resource in order to rescue passengers, is it not?
> Hendrickson – Yes.
> 5132. What I do not quite understand is, that there being seven of the crew, why you did not, despite the protests of these First Class passengers, go back to some of the drowning people?
> Hendrickson – Well, that is right enough, but the coxswain was in charge of the boat.
> The Commissioner – Speak a little louder so that I can hear?
> Hendrickson – There was a man in charge of the boat; he should know what to do best. It would not do for everybody to be in charge of a boat that is in her. When a man gets in a boat the coxswain takes charge and

The Perfect Calm

does everything.

5133. And the coxswain of your boat showed no inclination to pull back?

Hendrickson – No, none whatever.

5134. You say that that attitude of his was due to the protests of the Duff-Gordon's?

Hendrickson – Yes.

...5141. (The Commissioner.) I cannot understand this. Was there any discussion on board this boat as to whether you should go to these drowning people – any talk?

Hendrickson – No, only when I proposed going back, that is all.

5142. Do you mean to tell me that you were the only person that proposed to go back?

Hendrickson – I never heard any others.

5143. And to whom did you speak?

Hendrickson – Anyone who was there who was listening.

5144. Did you speak to everybody?

Hendrickson – I spoke to everyone there; I shouted out in the boat.

5145. Now tell me what each person said.

Hendrickson – They said it would be too dangerous to go back, we might get swamped.

5147. Who said that?

Hendrickson – Sir Duff-Gordon.

5148. Did anyone else say it?

Hendrickson – No; his wife as well, that was all.

5149. Those two – two of the five passengers. Did anyone else say it?

Hendrickson – I never heard anyone else.

5150. Was it Simmons [Symons] who was in charge of this boat?

Hendrickson – Yes.

Seaman George Symons is in charge of Emergency Clipper 1 and, "being Master of the situation," determines it is not safe to go back.

British Wreck Commissioner's Inquiry – Testimony of George Symons, examined by the Attorney General.

11526. When you saw the "Titanic" go down did you hear any cries from the people that went down with the boat?

Symons – Yes.

11527. Did you try to rescue them?

Symons – I thought at the time, being Master of the situation, it was not safe in any case to go back at that time.

11528. Do I understand from that, then, that your answer is that you did not try?

Symons – Not at that time; not as soon as the ship disappeared.

...11534. If you could have reached any one of those persons you could

have saved the life of that person?
Symons – Yes, but I thought at the time, by using my own discretion, that it was not safe in any way to have gone back to that ship as she disappeared.

…11537. You were there with ample room?
Symons – Yes; we had room say for another eight or a dozen more in the boat. I do not know what the boat's complement is.

11538. The boat's complement is 40, and you had 12?
Symons – If there were 40 in that boat there would not be room.

…11541. Do you tell my Lord that you determined, without consultation with anybody, that you would not go back?
Symons – I determined by my own wish, as I was Master of the situation, to go back when I thought that most of the danger was over.

11542. What?
Symons – I used my own discretion, as being Master of the situation at the time, that it was not safe to have gone back at that time until everything was over.

…11545. Never mind, it had disappeared, and had gone down to the bottom, two miles down, or something like that. What were you afraid of?
Symons – I was afraid of the swarming.

11546. Of what?
Symons – Of the swarming of the people – swamping the boat.

The Commissioner – I am not satisfied at all.

…11549. (The Attorney General.) Now, I want to know a little more about that. Was the question raised about your going back to the people who were shrieking at this time?
Symons – None whatever.

11550. Do you mean to tell my Lord that nobody ever mentioned, amongst the people that you had in that boat, going back to try to save some of the people who were in the water drowning?
Symons – I never heard anybody of any description, passengers or crew, say anything as regards going back. Had there been anything said I was almost sure to have heard it.

11551. You mean nothing was said, either by you or anybody?
Symons – I used my own discretion.

11552. You have told us that several times. I understand that you used your discretion, and that you were master of the situation; we have got those phrases. What I am asking you about now is whether at that time you heard anything said by anybody on the boat about going back?
Symons – None whatever.

11553. Either by you or by any of the crew?
Symons – No.

11554. Or by any of the passengers?
Symons – No.
11555. Then, if I understand correctly what you say, your story to my Lord is; the vessel had gone down; there were the people in the water shrieking for help; you were in the boat with plenty of room; nobody ever mentioned going back; nobody ever said a word about it; you just simply lay on your oars. Is that the story you want my Lord to believe?
Symons – Yes, that is the story.

Along with Symons and Hendrickson the other crewmembers aboard are Fireman Samuel Collins, Seaman Albert E. J. Horswell, Fireman Robert W. Pusey, Trimmer Frederick Sheath, and Fireman James Taylor. First Class passengers aboard are the Duff-Gordons and Lady Duff-Gordon's secretary, Miss Laura Mabel Francatelli, Businessmen Mr. Abraham Lincoln Salomon and Mr. Charles Emil Henry Stengel.

British Wreck Commissioner's Inquiry – Testimony of Fireman James Taylor, examined by the Solicitor General.
12051. Did you, or did you not, hear any suggestion made that the boat should return to the place where the "Titanic" had sunk?
Taylor – There was a suggestion of going back.
12052. There was?
Taylor – But who made it, I do not know.
…12057. Just tell us what you do remember. What did you hear?
Taylor – The suggestion was made, there was a talk in the boat of going back, and there was a lady passenger who talked of the boat being swamped if we went back.
12058. A lady passenger talked of the boat being swamped if you went back?
Taylor – Yes, and two other gentlemen in the boat replied to the same question, "We shall be swamped if we go back. It would be dangerous to go."

British Wreck Commissioner's Inquiry – Testimony of Fireman Robert Pusey, examined by Mr. Asquith.
13104. After the ship went down, did you hear any cries?
Pusey – I did.
13105. How long did they continue?
Pusey – I should say about a quarter of an hour or 20 minutes, something like that.
13106. While those cries went on were you standing still the whole time or did you begin to row again?
Pusey – No, I believe we were lying on our oars.

13107. All the time the cries went on?
Pusey – Yes, as far as I can recollect.
13108. Did anybody in the boat say anything about the cries?
Pusey – Not in my estimation; I cannot bring it to recollection.
13109. Did anybody suggest that you should go back in the direction of the cries?
Pusey – Not to my knowledge.

Fireman Robert Pusey does recollect a discussion about the crew having lost all their belongings, their "kit," and that their pay ended when the ship sank. Upon hearing this Sir Cosmo Duff-Gordon offers all the crewmen in the boat five pounds each to help them get back on their feet after they're rescued.

British Wreck Commissioner's Inquiry – Testimony of Fireman Robert Pusey, examined by Mr. Harbinson.
13117. Do you remember hearing anything said in the emergency boat about presents or about money?
Pusey – Yes, I did.
13118. That is to say you do not remember any conversation about going back to where the cries were?
Pusey – No.
13119. But you remember the conversation about the money?
Pusey – Yes. I do, and I will explain to you how it came about too. Lady Gordon said to Miss Franks, "There is your beautiful nightdress gone," and I said, "Never mind about your nightdress madam, as long as you have got your life"; and then I heard someone forward at the fore end of me say – I said we had lost our kits and that our pay was stopped from the time she was a wreck – "We will give you a little to start a new kit." That was all I heard.

British Wreck Commissioner's Inquiry – Testimony of Sir Cosmo Duff-Gordon, examined by Mr. Harbinson.
12706. The question I put to you is this: When you first heard this observation made with reference to the direction in which this emergency boat should go, was it then, 20 minutes after the "Titanic" sank, that you suggested that you would give them a fiver each?
Duff Gordon – No, I see what you mean now. No, it was not; not in any connection with it. The man calling out to go this way and that had no effect, I think on anybody, nor on this subject at all. It had nothing to do with it.
The Commissioner:
If you will put your question plainly it would perhaps be understood better. Your question, as I understand it, really is this: "Did you promise a £5 note in order to induce the men in the boat to row away from the

drowning people?" That is what you want to ask.
Mr. Harbinson:
That is the effect of it.

With Seaman George Symons using his "own discretion, as being Master of the situation at the time," Emergency Clipper 1, with a capacity of 40 but holding only 12, makes no attempt to return and save any of the hundreds of people crying for help and struggling for life in the North Atlantic.

Other lifeboats with room make the same choice.

Emergency Clipper 2

The Emergency Clipper from the port side, is commanded by Fourth Officer Joseph Boxhall. The boat, with a capacity of 40 carries only 17 including Boxhall and four other crewmembers.

> **British Wreck Commissioner's Inquiry** – Testimony of Joseph Boxhall, examined by Mr. Asquith.
> 15467. How far were you from the ship when she did sink?
> Boxhall – Approximately, half-a-mile.
> 15468. That means that you could not see what happened?
> Boxhall – No, I could not.
> 15469. After she sank, did you hear cries?
> Boxhall – Yes, I heard cries. I did not know when the lights went out that the ship had sunk. I saw the lights go out, but I did not know whether she had sunk or not, and then I heard the cries. I was showing green lights in the boat then, to try and get the other boats together, trying to keep us all together.
> 15470. Were there other boats round about near yours?
> Boxhall – I could not see any boats, not when I had got so far away as that. Some of them had gone in a more northerly direction than I had gone.
> 15471. Did you go back at all towards the ship, when you heard those cries?
> Boxhall – No, I did not.

Lifeboat 5

Third Officer Herbert Pitman is in command of lifeboat 5 with room for 29 more. His boat is 400 yards away when the *Titanic* goes under. Pitman and the survivors aboard boat 5 can't see anyone in the water but can hear the shrieks and pleading cries of those struggling against the ice cold sea. Pittman orders the boat to pull toward those cries for help but he is soon dissuaded by his boat full of reluctant First Class passengers.

> **United States Senate Inquiry** – Testimony of Third Officer Herbert Pitman, questioned by Senator Smith.
> Mr. Pitman – They commenced pulling toward the ship, and the passengers in my boat said it was a mad idea on my part to pull back to the ship, because if I did, we should be swamped with the crowd that was in the water, and it would add another 40 to the list of drowned, and I decided I would not pull back.
> Senator Smith – Officer, you really turned this No. 5 boat around to go in the direction from which these cries came?
> Mr. Pitman – I did.
> Senator Smith – And were dissuaded from your purpose by your crew?
> Mr. Pitman – No, not crew; passengers.
> Senator Smith – One moment; by your crew and by the passengers in your boat?
> Mr. Pitman – Certainly.
> Senator Smith – Then did you turn the boat toward the sea again?
> Mr. Pitman – No; just simply took our oars in and lay quiet.

Lifeboat 7

Lookout George Hogg is in charge of lifeboat 7 with 28 aboard including Dick and Helen Bishop. After the ship sinks, Hogg has the boat rowing back to pick up survivors.

> **United States Senate Inquiry** – Testimony of George Hogg, questioned by Senator Perkins.
> Mr. Hogg – … As soon as she went down, I went to try to assist them in picking up anybody if I could. I met another boat on my way, and they said to pull away. They said: "We have done all in our power and we can not do any more." I can not remember the number of the boat or who the man was who spoke to me. I laid off, then, until I saw the lights of the Carpathia.
> Senator Perkins – But you pulled around in search of other people?
> Mr. Hogg – I pulled around in search of other people before I could pull to the wreck. One man said: "We have done our best. There are no more people around. We have pulled all around." I said: "Very good. We will get away now."
> Senator Perkins – And you were then within about half a mile of the *Titanic*?
> Mr. Hogg – About that, sir.

While they wait for rescue Helen Bishop tells a story to pass the time and lift the spirits of her fellow lifeboat passengers. While the Bishops were in Egypt Helen received news of her future from a fortune teller. She had been told that she would survive a shipwreck, and then an earthquake, but would later die in an automobile accident. "We must be rescued," Helen announced, "for the rest of my prophecy to come true."

Lifeboat 9

Boatswain Albert Haines, in command of lifeboat 9, also believes his boat with 40 aboard is too full to safely return.

> **United States Senate Inquiry** – Testimony of Albert Haines, questioned by Senator Smith.
> Senator Smith – Did you hear any cries for help?
> Mr. Haines – Yes, sir; we heard some cries after the ship went down.
> Senator Smith – Did anybody in your boat urge you to return?
> Mr. Haines – No, sir. I called the sailors aft, and I passed the remark to them: "There is people in the water." I said, "Do you think it advisable?" I said, "We can't do nothing with this crowd we have in the boat," because we had no room to row, let alone do anything else, sir; and it was no good of our going back. By the time we got back there, we could not have done anything. We could not move in the boat, let alone row. I thought it unsafe to go back there, sir, having so many in the boat.
> Senator Smith – What did you do after the ship went down?
> Mr. Haines – I told the men it was no good rowing; that we could not do anything until the morning, and I just lay there all night, sir.

Lifeboat 3

Lifeboat 3 has 32 people aboard and Seaman George A. Moore in charge.

> **United States Senate Inquiry** – Testimony of George Moore, questioned by Senator Newlands.
> Senator Newlands – Did your boat make any effort to go back?
> Mr. Moore – No, sir.
> Senator Newlands – Why not?
> Mr. Moore – All the people in the boat wanted to get clear of the ship. They did not want to go near her. They kept urging me to keep away; to pull away from her. In fact, they wanted to get farther away.
> Senator Newlands – Why did you not go back and attempt to rescue some of the people who were sinking?
> Mr. Moore – Well, sir, we were about a quarter of a mile away, and the cries did not last long. I do not think anybody could live much more than 10 minutes in that cold water. If we had gone back, we would only have had the boat swamped.
> Senator Newlands – Do you think it would have been swamped?
> Mr. Moore – Yes; if there were any alive. Five or six pulling on that boat's gunwales would no doubt have capsized the boat.

Lifeboat 11

Quartermaster Sidney James Humphries is in command of lifeboat 11 with 50 people aboard including Seaman Walter Brice.

> **United States Senate Inquiry** – Testimony of Walter Brice, questioned by Senator Bourne.
> Senator Bourne – Did you figure that your boat was loaded to full capacity when you rowed away from the ship?
> Mr. Brice – You could not get to pull a stroke on the oar at all; she was packed.
> Senator Bourne – How long did you rest on your oars after you had gotten about a mile from the ship?
> Mr. Brice – We did not do any pulling at all, sir; only keeping the boat up head to the wind.
> Senator Bourne – How long did you remain that way?
> Mr. Brice – Until we saw the "Carpathia."

Lifeboat 8

Seaman Thomas William Jones commands lifeboat 8 with only 25 aboard including Lucy Noël Martha, the Countess of Rothes who told her story to the *New York Herald*. Excerpt from the *New York Herald* article published Sunday April 21, 1912:

> "…The most awful part of the whole thing was seeing the rows of portholes vanishing one by one. Several of us—and Tom Jones—wanted to row back and see if there was not some chance of rescuing any one that had possibly survived, but the majority in the boat ruled, that we had no right to risk their lives on the bare chance of finding any one alive after the final plunge. They also said that the captain's own orders had been to 'row for those ship lights over there,' and that we who wished to try for others who might be drowning had no business to interfere with his orders. Of course that settled the matter, and we rowed on.
> "…For three hours we pulled steadily for the two masthead lights that showed brilliantly in the darkness. For a few minutes we saw the ship's port light, then it vanished, and the masthead lights got dimmer on the horizon until they, too, disappeared.
> "…When the awful end came, I tried my best to keep the Spanish woman from hearing the agonizing sound of distress. They seemed to continue forever, although it could not have been more than ten minutes until the silence of a lonely sea dropped down. The indescribable loneliness, the ghastliness of our feelings never can be told. We tried to keep in touch with the other boats by shouting and succeeded fairly well. Our

boat was the furthest away because we had chased the phantom lights for three hours. Yes, I rowed for three hours."

Lady Rothes' cousin Miss Gladys Cherry was also in boat 8 and later wrote the following letter to *Titanic* Seaman Thomas Jones:

> I feel I must write and tell you how splendidly you took charge of our boat on the fatal night. There were only four English people in it-my cousin Lady Rothes, her maid, you and myself-and I think you were wonderful.
> The dreadful regret I shall always have, and I know you share with me, is that we ought to have gone back to see whom we could pick up; but if you remember, there was only an American lady, my cousin, self and you who wanted to return. I could not hear the discussion very clearly, as I was at the tiller; but everyone forward and the three men refused; but I shall always remember your words: 'ladies, if any of us are saved, remember, I wanted to go back. I would rather drown with them than leave them.' You did all you could, and being my own countryman, I wanted to tell you this.
> Yours very truly, Gladys Cherry.

Lifeboat 6

There is tension in lifeboat 6 from the beginning as Quartermaster Robert Hichens chooses to man the tiller while Major Peuchen, Lookout Frederick Fleet, and at various times several women are told to row. Hitchen's emotional manner presents the impression he is unstable and some of the ladies in the boat would later accuse him of being drunk and cowardly. Hichens denied these allegations with his final statement at the United States Senate Inquiry;

> I would like to make a little statement as regarding Mrs. Mayer's [Meyer] statement in the newspapers about my drinking the whisky sir, and about the blankets. I was very cold, sir, and I was standing up in the boat. I had no hat on. A lady had a flask of whisky or brandy, or something of that description, given her by some gentleman on the ship before she left, and she pulled it out and gave me about a tablespoonful and I drank it. Another lady, who was lying in the bottom of the boat, in a rather weak condition gave me a half wet and half dry blanket to try keep myself a little warm, as I was half frozen. I think it was very unkind of her, sir, to make any statement criticizing me. When we got to the ship I handled everyone as carefully as I could, and I was the last one to leave the boat, and I do not think I deserve anything like that to be put in the papers. That is what upset me and got on my nerves.

Margaret Brown, later known as "the Unsinkable Molly Brown," is one of the 20 women aboard lifeboat 6. After the *Titanic* sank, she and others urge Hichens to return to look for survivors. Hitchens refuses and at one point argues with Brown who threatens to toss him overboard. Frederick Fleet, the lookout who spotted the iceberg, testified at the U.S. Senate inquiry.

> **United States Senate Inquiry** – Testimony of Frederick Fleet, questioned by Senator Smith.
> Senator Smith – Did anybody propose to pull toward the place where the *Titanic* went down?
> Mr. Fleet – All the women asked us to pull there, before she went down; but the quartermaster was in charge, and he would not allow it. He told us to keep on pulling.
> Senator Smith – Did the women in your boat persist in their efforts to get him to go back to the scene of the wreck?
> Mr. Fleet – They asked him, but he would not hear of it; he told us to keep on pulling.
> Senator Smith – Did you say anything about it to the quartermaster?
> Mr. Fleet – No; I never said a word; I just pulled an oar; I just kept quiet.
> Senator Smith – At that time could you hear cries of distress?
> Mr. Fleet – Very faint.

Major Peuchen also testifies at the U.S. Senate inquiry.

> **United States Senate Inquiry** – Testimony of Major Arthur Godfrey Peuchen, questioned by Senator Smith.
> Maj. Peuchen – …We heard a sort of a call for help after this whistle I described a few minutes ago. This was the officer calling us back. We heard a sort of a rumbling sound and the lights were still on at the rumbling sound, as far as my memory serves me; then a sort of an explosion, then another. It seemed to be one, two, or three rumbling sounds, then the lights went out. Then the dreadful calls and cries.
> Senator Smith – For help?
> Maj. Peuchen – We could not distinguish the exact cry for assistance; moaning and crying; frightful. It affected all the women in our boat whose husbands were among these; and this went on for some time, gradually getting fainter, fainter. At first it was horrible to listen to.
> Senator Smith – How far was it away?
> Maj. Peuchen – I think we must have been five-eighths of a mile, I should imagine, when this took place. It was very hard to guess the distance. There were only two of us rowing a very heavy boat with a good many people in it, and I do not think we covered very much ground.
> Senator Smith – While these cries of distress were going on, did anyone in the boat urge the quartermaster to return?
> Maj. Peuchen – Yes; some of the women did. But, as I said before, I had

had a row with him, and I said to the women, "It is no use you arguing with that man, at all. It is best not to discuss matters with him." He said it was no use going back there, there was only a lot of stiffs there, later on, which was very unkind, and the women resented it very much. I do not think he was qualified to be a quartermaster.
Senator Smith – As a matter of fact, you did not return to the boat?
Maj. Peuchen – We did not return to the boat.

Lifeboat 16

Master-at-Arms Henry Joseph Bailey is in charge of lifeboat 16 with 52 aboard including Seaman Ernest Archer. Bailey ties his nearly full boat along side Hitchen's boat 6 to wait for a rescue ship.

> **United States Senate Inquiry** – Testimony of Ernest Archer, questioned by Senator Bourne.
> Senator Bourne – Then what did you do after the ship had sunk?
> Mr. Archer – It was spoken by one of the lady passengers to go back and see if there was anyone in the water we could pick up, but I never heard any more of it after that.
> Senator Bourne – And the boat was in charge of the master-at-arms?
> Mr. Archer – The master-at-arms had charge of the boat.
> Senator Bourne – Did this lady request you to go back?
> Mr. Archer – Yes, sir; she requested us to go back.
> Senator Bourne – What did he say?
> Mr. Archer – I did not hear; I was in the forepart of the boat.
> Senator Bourne – There were 50 people in the boat?
> Mr. Archer – Yes, sir.

Lifeboat 13

Lead Fireman Frederick Barrett is in command of lifeboat 13 and determines she is too full to return. Fireman George Beauchamp is among the 55 aboard.

> **British Wreck Commissioner's Inquiry** – Testimony of George Beauchamp, examined by Mr. Butler Aspinall.
> 760. Did you see anyone in the water after the ship went down?
> Beauchamp – No; you could hear the cries after the ship sank.
> 761. Did you go back to the place where the cries came from or not?
> Beauchamp – No; no order was given.
> 762. You did not go back?
> Beauchamp – No.
> 764. Had you any room for more people in your boat or not?
> Beauchamp – No. Had we had any more room we should have gone back, but we could not go back owing as we were full up.

Second Class passenger Lawrence Beesley is also in boat 13. He describes the aftermath of the sinking in his book – *The Loss of the SS. Titanic*.

> "And in place of the ship on which all our interest had been concentrated for so long and towards which we looked most of the time because it was still the only object on the sea which was a fixed point to us—in place of the *Titanic*, we had the level sea now stretching in an unbroken expanse to the horizon: heaving gently just as before, with no indication on the surface that the waves had just closed over the most wonderful vessel ever built by man's hand; the stars looked down just the same and the air was just as bitterly cold.
>
> "There seemed a great sense of loneliness when we were left on the sea in a small boat without the *Titanic*: not that we were uncomfortable (except for the cold) nor in danger: we did not think we were either, but the *Titanic* was no longer there.
>
> "We waited head on for the wave which we thought might come—the wave we had heard so much of from the crew and which they said had been known to travel for miles—and it never came. But although the *Titanic* left us no such legacy of a wave as she went to the bottom, she left us something we would willingly forget forever, something which it is well not to let the imagination dwell on—the cries of many hundreds of our fellow-passengers struggling in the ice-cold water.
>
> "…So that unprepared as we were for such a thing, the cries of the drowning floating across the quiet sea filled us with stupefaction: we longed to return and rescue at least some of the drowning, but we knew it was impossible. The boat was filled to standing-room, and to return would mean the swamping of us all, and so the captain-stoker told his crew to row away from the cries. We tried to sing to keep all from thinking of them; but there was no heart for singing in the boat at that time.
>
> "The cries, which were loud and numerous at first, died away gradually one by one, but the night was clear, frosty and still, the water smooth, and the sounds must have carried on its level surface free from any obstruction for miles, certainly much farther from the ship than we were situated. I think the last of them must have been heard nearly forty minutes after the Titanic sank. Lifebelts would keep the survivors afloat for hours; but the cold water was what stopped the cries."

Collapsible C

Collapsible C is the last starboard-side lifeboat launched by the crew with Quartermaster George Rowe in command. Amy Stanley is aboard the nearly full boat and later relates her experience in a letter to her parents.

Partial content of Amy Stanley's letter:

> "We were rowing for several hours. I seemed to have extra strength

that night to keep up my nerves, for I even made them laugh when I told them we had escaped vaccination, for we were all to have been vaccinated that day (meaning the Monday). I will say no more of that awful row ..."

Lifeboat 15

Lifeboat 15 is the fullest boat launched from the *Titanic* with 68 aboard, three over capacity and is in command of Fireman Frank Dymond. With most of the passengers being the women and children from Steerage that were led to the boat by Third Class Steward John Hart, the boat is too full to do anything other than to wait for rescue.

Lifeboat 4

Quartermaster Walter Perkis is in command of Lifeboat 4 with 36 aboard after picking up six surviving swimmers shortly after being launched.

> **United States Senate Inquiry** – Testimony of Walter Perkis, questioned by Senator Perkins.
> Mr. Perkis – No. 4 was the boat I got away in; the last big boat on the port side to leave the ship.
> Senator Perkins – You picked up eight in the water?
> Mr. Perkis – Yes; and two died afterwards, in the boat.
> Senator Perkins – Were they passengers or men of the crew?
> Mr. Perkis – No, sir; one was a fireman and one was a steward.
> Senator Perkins – The others were all passengers?
> Mr. Perkis – Yes, sir.
> Senator Perkins – Tell us what you did after that.
> Mr. Perkis – After that, after we had picked up the men, I could not hear any more cries anywhere. Everything was over. I waited then until daylight, or just before daylight, when we saw the lights of the "Carpathia".

Lifeboat 10

In lifeboat 10 Seaman Edward Buley is in charge. His boat is nearly full with 57 aboard.

> **United States Senate Inquiry** – Testimony of Edward Buley, questioned by Senator Fletcher.
> Mr. Buley – ...The people in the boat were very frightened that there would be some suction. If there had been any suction we should have been lost. We were close to her. We couldn't get away fast enough. There was nobody to pull away.
> Senator Fletcher – How far were you when she went down?
> Mr. Buley – We were about 200 yards.

Japanese passenger Masabumi Hosono is aboard boat 10 and later described his experience in his diary:

> "After the ship sank there came back again frightful shrills and cries of those drowning in the water. Our lifeboat too was filled with sobbing, weeping children and women worried about the safety of their husbands and fathers. And I, too, was as much depressed and miserable as they were, not knowing what would become of myself in the long run."

Collapsible D

The last lifeboat launched by the crew of the *Titanic* was the collapsible D. With Quartermaster Arthur John Bright in charge it left with 19 aboard and picked one person out of the water.

> **United States Senate Inquiry** – Testimony of Arthur Bright, questioned by Senator Bourne.
> Senator Bourne – Were you the last boat to leave the ship?
> Mr. Bright – Yes, sir.
> Senator Bourne – And you were from 50 to 100 yards from the ship when she sank?
> Mr. Bright – Yes, sir.
> Senator Bourne – And you rowed from the ship without cessation?
> Mr. Bright – Without what?
> Senator Bourne – Without stopping.
> Mr. Bright – Yes.
> Senator Bourne – Until she sank. How long a period was it from the time you left the ship until she sank?
> Mr. Bright – I only had two oars pulling, you know.
> Senator Bourne – How long a time do you think it was – how many minutes?
> Mr. Bright – I should say it was nearly a half an hour. We were not pulling in a straight direction.
> Senator Bourne – You were circling around?
> Mr. Bright – Yes, sir; trying to find the other boats.
> Senator Bourne – Oh, you were not trying to get away from the ship.
> Mr. Bright – We were told to get together if we could do so, and keep together, and as soon as I located a boat I would pull for that.
> Senator Bourne – But at no time were you more than 100 yards from the ship from the time you left it?
> Mr. Bright – Not when she went down.
>
> ---
>
> Questioned by Senator Smith.
> Senator Smith – You did not go back to the scene of this disaster after you pulled out into the sea, away from the *Titanic*?
> Mr. Bright – No; by the time we got clear we did not have time to go

back. We were told to keep together, you see –
Senator Smith – You kept together and did not return again to the scene of the disaster?
Mr. Bright – No, sir. Mr. Lowe, who gave us the order to stay together, went back.

Lifeboat 12

Seaman John Poingdestre commands lifeboat 12 with 40 women aboard and only one other seaman. After the *Titanic* goes under they pull back toward the wreck site but don't get close enough to pick up survivors.

British Wreck Commissioner's Inquiry – Testimony of John Poingdestre, examined by Mr. Butler Aspinall.
2992. After she sank did your boat pull in towards the place where she sank?
Poingdestre – Yes.
2993. For what purpose?
Poingdestre – To pick up anybody who was there.
2994. Was there anybody there?
Poingdestre – I never saw anybody.
2995. Did you see any corpses?
Poingdestre – No.
2996. You saw nothing?
Poingdestre – I saw some by daylight.
2997. Did you hear any cries?
Poingdestre – Yes.
2998. Did not the cries guide you so as to enable you to go to them?
Poingdestre – Certainly.
2999. Did you go in that direction?
Poingdestre – I pulled in the direction the cries came from.
…3003. When you pulled in that direction, did the passengers on board your boat approve of your doing so?
Poingdestre – Yes.
3004. And you went and searched and found nobody?
Poingdestre – Yes.
3006. Because you had a good deal of room in your boat?
Poingdestre – Well, it did not look much room to my idea.
3007. According to your numbers your boat had 42?
Poingdestre – Yes.
3008. And you and Clinch?
Poingdestre – Yes, 40; and Clinch and me is 42.
The Commissioner – And it is constructed to carry 65.
…3012. So that at that time there was a great deal of spare room in

your boat. You think not you say?
Poingdestre – No.
3013. We know what the capacity of the boat is. How long did you remain looking, do you suggest, for the people?
Poingdestre – About a quarter of an hour.
3014. And you saw nothing?
Poingdestre – Nothing at all.
3015. Did you see wreckage?
Poingdestre – Only about a couple of hundred deck chairs.
3016. But you saw no bodies?
Poingdestre – No bodies whatever.
3017. During that quarter of an hour, while you were looking, how long did the cries continue?
Poingdestre – All the time that we were looking we heard the cries.
…3020. What was the nearest do you think that you got to any of these cries?
Poingdestre – I reckoned about 100 yards.
3021. And then did they cease?
Poingdestre – Yes.
3022. Can you account for that?
Poingdestre – I can account for not going to the position where I ought to have been.
3023. Well, will you tell us?
Poingdestre – There were not enough sailors in my boat, only me and my mate, and we could not get there.
3024. (The Commissioner.) Get where?
Poingdestre – To where the halloes were coming from – the cries.
…3029. At the end of this quarter of an hour what did you do then?
Poingdestre – I hailed for other boats.
3031. What do you mean by that?
Poingdestre – Called to see if there were any in the vicinity of where I was.
…3040. What answer did you get?
Poingdestre – I heard somebody call out, and they came up to us – another lifeboat.
…3047. (The Commissioner.) What did you hail it for?
Poingdestre – To tie up, to keep together.

United States Senate Inquiry – Testimony of Seaman Frank Evans, questioned by Senator Smith.
Mr. Evans – I was in No. 10, and we tied up to No. 12. We gave the man our painter and made fast, and we stopped there.
Senator Smith – How long did you stop there?
Mr. Evans – We stopped there about an hour, I think it was, sir, when

No. 14 boat came over with one officer.
Senator Smith – What officer?
Mr. Evans – The fifth officer. I think it was.

Lifeboat 14 Returns

Fifth Officer Harold Lowe gathers and ties lifeboat 4 and collapsible D together with Edward Buley's boat 10 and Poingdestre's boat 12. He then redistributes the survivors, including a stowaway disguised as a woman, from his boat 14 to the other boats.

As multitudes lose their battle to survive, the sounds of the desperate and dying slowly wane and give way to the last muffled sounds of frozen death. Only then does Lowe deem it safe to return.

> **British Wreck Commissioner's Inquiry** – Testimony of Harold Lowe, examined by Mr. Rowlatt.
> 15862. What did you do after you got the four boats out there?
> Lowe – I tied them together in a string, and made them step their masts.
> 15863. What was that for?
> Lowe – In case it came on to blow, and then they would be ready.
> 15864. Did you transfer any of your passengers?
> Lowe – Yes, I transferred all of them.
> 15865. Among the other boats?
> Lowe – Into the other four boats.
> 15866. Why did you do that?
> Lowe – So as to have an empty boat to go back.
> 15868. Was that before the "Titanic" foundered or after?
> Lowe – No, that was after she went down.
> 15869. Having got an empty boat, did you go back to the wreckage?
> Lowe – I did.
> 15870. Was there much wreckage?
> Lowe – No, very little.
> The Commissioner – How many men had you on the boat?
> Lowe – I do not know; I should say seven.
> …15873. Including yourself?
> Lowe – Yes, I should say six and myself.
> 15874. (Mr. Rowlatt.) Did you row six oars back to the wreck?
> Lowe – No, five oars, I think, and I had a man on the look-out.
> 15875. I understand what you say is that you got rid of the passengers. You got rid of the people who could not do anything, and went back with a working crew to look for people who were drowning; that is what you mean?

One Lifeboat Returns

Lowe – Yes; it would be no good me going back with a load of people.
15876. Certainly; I am not complaining; I am only trying to bring it out in your favor, if I may say so. You rescued some people, did not you?
Lowe – I picked up four.
15877. I think one died in the boat, did he not?
Lowe – One died, a Mr. Hoyt, of New York. [Mr. William F. Hoyt.]

Frank Evans, Edward Buley, and four other seamen join Lowe in boat 14 to go back and look for anyone hardy enough to still be alive.

United States Senate Inquiry – Testimony of Seaman Frank Evans, questioned by Senator Smith.
Mr. Evans – ... He (Fifth Officer Lowe) came over in No. 14 boat, and he says, "Are there any seamen there?" We said, "Yes, sir." He said, "All right; you will have to distribute these passengers among these boats. Tie them all together and come into my boat," he said, "to go over into the wreckage and pick up anyone that is alive there." So we got into his boat and went straight over toward the wreckage. We picked up four men there, sir; alive.
Senator Smith – Any dead?
Mr. Evans – One died on the way back, sir. There were plenty of dead bodies about us.
Senator Smith – How many? Scores of them?
Mr. Evans – You couldn't hardly count them, sir. I was afraid to look over the sides because it might break my nerves down.
Senator Smith – Did these bodies have life preservers on?
Mr. Evans – Yes, sir; from here upward (indicating) they were clear of the water. They were like that (indicating). They simply had perished, sir.

Boat 14 is the only lifeboat to return and only rescued three survivors.

Now there are no more screams and no more pleading cries. The groans and fading sounds of collective agony have been replaced by silence; icebergs in the perfect calm and silence; the brilliant starlit night and silence. The sea, the ice, and the stars mingling with the horizon–all as it was before–and everyone in every lifeboat clearly understands the meaning of the haunting silence.

Just after 3:30 a.m., a little over an hour after the *Titanic* disappeared into the glass smooth ocean, the survivors in their lifeboats spot the approaching *Carpathia's* rockets.

Chapter 18

Rescue

When *Titanic's* bow dove into the sea only two collapsible lifeboats remained aboard as the crew desperately worked to release them. Collapsible B floated free but upside down, while Collapsible A was launched by the sea upright but swamped and without the sides raised. Some of the passengers and crew that managed to reach one of these boats are still alive but won't be able to hold on much longer.

Collapsible B

Balancing aboard the precarious Collapsible B, Marconi Operator Harold Bride informs Second Officer Charles Lightoller that the *Baltic*, *Olympic* and *Carpathia* are on their way to the rescue. Lightoller calculates that the *Carpathia* would arrive around dawn. Three men die on Collapsible B that night, one of them Bride's partner Senior Wireless Operator Jack Phillips.

Colonel Gracie described his experience on Collapsible B in his book – *The Truth About The Titanic*.

> "When dawn broke there were thirty of us on the raft, standing knee deep in the icy water and afraid to move lest the cranky craft be overturned. Several unfortunates, benumbed and half dead, besought us to save them and one or two made an effort to reach us, but we had to warn them away.
>
> "The hours that elapsed before we were picked up by the *Carpathia* were the longest and most terrible that I ever spent. We were afraid to turn around and look to see whether we were seen by passing craft, and when some one who was facing the stern passed the word that something that looked like a steamer was coming up, one of the men became hysterical under the strain. The rest of us, too, were near the breaking point."

Chief Baker Charles Joughin survives in the water for over two hours before being rescued by a lifeboat.

British Wreck Commissioner's Inquiry – Testimony of Charles Joughin, examined by the Solicitor General.

6078. How long do you think you were in the water before you got anything to hold on to?

Joughin – I did not attempt to get anything to hold on to until I reached a collapsible, but that was daylight.

... 6085. ... Tell us shortly about it.

Joughin – Just as it was breaking daylight I saw what I thought was some wreckage, and I started to swim towards it slowly. When I got near enough, I found it was a collapsible not properly upturned but on its side, with an Officer and I should say about twenty or twenty-five men standing on the top of it.

...6095. Was there any room for you?

Joughin – No, Sir.

...6098. Did you stay near it?

Joughin – I tried to get on it, but I was pushed off it, and I what you call hung around it.

6099. How much later on was it that you were picked up?

Joughin – I eventually got round to the opposite side, and a cook that was on the collapsible recognized me, and held out his hand and held me—a chap named Maynard.

...6103. So that your feet would be in the water?

Joughin – Yes, and my legs.

6104. And you supported yourself by your lifebelt. I do not want to be harrowing about it, but was the water very cold?

Joughin – I felt colder in the lifeboat—after I got in the lifeboat.

6105. You were picked up, were you, by a lifeboat later on?

Joughin – We were hanging on to this collapsible, and eventually a lifeboat came in sight.

6106. And they took you aboard?

Joughin – They got within about 50 yards and they sung out that they could only take 10. So I said to this Maynard, "Let go my hand," and I swam to meet it, so that I would be one of the 10.

6108. You have said you thought it was about two hours before you saw this collapsible, and then you spent some time with the collapsible. How long do you suppose it was after you got to the collapsible that you were taken into the lifeboat?

Joughin – I should say we were on the collapsible about half-an-hour.

6109. That means that for some two and a half hours you were in the water?

Joughin – Practically, yes.

Chief Baker Charles Joughin survived for two and half hours in the water, well past the time it takes for the freezing North Atlantic to claim most of its victims. Some believe his blood alcohol level helped him survive in the freezing Atlantic while floating in his lifebelt.

British Wreck Commissioner's Inquiry – Testimony of Charles Joughin, examined by Mr. Cotter.
6247. When you found your boat had gone you said you went down below. What did you do when you went down below?
Joughin – I went to my room for a drink.
6248. Drink of what?
Joughin – Spirits.
The Commissioner: Does it very much matter what it was?
Mr. Cotter: Yes, my Lord, this is very important, because I am going to prove, or rather my suggestion is, that he then saved his life. I think his getting a drink had a lot to do with saving his life.
The Commissioner: He told you he had one glass of liqueur.
6249. (Mr. Cotter.) Yes. (To the Witness.) What kind of a glass was it?
Joughin – It was a tumbler half-full.
6250. A tumbler half-full of liqueur?
Joughin – Yes.

At 17, Jack Thayer Jr. is no longer a child that could expect a seat in a lifeboat but after being separated from his parents he survives by reaching Collapsible B. As dawn approaches a swell begins to replace the flat calm sea and Second Officer Lightoller lines the men up into a double column, facing the bow of the overturned Collapsible. Then as the boat sways he orders them to lean to the left or right, to counteract the swell but Lightoller realizes the collapsible is slowly sinking. In the dawn light he sees Boats 4, 10, and 12 strung together in a line about 400 yards away and uses his officers whistle to get their attention. Boats 4 and 12 row over. Boat 4 arrives first and takes on twelve of the survivors from the foundering collapsible and the remaining ten transfer to boat 12. While the collapsible survivors are being transferred, Jack Thayer Jr. doesn't recognize his mother in lifeboat 4 and his mother doesn't see him get into lifeboat 12. Second Officer Charles Lightoller is the last to leave the sinking collapsible and takes over command of lifeboat 12 from Seaman John Poingdestre. Lifeboat 12 is designed to hold 65 but she now carries the hopes of 69 survivors.

Collapsible A

After Lowe and his crew find only four survivors to pull from the water, with one man dying minutes later, they rig a sail and boat 14 then picks up Collapsible D. With Collapsible D in tow they head in the direction of the *Carpathia's* rockets, but soon come upon the swamped Collapsible A. Standing knee deep in freezing cold water are twelve survivors, including R. Norris Williams, hoping for rescue before they sink or succumb to hypothermia.

United States Senate Inquiry – Testimony of Fifth Officer Harold Lowe, questioned by Senator Smith.
Mr. Lowe – I had taken this first collapsible (D) in tow, and I noticed

that there was another collapsible in a worse plight than this one that I had in tow. I was just thinking and wondering whether it would be better for me to cut this one adrift and let her go, and for me to travel faster to the sinking one, but I thought, "No, I think I can manage it"; so I cracked on a bit, and I got down there just in time and took off, I suppose, about 20 men and 1 lady out of this sinking collapsible.

Senator Smith – Did you leave any bodies on there?

Mr. Lowe – I left three bodies on it.

Senator Smith – What was the number of that boat?

Mr. Lowe – I do not know, sir; it was one of the collapsibles.

Senator Smith – But you took off of it 20 men?

Mr. Lowe – About 20 men.

Senator Smith – And three women?

Mr. Lowe – One woman.

Senator Smith – And left on board how many?

Mr. Lowe – Three male bodies.

Senator Smith – So that in this damaged collapsible there were 24 people, all together?

Mr. Lowe – Twenty–one and three are twenty-four, all together; yes, sir.

Senator Smith – What became of the other three that you left on it?

Mr. Lowe – As to the three people that I left on her – of course, I may have been a bit hard hearted, I can not say – but I thought to myself, "I am not here to worry about bodies; I am here for life, to save life, and not to bother about bodies," and I left them.

Senator Smith – Were they dead when you left them?

Mr. Lowe – They were dead; yes, sir. The people on the raft told me they had been dead some time. I said, "Are you sure they are dead?" They said, "Absolutely sure." I made certain they were dead, and questioned them one and all before I left this collapsible.

Senator Smith – Did you attempt to find anything on their persons that would identify them?

Mr. Lowe – No, sir; I did not.

Senator Smith – Do you know whether anyone did?

Mr. Lowe – No, sir; nobody; because they were all up to their ankles in water when I took them off. Another three minutes and they would have been down.

The *Carpathia* Arrives

Despite their heroic efforts, Captain Rostron and the crew of the *Carpathia* are only able to rescue the 712 souls that were fortunate enough to have a place in one of *Titanic's* lifeboats.

United States Senate Inquiry – Testimony of *Carpathia's* Captain Arthur H. Rostron, questioned by Senator Smith.

Senator Smith – Just proceed, in your own way.

Mr. Rostron – After interviewing the heads of the departments, I went on the bridge and remained there. While I was up there made inquiries making sure that my orders were all being carried out, and that everything possible was being done.

At 2:40, I saw a flare, about half a point on the port bow, and immediately took it for granted that it was the *Titanic* itself, and I remarked that she must be still afloat, as I knew we were a long way off, and it seemed so high.

However, soon after seeing the flare I made out an iceberg about a point on the port bow, to which I had to port to keep well clear of. Knowing that the *Titanic* had struck ice, of course I had to take extra care and every precaution to keep clear of anything that might look like ice.

Between 2:45 and 4 o'clock, the time I stopped my engines, we were passing icebergs on every side and making them ahead and having to alter our course several times to clear the bergs.

At 4 o'clock I stopped.

At 4:10 I got the first boat alongside.

Previous to getting the first boat alongside, however, I saw an iceberg close to me, right ahead, and I had to starboard to get out of the way. And I picked him up on the weather side of the ship. I had to clear this ice.

I am on the scene of action now. This is 4:10 with the first boat alongside.

Senator Smith – You are picking up these people now?

Mr. Rostron – Yes.

The *Carpathia* is first sighted around 4:00 a.m. and lifeboat 2, under the command of Fourth Officer Joseph Boxhall, reaches the *Carpathia* at 4:10 a.m. Elizabeth Walton Allen is the first passenger brought aboard the *Carpathia* and confirms that the *Titanic* has sunk. The other lifeboats, some huddled together and laying on their oars, also see the ship and start rowing to their rescue.

Testimony of *Carpathia's* Captain Arthur H. Rostron continues.

Senator Smith – Please describe that in your own way.

Mr. Rostron – We picked up the first boat, and the boat was in charge of an officer. I saw that he was not under full control of this boat, and the officer sung out to me that he only had one seaman in the boat, so I had to maneuver the ship to get as close to the boat as possible, as I knew well it would be difficult to do the pulling. However, they got alongside, and they got them up all right.

By the time we had the first boat's people it was breaking day, and then I could see the remaining boats all around within an area of about 4 miles. I also saw icebergs all around me. There were about 20 icebergs that would be anywhere from about 150 to 200 feet high and numerous smaller bergs; also numerous what we call "growlers." You would not call them bergs. They were anywhere from 10 to 12 feet high and 10 to 15 feet long above the water…

When *Titanic's* lifeboats come alongside the *Carpathia* the survivors are brought aboard using rope ladders, slings, and chairs. Children are hoisted up in the canvas ash bags that Captain Rostron had ordered for that purpose.

At 6:00 a.m. the *Californian* turns her wireless back on. She learns of the disaster from the *Frankfort* and steams toward *Titanic's* last reported position.

> Testimony of *Carpathia's* Captain Arthur H. Rostron continues.
> Mr. Rostron – …I maneuvered the ship and we gradually got all the boats together. We got all the boats alongside and all the people up aboard by 8:30.
> I was then very close to where the *Titanic* must have gone down, as there was a lot of, hardly wreckage, but small pieces of broken-up stuff nothing in the way of anything large.
> At 8 o'clock the Leyland Line steamer *Californian* hove up, and we exchanged messages. I gave them the notes by semaphore about the *Titanic* going down, and that I had got all the passengers from the boats; but we were then not quite sure whether we could account for all the boats. I told them: "Think one boat still unaccounted for." He then asked me if he should search around, and I said, "Yes, please." It was then 10:50…

The *Californian* searches but finds nothing because all the boats with surviving passengers had already been rescued by the *Carpathia*.

Survivors Aboard the *Carpathia*

> Testimony of *Carpathia's* Captain Arthur H. Rostron continues.
> Mr. Rostron – …At 8:30 all the people were on board. I asked for the purser, and told him that I wanted to hold a service, a short prayer of thankfulness for those rescued and a short burial service for those who were lost. I consulted with Mr. Ismay. I ran down for a moment and told them that I wished to do this, and Mr. Ismay left everything in my hands.
> I then got an Episcopal clergyman, one of our passengers, and asked him if he would do this for me, which he did, willingly.
> While they were holding the service, I was on the bridge, of course, and I maneuvered around the scene of the wreckage. We saw nothing except one body.
> Senator Smith – Floating?

Mr. Rostron – Floating, sir.
Senator Smith – With a life preserver on?
Mr. Rostron – With a life preserver on. That is the only body I saw.
Senator Smith – Was it male or female?
Mr. Rostron – Male. It appeared to me to be one of the crew. He was only about 100 yards from the ship. We could see him quite distinctly, and saw that he was absolutely dead. He was lying on his side like this (indicating) and his head was awash. Of course he could not possibly have been alive and remain in that position. I did not take him aboard. For one reason, the *Titanic's* passengers then were knocking about the deck and I did not want to cause any unnecessary excitement or any more hysteria among them, so I steamed past, trying to get them not to see it.
From the boats we took three dead men, who had died of exposure.
Senator Smith – From the lifeboats?
Mr. Rostron – From the lifeboats; yes, sir.
Senator Smith – Do you know from which boats they were taken?
Mr. Rostron – No, sir; I am only giving you the general news now. We took three dead men from the boats, and they were brought on board. Another man was brought up—I think he was one of the crew—who died that morning about 10 o'clock, I think, and he, with the other three, were buried at 4 o'clock in the afternoon.
Senator Smith – At sea?
Mr. Rostron – At sea.
…Senator Smith – Were they men or women?
Mr. Rostron – Men. There were several ladies in the boats. They were slightly injured about the arms and things of that kind, of course; although I must say, from the very start, all these people behaved magnificently. As each boat came alongside everyone was calm, and they kept perfectly still in their boats. They were quiet and orderly, and each person came up the ladder, or was pulled up, in turn as they were told off. There was no confusion whatever among the passengers. They behaved magnificently—every one of them.
As they came aboard, they were, of course, attended to. My instructions had already been given to that effect.
…Senator Smith – Have you concluded that you did not see the ill-fated ship at all?
Mr. Rostron – Oh, no; we arrived an hour and a half after she went down; after the last of her was seen.

Some of the surviving passengers are in shock, some are crying, and others are simply quiet, but many still hold out hope that they will be reunited with loved ones when all the lifeboats are rescued. Once on board the *Carpathia*, rescued passengers search for loved ones who may already be aboard. All three of Charles H. Marshall's nieces are among the survivors and are pleasantly surprised to find that their uncle is a *Carpathia* passenger. But, when wives don't find their husbands, and mothers don't find their sons, they anxiously watch as the remaining lifeboats come into view.

First Class passenger William Carter saw to it that his family was safely loaded into lifeboat 4 before he found a spot alongside Bruce Ismay in Collapsible C. His lifeboat is rescued before lifeboat 4 and, when he spots boat 4 from the deck of the *Carpathia,* he sees his wife and daughter but doesn't see his son William. He is relieved when he discovers 11 year old William Jr. is indeed in the boat still wearing the lady's hat that his mother had placed on his head to secure him a spot in the lifeboat.

After refusing a spot next to his wife and son in lifeboat 5, Dr. Washington Dodge takes one of the last spots in lifeboat 13. He is also happily reunited with his family, but there will be very few such happy endings aboard the *Carpathia* this day.

By 8:15 a.m. all but lifeboat 12, with 69 aboard, has been rescued. As boat 12 heads toward the *Carpathia* several waves break over the bow and Second Officer Lightoller worries if she'll stay afloat long enough to reach the rescue ship. She does.

One by one, as the survivors from lifeboat 12 are brought aboard, hope fades and the cruel reality starts to set in as prayers of finding loved ones aren't answered. Those coming aboard from boat 12 also cling to the hope of being reunited with family members aboard the *Carpathia*. Marian Thayer is momentarily thrilled when she finds her son, Jack Thayer Jr. Then she asks her son, "Where's daddy?" to which Jack Jr. replies, "I don't know, mother." Soon thereafter they would both learn what many others had already discovered—there have been precious few reunions with fathers or husbands aboard the *Carpathia*. Lifeboat 12 is empty after Second Officer Charles Lightoller is the last *Titanic* survivor taken aboard.

Chapter 19

The World Learns of Disaster

Amid much confusion, reports of the sinking reach many parts of the world through wireless transmission and newspaper accounts. There is little doubt that the unsinkable assumption plays a part in many of the early reports and statements—whatever happened couldn't possibly pose a danger to the *Titanic* or be anything other than an "inconvenience" to the passengers.

All the major newspapers pick up on the rumors, false hope, and mistimed wire stories to publish versions of the event. The Managing Editor of the *Wall Street Journal*, Maurice L. Farrell, 35, was later called to testify at the United States Senate Inquiry.

"No Danger of Loss of Life"

> **United States Senate Inquiry** – Testimony of Maurice L. Farrell, questioned by Senator Smith.
> Senator Smith – ... From your bulletin Local "A"-3, headed "Bulletin," I read as follows:
> NEW YORK, April 15
> *A dispatch received here from Halifax. N. S., this morning reports that all the passengers of the Titanic had left the steamship after 3:20 o'clock this morning.*
> ...Following that on your original memoranda appears the following:
> *Titanic – A dispatch from Halifax reports that all passengers had left the Titanic in boats shortly after 3:30 this morning.*
> Senator Smith – Have you that?
> Mr. Farrell – We published that dispatch on our ticker at 8:58 on the morning of April 15. We received it from the Boston News Bureau, our Boston correspondent.
> Senator Smith – Did you make any attempt to verify that statement at the White Star Line offices or through Mr. Franklin personally?
> Mr. Farrell – We did.
> Senator Smith – With what results?
> Mr. Farrell – Prior to that we had received from the White Star offices a statement somewhat similar.
> Senator Smith – Have you got it there?

Mr. Farrell – I have; …This was published at our tickers at 8:35, or thereabouts. It was obtained by Mr. Gingold, one of our reporters, who is now in London. He went to London on a vacation very shortly after that. I will read the statement as it appeared on our tickers, headed "Titanic." It reads:

"Officers of White Star Line stated at 8 o'clock this morning that passengers on the *Titanic* were being taken off in boats and that there was no danger of loss of life. The *Baltic* and the *Virginian*, they stated, were standing by to assist in the rescue work."

… Senator Smith – From whom was that information received?
Mr. Farrell – That was received at the White Star offices from some of the junior officials. Mr. Franklin had not yet arrived at the office.
Senator Smith – Can you give me the name of your informant?
Mr. Farrell – No, sir; I can not. Let me explain the relation of this. This was early in the morning. The early newspaper accounts had been published. There was a great crowd, and there was great excitement at the White Star offices. Dozens of newspaper men and also the relatives of passengers on the *Titanic* were all clamoring for information. In response to questions, this was the information given out by some of the representatives of the White Star Line. This particular information was not given by Mr. Franklin.
Senator Smith – Did you make any attempt to verify it?
Mr. Farrell – Yes; we made every attempt we could.
Senator Smith – What did you do?
Mr. Farrell – Then, subsequent to that, came the dispatch from Boston which you have just mentioned:
A dispatch from Halifax reports that all passengers had left the *Titanic* in boats shortly after 3:30 this morning.
Senator Smith – Did you regard that as confirmatory?
Mr. Farrell – We did.

"No Danger That Titanic Will Sink."

In later testimony Maurice Farrell, at Senator Smith's urging, read statements published by Dow, Jones & Co. He also provided the source of each item.
Testimony of Maurice L. Farrell continues.

Mr. Farrell – The first item we published was at approximately 8:10 a.m., April 15, as follows:

"At 10.25 Sunday night new White Star liner *Titanic* called C.Q.D. and reported having struck an iceberg. Wireless received stated steamship needed immediate assistance as she was sinking at the bow."

Another message received half hour later reported the women were being put off in lifeboats. Marconi station at Cape Race notified Allen Line steamship *Virginian*, which immediately headed for the *Titanic*. At midnight the *Virginian* was about 170 miles distant from the *Titanic* and expected to reach that *Titanic* about 10 o'clock this morning. Steamship *Baltic* is headed toward the disaster, being 200 miles away at midnight. Last word received from sinking *Titanic* was a wireless heard at 12:27. ... these signals were blurred and ended abruptly.

Mr. Farrell – ... This was a brief summary of what appeared in the morning papers, principally taken from the Herald.

Senator Smith – Some of that information, however, you obtained direct from the White Star office—that to which I have previously called your attention?

Mr. Farrell – I believe that one of our men, about 7:30 in the morning, went to the White Star office and got some information there, but as I recall it, he did not get much additional to what had been published in the morning papers. The Herald, the Times, and some of the other papers had rather complete accounts of it up to that time.

Senator Smith – That was on April 15?

Mr. Farrell – Yes.

... At 9:02 a.m., April 15, we published the following:

"An official of White Star Line said: 'There is no danger that *Titanic* will sink. The boat is unsinkable, and nothing but inconvenience will be suffered by the passengers.' Latest information which has come to White Star office is that the *Virginian* is due alongside the *Titanic* at 10 a.m., the *Olympic* at 3 p.m., and the Baltic at 4 p.m.."

That was obtained from Mr. Franklin by two of our reporters ...

At 9:22 a.m., or thereabouts, April 15, we published the following:

"Vice President Franklin, of International Mercantile Marine, says, regarding reported accident to *Titanic*: 'It is unbelievable that *Titanic* could have met with accident without our being notified. We had a wireless from her late Sunday giving her position, and are absolutely satisfied that if she had been in collision with an iceberg we should have heard from her at once. In any event, the ship is unsinkable, and there is absolutely no danger to passengers.'"

That was received from Mr. Franklin by Mr. Trebell, one of our reporters.

At 9:25 a.m., April 15, we published the following:

"Wireless advices from steamship *Virginian* said last word from wireless telegrapher on *Titanic* was received at 3:05 o'clock this morning. He said women and children were being taken off in calm sea. It is thought that *Titanic* wireless has failed, due to some local cause."

"Titanic is Moving Under Her Own Engines"

Senator Smith – Proceed with your reading of the messages.
Mr. Farrell – Yes.
... At 10:45, or thereabouts, on April 15, we published the following:

"Dispatch from Montreal received by White Star officials says *Titanic* was afloat at 8:30 and that women and children had not yet been taken off, though lifeboats were ready in case of emergency. The steamship is heading in direction of Halifax, from which the *Virginian* is approaching. It is thought that bulkheads will prevent ship from sinking. *Titanic* is moving under her own engines."

... At 11:25 a.m., or thereabouts, on April 15, we published the following:

"A. S. Franklin, of International Mercantile Marine, says: 'We can not state too strongly our belief that the ship is unsinkable and passengers perfectly safe. The ship is reported to have gone down several feet by the head. This may be due from water filling forward compartments, and ship may go down many feet by the head and still keep afloat for an indefinite period.'
"Interruption of wireless communication with the ship, according to company officials, does not indicate danger."

That was received from Mr. Franklin by Mr. Byrne and Mr. Smallwood, two of our reporters.
... At 12:12 p.m., or thereabouts, on April 15, we published the following:

"The Sandy Hook marine operator received the following wireless on his machine at 11:36 o'clock this morning: 'Wireless says *Titanic* is under way and proceeding to New York.'"

"Titanic Being Towed to Halifax by the Virginian"

Mr. Farrell – About 3:15 p.m. or thereabouts, on April 15, we published the following:

"CANSO, NOVA SCOTIA
At 2 o'clock the *Titanic*, having transferred her passengers to the *Parisian* and *Carpathia*, was being towed to Halifax by the *Virginian*."

... Senator Smith – And that came from the Laffan News Bureau?
Mr. Farrell – Yes. That is all we published in our news ticker on April 15 concerning this accident.
... Senator Smith – How about the succeeding days? If you have the ticker tape for Tuesday and Wednesday, I would like that.

Tuesday April 16th

Mr. Farrell – At 8:02 a.m., April 16, we published the following:

"White Star liner *Titanic* sank at 2:20 a.m. Monday, five hours after crashing into an iceberg. More than 1,500 persons have been drowned."

... This is the 16th, Tuesday. You recollect that the information really came out after 6 o'clock Monday night. (Continuing reading):

"At 7:30 a.m. this morning an officer of the Mercantile Marine stated that company had been receiving names of those saved all night and that so far they had received 200. He stated the captain of *Carpathia* estimated there were between 800 and 850 persons saved. The names of Mrs. J. J. Astor and maid are among those received, but no mention is made Col. Astor or J. Archibald Butt.

"Latest message is *Carpathia* has 806 passengers aboard. Grave fears for rest of *Titanic's* passengers.

"First definite message received was from Capt. Haddock, *Olympic*, which stated: '*Carpathia* reached *Titanic* position at daybreak. Found boats and wreckage only. *Titanic* sank about 2:20 a.m. In 41.46 north, 50.14 west. All her boats accounted for containing about 675 souls saved, crew and passengers included. Nearly divided women and children. Leyland liner *Californian* remained and searching exact position of disaster. Loss likely total 1,800 souls.'"

That was a summary gleaned from the morning newspapers, which were at hand, and by a reporter who visited the White Star offices that morning; but they had practically nothing more than all the newspapers had at the same time.

...About 9:56 a.m. we published this:

"White Star officials this morning say first news they had directly yesterday was received after 6 p.m. They gave out to all inquirers the indirect information they had received in newspaper reports from various quarters and unofficial wireless dispatches said to have been received at Montreal, Halifax, and other places.

"The news men took the reports from White Star office and believed them to be official, and White Star officials believed them to be authentic, although not directly received."

I got that message out from the White Star offices, as I mentioned a while ago. I went down there to find out why they had given out these dispatches and published them, which had subsequently proven to be false. I went to see Mr. Franklin, but he was held up in a conference and I wanted to get at someone in authority as soon as I could, so that I was turned over to one of his assistants, and I asked him, "How is it that these dispatches were given? This information came from your office yesterday." I said, "Did you receive that news?"

"He said, 'No; the first definite news we received was after 6 o'clock last night, and directly after that we called up the newspapers and gave it out.' I said, "Well, our reporters were down here yesterday at the White Star Line offices all day." He said, 'Well, that was not official. We had received that information from various sources, and we just gave it out.'"

Wednesday, April 17th

... Senator Smith – ...On Wednesday, if you have your ticker-tape references to the *Titanic* disaster, I would like to have you give them.
Mr. Farrell – The first item published on Wednesday, April 17, was at 5 a.m., and reads as follows:

"The overnight news concerning the *Titanic* reveals little which was not published by Dow Jones & Co. yesterday. No word has yet been heard from Col. John Jacob Astor, Isidor Straus, Maj. Archibald W. Butt, George D. Widener, Harry Widener, Benjamin Guggenheim, Edgar I. Meyer, Frank D. Millet, W. T. Stead, Washington A. Roebling, or John B. Cummings of stock-exchange firm of Cummings & Marckwald, and Jacques Futrelle the author, and Henry B. Harris the theatrical man."

That was simply a brief summary for the information of our readers of the situation as it stood at 8 o'clock Wednesday morning.
...Senator Smith – Have you here the bulletins which correspond with the items you have just read into the record?
Mr. Farrell – I find one here which I think would be of interest which I do not think appeared on the tape. It is headed, "Those false reports." It reads:

"Uncle of Phillips, wireless operator of *Titanic*, solved one of the mysterious wireless messages that at first gave hope vessel was saved. He acknowledged that he sent the following messages from London to Mr. and Mrs. Phillips, Godalming, Surrey, England, parents of the wireless operator, to reassure them: 'Making slowly for Halifax; practically unsinkable; don't worry.'"

Senator Smith – From whom did you obtain that information?
Mr. Farrell – From the Laffan News Bureau.
Senator Smith – Mr. Farrell, do you know of any news item or information possessed by your company or by any of its officers or agents that was attempted to be suppressed?
Mr. Farrell – No, sir; I do not.
Senator Smith – Do you wish to be understood as saying that no pressure of any kind or character was brought to bear upon you?

Mr. Farrell – Oh, absolutely none.
Senator Smith – For the purpose of suppressing news concerning this matter?
Mr. Farrell – Absolutely none whatever. It would not have been tolerated if there had been; and there really was no pressure. There was not a suggestion of that sort.

Additional Statement of Maurice L. Farrell

Maurice Farrell attempts to explain the rash of erroneous statements initially reported to the world through the Dow-Jones ticker, the *Wall Street Journal*, and other prominent newspapers.

> **United States Senate Inquiry** – Testimony of Maurice L. Farrell, questioned by Senator Smith.
>
> Senator Smith – This summary which you have handed to the committee you desire to appear as a part of your testimony?
> Mr. Farrell – I would like to have it appear if you have no objection. While, as I say, it contains a good deal that is matter of opinion, it seems to me it helps a good deal to explain how some of these things got so badly twisted.

Maurice Farrell, managing news editor of Dow, Jones & Co., news agency, of New York, made the following statement to the U.S. Senate subcommittee investigating the *Titanic* disaster:

> Reports published by Dow, Jones & Co. on Monday, April 15, regarding the *Titanic* disaster came chiefly from three sources—office of the White Star Line, the Laffan News Bureau, and the Boston News Bureau. At 8 a.m. on that day, upon interviewing representatives of the White Star Line in their New York office, a reporter received information which was summarized on the Dow, Jones & Co. news tickers as follows:
> Officers of the White Star Line stated at 8 o'clock this morning that passengers on the *Titanic* were being taken off in boats and that there was no danger of loss of life. The *Baltic* and the *Virginian*, they stated, were standing by to assist in the rescue.
> On account of misconstruction of the expression "standing by" this item may have given rise to subsequent erroneous reports. To the lay mind "standing by" conveyed the meaning that the vessels were in the immediate vicinity, holding themselves in readiness to render aid. Its use, however, appears to have been in the technical sense, indicating that the vessels had received the C. Q. D., responded to it, and had headed their course toward the *Titanic*. The expression used in its nautical sense meant response to direction or the setting a course toward, rather than being in the immediate presence of the *Titanic*.

The statement was called to London, and later in the day at least two dispatches of similar purport, but different verbiage, were received from different quarters, and may have represented merely a return of the same report from other parts of the world. In New York they were at the time taken as confirming the earlier statement made at the White Star office. No one was willing to believe, and, in fact, at the time could believe, that the *Titanic* had sunk. Every scrap of what purported to be news indicating safety of the passengers was seized with avidity and rushed by telephone, telegraph, or cable to all parts of America and Europe. This process doubtless entailed duplication of the same messages flying back and forth, which was erroneously construed as confirmatory evidence.

As an example of the misunderstandings arising, I am informed that the White Star office at Boston called up the Allen Line in Montreal by telephone to get confirmation of a report that all *Titanic* passengers were transferred to the *Virginian* and the *Titanic* was proceeding to Halifax under her own steam. The Allen Line replied that they had such a statement, meaning that they had heard such a report. The White Star Boston office took this as substantiating the rumor, and accordingly called up the White Star office in New York confirming the message to Vice President Franklin. Doubtless many similar cases of unintentional errors occurred in the same way, the chances of error, of course, being increased as the reports went through different channels.

President Taft Concerned for Safety of Major Butt

President William Howard Taft had followed the early accounts of the collision and flawed reports of the passengers' safety. On Tuesday April 16, 1912 the *New York Times* reported his reaction and concern for his friend and aide, Major Archibald Butt, when he learned the truth.

PRESIDENT TAFT STUNNED

Wires White Star Line for News of Major Butt

WASHINGTON, April 15---President Taft did not know of the sinking of the *Titanic* or of the danger of his old friend, Major Archibald Butt, when he went to spend the evening at Poll's Theatre, formerly Chase's vaudeville, where "Nobody's Widow" was the play.

The President had read the erroneous accounts of the *Titanic's* accident that appeared in the afternoon papers and thought all on board had been saved and the ship would be taken safely into Halifax. He was nearly frantic when he learned the truth about 11 o'clock, and went at once to the telegraph room at the White House to read the Associated Press bulletins and the bulletins from THE NEW YORK TIMES Washington office. Mr. Taft told the operator to use every effort to get him the news and let him know anything during the night when any was received.

Word was also sent to the telephone operators at the War and Navy Department to forward to the President any information they might get from the wireless stations about the *Titanic*. President Taft for the past three years has regarded Major Butt as his inseparable companion and friend. His fidelity, practical sense, and jovial nature made him exactly the sort of a comrade a man worried with innumerable heavy burdens would desire to have. The President as he appeared at the White House offices to-night was deeply moved. When he knew all that the newspaper dispatches told he turned like a man that had been stunned with a heavy blow and went slowly back to the Executive mansion.

The following telegram from President Taft was received in the offices of the White Star Line shortly after midnight:

Have you any information concerning Major Butt? If you communicate at once I will greatly appreciate. WILLIAM HOWARD TAFT.

The following reply was sent:

Sorry to say we have no definite information. Soon as receive it will notify you. P. A. S. FRANKLIN.

President Taft's inquiry was one among hundreds from all over the country received at the White Star offices.

A Survivor's Letter Home

Miss Amy Stanley – Amy, 24, survived in collapsible boat C. Enroute to New York, the *Carpathia's* wireless operator accepted the following Marconigram from Miss Stanley:

To: Mrs. Stanley, Wolvercote, Oxford.
"Saved *Carpathia*. – Amy".

Due to the volume of messages and lack of time it was never transmitted. She later sent a letter to her parents from New York. The letter was printed in *The Oxford Times* on May 18, 1912.

Partial content of Amy Stanley's letter:

"...I was able to fix the rope round the women for them to be pulled up on the *Carpathia* while the men steadied the boat—the women seemed quite stupefied—yet when I was safe myself, I was the first to break down. The sight on board was awful, with raving women—barely six women were saved who could say they had not lost a relative. Oh! the widows the *Titanic* has made! The last three days have been terrible. I attended to a woman who was picked up on a raft with four men. The latter died, but she lived. She has lost two sons on the *Titanic*.

"Their cabin was next to mine. She was the last woman I spoke to on the ship's deck. I am staying in a Woman's League Hotel, but I am quite well, and these people are fitting me up with clothes. I have telegraphed to Grace but have not yet received a reply. I long now to be with her. I will not write again until I am safe in Newhaven. Don't you think I have been lucky throughout?

"I remain your loving Daughter

"Amy."

1503 Perish

There were no Marconigrams or letters home from 1503 of the passengers and crew that traveled or worked in First, Second, or Third Class. They were old or young, accomplished or striving to be—they were fathers or mothers, husbands or wives, brothers or sisters, friends or acquaintances, or complete strangers. Their stories, their journey, and their lives ended together on April 15, 1912, in the North Atlantic.

Fifteen of the 1503 who perished:

- Mr. William Alexander, 23, Labourer, Third Class passenger
- Dr. Arthur Jackson Brewe, 45, Physician, First Class passenger
- Mr. Francesco Celotti, 24, Stoker, Third Class passenger
- Miss Maggie Ford, 7, Third Class passenger
- Mr. Mark Fortune, 64, Real Estate spec., First Class passenger
- Mr. George Gumery, 24, Mess Steward, Engineering Crew
- Rev. John Harper, 39, Minister, Second Class passenger
- Mr. Denzil Jarvis, 47, Engineer, Second Class passenger
- Mrs. Mary Mack, 57, Widow, Second Class passenger
- Mr. Richard Otter, 38, Stone Cutter, Second Class passenger
- Mr. Marius Petersen, 24, Dairy Worker, Third Class passenger
- Mr. Harry J. Slight, 33, 3rd Class Steward, Victualling Crew
- Master Walter Van Billiard, 9, Third Class passenger
- Mr. Percival W. White, 54, Manufacturer, First Class passenger
- Sig. L. Zarracchi, 26, Wine Butler, À la Carte Restaurant Staff

These 15 people represent unfinished stories and abruptly finished lives. That their fate was shared 100 fold is unfathomable. The 1503 souls that were lost is the disaster of the *Titanic*.

Chapter 20

SEARCH AND RECOVERY

Four days after the *Titanic* sank, the *Bremen* passes through the site. The Thursday, April 25th edition of the *London Daily Sketch* reports what the passengers and crew witnessed:

> "New York, Wednesday. The North German liner *Bremen*, which arrived here (New York) this morning, reports having passed seven icebergs on Saturday last (4/19) in the locality where the *Titanic* disaster occurred. Many bodies were seen floating in the water around the spot where the liner sank. All bore lifebelts. Some of them are described as clasping the bodies of children, and others as still gripping deck chairs and other objects. The officers of the *Bremen* estimated that in one group there were two hundred corpses."

When the scope of the tragedy is realized, White Star Line charters four Canadian ships to search for and recover bodies. The first ship to take up the search is the cable ship *CS Mackay-Bennett* from Halifax, Nova Scotia, soon to be followed by the cable ship *Minia*, lighthouse supply ship *Montmagny*, and the *Algerine*, a sealing vessel.

To comply with health regulations only embalmed bodies could be returned to port so each vessel carries undertakers and embalming supplies as well as clergy. The *Mackay-Bennett* is the first ship to reach the scene and encounters more bodies than can be embalmed with the supplies on board. This leads to the decision by Captain Larnder and the undertakers to only embalm the bodies of First Class passengers. They believe this is necessary to provide visual identification to facilitate the settlement of large estates. Estates not being an issue for Third Class passengers and crew, those bodies are buried at sea. Considered an honor for the mariners, this is a necessity for the many, mostly unidentified, Third Class passengers.

Bodies that are preserved are transported to Halifax, the closest city with direct rail and steamship connections. A curling rink serves as a temporary morgue and the Halifax coroner, John Henry Barnstead, calls for assistance from undertakers from all across Eastern Canada. Some bodies are shipped to their hometowns in Europe and North America for burial but the vast majority of the bodies that reached Halifax are buried there, adding 150 graves to three cemeteries; 121 are buried in the non-denominational Fairview Lawn Cemetery; 19 are buried in the Roman Catholic Mount Olivet Cemetery, and 10 in the Jewish Baron de Hirsch Cemetery. About a third of these bodies could not be identified and are buried with the date of death and the number assigned based on the order of discovery, including the first body recovered.

> NO. 1. – MALE.—ESTIMATED AGE.—10-12.—HAIR. LIGHT.
> CLOTHING – Overcoat, grey; one grey coat; one blue coat; grey woolen jersey; white shirt; grey knickers; black stockings; black boots
> EFFECTS – Purse containing few Danish coins and ring; two handkerchiefs marked "A".
> PROBABLY THIRD CLASS

Other bodies recovered by the *Mackay-Bennett* include:

> NO. 96 – MALE—ESTIMATED AGE, 65—FRONT GOLD TOOTH (Partly)—GREY HAIR AND MOUSTACHE
> CLOTHING – Fur-lined overcoat; grey trousers, coat and vest; soft striped shirt; brown boots; black silk socks.
> EFFECTS – Pocketbook; gold watch; platinum and pearl chain; gold pencil case; silver flask; silver salts bottle; £40 in notes; £4 2s 3d in silver.
> FIRST CLASS – NAME – ISADOR STRAUSS

> NO. 124 – MALE—ESTIMATED AGE 50—LIGHT HAIR & MOUSTACHE
> CLOTHING – Blue serge suit; blue handkerchief with "A.V."; belt with gold buckle; brown boots with red rubber soles; brown flannel shirt; "J.J.A." on back of collar.
> EFFECTS – Gold watch; cuff links, gold with diamond; diamond ring with three stones; £225 in English notes; $2440 in notes; £5 in gold; 7s. in silver; 5 ten franc pieces; gold pencil; pocketbook.
> FIRST CLASS – NAME – J.J.ASTOR

> NO.224 – MALE—ESTIMATED AGE, 25—HAIR, BROWN
> CLOTHING – Uniform (green facing); brown overcoat; black boots; green socks.
> EFFECTS – Gold fountain pen, "W.H.H."; diamond solitaire ring; silver cigarette case; letters; silver match box, marked "W.H.H., from Collingson's staff. Leeds"; telegram to Hotley, Bandmaster "Titanic"; nickel watch; gold chain; gold cigar holder; stud; scissors; 16s; 16 cents; coins.
> BANDMASTER WALLACE H. HOTLEY

NO. 249 – MALE—ESTIMATED AGE, 65—HAIR, GREY
CLOTHING – Light overcoat; black pants; grey jacket; evening dress
EFFECTS – Gold watch and chain; "F.D.M." on watch; glasses; two gold studs; silver tablet bottle; £2 10s in gold; 8s in silver; pocketbook
NAME – FRANK D. MILLET (?)

The *Minia* recovered:

NO. 307. – MALE.—ESTIMATED AGE, 56.—HAIR,
FIRST CLASS – NAME – CHARLES MELVILLE HAYS. Montreal, Canada.

NO. 313. – ESTIMATED AGE, 36.
EFFECTS – Gold watch and chain; sovereign case; Kruger sovereign; silver match box; $6 American notes; pair cuff links marked "L. G."; diamond ring; 2 collar buttons; knife marked "Imperial Restaurant"; key; rubber eraser; lead pencil; in case, 7 sovereigns, 2 half sovereigns, 5/6d in silver, copper coins; bunch of keys with the following tags: "Comptroller's Office restaurant 1st class entrance to "B" deck; the other "Restaurant Manager, entrance to Cafe Parisian"; laundry, marked on linen collar "H. R."; two pocket knives marked "H. R. ; one pair gloves.
MANAGER (r)
NAME – LUIGI GATTI.
Montalto, Harborough Rd., Southampton.

The Canadian vessels recover a total of 328 bodies, but during one of the final searches in early June they report that the life jackets are coming apart and releasing the floating corpses to a burial at sea.

Five additional bodies are recovered by passing ships including the three bodies left in Collapsible A. The boat is discovered 200 miles from the site of the sinking in mid-May by the *RMS Oceanic*. The bodies were buried at sea.

This report appeared in the *Cork Examiner* – Thursday May 16, 1912

"ECHO OF DISASTER : BOAT PICKED UP BODIES ON BOARD
"New York, Wednesday. The White Star Line has received a marconigram from the *Oceanic*, dated May 13th, latitude 39.56, longitude 47.01, reporting that she had picked up a collapsible boat of the *Titanic* containing three bodies. One body was apparently that of Thomas Beattie and the others were a sailor and a fireman. They were committed to the deep. In the boat were also a coat with letters addressed to Richard N. Williams; a can marked 'Dan Williams,' and a ring with the inscription, 'Edward and Gerda.' The collapsible boat is the one mentioned by Mr. Lowe in his testimony at Washington as that from which he took twenty men and three women, leaving three bodies. —Reuter.—"

A more gruesome account of how the three perished in Collapsible A appeared in the *St. Paul Daily News* the following day – Friday 17 May 1912

> "*Titanic* victims died of hunger—Tooth marks on cork and collapsible lifeboat tell grim tale—Liner found three—
>
> "New York, May 16.—Bits of cork in their mouths and tooth marks on the cork and wood portions of the boat indicated that starvation killed the three *Titanic* victims whose bodies were in a *Titanic* collapsible lifeboat picked up by the White Star liner *Oceanic*, which arrived here today.
>
> "Two of the bodies were secured to thwarts by pieces of chains. The body of a cabin passenger was identified by the clothing as that of Thompson Beattie, Chicago. The other two were members of the crew.
>
> "A fur coat with the name Williams inside the pocket and a woman's ring inscribed 'Edward to Cerda,' indicated that there had been others in the lifeboat. The bodies were buried at sea.
>
> "White Star line officials say that the lifeboat is that mentioned by Third Officer Lowe of the *Titanic*, who said he left three bodies in the lifeboat of which he had charge when his 21 passengers were transferred to the *Carpathia*. This does not conform with the evidence of starvation."

The bodies of only one in five of the over 1500 victims are recovered. Some victims sank with the *Titanic*, others followed soon after. Undiscovered bodies still supported by life vests were dispersed by the currents of the North Atlantic and eventually claimed by the sea.

Chapter 21

The Inquiries

United States Senate Inquiry

William Alden Smith, 52, was born in Dowagiac, Michigan in 1859, the same small town where *Titanic* survivor Dickinson Bishop was born 28 years later. Surviving First Class passengers Dick and Helen Bishop still call Dowagiac home, as will Third Class survivors Mrs. Hanna Touma, and her children.

The Smith family moved to Grand Rapids, Michigan in 1872. William eventually studied law and was admitted to the bar in 1882. While a practicing attorney William Smith became an expert on railroad law.

William A. Smith was elected as a Republican to Michigan's 5th congressional district and served from March 4, 1895, until he resigned February 9, 1907 to fill the Senate vacancy caused by the death of Russell A. Alger. Smith had already been elected to that Senate seat in January for the term beginning March 4, 1907. In his fourth and fifth terms in Congress Smith chaired the Committee on Pacific Railroads and, in that capacity, advocated for universal safety standards for railroads.

In 1906 then Congressman Smith had occasion to sail White Star Line and meet Captain Edward J. Smith. This, and his experience with railroad safety, apparently are the Senator's primary qualifications for investigating a shipwreck.

On the morning of April 17, 1912 Smith introduces a resolution calling for the Committee on Commerce to investigate the *Titanic* disaster. The resolution is immediately passed and Senator Smith is appointed by the Commerce Committee chairman to chair the *Titanic* investigation subcommittee. Three Democrats and three Republicans are selected to round out the subcommittee: Jonathan Bourne (R – Oregon), Theodore Burton (R – Ohio), Duncan Fletcher (D – Florida), Francis G. Newlands (D – Nevada), George Perkins (R – California), and Furnifold Simmons (D – North Carolina).

Also on April 17th Bruce Ismay sent this Marconigram to P.A.S. Franklin, manager of White Star Line in America;

From Ismay, Carpathia, To Islefrank, New York,

'Most desirable Titanic crew aboard Carpathia should be returned home earliest moment possible suggest you hold Cedric sailing her daylight Friday

unless you see any reason contrary propose returning in her myself please send outfit clothes including shoes for me to Cedric have nothing of my own please reply Yamsi'

All the Ismay messages from the *Carpathia* to White Star are signed 'Yamsi' (Ismay backwards).

The following day, April 18th, Senator Smith is contacted by the Department of the Navy with the news that they had intercepted several Marconigrams sent by Bruce Ismay. The messages indicate that Ismay and the *Titanic* crew intend to go directly back to England, without setting foot on American soil.

With the *Carpathia* set to arrive in New York that very day, Senator Smith immediately arranges to meet with President William Howard Taft at the White House. The president has just learned that his friend and military advisor Major Archibald Butt was not on the list of survivors. At this meeting Taft and Smith are assured by Attorney General George Wickersham that it is legal for the Senate subcommittee to subpoena British citizens as long as they are in the United States. President Taft then arranges for a naval escort to meet the Carpathia to ensure no one leaves the ship before it docks in New York. Senator Smith convenes the first meeting of the investigative subcommittee that same afternoon. The Ismay messages are discussed and the subcommittee decides that Senator Smith and Senator Francis G. Newlands of Nevada, will go to New York with subpoenas in hand for J. Bruce Ismay and key members of the crew. Accompanying the Senators are: U.S. Steamship Inspector General George Uhler; Smith's private secretary, Bill McKinstry; and to serve the subpoenas, Smith's friend, Sheriff Joe Bayliss of Chippewa County, Michigan (Bayliss being duly deputized as an Assistant Sergeant at Arms of the U.S. Senate).

The men travel by train to New York and arrive in time to meet the *Carpathia* as it docks that evening. Smith and his colleagues board the *Carpathia* and serve their subpoenas on Ismay and the surviving officers and crew. The subpoenas require them to remain in the United States and appear before the U.S. Senate subcommittee.

The hearings open at 10:30 a.m. the following morning, April 19th, at the Waldorf-Astoria Hotel in New York City. The hotel is owned by the estate of recently deceased Colonel John Jacob Astor. The first witness to testify is J. Bruce Ismay.

> **United States Senate Inquiry** – Day 1, partial testimony of J. Bruce Ismay, questioned by Senator Smith.
> Senator Smith – Mr. Ismay, for the purpose of simplifying this hearing, I will ask you a few preliminary questions. First state your full name, please?
> Mr. Ismay – Joseph Bruce Ismay.
> Senator Smith – And your place of residence?
> Mr. Ismay – Liverpool.
> Senator Smith – And your age?

Mr. Ismay – I shall be 50 on the 12th of December.
Senator Smith – And your occupation?
Mr. Ismay – Ship owner.
Senator Smith – Are you an officer of the White Star Line?
Mr. Ismay – I am.
Senator Smith – In what capacity?
Mr. Ismay – Managing Director.
Senator Smith – As such officer, were you officially designated to make the trial trip of the Titanic?
Mr. Ismay – No.
Senator Smith – Were you a voluntary passenger?
Mr. Ismay – A voluntary passenger, yes.
Senator Smith – Where did you board the ship?
Mr. Ismay – At Southampton.
Senator Smith – At what time?
Mr. Ismay – I think it was 9:30 in the morning.
Senator Smith – Of what day?
Mr. Ismay – The 10th of April.
Senator Smith – The port of destination was New York?
Mr. Ismay – New York.
Senator Smith – Will you kindly tell the Committee the circumstances surrounding your voyage, and, as succinctly as possible, beginning with your going aboard the vessel at Liverpool, your place on the ship on the voyage, together with any circumstances you feel would be helpful to us in this inquiry?
Mr. Ismay – In the first place, I would like to express my sincere grief at this deplorable catastrophe.
I understand that you gentlemen have been appointed as a Committee of the Senate to inquire into the circumstances. So far as we are concerned, we welcome it. We court the fullest inquiry. We have nothing to conceal; nothing to hide. The ship was built in Belfast. She was the latest thing in the art of shipbuilding; absolutely no money was spared in her construction. She was not built by contract. She was simply built on a commission.

A week later Senator Smith moves the inquiry to Washington, D.C. where the hearings are the first to be conducted in the new caucus room in the Russell Senate Office Building. The witnesses are asked about ice warnings, the inadequate number of lifeboats, the ship's speed, distress calls, and the evacuation of the ship.

The U.S. Senate inquiry is not popular with the British government and their Board of Trade in part because the inadequate regulation regarding lifeboats is exposed. The inquiry and Senator Smith are also vilified in the British press. The *Daily Express* calls Smith "a backwoodsman from Michigan"; the newspaper then characterizes Michigan as a state "populated by kangaroos and by cowboys with an intimate acquaintance of prairie schooners as the only kind of boat".

The *Chicago Tribune* reports additional attacks from the British press on April 26th.

> "London Papers Attack Smith
>
> "Several more papers severely attack the American inquiry. The Standard says Senator Smith 'is rather less qualified for such a task than any individual picked up in an American street car.'
>
> "The Morning Post says: 'a schoolboy would blush at Senator Smith's ignorance,' and adds, 'Honest Americans will feel with shame that not merely the White Star company but American civilization is on trial.'"

Senator Smith's line of questioning gives the British press plenty of ammunition for their attacks when taken out of context, an example being this question Senator Smith asks Fifth Officer Harold Lowe:

> Senator Smith – Do you know what an iceberg is composed of?
> Mr. Lowe – Ice, I suppose, sir.

Senator Smith, attempting to ascertain the Fifth Officer's knowledge of icebergs, follows up with these questions:

> Senator Smith – Have you ever heard of an iceberg being composed not only of ice but of rock and earth and other substances?
> Mr. Lowe – No, sir; never.
> Senator Smith – Did you hear the testimony of your fellow officer, Boxhall?
> Mr. Lowe – No, sir.
> Senator Smith – You did not hear him describe what composed an iceberg?
> Mr. Lowe – No, sir.
> Senator Smith – But you labor under the impression that they are composed entirely of ice?
> Mr. Lowe – Absolutely, sir.

Much of the British press takes to calling Senator Smith "Watertight Smith" because he asks witnesses if the watertight compartments were created to keep the *Titanic* afloat or were meant to shelter passengers. But there are other, supporting, voices in some British publications. The *Review of Reviews*, declares: "We prefer the ignorance of Senator Smith to the knowledge of Mr. Ismay. Experts have told us the *Titanic* was unsinkable – we prefer ignorance to such knowledge!" The *Review of Reviews* was founded by William Stead who went down with the unsinkable *Titanic*.

A total of 86 witnesses are brought in to testify during the 18 days of the U.S. Senate inquiry into the *Titanic* disaster. The inquiry concludes with Senator Smith visiting *Titanic's* sister ship *Olympic* in port in New York on May 25,

1912. The final report is presented to the United States Senate on May 28, 1912. The report is 19 pages long, includes 44 pages of exhibits, and summarizes 1,145 pages of testimony and affidavits.

The British Wreck Commissioner's Inquiry

The British Government also orders a formal investigation into the *Titanic* disaster and on April 22nd, Sydney Buxton, President of the Board of Trade, requests Lord Chancellor Robert Earl Loreburn to appoint a Wreck Commissioner to investigate. Lord Chancellor chooses Charles Bigham, "Lord Mersey" of Toxteth, President of the Probate, Divorce & Admiralty Division of the High Court, as the Wreck Commissioner for the *Titanic* inquiry.

Appointed as Assessors to assist the Right Hon. Lord Mersey, Wreck Commissioner of the United Kingdom, are these experts in the maritime and naval fields:

- Rear Admiral the Hon. S. A. GOUGH-CALTHORPE, C.V.O., Royal Navy Retired
- Captain A. W. CLARK, Trinity [House] Master in Admiralty Court
- Commander F. C. A. LYON, Royal Navy Retired
- Professor J. H. BILES LL.D., D.Sc., Chair: Naval Architecture at Glasgow
- Mr. E. C. CHASTON, Senior Engineer Assessor, Royal Navy Retired

Many others, representing the interests of the government, shipping unions, and businesses are also included in the proceedings:

- Attorney General, Sir Rufus Isaacs—representing the Board of Trade
- Solicitor General, John Simon—also representing the Board of Trade
- Mr. Thomas Scanlan—representing the Seamen's and Firemen's Union
- Mr. Clement Edwards—representing the dock labourers
- Mr. Robert Finlay—representing White Star Line
- The maritime law firm Hill Dickinson also representing White Star Line.

Other counsels include the prime minister's son Mr. Raymond Asquith, along with Mr. Sidney Rowlatt, and Mr. Edward Maurice Hill. Other organizations with counsel representing or observing on their behalf include the Chamber of Shipping of the United Kingdom, the British Seafarers' Union, the Imperial Merchant Service Guild, the Marine Engineers' Association, the National

Union of Stewards, the ship's builder Harland & Wolff, Allan Line Royal Mail Steamers, Canadian Pacific Railway, and the Leyland Line.

In his capacity as Attorney General, Sir Rufus Isaacs serves as the chief legal adviser to the Crown and government. Sir Isaacs presents the inquiry with a list of 26 key questions to be answered in the course of the investigation. These questions concern the ship's construction, how the *Titanic* had been navigated, and ice warnings received prior to the collision. A question concerning the role played by the *Californian* is added after the inquiry begins.

The British government will have to wait until the Americans are done with Mr. Ismay and the other surviving witnesses before it can start its own inquiry. The formal investigation ordered by the Board of Trade into the loss of the S. S. "TITANIC" opens in the Wreck Commissioner's Court, Scottish Drill Hall, Buckingham Gate, Westminster, on May 2, 1912.

Titanic's builders, Harland & Wolff, provide the inquiry with a 20 foot half-model of the ship showing the starboard side. They also provide a large map showing the North Atlantic shipping lanes and locations of sea ice.

The next two months include 36 days of official investigation with nearly 100 witnesses answering more than 25,000 questions before Wreck Commissioner, Lord Mersey and the various solicitors. Testimony is solicited from *Titanic's* officers and crewmembers, as well as captains and crewmembers of other ships in the vicinity. Expert witnesses, government officials, White Star Line officials, and the ship designers from Harland & Wolff are also called to testify. The only passengers to testify are Sir Cosmo Duff-Gordon and his wife. The Duff-Gordons had been accused of misconduct for their actions in leaving *Titanic* aboard a lifeboat with 40 seats but only 12 passengers. Sir Cosmo's motive for paying the lifeboat crewmembers after they were safely aboard the *Carpathia* is also questioned. The Duff-Gordon's testimony attract the largest crowds of the inquiry with many notable society figures in attendance.

The British Wreck Commissioner's Inquiry – Report on the Loss of the "Titanic." (s.s.) is published on July 30, 1912. The lines of questioning at the inquiry result in a detailed description of the ship, an account of the ship's journey, a description of the damage caused by the iceberg, an account of the evacuation and rescue. There is also a special section devoted to the circumstances of the *Californian*.

A summary of recommendations from the U.S. Senate Inquiry and the British Wreck Commissioner's Inquiry is included in Chapter 28. This will allow the root cause analysis, found in Part Two of this book, to be received by the reader without preconceived assignment of causes.

Part One Epilogue

Survived And Perished

"What a change! A short time ago we were on the 'Titanic,' partaking of the comforts and luxuries provided. I had many opportunities for conversation, and for dwelling on the object of my mission. I noted that, as in the greater world, there was a great gulf fixed between those who possessed wealth, demanding luxuries, and for whom the mighty vessel was designed, and others there who were permitted to travel and serve on the same floating world. When in the 'Titanic's' clutches, there was no gulf. Think of it, and let it burn into your souls. A terrific lesson on equality in the sight of God."

~Partial content of a message received by a medium from the spirit of W. T. Stead at a seance held in Rothsey, England on May 3rd 1912.

There were 2,215 crew and passengers aboard the *Titanic* when she began her maiden voyage across the North Atlantic. Only 712 survived to complete the voyage aboard the *Carpathia*.

Of the 1297 passengers aboard 500 (39%) survived. The 500 surviving passengers included 369 women and children and 131 men.

The crew and staff totaled 918 of which 212 (23%) survived.

The Captain and Officers of the *Titanic*

The Master and Officers were in charge of the ship and all decisions regarding speed and navigation. Although not directly blamed for the tragedy, no surviving officer from the *Titanic* would ever get their own command from White Star Line.

Captain Edward J. Smith – Ship's Master, age 62, perished. Captain Smith was last seen in the bridge area after he gave the final order to abandon ship. There are conflicting reports as to whether or not Smith made any attempt to save himself. His body was not recovered. Captain Smith left a widow and a daughter.

Mr. Henry T. Wilde – Chief Officer, age 38, perished. Wilde was transferred from the *Olympic* and appointed Chief Officer at the last minute causing Murdoch and Lightoller to move down in rank and bumping Second Officer David Blair from the transatlantic voyage. Wilde was last seen trying to free

Collapsible boat B from the roof of the officers' quarters. Wilde's body was not recovered. Wilde left four surviving children and a sister. The family received relief from the mansion house *Titanic* relief fund.

Mr. William T. Murdoch – First Officer, age 39, perished. Murdoch was the officer in charge of the bridge at the time of the collision. Three bells struck and the relayed telephone message, "Iceberg right ahead," triggered Murdoch's "Hard-a-starboard," order and port around attempt. The maneuver he attempted was textbook accurate but resulted in the damage that sunk the unsinkable ship. Unsubstantiated press reports, later portrayed in movies, indicate Murdoch shot himself but surviving witnesses saw him working diligently to the end and some claim to have seen him alive in the water. Murdoch left a widow. His body was not recovered.

Mr. Charles H. Lightoller – Second Officer, age 38, survived. Lightoller was in charge of loading the even-numbered port side lifeboats and strictly enforced the Captain's "women and children" general order. Lightoller survived by reaching the overturned Collapsible B. When lifeboats 4 and 12 eventually rescued survivors from Collapsible B, Lightoller took command of lifeboat 12 and was the last *Titanic* survivor taken aboard the *Carpathia*.

During the Great War that soon followed Lightoller joined the Royal Navy as a Lieutenant. He moved up in rank serving on and commanding various ships and was awarded the Distinguished Service Cross for attacking a zeppelin. Lightoller came out of the Royal Navy as a full Commander in 1918. On his return to White Star Line he was passed over for a position on the *Olympic* and appointed Chief Officer of the *Celtic*. Lightoller, not interested in remaining Chief Officer indefinitely, resigned from White Star Line after 20 plus years of service.

In 1940 the 66 year old Lightoller, with his 52 ft. yacht, *Sundowner*, participated in one of the greatest rescues of all time when he helped evacuate over 338,000 men of the British Expeditionary Force from French port of Dunkirk.

Charles H. Lightoller passed away on December 8, 1952 at the age of 78.

Mr. Herbert "Bert" Pitman – Third Officer, age 34, survived. Pitman left the *Titanic* in charge of lifeboat 5. His boat had room for 29 more people but Pitman was dissuaded from returning to rescue others by the reluctant passengers afraid their boat would be swamped.

Bert Pitman continued to serve with White Star Line and re-joined the *Oceanic* as Third Officer. He later served on the *Olympic* in the Purser's Section because of deteriorating eyesight. He eventually moved from White Star Line to Shaw, Savill and Albion Company Ltd. Pitman married Mildred Kalman in 1922. Pitman served as Purser aboard SS *Mataroa* during World War II before retiring in 1946. He lived out his retirement in Pitcombe, Somerset, passing away on December 7, 1961 at the age of 84.

Mr. Joseph Boxhall – Fourth Officer, age 28, survived. After the collision Boxhall was charged with working out the ship's position so distress calls could be sent out by the Marconi wireless operators. Boxall and two quartermasters then fired rockets in an unsuccessful attempt to contact a distant steamer. Captain Smith ordered Boxall to leave in charge of lifeboat 2, the emergency cutter on the port side. The boat, with a capacity of 40, only carried 17 but did not attempt to pick up survivors from the water. Boat 2 was the first boat picked up by the *Carpathia*.

After the disaster Boxhall suffered from pleurisy caused or exacerbated by exposure in the lifeboat. He returned to England and joined the *Adriatic* as Fourth Officer. During World War 1 he served on cruisers, a torpedo boat, and a shore base. After the war he was promoted to the rank of Lieutenant Commander. In May, 1919 Boxhall returned to the merchant service with White Star Line. Following the White Star-Cunard merger, he served as First and later Chief Officer of several ships but never received his own command. Boxhall retired in 1940.

Boxall served as technical advisor to the 1958 film "A Night to Remember" and was involved in the promotion of the film. Boxhall's health deteriorated sharply in the 1960s and he died on April 25, 1967, at 83. He was the last of the *Titanic's* surviving officers to pass away. According to his wishes, his cremated remains were scattered over the spot the *Titanic* had gone down - the very position he had calculated.

Mr. Harold G. Lowe – Fifth Officer, age 29, survived. *Titanic's* maiden voyage was Lowe's first trip across the North Atlantic. Lowe left the *Titanic* in charge of lifeboat 14 and, fearing his boat was already full and wouldn't take a sudden jolt, fired his pistol in the air to dissuade passengers from jumping aboard the lowering lifeboat. Later Lowe tied several lifeboats together and transferred survivors to free up space in his boat. Lowe and several seamen returned to pick up survivors from the water but were only able to save three. He then rescued 12 survivors from the swamped Collapsible A.

Harold Lowe never achieved a command in the merchant service but he did make commander in the Royal Naval Reserve during the first World War. He eventually retired to his home in North Wales with his wife Marion where he died on May 12, 1944 at the age of 61.

Mr. James Moody – Sixth Officer, age 24, perished. Moody answered the bridge telephone and relayed Lookout Fleet's message, "Iceberg right ahead," to First Officer Murdoch. Moody was last seen attempting to launch the remaining collapsible lifeboats. His actions were poignantly recalled by Geoffrey Marcus in *The Maiden Voyage*.

> "Wilde's efforts to avert panic, maintain order and discipline, and get the last of the boats loaded and lowered to the water were valiantly supported by the youngest of the officers, James Moody. Long before this, the latter should by rights have gone away in one of the boats along with the other junior officers. But the seamen left on board were all too few as it was for the work that had to be done. Moody therefore

stayed with the ship to the end and was the means of saving many a life that would otherwise have been lost."

James Moody's body was not recovered.

The Deck Crew

The 60 member Deck Crew ran the ship according to the officers' orders and many were ordered to command or crew the lifeboats. 68% survived.

- Able Officer Mr. James Callahan with rank over all crew except the officers – perished.
- 31 Able Bodied Seamen – 22 survived, nine perished.
- Two Boatswains – one survived, one perished.
- Master-at-Arms – survived,
- Assistant Master-at-Arms – perished.
- Seven Quartermasters – all survived.
- Two Window Cleaners – one survived, one perished.
- Two Lamp Trimmers – both survived.
- Two Carpenter/Joiners – both perished.
- Surgeon and Assistant Surgeon – both perished.
- Six Lookouts – all survived including the Lookouts who first spotted the iceberg.

Mr. Frederick Fleet – Lookout, age 24 , survived. Fleet spotted the iceberg from the crow's nest, struck three bells and phoned the bridge to report, "Iceberg right ahead." He survived helping crew Lifeboat 6.

Fleet served in the merchant service in World War I then served on *Titanic's* sister ship *Olympic* from 1920 to 1935. After being unemployed, he again joined the merchant service during World War II.

Fleet's wife died in December 1964 and he committed suicide two weeks later. He was buried in an unmarked grave at Hollybrook Cemetery, Southampton, until a headstone was erected by The Titanic Historical Society.

Mr. Reginald Lee – Lookout, age 41, survived. Lee was on duty with Fleet when the iceberg was spotted. Lee was ordered to man Lifeboat 13. Reginald Lee was the first surviving crew member to die when he succumbed to pneumonia on August 6, 1913 at the age of 43.

The Engineering Crew

The Engineering Crew operated the ship's boilers, engines, and other equipment below deck. 22% survived.

The 25 Engineers along with 10 electricians and boilermakers, responsible for keeping the engines, generators, and other mechanical equipment running, all perished. They remained below deck in the engine and boiler rooms attempting to keep the ship afloat by operating the pumps in the forward compartments. They also kept the generators running to provide power and lights up until minutes before the *Titanic* sank. Their actions and sacrifice may have delayed the sinking for over an hour and saved many lives.

The Engineering Crew also included:
- 13 Stoker Foremen – three survived, 10 perished.
- 163 firemen (Stokers) – 45 survived, 118 perished.
- 73 Coal Trimmers – 20 survived, 53 perished.
- 33 Greasers – four survived, 29 perished.
- Six Mess Hall Stewards – one survived, five perished.

The Memorial to the Engine Room Heroes of the *Titanic* in Liverpool honors the engineers, firemen, trimmers, and greasers who lost their lives.

The Victualling Crew

The Victualling Crew provided food service and took care of other needs for all three passenger classes. 19% survived.
- Two Pursers supervised the victualling staff—both perished.
- Four Clerks worked in the Purser's Office—all perished.
- 322 Stewards were responsible for multiple functions in each passenger class—only around 60 Stewards survived.
- There were 21 female crew on board including 20 stewardesses and one matron—20 survived.
- 62 Galley and Kitchen staff included chefs, cooks, bakers, butchers, and scullions (dishwashers)—13 survived including Chief Baker Charles Joughin.

Mr. Charles Joughin – Joughin survived for two and half hours in the freezing cold water after the *Titanic* went down. It was suggested at the British inquiry that multiple trips to his cabin to drink liquor that night provided a level of alcohol in his bloodstream that saved his life. Joughin later worked on the *SS Oregon* and was on board when it sank in the Boston Harbor. He also served on ships operated by the American Export Lines, as well as on World War II troop transports. Joughin died in Paterson, New Jersey on December 9, 1956 leaving a daughter and stepdaughter.

Builder's Guarantee Group

Mr. Thomas Andrews – Andrews, 39, was the chief naval architect and managing director of the design department at Harland & Wolff. *Titanic* was the first ship for which Andrews was responsible from start to finish. He was aboard as the leader of the nine-member Guarantee Group responsible for overseeing any unfinished work and fixing any problems that might arise during the voyage.

During *Titanic's* last hours, while the ship he built was sinking from under him on her maiden voyage, Andrews encouraged passengers to wear their lifebelts and to make their way to the lifeboats. Near the end Andrews was seen staring at a painting in the First Class Smoking Room without his lifebelt on. Another account has him throwing deck chairs into the water. Thomas Andrews and all members of the Guarantee Group perished. Andrews body was not recovered.

The Marconi Wireless Operators

The two Wireless Telegraphy Operators were employed by the Marconi Company and manned the wireless around the clock sending and receiving wireless messages for the passengers and crew.

Mr. John George "Jack" Phillips – Senior Marconi Wireless Operator, age 25, perished. Phillips continued to send out distress calls until the wireless room flooded and the equipment shutdown. He made it to the overturned Collapsible B but died prior to rescue.

Mr. Harold Sydney Bride – Junior Marconi Wireless Operator, age 22, survived. Bride relayed messages between Captain Smith and Jack Phillips and also remained on duty until no more could be done. He also reached Collapsible B but suffered from frozen and crushed feet due to the position he was sitting on the collapsible hull. After a spell in hospital Bride returned to England and eventually returned to work as a wireless operator. During World War One he served on the steamer *Mona's Isle* as a telegraphist. Bride married Lucy Johnstone Downie, and the couple had three children. Bride did not often discuss the *Titanic* disaster, being deeply disturbed by the experience and by the loss of his friend and colleague Jack Phillips. He wanted nothing to do with the celebrity that went along with being a *Titanic* survivor and moved his family to Scotland to escape the attention. Harold Bride worked there as a travelling salesman and lived out the rest of his live in relative obscurity. He died on April 29, 1956, at the age of 66.

The Postal Clerks

As the *Titanic* sank, the five Postal Clerks worked to bring some 200 sacks of registered mail up to a higher deck.

British Postal Clerks John Richard Jago Smith, 35, and James Bertram Williamson, also 35, both perished. Neither body was recovered. On May 5, 1912 a service was held at St. Peters Church in Southampton in memory of the men who had worked unfailingly in their duty right up to the time the ship sank. The service was attended by all the ranks of the Southampton postal staff.

American Postal Clerks John Starr March, Oscar Scott Woody, and William Logan Gwinn also died in the sinking.

After his wife died while he was at sea in 1911, John March's adult daughters tried to convince him to take a safer assignment. He assured them that he would never be lost at sea. His body was recovered by the *Mackay-Bennett*. March was buried at Evergreen Cemetery, Hillside, New Jersey.

Oscar Woody turned 44 on April 15, 1912, the day he died. His body was also recovered by the *Mackay-Bennett*. He was buried at sea.

William Gwinn's body was not recovered.

From the Sunday April 21, 1912 edition of the *New York Times* (partial content):

> "WASHINGTON, April 20—Postmaster General Hitchcock to-day addressed a communication to Chairman John A. Moon of the Postal Committee of the House of Representatives, recommending that a provision be inserted in the pending Post Office Appropriation bill authorizing the payment of $2,000, the maximum amount prescribed by law for payment to the representatives of railway postal clerks killed while on duty, to the families of each of the three American sea post clerks who lost their lives on the *Titanic*.
>
> "'The bravery exhibited by these men,' Mr. Hitchcock said, 'in their efforts to safeguard under such trying conditions the valuable mail intrusted to them should be a source of pride to the entire Postal Service, and deserves some marked expression of appreciation from the Government.'"

The Orchestra

The eight members of the orchestra were employed by the Liverpool firm, C.W. and F.N. Black who contracted with all of the major lines to provide musicians. Members of the orchestra played on the deck of the sinking ship until the very end. All the members of the orchestra perished.

Mr. W. Theodore Ronald Brailey, 24, Pianist, from London. Brailey, the son of well-known medium Mr. Ronald Brailey, is later said to have spoke through a medium at a London seance confirming spiritualist William Stead's afterlife assertion that he had requested the band play "Nearer, My God, To Thee." Brailey's body was not recovered.

The bodies of these members of the orchestra were not recovered:

Mr. Roger Marie Bricoux, 20, Cellist, from Lille, France.

Mr. John Frederick Preston Clarke, Bass Violist, 30, from Liverpool.

Mr. Georges Alexandre Krins, 23, Violinist, from Paris living in London.

Mr. Percy Cornelius Taylor, 32, Cellist, resided in London.

Mr. John Wesley Woodward, 32, Cellist, from Oxfordshire, England.

The bodies of Bandmaster Hartley and Violinist Hume were recovered.

Bandmaster Wallace H. Hartley – Hartley, 33, lead the orchestra and chose the requested "Nearer, My God, To Thee" as their final number.

Hartley's body was recovered by the *Mackay-Bennett*. On May 4, 1912 Hartley's body was transferred from Halifax to Boston for its return to Liverpool on-board the *Arabic*. From Liverpool the body was taken to its final resting place, Hartley's boyhood hometown of Colne, Lancashire.

Mr. John "Jock" Law Hume – Hume, 21, was a Violinist in the orchestra. His body was also recovered by the *Mackay-Bennett*. Hume was buried at the Fairview Cemetery, Halifax, Nova Scotia.

The C.W. and F.N. Black firm still had a business to run and two weeks after the *Titanic* disaster claimed 1503 lives including that of 21 year old Jock Hume, his father received this note from their firm:

> Dear Sir:
> We shall be obliged if you will remit us the sum of 5s. 4d., which is owing to us as per enclosed statement. We shall also be obliged if you will settle the enclosed uniform account.
>
> Yours faithfully,
> C.W. & F.N. Black

The uniform account included two shillings for the lyre lapel insignia, and one shilling for sewing White Star buttons on the tunic. The total bill was 14 shillings and seven pence.

First Class À la Carte Restaurant Staff

Only one male clerk and two female cashiers survived from a staff of 68 employees who operated the First Class À la Carte Restaurant. Unconfirmed reports indicated that the restaurant employees, most Italian or French nationals, were locked in their quarters to prevent them from rushing the lifeboats.

The restaurant was a private concession managed by Italian businessman A.P. Luigi Gatti, who also perished. The *Minia* recovered Gatti's body and he was buried in Fairview Cemetery, Halifax, Nova Scotia.

First Class Passengers

J. Bruce Ismay – Ismay, President and Managing Director of International Mercantile Marine owner of White Star Line, traveled as a First Class passenger aboard the *Titanic*. Ismay, who had complete control of the design and equipment decisions during the construction of the *Titanic*, helped load and launch several of the lifeboats following the collision. With full knowledge that the ship would sink and the lifeboat capacity was grossly inadequate, Bruce Ismay chose to take a spot in the last starboard lifeboat while it was being lowered away with space available.

Some believed Ismay owed his life in exchange for the decisions made concerning the number of lifeboats the *Titanic* would carry.

British Wreck Commissioner's Inquiry – Testimony of Bruce Ismay, examined by Mr. Clement Edwards.

18848. You were one of those, as the managing Director, responsible for determining the number of boats?

Ismay – Yes, in conjunction with the shipbuilders.

18849. When you got into the boat you thought that the "Titanic" was sinking?

Ismay – I did.

18850. Did you know that there were some hundreds of people on that ship?

Ismay – Yes.

18851. Who must go down with her?

Ismay – Yes, I did.

18852. Has it occurred to you that, except perhaps apart from the Captain, you, as the responsible managing Director, deciding the number of boats, owed your life to every other person on that ship?

Ismay – It has not.

…The Commissioner: Your point, Mr. Edwards, as I understand is this: That, having regard to his position, it was his duty to remain upon that ship until she went to the bottom. That is your point?

Mr. Edwards: Yes, and inasmuch—

The Commissioner: That is your point?

18867. (Mr. Clement Edwards.) Frankly, that is so; I do not flinch from it a little bit. But I want to get it from this Witness, inasmuch as he took upon himself to give certain directions at a certain time, why he did not discharge the responsibility even after that, having regard to other persons or passengers?

Ismay – There were no more passengers to get into that boat. The boat was actually being lowered away.

18868. That is your answer?

Ismay – Yes.

Ismay was unfairly vilified in the U.S. press for escaping the sinking ship, his ship, while fellow passengers perished. This incriminating but untrue item appeared in the *New York Times* on Friday April 19, 1912.

"SAYS ISMAY TOOK FIRST BOAT

"Titanic Fireman Declares He Got in 'with Millionaires'

"Harry Senior, a fireman on the *Titanic*, said last night:

'I was in my bunk when I felt a bump. One man said. "Hello, she has been struck." I went on deck and saw a great pile of ice on the well deck below the forecastle, but we all thought the ship would last some time, and we went back to our bunks. Then one of the firemen came running down and yelled, "All muster for the lifeboats!" I ran on deck, and the Captain said, "All firemen keep down on the well deck. If a man comes up I'll shoot him."

'Then I saw the first boat lowered. Thirteen people were on board, eleven men and two women. Three were millionaires and one was Ismay.'"

The millionaires lifeboat from the Times story may have been the starboard emergency clipper with Sir Cosmo and Lady Lucile Duff-Gordon and only 10 others (but not Ismay) aboard.

J. Bruce Ismay donated $50,000 to the pension fund for widows of seamen on the *Titanic* shortly after the disaster. In 1924 he inaugurated the National Mercantile Marine fund with a gift of $125,000. Ismay was the first witness called to testify before the United States Senate's inquiry but did not make any further public statements about the *Titanic* or his conduct following his testimony before the Senate committee and Lord Mersey's Board of Trade investigation. The British Inquiry exonerated Ismay but, because he survived, history continues to judge him harshly.

Joseph Bruce Ismay died in 1937 at the age of 74.

No Lifeboat for Millionaires

There was no lifeboat for the millionaires but there could have been. Colonel John Jacob Astor IV, the richest man in the world, and some of the richest men to call Pennsylvania home, could afford the luxuries of a First Class voyage but seats on a port side lifeboat weren't for sale. Second Officer Charles Lightoller held firm, allowing women and children *only* to board lifeboat 4, one of the last large boats to leave the *Titanic*. The men could only watch as the lifeboat was lowered away with their wives and children and 36 empty seats.

Colonel and Mrs. John Jacob Astor IV – Colonel John Jacob Astor IV, 47, perished. Mrs. Astor (Madeleine Force), 18, survived. After helping his pregnant 18 year old wife into lifeboat 4, Colonel Astor was refused entry to the boat by Second Officer Lightoller. Only Collapsible boats C and D would be launched by the crew after lifeboat 4. At some point as he watched the crew filling these boats Colonel John Jacob Astor IV, the richest man on the *Titanic*, must have realized that his money would do nothing to help him survive the disaster.

Astor's body was recovered on Monday April 22nd by the *Mackay-Bennett* and was delivered to New York City on May 1st. He was buried at Trinity Cemetery, New York.

Madeleine's inheritance included the income from a five-million-dollar trust fund and the use of the Astor homes on Fifth Avenue and in Newport as long as she did not remarry. She gave birth to a son in August 1912 and named him John Jacob Astor.

During World War One Madeleine relinquished all claims to the Astor fortune when she married William K. Dick. They had two sons before divorcing in 1933. Madeleine later married prize-fighter Enzo Fiermonte but they too divorced in 1938 and she took back the surname Dick. She died in Palm Beach, Florida in 1940 at the age of 47.

Mr. and Mrs. Arthur Larned Ryerson – Arthur Ryerson, 61, perished. After Ryerson's family and Mrs. Ryerson's maid, Victorine Chaudanson, are safely aboard lifeboat 4, Second Officer Lightoller attempted to remove Ryerson's 13 year old son John. The elder Ryerson persuaded Lightoller to allow his son to remain in the lifeboat with the rest of his family. Young John was apparently very near Lightoller's limit for a child allowed to survive versus a man allocated to go down with the ship. Arthur Ryerson's body was not recovered.

Mr. and Mrs. William Ernest Carter – William Carter and his wife Lucile, both 36, survived as did their children. After seeing his wife and children into lifeboat 4 Carter suggested it was time for the Pennsylvania men to find their own boat. The others declined but Carter succeeded when he joined Bruce Ismay taking a spot in collapsible lifeboat C as it was being lowered away with a few vacant seats. Mr. Carter's manservant Alexander Cairns, and his chauffeur, Charles Aldworth both perished.

The Carter's were divorced in 1914. Lucile Carter later married steel executive George Brooke. Lucile Brooke died on October 26, 1934 at the age of 59. William Carter died on March 20, 1940 in Florida at the age of 64.

Mr. and Mrs. John Borland Thayer – John Thayer, 49, Second Vice-President of the Pennsylvania Railroad, perished. His body was not recovered.

Marian Thayer and her maid, Margaret Fleming, survived in lifeboat 4. Their son Jack survived after jumping in the sea and reaching Collapsible B.

Marian Thayer never remarried. She lived in Haverford, Pennsylvania until her death on April 14, 1944, the 32nd anniversary of the collision.

Jack Thayer attended the the University of Pennsylvania and went into banking. He married and he and his wife had two sons. Jack produced a pamphlet relating his experiences on the *Titanic* in 1940. In 1945, at the age of 50, Jack took his own life after losing his son Edward in WWII. He was laid to rest at the Church of the Redeemer Cemetery, Bryn Mawr, Pennsylvania.

Mr. and Mrs. George Dunton Widener – George Widener, 50, and his son Harry, 27, both perished. Eleanor Widener survived. George and Harry helped Eleanor and her maid into lifeboat 4 then watched along with Colonel Astor, John Thayer, Arthur Ryerson, and William Carter while the boat saving their wives and children was lowered to the sea with room for many more. The bodies of George and Harry Widener were not recovered.

Eleanor Widener donated $2,000,000 for the construction of the Harry Elkins Widener Memorial Library at Harvard which would house her son's extensive collection of books. Mrs. Widener stipulated that no brick, stone, or piece of mortar could be changed while the library stands and also requested that each Harvard graduate pass a swimming test in support of her belief that Harry might have been saved had he been able to swim.

In 1915 Mrs. Widener married Dr. Alexander Hamilton Rice of New York, NY. Rice was an explorer and Eleanor would accompany him on expeditions in South America. The couple also travelled extensively in Europe and India. Eleanor died in Paris in July 1937 at the age of 75.

Other First Class Passengers

Of the 319 First Class passengers aboard, 200 (63%) survived but other rich, famous, and prominent First Class passengers suffered the same fate as the men not allowed to join their families in lifeboat 4.

Mr. and Mrs. Lucian P. Smith – Lucian Smith, 24, perished. His body was not recovered. Lucian and his eighteen-year-old bride, Eloise (Hughes) Smith, were returning to their West Virginia home following their honeymoon. Eloise was saved when Lucian convinced her to board port side lifeboat 6.

Eloise (Hughes) Smith was one of three First Class brides returning from honeymoons with child; the others being Madeleine Astor and Helen Bishop whose husband survived.

Aboard the *Carpathia* Eloise met and was consoled by Robert W. Daniel, 27, a Philadelphia banker. Daniel was returning home on the *Titanic* with his newly acquired French bulldog. He survived taking a spot in lifeboat 3 – his bulldog perished. A romance aboard the *Carpathia* was rumored and it was reported that after the *Carpathia* landed Robert carried Eloise off and delivered her into the waiting arms of her father, Representative James Hughes of West Virginia.

Members of Eloise's family used to say that she was probably the only woman in the world who made her debut, got engaged, married, became a widow, and then a mother in just a year's time. Lucian P. Smith, Jr., was born on November 29, 1912. Madeleine Astor was among those sending congratulatory telegrams.

Eloise stayed in touch with Robert Daniel and the *Titanic* survivors were secretly married on August 18, 1914 in a ceremony in New York's Church of the Transfiguration. They did not announce the marriage for two months so that they could honeymoon in London and Robert could attend to pressing business matters there. The marriage of the *Titanic* survivors lasted nine years before the couple divorced in 1923. That same year Eloise married Capt. Lewis H. Cort, a World War One veteran from a wealthy family. The Captain died of war-related injuries in 1927, at the age of 36.

Two years later Eloise married her fourth husband, C.S. Wright, a state auditor of West Virginia. She started using her married name of Smith, the name of her only child, after this marriage also ended in divorce.

Eloise Smith was active in the Republican Party and campaigned for candidates in several West Virginia elections. Being a *Titanic* survivor, the daughter of prominent U.S. Congressman, and a talented speaker, Eloise was in great demand as a public speaker. She used this popularity to campaign for women's right to vote prior to the enactment of the 19th Amendment in 1920.

Eloise (Hughes) Smith died of a heart attack in May, 1940 at the age of 46. Her fellow *Titanic* survivor and ex-husband, Robert W. Daniel, died in December of the same year.

Mr. and Mrs. Charles M. Hays – Hays, 55, General Manager of the Grand Trunk Pacific Railway, with his wife Clara, their daughter Orian, and her husband Thornton Davidson were returning to their home in Montreal as guests of Bruce Ismay. After seeing Clara, her maid Anne Perreault, and daughter Orian into lifeboat 3, Charles Hays and his son-in-law chose not to take any of the 33 remaining spaces in the lifeboat at a time when men were being allowed in the starboard lifeboats. Charles Hays and Thornton Davidson both perished. Davidson's body was not recovered but the *Minia* recovered the body of Charles Hays.

His coffin was transported aboard his private railway car to Montreal, Canada, where simultaneous funerals were held on May 8th at the American Presbyterian Church in Montreal and at the Church of St. Edmund King and Martyr in London.

Mr. and Mrs. Isidor Straus – Isidor Straus, 67, and his wife Ida both perished after Ida steadfastly refused to get in a lifeboat if it meant leaving behind her husband of 40 years. Ida's newly employed maid Ms. Ellen Bird survived in lifeboat 8, the same boat Ida refused to enter.

Mrs. Straus' body was not recovered but the body of Isidor Straus was recovered by the *Mackay-Bennett*. An estimated 40,000 people gathered for the couple's memorial service in New York City. Eulogies included one by William J. Gaynor, Mayor of the City of New York and by Andrew Carnegie. Two years later the Straus Square on Broadway and 107th Street was established.

A memorial plaque on the main floor of Macy's Department Store in Manhattan reads:

IDA STRAUS ... ISIDOR STRAUS
BORN FEB. 6. 1849 ... BORN FEB. 6. 1845.
DIED. APRIL. 15. 1912
"THEIR LIVES WERE BEAUTIFUL AND THEIR DEATHS GLORIOUS."
THIS TABLET IS THE VOLUNTARY TOKEN OF SORROWING EMPLOYEES.

Mr. William Thomas Stead – William Stead, 62, perished. Stead was a well known journalist, author, spiritualist, and peace activist. He was traveling to America to participate in a peace congress at Carnegie Hall at the request of President William Howard Taft.

Excerpt from, "William T. Stead" by Albert Shaw, published in *The American Review of Reviews*, June 1912)

"In private life Mr. Stead was always a man of the utmost simplicity. He was generous to everyone who seemed to be in distress, and his kindness was lavished in particular upon those who deserved it so little that nobody else would help them. For, as he always reasoned, deserving cases could usually find help and relief, while the really needy were the others. He was like an elder brother to his sons and daughters, and a delightful companion and loyal friend to those who had come into the circle of his life. He had always been a believer in extending to women every legal and political responsibility, as well as every right, that had been granted to men.

"His great interest in psychic research and 'occultism,' so called, is well known. Many of his friends had deplored his activities as a spiritualist, and doubtless in certain circles his influence was diminished by his editing, for some years, a periodical called Borderland and his publishing what he regarded as communications from the spirit world. As for those of us who have not given much study to these matters, and who are not influenced by the things which brought absolute conviction to Mr. Stead's mind, it is at least permissible to be tolerant and to admit that some of our fellow men may be gifted with natures more sensitive than ours and more perfectly attuned to things not of this world."

Stead's occultism and psychic beliefs led to several alleged reports of contact at seances and through mediums including his daughter Estelle. Estelle W. Stead would later publish *When We Speak With The Dead* and become the director of Stead's forum of psychics called "Julia's Bureau."

William Stead's body was not recovered but a symposium published in 1913 asked the question with its title, *Has W.T. Stead Returned?* In purporting to answer this question the book's introduction includes:

"To the bulk of mankind W. T. Stead is dead. Nevertheless, 'he was the last person who would admit he was dead, and would object'—as the Rev. Herbert Stead said at the Memorial Meeting held in Queen's Hall, June 26th— 'to be spoken of as dead, for he is not dead but alive, more fully alive than ever.' A statement which was greeted with a hearty round of applause."

Major Archibald W. Butt – Major Archibald "Archie" Butt, age 46, perished. Major Butt was a military aide to President William Howard Taft and was traveling back to Washington with his longtime friend the artist Francis Millet who also perished. Major Butt's body was not recovered. President Taft gave the eulogy for his friend, Major Butt, at his memorial service. The Millet-Butt Memorial Fountain was erected to their memory near the White House on the Ellipse in the President's Park and dedicated in October, 1913.

Miss Marie Grice Young was rescued in lifeboat 8 and while on board the *Carpathia* she started an account of the sinking which was later published in the National Magazine. Rumors, bolstered by newspaper stories, circulated that Miss Young had conversed with Major Butt during the sinking. This story appeared in the *Cleveland Plain Dealer* on Saturday, April 20, 1912:

"Butt A Courtier to Death, Says Woman

"Washington, April 19—A graphic story of the heroism of Maj. Archibald W. Butt on the *Titanic* was told today in an interview given by Miss Marie Young, a former resident of Washington. Miss Young is believed to have been the last woman to leave the *Titanic* and the last of the survivors to have talked with the president's military aid. She and Maj. Butt long had been friends, Miss Young having been assistant music instructor to the children of former President Roosevelt. Miss Young said:

'The last person to whom I spoke on board the *Titanic* was Archie Butt, and his good, brave face, smiling at me from the deck of the steamer was the last I could distinguish as the boat I was in pulled away from the steamer's side.

'Archie put me into the boat, wrapped blankets around me, and tucked me in as carefully as if we were starting for a motor ride. He entered the boat with me, performing the little courtesies as calmly and with as smiling a face as if death was far away, instead of being but a few moments removed from him.

'When he had carefully wrapped me up, he stepped upon the gunwhale of the boat and lifting his hat smiled down at me.

'"Goodbye, Miss Young," he said, bravely and smilingly. "Luck is with you. Will you kindly remember me to the folks back home?"

'Then he stepped to the deck of the steamer and the boat I was in was lowered to the water. It was the last boat to leave the ship; of this I am certain. And I know that I am the last of those who were saved to whom Archie Butt spoke.

'As our boat was lowered and left the side of the steamer, Archie was still standing at the rail, looking down at me. His hat was raised and the same old, genial, brave smile was on his face. The picture he made as he stood there, hat in hand, brave and smiling, is one that will always linger in my memory.'"

Later Miss Young wrote to President Taft to set the record straight:

Briarcliff Lodge,
Briarcliff Manor,
New York.
May 10, 1912

President William H. Taft

Dear Mr. President:
I have read an account of the Memorial Service held in Washington recently in honor of Major Archibald Butt, at which service the Secretary of War alluded to a farewell conversation supposed to have taken place between Major Butt and myself. Had such a conversation taken place I should not have delayed one hour in giving you every detail of the last hours of your special Aide & friend.

Although a Washingtonian I did not know Major Butt, having been in deep mourning for several years. The alleged "interview" is entirely an invention, by some officious reporter; who thereby brought much distress to many of Major Butt's near relatives and friends…for when they wrote me of what a comfort the story was to them, I had to tell them it was untrue, as no such deception could be carried through.

They wrote me that through Mrs. Sloan's kindness, they obtained my address…and I immediately wrote Mrs. Sloan that there was no truth in this newspaper story.

When I last saw Major Butt, he was walking on deck, with Mr. Clarence Moore, on Sunday afternoon.

With deep regret that I could not be his messenger to you,
Believe me,
Very sincerely yours
(Miss) Marie G. Young

Mr. Francis Davis Millet – Artist, 65, perished. Millet was returning to Washington with his friend Major Archibald Butt. Millet's body was recovered by the *Mackay-Bennett*. His body was sent on to Boston and he was buried at East Bridgwater Central Cemetery. The Millet-Butt Memorial Fountain was erected to his and Major Butts memory on the Ellipse in the President's Park near the White House in October, 1913.

Mr. Clarence Bloomfield Moore – Banker and sportsman, 47, perished. His body was not recovered. Moore was returning home to Washington with friends Major Butt and Frank Millet.

From the *New York Times*, Tuesday April 16, 1912 edition (partial content):

"WASHINGTON, April 15—Clarence Moore of 1748 Massachusetts Avenue, a passenger on the *Titanic*, is one of the best-known sportsmen in America. He is Master of Hounds of the Chevy Chase Hunt, and on his visit to England from which he is returning he is said to have purchased twenty-five brace of hounds from the best packs in the north of England. His present wife is Miss Mabelle Swift, daughter of the late E. C. Swift of Chicago. She said to-day that her husband's trip abroad had been for pleasure.

"Mr. Moore is a member of the New York Yacht Club and the Travelers' Club of Paris, besides the Metropolitan, the Chevy Chase, and the Alibi Clubs of Washington. Socially he is one of the best-known men in Washington."

Mr. Benjamin Guggenheim – Industrialist, 46, perished. His body was not recovered. Guggenheim was returning home from a three month business trip with his valet, Mr. Victor Giglio, who also perished. Guggenheim was also accompanied by his French mistress, Mme. Léontine Pauline Aubart.

First Class Bedroom Steward James Etches who survived in lifeboat 5, the second boat launched, had a message from Benjamin Guggenheim for his wife and, as it turned out, the readers of the *New York Times*.

Partial content of *New York Times* article published April 20, 1912:

"James Etches, assistant steward in the first cabin of the *Titanic*, appeared at the St. Regis Hotel early yesterday morning and inquired for Mrs. Benjamin Guggenheim. He said that he had a message from Benjamin Guggenheim, one of the victims of the sea disaster. He said that it had to be delivered in person.

"Mrs. Guggenheim was in the care of Daniel Guggenheim whose apartments are at the St. Regis. The steward was admitted, but was not permitted to see Mrs. Guggenheim, who is prostrated with grief. He insisted that he must see her personally, but finally consented to transmit the message through her brother-in-law.

"'We were together almost to the end,' said the steward. 'I was saved. He went down with the ship. But that isn't what I want to tell Mrs. Guggenheim.'

"Then the steward produced a piece of paper. He had written the message on it, he said, to be certain that it would be correct. This was the brief message: 'If anything should happen to me, tell my wife in New York that I've done my best in doing my duty.'

"'That's all he said,' added the steward. 'There wasn't time for more.'

"Little by little Mr. Guggenheim got the whole story of his brother's death from the steward. It was the first definite news that he had received from his brother.

"'Mr. Guggenheim was one of my charges,' said the steward anew. 'He had his secretary with him. His name was Giglio, I believe, an Armenian, about 24 years old. Both died like soldiers.

"'When the crash came I awakened them and told them to get dressed. A few minutes later I went into their rooms and helped them to get ready. I put a life preserver on Mr. Guggenheim. He said it hurt him in the back. There was plenty of time and I took it off, adjusted it and then put it on him again. It was all right this time.

"'They wanted to go out on deck with only a few clothes on, but I pulled a heavy sweater over Mr. Guggenheim's lifebelt, and then they both went out. They stayed together, and I could see what they were doing. They were going from one lifeboat to another, helping the women and children. Mr. Guggenheim would shout out. "Women first," and he was of great assistance to the officers.

"'Things weren't so bad at first, but when I saw Mr. Guggenheim about three-quarters of an hour after the crash there was great excitement. What surprised me was that both Mr. Guggenheim and his secretary were dressed in their evening clothes. They had deliberately taken off their sweaters, and as nearly as I can remember they wore no lifebelts at all.

"'What's that for?' I asked.

"'We've dressed up in our best,' replied Mr. Guggenheim, 'and are prepared to go down like gentlemen.' 'It was then that he told me about the message to his wife, and that is what I have come here for.'"

Mr. James Clinch Smith – Smith, 56, perished. One of Smith's oldest friends, Colonel Archibald Gracie, was also on the voyage. Together Smith and Gracie worked to assist the crew with loading the lifeboats with women and children and were among those attempting to free the last collapsible when the bridge went under. Clinch Smith disappeared with the waves. His body was not recovered.

On May 11, 1912 a memorial service was held for Smith at St. James Episcopal Church, St. James, Long Island. Smith's wife Bertha never recovered from the loss of her husband and survived him by a little more than a year. There is a memorial stone in memory of Bertha and James Clinch Smith in the St. James Episcopal Church.

Colonel Archibald Gracie – Archibald Gracie IV, 54, survived. Gracie was able to reach the overturned Collapsible B after being swept off the *Titanic* as she sank. Colonel Gracie wrote *The Truth About The Titanic*, published in 1913 after his death on December 4, 1912. Gracie was the third *Titanic* survivor to die.

On Thursday, December 5, 1912 the *New York Times* published this story (partial content):

"Haunted by his memories of the wreck of the *Titanic* and never completely recovered from the shock of his experiences in that disaster, Col. Archibald Gracie, U. S. A., retired, died yesterday morning at his apartment at the Hotel St. Louis, in East Thirty-second Street. Death was immediately due to a complication of diseases, but the members of his family and his physicians felt that the real cause was the shock he suffered last April when he went down with the ship and was rescued later after long hours on a half-submerged raft.

"After the *Carpathia* had brought the *Titanic* survivors to New York Col. Gracie did nothing to banish the tragedy from his thoughts. On the contrary, he spent the succeeding months in correspondence with other survivors, gathering data for his book, 'The Truth About the *Titanic*.' The events of the night of the wreck were constantly on his mind. The manuscript of his work on the subject had finally been completed and sent to the printers when his last illness came. In his last hours the memories of the disaster did not leave him. Rather they crowded thicker, and he was heard to say, 'We must get them into the boats. We must get them all into the boats.'"

Major Arthur Godfrey Peuchen – Peuchen survived in lifeboat 6 after volunteering to join the boat as it was being lowered with only Quartermaster Hichens and one seaman (Lookout Frederick Fleet) on board. Peuchen, a Vice Commodore of the Royal Canadian Yacht Club, is allowed in the boat by

Second Officer Lightoller if he was sailor enough to shimmy down a rope into the boat. He was. He was also the only adult male passenger Lightoller allowed into a lifeboat that night.

Major Peuchen, a military officer, was criticized for not asserting himself into a leadership role with the questionable behavior of Quartermaster Hichens, instead choosing not to second guess the decisions and orders of the man in charge.

Back home in Toronto, Peuchen, like many of the men who survived, had to defend his reputation against accusations of cowardice. One common insult about the circumstances that put him in a lifeboat was that he was a yachtsman so he could get off the *Titanic*, and if there had been a fire, he would have been a fireman.

In spite of the adverse publicity Major Peuchen received his expected promotion to Lieutenant-Colonel in the Queen's Own Rifles on May 21, 1912. Peuchen was also awarded the Officer's Long Service Decoration. Peuchen retired as head of Standard Chemical to command the Home Battalion of the Queen's Own in World War One.

Peuchen's social standing ultimately suffered in his later years because he managed to survive both the sinking of the *Titanic* and the World War. He lost much of his fortune in bad investments in the 1920s and spent the last years of his life living in a company dormitory in Hinton, Alberta. He returned to Toronto in 1929 where he died at his home on December 7th at the age of 69.

Sir Cosmo and Lady Lucile Duff-Gordon – The Duff-Gordons both survived the sinking along with Lady Duff-Gordon's maid, Laura Mabel Francatelli, when First Officer William Murdoch allowed them in lifeboat 1, the emergency clipper on the starboard side. The Duff-Gordon's concern about the lifeboat being swamped if they returned for survivors, and the five pounds given to each boat 1 crewmember by Sir Cosmo was called into question by the British Inquiry. The Duff-Gordons were the only passengers who were called to testify.

Sir Cosmo Duff-Gordon died on April 20, 1931 at the age of 69. Lady Duff-Gordon died four years later at the age of 71 and was buried next to her husband at Brookwood Cemetery, near London.

Mrs. Charlotte Drake Cardeza – Charlotte Drake Cardeza and her son Thomas Drake Martinez Cardeza survived in lifeboat 3 along with her maid Anna Ward, and his manservant Gustave Lesueur. All of their fourteen trunks, four suitcases and three crates of possessions went down with the ship. Charlotte would later file the largest claim against White Star Line for the lost contents. At $177,353 the claim included her vast wardrobe and the contents of her jewel case including a Burmese ruby ring and a seven-carat pink diamond from Tiffany's. These two pieces alone were valued at $34,000 in 1912 ($750,000 in today's dollars).

Charlotte Cardeza died of heart failure on August 1, 1939. She was buried at West Laurel Hill Cemetery, Bala Cynwyd, Pennsylvania. Her son Thomas inherited the bulk of her estate and he later endowed a foundation in his mother's name to study blood diseases at Thomas Jefferson University. Thomas Cardeza died in June 1952 and was buried beside his mother.

Mrs. Margaret Brown – Margaret (Tobin) Brown, 44, survived. Brown was returning to her home in Denver, Colorado after learning that her first grandchild was ill. Because of her quick decision to return home most of her family and friends had no idea she was traveling aboard the *Titanic*.

Following the collision Brown helped load lifeboats until Second Officer Lightoller, with no other passengers available, insisted she board lifeboat 6. While aboard the *Carpathia*, Margaret Brown attended to survivors, and by the time they reached New York she had helped establish the Survivor's Committee that raised almost $10,000 for destitute survivors. Brown could communicate in English, French, German, and Russian and remained on the *Carpathia* until all *Titanic* survivors had met with friends, family, or medical/emergency assistance. In May Brown, as chair of the Survivor's Committee, presented a silver cup to Captain Rostron of the *Carpathia* and medals to the *Carpathia* crew members. In later years Margaret Brown was upset that, as a woman, she was not allowed to testify at the *Titanic* inquiries and responded by writing her own version of events which was published in newspapers in Denver, New York, and Paris.

Margaret Tobin Brown was never known as "Molly." The name was a Hollywood invention and the basis for the Broadway play, and later the MGM movie, "The Unsinkable Molly Brown."

Margaret Tobin Brown died of a brain tumor on October 26, 1932, at the age of 65. She was buried in Long Island's Holy Rood Cemetery next to her husband J.J. Brown, who died in 1922.

The Countess of Rothes – Lucy Noël Martha Dyer-Edwards, Scotland's Countess of Rothes, 33, survived as did her cousin, Gladys Cherry, and her maid Roberta Maioni. Her party was traveling to Vancouver, BC, Canada. All survived in lifeboat 8. After being lowered to the sea the Countess offered to take the tiller and steer the lifeboat. ABS Thomas W. Jones took her up on the offer so he could row. Jones admired how the Countess handled herself aboard the lifeboat and later presented her with the brass number plate from the boat. The Countess died September 1956, at the age of 77.

Mr. and Mrs. Dickinson H. Bishop – Dick Bishop and his wife Helen both survived. The Bishops, from Dowagiac, Michigan, were returning from a four-month honeymoon with Helen pregnant. They delayed their departure so they could return on *Titanic's* maiden voyage.

News of the Bishop's rescue was confirmed in this report by the *Dowagiac Daily News* on Friday, April 19, 1912 (partial content):

> "Mr. and Mrs. Bishop, passengers on the wrecked steamship *Titanic* and rescued by the *Carpathia* hours after the wrecked ship sank into the sea, landed safely in New York City last night about 8 o'clock, when the *Carpathia* , of the Cunard Steamship Line, docked with it's freight of 662 people, all that were saved from the *Titanic*. Immediately advices

came to this city announcing they were well and safe. Shortly before the *Carpathia* reached harbor, Mr. Bishop sent a wireless dispatch to Manager F. E. Lee, of the Round Oak Stove Works as follows: 'On board the *Carpathia*, April 18 All are well. Signed, Dick' At 6:30 this morning Mrs. G. E. Bishop, of Dowagiac, mother of D. H. Bishop, received a message, transmitted by wire at New York City, bearing the same intelligence."

The Bishops were delayed in returning to their home in Dowagiac while both stayed to testify before the U.S. Senate Inquiry headed by the Dowagiac-born Senator from Michigan, William A. Smith.

Bad luck followed the Bishops. Helen gave birth to a baby boy on December 8, 1912 but the child died 2 days later.

While they waited for rescue in lifeboat 7 Helen Bishop had told her fellow passengers of an Egyptian fortune teller's prophecy to reassure them that they would be rescued. According to the fortune teller, she was destined to survive a shipwreck, then an earthquake, before losing her life in an automobile accident. Part two of the prophecy came to pass during a vacation in California when the Bishops experienced an earthquake. Then, on November 15, 1913, the Bishops were returning to Dowagiac from Kalamazoo, Michigan, when their car lost control and struck a tree. Helen didn't die but suffered a severely fractured skull that left her with a steel plate in her head and in a changed mental condition. After the accident the Bishop's marriage unraveled and they were divorced in January 1916. Helen suffered a fall three months later and died, belatedly fulfilling her honeymoon prophecy at age 23. News of Helen's death was announced on the front page of the Dowagiac Daily News. Dick Bishop's marriage to his third wife, Sidney Boyce of Chicago, also appeared in the Dowagiac Daily News, on the same day, also on the front page.

Dickinson Bishop died of a stroke in February 1961 at the age of 73.

Miss Edith Russell – Edith Louise Rosenbaum, a journalist better known as Edith Russell, survived. She was returning to the states after covering French fashion at Paris' Easter Sunday races. Edith escaped in lifeboat 11 after having her steward retrieve a small toy pig covered with white fur from her stateroom. It was one of her treasured possession; winding its tail caused it to play a Latin dance piece called "The Maxixe".

During World War One Edith was with the troops in the trenches and was likely the first female war correspondent. During her lifetime Edith survived other catastrophes including car accidents, tornadoes, and another shipwreck. She wrote an account of the *Titanic's* sinking but was unable to find a publisher.

In her latter years she became increasingly eccentric and disagreeable. Her final years were spent in London threatening lawsuits against everyone who committed any perceived transgression against her, including hotel maids and those who delivered her food.

Edith never married and died in London in April 1975 at the age of 98.

Miss Dorothy Gibson – Model and Broadway and motion picture star Dorothy Gibson, survived. Dorothy was traveling with her mother, Mrs. Leonard Gibson, who also survived. The pair were returning home from a European vacation so Dorothy could start a new film for her producer and married lover Jules Brulatour.

A month after the disaster Dorothy starred in the first film produced about the sinking of the *Titanic*. Dorothy played herself in, "Saved From the *Titanic*" which got good reviews from the trade magazines of the time. No copy of the film survives. After the movie was finished Dorothy gave up her acting career to pursue a short-lived career in opera.

In May 1913 her affair with Jules Brulatour was made public after Gibson struck and killed a man while driving Brulatour's car. Brulatour eventually divorced his wife and married Dorothy in 1917. The couple separated in 1919 and Dorothy never remarried. She settled in France to be with her mother and like her mother, became involved in Fascist politics and later intelligence work. After switching her allegiance during World War II she was arrested by the Gestapo in Italy and imprisoned at San Vittore in Milan. She escaped in 1944.

Dorothy Gibson died of heart failure on her birthday in 1946 at the age of 57.

Mme. Léontine Pauline Aubart – Madame Aubart, also known as "Ninette", was a singer from Paris, France and was the mistress of millionaire Benjamin Guggenheim. Aubart and her maid Emma Sägesser were accompanying Guggenheim to New York. Both survived.

She sent a Marconigram from the *Carpathia* to Paris on April 18, 1912:

Aubart 42 rue Monge Paris
Moi sauvee mais Ben perdu (I'm saved but Ben lost)

After her rescue Madame Aubart wrote the following letter to the White Star Line, itemizing her lost possessions:

New York, May 1st, 1912.

Dear Sir,

Before returning tomorrow to Paris, I beg to send you a list of the effects and jewelry that I have lost on the "Titanic."

TRUNKS:
1 trunk "Innovation" for hats
1 trunk "Innovation" for dresses
1 trunk "Innovation" for lingerie
1 trunk "Vuitton"
1 toilet-bag with silver fittings .... 3,500 Frs.

24 dresses and wraps .... 25,000 Frs.
7 hats and 2 with aigrettes .... 2,400 Frs.

SHOES:
6 pairs black
6 pairs evening
6 pairs satin with jewelled buckles
6 pairs (without description) .... 1,800 Frs.

LINGERIE:
24 chemises
6 chemisettes
12 sets of knickers
24 night costumes of silk lace, corsets, corset-covers, handkerchiefs and neck-wear .... 6,000 Frs.

Gloves and opera glasses ... 400 Frs.

JEWELRY:
1 gold bag with sapphires .... 4,000 Frs.
1 purse, gold with emeralds .... 2,000 Frs.
1 money and powder purse, gold with sapphires .... 4,000 Frs.
1 bracelet .... 3,000 Frs.
1 tiara of brilliants .... 9,000 Frs.

Total: 61,100 Frs ($12,220)

For the greater part of these articles I think *I am* able to produce the invoices. I would inform you that on my arrival in Paris I shall put the matter in the hands of my lawyer.

Ninette Aubart
17, rue Le Sueur
Paris
Passenger on "Titanic," Deck B-35.

The Sportsmen

Three *Titanic* passengers were identified as "Sportsman." All wielded rackets. All survived. Karl Behr was an established tennis player but was pursuing a different "sport" aboard the *Titanic*. The other two men were named Williams but weren't related. They were up-and-coming tennis player R. Norris Williams and squash racquet world title holder Charles Eugene Williams (who traveled Second Class).

Mr. Karl Howell Behr – Behr was pursuing a relationship with Helen Newsom and was returning from Europe on the *Titanic* in order to be on the same ship that Helen and her parents had booked for their return passage. He was with them on the Boat Deck when Bruce Ismay ushered their party into lifeboat 5.

Behr was among the group of survivors who formed a committee to honor the *Carpathia's* Captain Rostron and his crew.

Behr was a well known lawn tennis champ who ranked in the Top 10 in the world for eight years. Twelve weeks after he survived the *Titanic* disaster, Behr defeated fellow survivor Norris Williams at the Longwood Challenge Bowl. The thrilling fourth round match saw Behr come back from two sets down to win 0-6, 7-9, 6-2, 6-1, 6-4. The two survivors eventually teamed up for Davis Cup doubles and were members of the American team that won the Davis Cup challenge round in 1914. Karl Behr's other tennis achievements included a victory over then top-ranked Maurice McLoughlin for the 1915 Achelis Cup. Also in 1915, Behr led the campaign that brought the U.S. Championships (today's U.S. Open) from Newport, Rhode Island to New York.

Karl Behr did succeed in winning the adulation of Helen Newsom. With her mother's blessing, they were married in the Church of the Transfiguration in March, 1913. The couple had 4 children, three sons and a daughter.

Behr was a successful attorney but ultimately turned to banking as his chief profession. Karl Behr died on October 15, 1949. After his death Helen married one of his best friends and tennis partner, Dean Mathey. Helen died in Princeton, New Jersey in 1965.

Mr. Richard Norris Williams II – Norris Williams was travelling with his father Charles D. Williams from Geneva to Radnor, PA. He planned to take part in some tennis tournaments before enrolling at Harvard.

After both abandoned the sinking ship, Norris saw his father crushed to death when the forward funnel collapsed. The resulting wave carried him to Collapsible A.

All the survivors from Collapsible A suffered terribly in near waist-deep freezing water before they were transferred to lifeboat 14. After being rescued the *Carpathia's* doctor recommended Norris Williams have both legs amputated. He refused, choosing instead to work his legs back into shape by walking every 2 hours, each day aboard the *Carpathia*. Williams did enter Harvard and continued his tennis career with a good deal of success. After losing to fellow *Titanic* survivor Karl Behr just 12 weeks after the disaster, he went on to win the United States mixed doubles title (with Ms. Mary Browne) later that year. He was United States singles champion in 1914 and again in 1916. He was the 1920 Wimbledon men's doubles champion (with Mr. C. S. Garland) and runner up (with Mr. W. M. Washburn) in 1924. Williams was also the 1924 Olympic gold medalist. He was a member of the United States Davis Cup team from 1913 to 1926, teamed with Karl Behr in 1914.

Williams also served in the U.S. Army in World War I and was awarded the Chevalier de la Legion d'Honneur and Croix de Guerre.

He eventually became a successful investment banker in Philadelphia and was the President of the Historical Society of Pennsylvania. He died in 1968 at the age of 77.

Three Dogs Survive

There were nine dogs on board the *Titanic*, all belonging to First Class passengers. Francis Millet, in a letter to a friend, stated that among the passengers aboard there are "…a number of obnoxious ostentatious American women, the scourge of any place they infest and worse on shipboard than anywhere. Many of them carry tiny dogs and lead husbands around like pet lambs." Three of those tiny dogs survived; many of the husbands didn't. The three lap-sized dogs that survived were *Lady*, a Pomeranian belonging to Margaret Hays, in lifeboat 7; Elizabeth Rothschild's Pomeranian in lifeboat 6; and Henry Sleeper Harper's Pekingese, named *Sun Yat-Sen*, in lifeboat 3.

Among the dogs that didn't make it was Robert Daniel's champion French Bulldog, *Gamin de Pycombe*, that Norris Williams encountered swimming in the sea just before the forward funnel collapsed. A St. Bernard, a King Charles Spaniel, and Colonel Astor's Airedale were also lost.

Second Class Passengers

Second Class totaled 269 passengers; 119 (44%) survived.

Mr. Charles Eugene Williams – Williams, from Harrow, England, was bound for New York to defend his squash racquet world title against the American champion for a $5000 purse. The press initially reported that he had perished but Williams put a quick end to the erroneous reports with a reply from the *Carpathia*.

Published in the *Chicago Tribune*, Thursday, April 18, 1912:

> "Champion at Racquets Lost
> "London, April 17—Among the *Titanic's* passengers was Charles Williams, The professional racquet champion of the world who was on his way to New York to play Standing, the American champion for a stake of $5,000."

From the *London Daily Sketch*, April 20, 1912:

> "Mr. Peterman, hon. secretary of the Racquets Association, stated last night that he received a cable from Williams, the professional racquets champion, who was on board the *Titanic*. Williams was to have played a match in New York against G. Standing on April 29 for the championship of the world. The cable reads: 'Match postponed; return next week. Williams.'"

Williams eventually made it to the tournament and defeated the American champion retaining the World title for England. A year later his squash partner Jock Soutar from Philadelphia defeated Williams and became the first American World Champion. Soutar held the title until 1929 when Williams, who had moved his family to Chicago, regained the World Title and held it until his death in 1935.

Mr. Masabumi Hosono – Civil Servant, 42, survived. Hosono was the only Japanese passenger aboard and survived by leaping into lifeboat 10 while it was being lowered with room for more passengers. After reaching New York on the *Carpathia* Hosono borrowed money from friends in order to get home to Japan by way of San Francisco. He was interviewed by the Japanese press after arriving in Tokyo and was pictured with his family in several publications but was soon ostracized by the Japanese public and press. This public condemnation was in part due to rumors and erroneous reports that Hosono was in the lifeboat as a stowaway or had dressed as a woman to gain access. These allegations, and the fact that Hosono had lived, were considered a disgrace and embarrassment to Japan. He lost his ministry post (but was later hired back on a contract basis), denounced by a professor of ethics, and even described in Japanese textbooks as an example of dishonor. The furor eventually died down but Hosono never spoke of his *Titanic* experience. After regaining his Ministry position he worked until his death in 1939 at the age of 69.

Mr. Lawrence Beesley – Teacher, 34, survived. Beesley, a widower, left his young son behind when he boarded the *Titanic* en route to a holiday in the States before visiting his brother in Toronto. Beesley was allowed in lifeboat 13 just before it was lowered away because there were no women immediately available. After the disaster Beesley wrote *The Loss of the SS Titanic,* and it was published by Houghton-Mifflin only six weeks after the sinking. He remarried in 1919 and had three more children with his wife Mollie. He later served as a technical advisor (uncredited) on the movie "A Night To Remember."

Lawrence Beesley died on February 14, 1967 at the age of 89.

Third Class Passengers

Of the 709 Third Class passengers only 181 (26%) managed to survive.

Mr. Daniel Buckley – Buckley, 21, an Irish farm laborer, survived. According to his testimony at the United States Senate inquiry he survived after boarding lifeboat 13 with several other men. He was crying and shivering in the boat when a lady, mistakenly identified as Mrs. Astor, covered him with a shawl. Buckley remained in the boat when the other men were forced out by a gun wielding officer.

Daniel Buckley gave his life to his newly adopted country when he perished in World War One in 1918.

Mr. Olaus Jørgensen Abelseth – Farmer, 25, survived. Abelseth, a Norwegian native who had emigrated to America in 1902, was returning to Minnesota after visiting with his relatives in Norway. Abelseth is one of only twelve people who survived after reaching the swamped Collapsible A. Of the five other Norwegians traveling in the same party only 16 year-old Karen Marie Abelseth (not related) and Miss Anna Kristine Salkjelsvik, 21, survived. Karen Marie in lifeboat 16 and Miss Anna Kristine in collapsible C.

Karen Marie Abelseth eventually married and had two sons and three daughters. She died in Inglewood, California in 1969 at the age of 73.

Anna Kristine Salkjelsvik lived an additional 66 years after surviving the shipwreck.

Olaus Abelseth married Anna Grinde in July 1915. The couple had four children including their second son who died at the age of 3. The Abelseths worked their farm for 30 years until Olaus retired in 1946. Olaus Abelseth died at the age of 93 on December 4, 1980, sixty eight years after surviving the *Titanic*.

Mrs. Hanna Youssef Touma (née Razi) – Mrs. Touma, 29, and her children Maria, nine, and George, eight, survived in Collapsible C. The family from Assyria (now Lebanon) was emigrating to the United States to join Hanna's husband Darwis on the farm he had bought near Dowagiac, Michigan. The family lost most of their possessions but received assistance in New York from a woman's relief group connected with the St. Vincent's Hospital. On April 20th Hanna sent Darwis a telegram letting him know that they had been aboard the *Titanic* but were safe. Hanna and the children were reunited with Darwis on April 26th after taking a train from New York. Hanna later received $90 from the relief fund for destitute *Titanic* survivors.

The family lived for the next eight years in Dowagiac and the family name was anglicized to "Thomas." They never met fellow survivors Dick and Helen Bishop, who lived a world apart in the same small town. The Thomas family added three additional children and eventually settled in Burton, Michigan. Hanna Youssef Touma (Thomas) died on June 28, 1976.

Found Souls - *Titanic's* Discovery

Over the years numerous expeditions have tried and failed to locate the *Titanic* in part because of the tremendous depth of the ocean and because the precise location she sank was in doubt. In 1985 teams from the United States and France joined forces on an expedition to find the *Titanic*. The project team was led by Dr. Robert Ballard, chief of the Deep Submergence Laboratory at the Woods Hole Oceanographic Institute, and Jean-Louis Michel, his French counterpart. After reconstructing the most likely scenario based on the *Titanic's* speed, course, and reported position, the team identified a search area north of where the *Carpathia* encountered *Titanic's* lifeboats in 1912.

On June 28th the French ship *Le Suroit* started using her deep search sonar to systematically search 150-square miles of the ocean floor with a back and forth technique called "mowing the lawn." Using this technique the French ship explored 80% of the targeted search area over a two month period without locating the *Titanic*. The Americans searched the remainder of the target area with the Woods Hole research ship *Knorr* using side-scanning sonar and high-resolution real-time video on a new piece of equipment called "Argo." After towing Argo back and forth on the ocean floor one of *Titanic's* boilers was discovered 2.5 miles below the surface at 2:00 a.m. on September 1, 1985—73 years after the great ship went down. She was found approximately 350 miles southeast of Newfoundland.

The discovery team went on to find *Titanic's* hull section and, based on the evidence from the debris field photographs, determined that the hull had broken apart from the stern at an expansion joint. The break started just forward of the third funnel and continued at an angle toward the stern. The stern portion of the ship, discovered in a subsequent expedition, indicates the bow and stern sections sank independently (corroborating witness accounts from several lifeboats). The bow section, about 450 feet of *Titanic's* 882 foot length, had the gentler landing. It plowed 50 feet into the mud but is basically intact and upright on the ocean floor. The stern is also upright but shows the crushing effects of a more devastating crash landing and includes its own debris field.

The *Titanic* went down in an unusually calm North Atlantic sea in 1912 and has fittingly occupied the perfect calm of her final resting place ever since.

From Dr. Robert Ballard:

> "The *Titanic* itself lies in 13,000 feet of water on a gently sloping alpine-like countryside overlooking a small canyon below. Its bow faces north and the ship sits upright on the bottom. Its mighty stacks point upward…It is quiet and peaceful and a fitting place for the remains of this greatest of sea tragedies to rest. May it forever remain that way and may God bless these found souls."

Iceberg Photographed Near the Scene of the Disaster

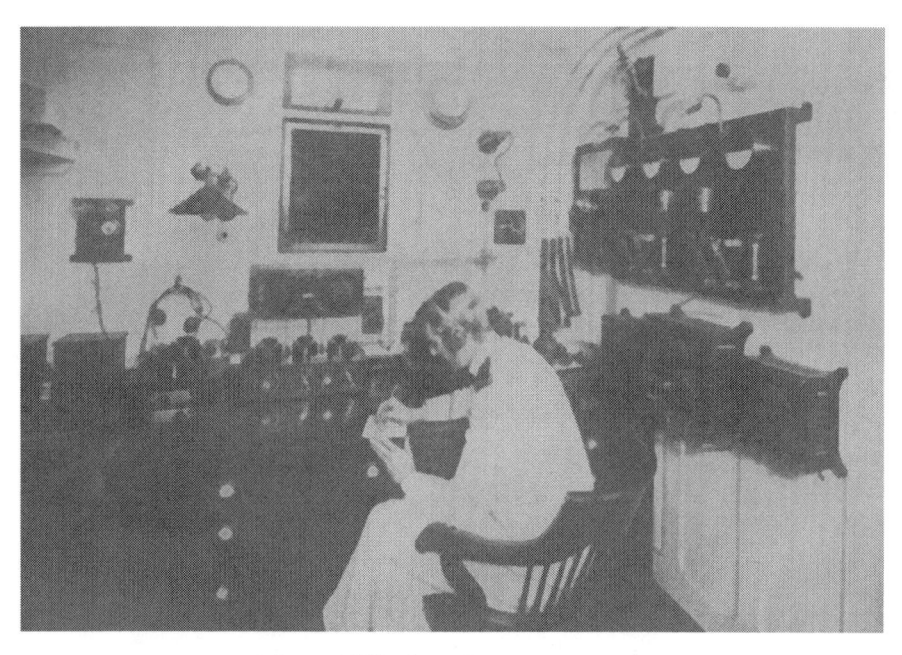

Marconi Wireless Operator at work

Lowering the Lifeboats – Illustration first published in 1912

The Sinking of the *Titanic* – Illustration first published in 1912

The Cunard Liner *Carpathia*

Captain Arthur H. Roston of the *Carpathia*

Collapsible Lifeboat C approaches the *Carpathia*

Newlyweds George and Dorothy Harder aboard the *Carpathia*

New York Newsboy

Wireless Operator Harold Bride being helped off the *Carpathia*

Surviving White Star Line Crewmembers in New York

J. Bruce Ismay testifies before the U.S. Senate Inquiry at the Waldorf-Astoria Hotel in New York

Part Two

Root Cause Analysis of the *Titanic* Disaster

Chapter 22

Root Cause Analysis Primer

Anyone who knows the *Titanic* was a real ship, not just an expensive prop for James Cameron's movie, also knows that she sank after hitting an iceberg in the North Atlantic on her maiden voyage in 1912. The world has been intrigued by the story and the people involved ever since. The disaster that sank the unsinkable ship has been the subject of official inquiries, popular speculation, and well researched theories as to the cause. It has also given rise to bogus myths, legends, and conspiracy theories with little or no supporting evidence. A good deal of the popular speculation as to the causes of the disaster comes from only looking at the tip of the iceberg or, in the case of the *Titanic*, the edge of the iceberg just below the surface of the sea.

Tip of the Iceberg

Icebergs float because their density is less than the density of seawater but a significant proportion of their volume is below the surface with only about one-ninth of the iceberg visible above the water. The shape of the underwater portion of an iceberg is hard to determine by looking at the small, visible portion above the surface. This is the source of the "tip of the iceberg" metaphor which refers to a small evident aspect of an issue when larger and potentially more serious underlying issues are yet to be discovered. "Tip of the iceberg" works well to describe the obvious cause of an incident versus underlying root causes.

If the "tip of the iceberg" metaphor wasn't based specifically on the *Titanic* disaster, it certainly could have been. Only the tip of the iceberg was seen when Lookout Fred Fleet reported, "Iceberg right ahead" and for an instance it appeared the *Titanic* would clear the iceberg with the port-around maneuver attempted by First Officer Murdoch but the unseen ice below the surface caused the damage that sank the unsinkable ship.

While the *Titanic* literally struck an iceberg, the collision and aftermath was only the tip of the iceberg with multiple, underlying root causes to be debated, identified, and corrected.

Much has been learned about the *Titanic's* unsinkable design and the materials used for her construction with some information surfacing only after the wreck was discovered in 1985, off the coast of St. John's, Newfoundland, 73 years after she struck the iceberg and sank in less than three hours. The ongoing curiosity, fueled by her discovery, has kept the *Titanic* story and investigation alive for over 100 years as new evidence and theories continue to emerge. Hitting that iceberg was the obvious event that led to *Titanic's* demise on that cold April night, but there were numerous other problems and contributing factors that, taken together, caused, or failed to prevent, the *Titanic* disaster.

Root Cause

Before beginning the root cause analysis of the *Titanic* disaster it is important to have a practical working definition of root cause and to understand some basic concepts of root cause analysis.

During the British Wreck Commissioner's Inquiry, Sir Rufus Isaacs, the Attorney General for Britain and Wales, aptly spoke about the objectives of the *Titanic* Inquiry when, during the final arguments, he stated, "Now, my Lord, speaking generally, the questions which your Lordship has to answer relate to what has happened in the past and what is to happen in the future. And no doubt different considerations must apply when you are forming a judgment as to past events, or making any recommendations as to what shall happen in the future for the guidance of those who have to navigate the North Atlantic."

The Attorney General then stated, "The main questions resolve themselves into two, I think. The first is whether there was any failure to take proper precautions which, if taken, would have avoided or would have materially minimised the loss both of life and property. That, of course, is the question that affects the past." Isaacs was pointing out the need to identify root cause and his statement is remarkably similar to a practical, contemporary definition of root cause.

Isaacs continued with, "Then the other, and I cannot help saying it appears to me to be the more important question in relation to this Inquiry, is: What precautions shall be taken in the future to guard against any similar calamity," demonstrating that he also understood the need to identify effective corrective and preventive actions.

Today "forming a judgment as to past events," when done correctly, is root cause analysis. Based on that analysis, "recommendations as to what shall happen in the future" are commonly referred to as Corrective and Preventive Actions (CAPAs). Effective CAPAs are necessary "to guard against any similar calamity" in the future, but, prior to identifying corrective and preventive actions, correctable root causes must be identified.

> **Definition of Root Cause** – Root cause is the most basic initiating and correctable cause for the problem being investigated which, if eliminated, would have prevented the problem or resulted in less severe consequences.

The above practical definition adds the "correctable" adjective to the most basic initiating cause because identifying a root cause that is not reasonably correctable—within the means of those who need it corrected—is an exercise in futility. If the most basic initiating cause can not be eliminated in a practical manner, it is not a root cause but may be a contributing factor that should still be considered when CAPAs are identified.

The upcoming analysis of the *Titanic* disaster will not identify the presence of icebergs in the North Atlantic as a root cause because they can't be eliminated and moving the east/west shipping lanes so far south that icebergs would never be encountered, while possible, was not economically viable for the passenger shipping trade. The presence of icebergs is not a root cause but is a contributing factor that could be mitigated by better tracking and reporting.

If the analysis determines that binoculars being unavailable for the crow's nest lookouts is a root cause, that root cause is easily correctable and can be eliminated by providing binoculars.

Basic Concepts of Root Cause Analysis

Key concepts for effective root cause analysis:
- The primary aim of root cause analysis is to identify the most basic initiating and correctable causes of the problem in order to identify Corrective and Preventive Actions – the solutions necessary to prevent a recurrence, or result in a better outcome if there is a recurrence.
- Well-defined problem statements and event descriptions are necessary for effective root cause analysis.
- There is often more than one problem to be defined for the event being investigated and there could be more than one root cause for each problem. The risk in only identifying the obvious root cause, or the easiest one to correct, is that the undetermined and unaddressed root causes could result in a repeat incident.
- To be effective the analysis must be performed systematically in conjunction with the investigation. Conclusions and root causes identified should be backed up by corroborated facts and proven evidence whenever possible.
- Human Performance (human error) is not a root cause – it is a cause category that requires further investigation.

Human Performance

Human Performance is a current term for the performance of the people involved with the process or problem. Human Performance is often referred to with a negative connotation as human error and human error is too often misidentified as a root cause. Human Performance is a cause category that requires further investigation to identify fixable root causes to prevent a recurrence of the undesired actions and results.

Discussion of Human Performance as a cause category needs to start with an understanding on where to draw the line. Ultimately, everything people have a hand in could be considered Human Performance, with only Mother

Nature escaping the category. A more useful place to start the analysis is with the performance of the people involved during the relevant timeline of the incident being investigated.

In that context the Human Performance aspects of the *Titanic* disaster will consider decisions made during construction and outfitting, the actions of *Titanic's* Captain and crew before and after the accident, and the inaction of the Captain and crew of the *Californian*.

Human performance as it relates to any problem being investigated is invariably the human errors that caused or contributed to the problem. Therefore, it is necessary to define human error before starting a deep dive into the *Titanic* root cause analysis.

> **Definition of Human Error** – Human error is an inappropriate action or omission that results in an undesirable outcome; a person acted improperly (wrong action or wrong time) or a person failed to act when action was necessary and expected.

This definition may seem to suggest that human error is a root cause with, in the case of the *Titanic*, some people more to blame than others. But playing the human error "blame game" does not lead to fixable root causes. Identifying human error as the root cause may allow for quick investigations with the common corrective actions of training or discipline, but this "blame and train" scenario is not likely to prevent a recurrence of the error if the fixable causes are left unidentified. While it may be quicker and easier to simply blame someone and attempt to "fix" that person with training or discipline, someone else in the same circumstances may repeat the error if underlying causes of the performance problem have not been identified or if the corresponding fixes have not been implemented. Further analysis is needed to identify root causes of Human Performance problems. A method for that analysis is discussed later in this Chapter.

Root Cause Analysis Methods

A description follows of two popular root cause analysis methods, 5-Whys and the fishbone, and the potential drawbacks of relying exclusively on one of these methods:

5-Whys Method – The 5-Whys method uses the question "why?" multiple times to explore cause/effect relationships underlying the defined problem. The "five" in 5-Whys is not an absolute; rather it is expected that asking why five times is usually adequate to get to a root cause. Often iterations beyond five start to lose their connection to the original problem or identify issues that are beyond reasonable means to correct and control. The ultimate goal of continuing to ask "why" is to determine a fixable root cause of the problem.

The following example uses the primary *Titanic* Problem Statement and explores a root cause based on one of many possible answers to the first why question.

Problem Statement: The *Titanic* hit an iceberg.
1. Why did the *Titanic* hit an iceberg? – The Lookouts didn't see the iceberg in time.
2. Why didn't the Lookouts see the iceberg in time? – The lookouts did not have binoculars.
3. Why didn't the lookouts have binoculars? – No one on board had the key to the locker containing their binoculars.
4. Why didn't anyone on board have the key to the locker? – Second Officer Blair, who did have the key, was replaced at the last minute and failed to turn over the key to his replacement.
5. Why did Blair fail to turn over the key to his replacement? – There was not an adequate handoff between Blair and his replacement.
6. Why wasn't there an adequate handoff? – Blair was in a hurry to get off the ship.
7. Why was Blair was in a hurry to get off the ship? – Blair had to get off before *Titanic's* departure.

The why questioning for this example was taken to the seventh "why?" level. While justifiable in some cases, Second Officer Blair being in a hurry to get off the ship prior to *Titanic's* departure can't reasonably be assigned as a root cause for the ship striking an iceberg six days later. So which why answer could be considered a *fixable* root cause?

To eliminate unnecessary "Why" iterations in order to identify a fixable root cause, each why answer can be tested in reverse order by asking, "So what?" If the answer to the "So what" question identifies a "Why" statement that, when solved, directly leads to preventing the problem (or making it less severe) that "Why" statement is a fixable root cause.

Testing the Whys from the above example by asking "So what?" in reverse order:

- Blair had to leave before *Titanic's* departure (answer 7). So what?
- So Blair was in a hurry to get off the ship (answer 6). So what?
  - So if Blair wasn't in a hurry to get off the ship he may or may not have turned over the key to the binoculars to his replacement. There is no evidence that more time would have resulted in Second Officer Blair passing on the key to his replacement or completing an adequate handoff, therefore "Why" answers 6 and 7 are not root causes.

Continuing with the "So What?" test:

- There was not an adequate handoff between Blair and his replacement (answer 5). So what?
- So Second Officer David Blair failed to turn over the key to his replacement (answer 4). So what?
- So no one on board had the key to the locker containing the binoculars (answer 3). So what?

- So crow's nest Lookouts did not have binoculars to use (answer 2). So what?
- So the Lookouts didn't see the iceberg in time (answer 1). So what?
- So the *Titanic* hit the iceberg (the Problem Statement).

According to the "So What" test the fifth why answer (convenient for a 5-Whys example) points to an inadequate or missing handoff process and directly connects with the fourth "Why," then the third, and so on to the problem statement. An adequate handoff between Blair and his replacement would have ensured the key to the binoculars was turned over, whereas any handoff that failed to transfer the key should not be considered adequate. An adequate handoff would have ultimately resulted in the lookouts having binoculars and a better chance of spotting the iceberg in time to avoid the collision so, per the 5-Whys method, an inadequate handoff process is a root cause.

This root cause also meets the fixable test. When corrected with an adequate handoff process all the preceding "Why?" answers fall like dominoes all the way to preventing the problem. A key concept of the 5-Whys approach is that the why answer that is ultimately identified as the root cause should point to a process, not a person or a concept that can't be corrected. A process can be improved or created; it is a fixable root cause. After asking "Why," and testing those answers by asking "So What," asking what process failed or was missing will also help identify corrective and preventive actions.

This *Titanic* 5-Whys example assumes agreement with the second why answer; that binoculars in the hands of the lookouts could have prevented the accident or resulted in a less severe collision. Only with that agreement is it reasonable to conclude that the lack of an adequate handoff process, resulting in the binoculars being unavailable, is a root cause.

Frederick Fleet, the Lookout in the crow's nest who spotted the iceberg, certainly believed binoculars (called glasses at the time) would have been useful. Fleet was examined by Mr. Scanlan during the British Wreck Commissioner's Inquiry and a portion of his testimony follows:

Scanlan – Do you think if you had had glasses you could have seen the iceberg sooner?

Fleet – Certainly.

Scanlan – How much sooner do you think you could have seen it?

Fleet – In time for the ship to get out of the way.

Scanlan – So that it is your view that if you had had glasses it would have made all the difference between safety and disaster?

Fleet – Yes.

After ascertaining that the lookouts needed binoculars to prevent the collision there is a risk in continuing to ask why. That risk is identifying a root cause that is too specific and doesn't consider other reasons the lookouts may be without binoculars. The binocular issue is used here to demonstrate the 5-Whys method but will be explored further in the root cause analysis chapter that focuses on why the collision with the iceberg occurred.

5-Whys is an easy concept that can be employed to quickly find root cause but it is best used for simple problems where there is likely a single root cause to be identified. 5-Whys, when used exclusively, is less effective when there are multiple factors to consider.

The same Problem Statement demonstrates what can happen when attempting the 5-Whys technique for complex problems with multiple root causes.

Problem Statement: The *Titanic* hit an iceberg.
1. Why? – The Lookouts didn't see the iceberg in time.
2. Why? – The Lookouts did not have binoculars.

Or

The *Titanic* hit an iceberg.
1. Why? – The ship was going too fast.
2. Why? – The Captain failed to order a slower speed.

Or

The *Titanic* hit an iceberg.
1. Why? – The ship steamed directly into an area that was reported to contain icebergs.
2. Why? – The Wireless Operator failed to deliver crucial ice warnings to the bridge officers.

In the above examples all the "why" answers are true and each immediately starts the analysis down a different path. It could be argued that multiple iterations of the 5-Whys exercise would lead to all the root causes but this example also illustrates the risk of exclusively relying on the 5-Why method for complex problems—the 5-Whys practitioner may not explore all the possibilities and instead be drawn to their own area of expertise or to an answer that satisfies a predetermined conclusion.

Fishbone Cause-and-Effect Method – Cause-and-effect Fishbone or Ishikawa diagrams, named for creator Kaoru Ishikawa, demonstrate cause and effect relationships for the problem being considered. They can reveal key relationships among several different variables and the possible causes may provide additional insight into processes and behaviors.

When using the fishbone method the head of the fish contains the Problem Statement while the fishbones are used to capture potential causes and contributing factors (Figure 22–1). These causes and factors are identified through investigation, consultation with subject matter experts, and brainstorming. The 5-Whys technique is useful for further analyzing factors identified on the fishbone model. The repeated why question drills down to help identify a cause or contributing factor as a root cause or to rule it out. In its most basic form the fishbone is simply a way to chart and compare multiple iterations of 5-Whys and in this form suffers from the same problem, the resulting fish may be a bone or two short of a keeper and practitioners may fail to hook all the root causes.

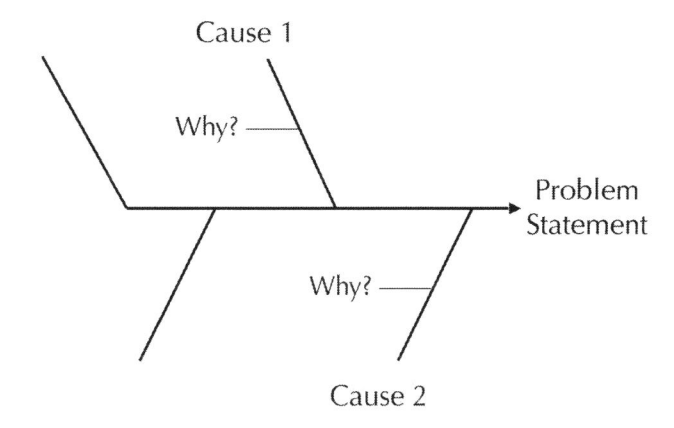

Figure 22 – 1, Cause and Effect fishbone diagram

The DMAIC Model for Incident Analysis

A comprehensive root cause investigation includes analysis of all contributing factors and potential root causes, but in today's just-in-time business environment competing priorities, business needs, regulation, and other realities influence the time available to complete an investigation and identify root causes. That is why a method and process needs to be established before there is an incident to investigate. DMAIC is the acronym for Define, Measure, Analyze, Improve, Control and is a proven and practical method for identifying, solving and controlling simple or complex problems. The DMAIC concept also works for investigating, analyzing and identifying root causes of specific incidents. Each DMAIC phase, as applied to incident analysis, is detailed below:

Define – Identify the Problem

It is important to clearly define each issue to be analyzed in a concise problem statement. Human Performance issues, if known, should also be identified and they should indicate what a person did, or failed to do, to cause or contribute to the problem being investigated.

For the *Titanic*, a root cause analysis that too broadly identifies the problem as, '*Titanic* sank during maiden voyage' doesn't define the specific problems to be corrected and avoided. Conversely if the Problem Statement is too narrowly focused it may not capture the entire scope of the problem. '*Titanic* hit an iceberg,' is an example of a Problem Statement that doesn't tell the entire story which includes the aftermath of the collision. If the *Titanic* had not sunk after hitting the iceberg, or if everyone had survived, a very different root cause analysis would result.

There is often more than one problem to be analyzed and there may be more than one root cause for each problem. Corrective and preventive actions need to be implemented for each root cause in order to prevent a recurrence or make the consequences of a recurrence less severe.

Determining how the *Titanic* accident could have been less severe will help define the specific problems that the root cause analysis should attempt to prevent. The *Titanic* colliding with an iceberg was the obvious problem and if other ships avoid colliding with icebergs, there will be no severity issues to contemplate. If another ship should collide with an iceberg, not sinking or staying afloat long enough to rescue the passengers and crew would be a much better (less severe) fate than was suffered by most of those aboard the *Titanic*. A Problem Statement that captures the appropriate severity of the *Titanic* incident could be stated as, '*Titanic* hit an iceberg and sank, causing 1503 people to perish.' Alternately three separate Problem Statements could be identified to help maintain focus as each one is analyzed:

- **The *Titanic* collided with an iceberg** – root cause analysis to focus on why the collision occurred in order to prevent ships from colliding with icebergs in the future.
- **The *Titanic* sank after the collision** – root cause analysis to focus on why the *Titanic* sank following the collision in order to identify design corrections or correctable Human Performance issues.
- **1503 people perished when the *Titanic* sank** – root cause analysis to focus on how more people could have been saved in order to prevent loss of life in future shipwrecks.

The where, when, and who details of the incident are also captured in the Define phase as is the Desired State. The Desired State is the goal or acceptable level of improvement and should determine if there is a tolerable error rate or, as in the case of the *Titanic*, that there is no tolerance for other ships to share her fate.

Measure – Sequence of Events and Relevant Facts

A sequence of events timeline is identified and relevant facts are collected in the Measure phase. Events leading up to the incident are listed in chronological order starting at a point prior to the incident that puts the sequence of events in context and includes potential contributing factors. For the root cause analysis of the problem statement, "The Titanic collided with an iceberg," the sequence of events timeline should start with the ship's departure and include the ice warnings received during the voyage. For the problem statement, "The *Titanic* sank after the collision," the timeline needs to include the ship's design and construction as well as events that contributed to the '"unsinkable" belief. For the problem statement, "1503 people perished when the *Titanic* sank," decisions concerning the number of lifeboats the ship would carry should be part of the timeline. As the timeline approaches the actual incident, the events should be described with an increasing level of detail and precise timing, when known.

Pertinent events that followed the incident should also be included.

The Measure phase also captures known facts and information that may be important to the issue being investigated. This data can help to clarify speculation concerning what apparently happened and, along with the timeline, identify what actually happened. It is a fact that the lookouts did not have binoculars available when the *Titanic* struck the iceberg; this may or may not be pertinent to the root cause analysis but this is a fact that should be captured. Speculation or information that can not be verified should not be captured as fact. A reasonable assumption based on other known facts can be included but should be identified as an assumption, or an event likely to have occurred.

It is important that the sequence of events and facts identified during an investigation validate the Problem Statement and/or Human Performance issues identified. If there is a disconnect, more investigation may be necessary or the validity of the Problem Statement or Human Performance issue should be reviewed (an example is provided at the end of this Chapter).

Analyze – Identify Root Cause(s)

In this phase the problem is analyzed to discover and verify cause-and-effect relationships and determine root cause. For a comprehensive root cause analysis all contributing factors and potential root causes need to be considered. The basic categories may vary based on the type of investigation but typically a fishbone Problem Solving Model that includes multiple cause categories is used to ensure a comprehensive analysis.

The three problem statements identified for the *Titanic* root cause analysis should each be analyzed separately to maintain focus on that problem and because there are likely different underlying root causes for each problem being analyzed. Additionally, Human Performance should be analyzed using a separate Human Performance Model.

All root causes should be identified during the Analyze phase. Too often less than titanic problems aren't fully investigated or properly analyzed. It may be tempting to stop after identifying the most obvious root cause, or the one that is the easiest to correct, but leaving one or more root causes on the table can allow a recurrence or similar preventable incidents. Those subsequent incidents, often under different circumstances but with the same underlying root causes, may not be recognized as repeats. Each of these unrecognized repeats will require another investigation to identify root causes that were missed in the previous investigation. This cycle of repeats will continue to plague any organization until all the root causes are eventually identified and corrected.

If root cause cannot be determined or if the root cause identified is not correctable, the Problem Statement or Human Performance issue may need to be clarified or further investigation and analysis may reveal a different, solvable root cause. Determining that icebergs in the North Atlantic is the root cause of the *Titanic* disaster is only appropriate if there is a way to eliminate or substantially reduce future icebergs in the North Atlantic. There isn't. Mother Nature simply won't be corrected.

Problem Solving Model – The Problem Solving Model (Figure 22 – 2) is a cause and effect fishbone that contains major categories with predetermined causal statements and questions to be answered. When an answer reveals a potential root cause, the 5-Whys technique can be employed to further drill down. The causal statement questions used in conjunction with the 5-Whys technique turns a simple fishbone diagram into a comprehensive problem-solving tool.

The Problem Solving Model can vary but generally cover these major categories:

- **Method/Procedure:** Description of how a process is performed and could include policies, procedures, rules, regulations, or unwritten accepted standards.
- **Equipment:** Category includes equipment, tools, etc. required to accomplish a task.
- **Measurement:** The information and data captured from the process.
- **Materials:** Including raw materials, manufactured parts, etc. used to produce a product.
- **Environment:** The inside or outside environment – the conditions at the time the problem occurred, including location, temperature, and visibility.

The major categories each contain questions to be considered for the problem being analyzed. Suggested causal statements and questions for each major category follow:

Method/Procedure

- No Procedure – If there is no procedure, was a procedure or written document necessary to complete the task?
- Procedure unclear/lacking detail – Did procedure use contribute to the incident because of insufficient detail or because expected scenarios weren't covered? Or did document design issues contribute to the incident?
- Procedure incorrect – Did procedure use contribute to the incident because facts, steps, or order were incorrect?
- Procedure unavailable – If a procedure exists but wasn't used; was it because the procedure was unavailable?
- Alternate Practice – Was an alternate practice followed instead of the written procedure or expected standard?
- Significant Change – Did a major change to a standard/reliable method contribute to the incident?
- Other – Note the specific issue and if normal or unusual.

Equipment

- Breakdown – Did mechanical failure contribute to the incident?
- Performance – Was the equipment running properly?
- Maintenance – Did inadequate or ineffective maintenance contribute to the incident?
- Design – Was the equipment designed for the task?
- Significant Change – Did significant equipment changes contribute to the incident?
- Other – Note the specific issue and if normal or unusual.

Measurement

- Missing – Were necessary measurements unavailable?
- Inaccurate – Did the use of inaccurate measurements contribute to the incident?
- Capability – Did instrument capability, including inadequate design, contribute to the incident?
- Other – Note the specific issue and if normal or unusual.

Materials

- Supplier Quality – Did the supplier deliver the expected material quality?
- Defective Material – Did defects not attributed to the supplier contribute to the incident?
- Damaged Material – Did damaged material contribute to the incident?
- Physical Properties – Did unexpected or unusual material physical properties contribute to the incident?
- Container/Labeling – Did significant changes in size/material of construction or container labeling/identification contribute to the incident?
- Handling and Storage – Was material handled, stored, and/or staged within the specified controls and procedures?
- Other – Note the specific issue and if normal or unusual.

Environment

- Layout/Design – Did facility design or work area layout contribute to the incident?
- Utilities – Did a utility fail or not function properly?
- Housekeeping – Did inadequate housekeeping contribute to incident?
- Hazardous Conditions – Did a hazardous condition exist and contribute to incident?

- Inside Environment – Did temperature, humidity, noise, vibration, or poor visibility contribute to the incident?
- Outside environment – Did the outside environment contribute to the incident?
- Other – Note the specific issues and if normal or unusual.

The Problem Solving Model is best used to explore five of the six basic cause categories. Factors and ultimately root causes that do not involve Human Performance will typically fall into one of the established categories mentioned above with casual statement variation based on the industry, business, and the types of problems for which the model is generally used. The 6th category is People and is best analyzed with a separate model.

Problem Solving Model

Method	Equipment	Measurement
No Procedure	Breakdown	Missing
Procedure Unclear	Performance	Inaccurate
Procedure Incorrect	Maintenance	Capability
Procedure Unavailable	Design	Other
Alternate Practice	Significant Change	
Significant Change	Other	
Other		

Material	Environment	People
Supplier Quality	Layout / Design	See Human Performance Model
Defective	Utilities	
Damaged	Housekeeping	
Physical Properties	Hazardous Conditions	
Container / Labeling	Inside Environment	
Handling / Storage	Outside Environment	
Other	Other	

→ Problem Statement

Figure 22 – 2, Problem Solving Model with causal statements

Human Performance Model – The Human Performance Model (Figure 22 – 3) is a separate cause and effect fishbone with predetermined categories and causal statement questions. The model is used in conjunction with the Problem Solving Model when a Human Performance issue has been identified. The model is designed to provide a systematic approach to Human Performance analysis that identifies fixable root causes. A systematic approach is necessary to ensure the investigating entity doesn't simply blame people for Human Performance problems but instead focuses on how to solve them. A systematic approach is also necessary for the people who work in the process and who may tend to avoid considering Human Performance as a cause due to the consequences of a "blame and train" culture. Even in a blame-free culture, where people generally admit their mistakes, some people may not be able to get past their own "It's my fault" admission in order to identify underlying root causes. No matter the reason, there is diminished opportunity to implement effective solutions if the analysis stops with "human error" as a root cause.

The Human Performance Model is based on Human Performance Technology (HPT) – a methodical approach to addressing performance issues through diagnosis and implementation of solutions to close Human Performance gaps. The HPT approach assumes positive intent by those involved while dealing directly with Human Performance issues through thorough evaluation and understanding of the work, the work environment, and individual workers.

The three central problem statements identified for the *Titanic* root cause analysis all contain Human Performance issues. Each Human Performance issue should be analyzed separately to maintain focus on that issue and because there are likely different underlying root causes for each.

For Human Performance issues associated with the problem statement "The *Titanic* collided with an iceberg,"

- The "work" is navigating the *Titanic* across the Atlantic ocean.
- The "work environment" is the *Titanic* and the North Atlantic.
- The "individual workers" are *Titanic*'s Captain, Officers, and crew.

Analysis of decisions made during *Titanic*'s construction and outfitting, on the other hand, will have altogether different work, work environment, and individual worker scenarios to consider.

The Human Performance Model is comprehensive and is designed to follow, in order, each of the broad categories covering the work, work environment, and the individual for the performance issue being analyzed. The questions in these categories will help identify Human Performance root causes or could help rule out Human Performance as a cause. The Human Performance Model categories covering the work and work environment are:

- **Expectations and Feedback:** The data people need to do their job, including performance expectations and timely feedback to tell them how they are performing and achieving.
- **Tools and Resources:** The tools, technologies, and processes people employ to do the job.
- **Consequences and Incentives:** The incentives and disincentives for task performance and application of consequences when performance does not meet expectations.

These are followed by categories that explore individual performance:

- **Skills and Knowledge:** Skills the individual already has and knowledge that is necessary for performing the job.
- **Capacity:** The personal qualities a person brings to the job including social skills and their ability to learn. This category also includes their capacity to perform during the timeline of the issue being investigated.
- **Motivation:** A person's attitude toward their job and factors that comprise their satisfaction.

Causal statements and questions for each category follow:

Expectations and Feedback
- Complex Process/Distractions – Was the worker distracted or overloaded due to multiple tasks, complex activities, and/or surroundings?
- What/When Instructions – Did workers receive adequate instructions about what to do and when to do it?
- Importance of Performance – Can the worker explain why the task is important? [The worker may know how to do the task but if they don't know why they need to do it (why it's important) there is a training/learning gap.]
- Goals/Expectations – Do workers feel the goals and expectations for the task are fair and realistic? [Workers may need more information to gain their buy-in.]
- Time/Duration Prompts – Are there reminders to prompt the appropriate steps for the task at the correct time or duration?
- Process/Equipment Feedback – Did the process or equipment deliver clear and adequate feedback to help workers know the task was done correctly?
- Worker Feedback – Do workers receive timely feedback (positive or constructive) on task performance?

Tools and Resources
- Availability – Was the required equipment available when and where the task was performed?
- Equipment Choice – Did the worker choose to use equipment known to be unreliable or not in good working order?
- Equipment Use – Did the worker use the equipment correctly?
- Inadequate Time – Was there adequate time available to correctly perform the task?

Consequences and Incentives
- Initial Incentive – Did the worker's initial consideration determine the desired task or performance was not value-added and therefore unnecessary?
- Competing Behavior – Were there alternate priorities, practices or procedures competing with the desired task performance?
- Applied Consequences – Are consequences consistently applied when performance doesn't meet expectations?

Human Performance Model

Figure 22 – 3, Human Performance Model with causal statements

Skills and Knowledge

- Performance Timing – Can the worker correctly identify when to do and not do the task?
- Training – Can the worker properly demonstrate the complete task?
- On-the-Job Proficiency – Has the worker ever successfully completed the task in the work environment under normal working conditions?
- Technique – Did allowable flexibility (worker technique) lead to an undesirable outcome?

Capacity

- Ability to Learn – Does the worker have the mental capacity to learn the task, technology, or equipment necessary to perform their job?
- Social Skills – Does the worker have the social skills necessary to adequately interact with other workers in order to perform their job?
- Temporarily Incapacitated – Was the worker impaired due to illness, drug/alcohol use, being overly tired, or sleeping on the job?

Motivation

- Job Satisfaction – Is the worker satisfied with the nature of the work or the work environment?
- Available Incentives – Is the worker motivated by available incentives including monetary and nonmonetary rewards?

The "Capacity" and "Motivation" sections of the Human Performance Model are included to complete the model but, with the exception of the "Temporarily Incapacitated" cause, are rarely the cause of a specific problem. If one or more of the other causal statements are identified in these categories, corrective and preventive actions may involve the worker selection/hiring process and are often referred to the Human Resources department.

The Analyze phase can be time consuming but is arguably the most important part of the process because that is the phase where fixable root causes are identified. The time spent identifying root causes will be wasted if corrective and preventive actions are not implemented and monitored in the Improve and Control phases that complete the DMAIC model.

Improve – Identify Corrective and Preventive Actions

After root causes have been identified they need to be addressed with corrective and preventive actions (CAPAs). In some cases it is possible that a single CAPA will address multiple root causes, while in other cases multiple CAPAs are necessary to address a single root cause. To be effective the CAPAs should be comprehensive and address all identified root causes in order to prevent a recurrence of the incident. Broader application of incident specific CAPA items should also be considered if any of the root causes identified are generic problems. In the case of the *Titanic* disaster the CAPAs could apply specifically to the *Olympic, Titanic's* sister ship, or could have broad application to shipbuilding and the shipping trade.

Control – Implement and Monitor

Control is the last phase in the DMAIC process. In this phase a plan is formulated to verify the identified CAPAs are appropriately implemented and are effective in preventing a repeat or similar problem. The control plan should align to achieve the Desired State identified in the Define phase.

Using DMAIC - Root Cause Analysis of Thomas Whiteley's Account

Whiteley's account – Thomas Whiteley was an eighteen-year-old First Class Saloon Steward who had transferred from the *Olympic* to the *Titanic* for her maiden voyage. Whiteley survived the ordeal with a fractured leg and remained in New York's St. Vincent's Hospital while most of the surviving crew returned to England. A *New York Herald* newspaper reporter interviewed Whiteley in the hospital on April 20th. The bedridden Whiteley had a story to tell and the reporter was eager to feed a sensation-hungry public. The *New York Herald* story published Sunday, April 21, 1912 follows:

LOOKOUTS' WARNINGS OF ICEBERGS THRICE DISREGARDED WITHIN HALF HOUR OF CRASH DECLARES STEWARD

Thomas Whiteley, Tells of Hearing Men Who Were in Crows Nest Express Indignation Because Mr. Murdock, the First Officer, Repeatedly Refused to Act on Their Report of Danger.

"NO WONDER MR. MURDOCK SHOT HIMSELF," SAID SAILOR WHO TOLD OF ICE AHEAD

Conversation of Two Men Who Saw Mountain of Ice That Caused the Disaster Overheard in Lifeboat by Man Now in St. Vincent's Hospital.

That three warnings were given to the officer on the bridge of the *Titanic* that icebergs were ahead, less than half an hour before the fatal crash, was the declaration made last night by Thomas Whiteley, a first [class] saloon steward who now lies in St Vincent's Hospital with frozen and lacerated feet.

Mr. Whitney [sic] also says he understands that the first officer of the *Titanic*, Mr. Murdock [sic], did shoot himself after the crash. This has been rumored, but never verified.

Mr. Whiteley does not attempt to explain why the warnings were ignored or why the speed of the vessel was never reduced or the course changed, but he is positive, he asserts, that the first officer was warned distinctly three times. The warnings came from the two men in the crow's nest, Mr. Whiteley said, and the fact that their warning was unheeded caused the lookouts much indignation and much astonishment.

After being thrown from the *Titanic* while helping to lift women and children into the small boats, Mr. Whiteley finally swam to a small boat and was helped in. It was while there that he heard a conversation between the two lookouts, neither of whom he recalled having seen before, but who, he is confident, were on board the steamship.

WONDERED AT INDIFFERENCE OF OFFICER

The two men talked freely in his hearing and expressed wonderment that their attempts to get the officer to slow up or take other precautionary methods to avoid the bergs had failed. Mr. Whiteley says he carefully marked every word they uttered.

"I don't recall the exact words of the men, but I am certain of the sentiment they expressed. They were very indignant. I was particularly astonished when I heard one of them say: – 'No wonder Mr. Murdock shot himself.'"

Asked if he knew how the reports from the crow's nest to the first officer were made, whether in person or by telephone, the steward said he did nott (sic) know, but his idea was it was done by bells – three bells meaning danger straight ahead, two bells starboard and one bell port.

"My only information is that I heard one of the two men say that he had reported to the first officer that he saw an iceberg."

"I heard one of them say," he said last night in the hospital, "that at a quarter after eleven o'clock on Sunday night, about twenty-five minutes before the great ship struck the berg, that he had told First Officer Murdock that he believed he had seen an iceberg. He said he was not certain, but that he saw the outline of something which he thought must be a berg. A short time later, the lookout said, he noticed what he thought was another mountain of ice. Again, he called the attention of the first officer to it.

"A third time he saw something in the moonlight which he felt certain was an iceberg. The air was cool and there were indications in his mind that there were bergs in the neighborhood. A third time he reported to the first officer that he had seen an iceberg. This time, as I recall it, he did not say merely that he fancied he saw one, but that he had actually seen one.

"His words to the officer, as I remember them, were – 'I saw the iceberg. It was very large, and to me it looked black, or rather a dark gray instead of white.'"

Mr. Whiteley is not in a serious condition and will be out soon. He is a man above the average intelligence and seems very certain of what he says.

The following root cause analysis uses the DMAIC process and is based on *Titanic* Saloon Steward Thomas Whiteley's account of events as reported by the *New York Herald*.

DEFINE
Problem Statement: The *Titanic* hit an iceberg.
When: April 14, 1912
Where: North Atlantic, 41.46 N., 50.14 W
Who: First Officer William T. Murdoch, Lookout Frederick Fleet, and Lookout Reginald Lee
Human Performance: First Officer Murdoch, senior officer on the bridge, ignored the first warnings of icebergs from the Lookouts Fleet and Lee.
Description: Saloon Steward Thomas Whiteley shared a lifeboat with Lookouts Fleet and Lee. Whiteley heard the Lookouts state that they warned First Officer Murdoch on the bridge of icebergs three times with the first warning delivered 25 minutes prior to the collision. First Officer Murdoch ignored the early iceberg warnings that could have prevented the collision.

MEASURE
The Measure phase verifies and captures the sequence of events and pertinent facts (something the New York Herald failed to do).
Sequence of Events (known timeline and Thomas Whiteley's account):
April 14, 1912
9:30 p.m.: Second Officer Lightoller sends message to crow's nest to watch carefully for icebergs until morning.
10:00 p.m.: Lightoller relieved on bridge by First Officer Murdoch. Crow's nest Lookouts relieved by Fleet and Lee. Warning to watch for icebergs passed between the watches.
11:15 p.m.: Lookouts Fleet and Lee report suspected iceberg to the bridge. No action taken by First Officer Murdoch.
Shortly thereafter: Lookouts Fleet and Lee again report suspected iceberg to the bridge. No action taken by First Officer Murdoch.
11:40 p.m.: Lookout Fleet sees *"something in the moonlight which he felt certain was an iceberg."* Fleet immediately strikes three bells and telephones the bridge, *"I saw the iceberg. It was very large, and to me it looked black, or rather a dark gray instead of white."*
First Officer Murdoch takes evasive action but can't avoid the iceberg.
Facts
- There was no moon showing in the North Atlantic on the night of April 14, 1912.
- Frederick Fleet survived in lifeboat 6.
- Reginald Lee survived in lifeboat 13.
- Thomas Whiteley survived in collapsible boat B.

There are many other pertinent and provable facts concerning the Lookouts warning and the First Officer's actions prior to the collision. The fact that

Lookouts Frederick Fleet and Reginald Lee, and Thomas Whiteley were all in separate lifeboats discredits Whiteley's assertion that he overheard the Lookouts, in his lifeboat.

Thomas Whiteley may have seemed to be a reputable source. However, closer scrutiny of his story reveals the danger of relying on a single source of information and being too quick to judgement. This example demonstrates the importance of gathering and verifying the facts during the investigation. Prior to identifying a Human Performance issue based solely on one person's account, that account should be corroborated with verifiable facts.

Whiteley Got it Wrong

Thomas Whiteley and the New York Herald got part of the story right—both Frederick Fleet and Reginald Lee survived. However, their corroborated testimony tells a different story.

11:30 p.m.: With the *Titanic* cruising at 21 knots Lookouts Fleet and Lee in crow's nest noted a slight haze appearing directly ahead of *Titanic*. The haze was not reported to the bridge.

11:40 p.m.: Fleet sees an iceberg dead ahead about 500 yards away towering some 55-60 feet above the water, immediately struck three bells and telephoned the bridge. He reported "Iceberg right ahead." Sixth Officer Moody on bridge replied "Thank you," and relayed the message to First Officer Murdoch who instinctively called "hard-a-starboard" to helmsman and ordered stop engines and then full astern. Less than 30 seconds elapsed from the iceberg sighting to the collision.

Thomas Whiteley never testified or gave any deposition on the disaster to the United States Senate Inquiry or the British Wreck Commissioner's Inquiry or any solicitor for the White Star Line. No one who did give testimony corroborated Whiteley's account. The timeline and proven facts show the Human Performance aspect from Whiteley's account—that the First Officer ignored early iceberg warnings from the Lookouts—to be false.

Thomas Whiteley's account, the account he had five days to contemplate, was not supported by the evidence, but did Thomas Whiteley lie? Perhaps. The chance to tell a reporter a front-page worthy story may have been too tempting and led to embellishment or outright deception. Or perhaps not. It is also possible that his mind simply filled in the missing pieces; a snippet of conversation here, a repeated rumor there, and these overheard theories and speculation, combined with what he did experience, filled in the gaps for him. Those five idle days in the hospital may have contributed to blurring the line between what he actually knew and what he thought he knew.

This Human Performance example serves to demonstrate that misinformation or exaggerated fact can make its way into any investigation if the facts aren't ascertained and corroborated as soon as possible following an incident. The human mind needs the whole story and will unconsciously fill in the gaps with plausible detail. Later these filled-in details can be honestly "remembered" along with other facts. In a blame-free work environment, where the focus is finding root cause, time-affected memory could be one of the few significant impediments to an effective incident investigation.

Other Myths and Legends

Some stories emerge with very little factual basis but become more sensational and popular with every telling.

Titanic's Hull Number – It was widely rumored that *Titanic's* hull number was 390904 (it wasn't), and when viewed in a mirror appeared to read as "NO POPE." How could *Titanic* possibly survive her maiden voyage without one?

Worker Trapped in Hull – This rumor purports that a worker was trapped and died in *Titanic's* double-bottom hull during construction and haunted the ship. This rumor wasn't true and may have started with old timers attempting to scare newly hired workers.

The Christening – This one reasons that the *Titanic* sank because the bottle of champagne used to christen her did not break on the first swing—a short lived reprieve for the champagne but considered very bad luck for the ship. This one fails to recognize that White Star Line did not christen their ships.

Room 13 – The presence of unlucky room number 13 was responsible for *Titanic's* bad luck. A common preventive measure for the number 13 superstition was to avoid it as a hotel floor and as a room number. There was no room number 13 on *Titanic*. Perhaps if there was, it could have been reserved for the absent Pope.

The Mummy Curse – The Priestess of Amen-Ra (a.k.a. ship wrecker) lived in Egypt in 1500 B.C. (well before the relevant timeline for the root cause analysis). After her discovery in the 1890s, various owners of the mummy ran into a series of troubles. The mummy was then donated to the British Museum where it continued to cause mysterious problems for visitors and staff. First Class passenger the British journalist and spiritualist William Stead told stories of the mummy's curse during *Titanic's* voyage and implied the mummy was secretly being transported aboard the ship to New York.

Conclusion – Could it be that the *Titanic* sank because William Stead didn't buy this mummy a ticket and, in the absence of the Pope, a vengeful ghost conspired with Stead's mummy priestess in non-existent room 13 to wreak maiden voyage havoc–causing the ship to break in two when it struck the iceberg because a champagne bottle didn't break when it struck the ship? Probably not.

These myths and legends are not included in the timeline or root cause analysis presented in the following chapters. These chapters will demonstrate the DMAIC process and utilize the Problem Solving and Human Performance models to identify the root causes of the *Titanic* disaster.

Chapter 23

DEFINE AND MEASURE

DMAIC Define

The Define phase of the DMAIC process identifies the when, where, and what for the incident being investigated. The Desired State is also identified in this phase. The "what" for the *Titanic* disaster includes three separate Problem Statements along with a desired state for each.

DEFINE:

When: April 14, 1912 at 11:40 p.m.

Where: North Atlantic, 41.46 N., 50.14 W.

What: The *RMS. Titanic*, on her maiden voyage to the United States, collided with a massive iceberg and sank in less than three hours. 2215 passengers and crew were aboard but only 712 survived the disaster.

Problem Statements and Desired State:

1. **The *Titanic* collided with an iceberg** – the root cause analysis will focus on why the collision occurred.
   Desired State: The goal and acceptable level of improvement is for ships at sea to avoid collisions with icebergs.

2. **The *Titanic* sank after the collision** – the root cause analysis will focus on why the *Titanic* sank following the collision.
   Desired State: The goal is to prevent ships from sinking following a collision at sea.

3. **1503 people perished when the *Titanic* sank** – the root cause analysis will focus on how more people could have been saved.
   Desired State: The goal and acceptable level of improvement is to prevent or minimize loss of life in future shipwrecks.

These problem statements will be analyzed separately for root causes in subsequent Chapters in order to maintain focus on the separate problems. Human Performance issues, if known, should also be identified in the define phase and indicate what a person did, or failed to do, to cause or contribute to the problem being investigated. Potential Human Performance issues associated with each of the above problem statements will be identified in the Chapter that analyzes that problem.

The information contained in the root cause analysis of each of these problem statements and the information included in the following timeline are consistent with the testimony, known facts, and other information contained in the preceding Chapters of this book.

DMAIC Measure

In the Measure phase of the DMAIC process a sequence of events timeline is compiled. The entire timeline, including details that may not seem relevant, is detailed on the following pages. The timeline details applicable to a specific problem statement should be considered during the DMAIC Analyze phase of the root cause analysis.

The Measure phase should also capture known facts and information that may be important to each problem statement being analyzed. The facts that are relevant to a specific problem statement are included in the analysis of that problem in the coming Chapters.

Titanic Timeline:

Background

1886 — Renowned journalist William T. Stead published an article entitled "How the Mail Steamer Went Down in Mid-Atlantic, by a Survivor." The story is about an unnamed steamer that collides with another ship with a large loss of life due to a shortage of lifeboats. Stead wrote, "This is exactly what might take place and will take place if liners are sent to sea short of boats."

1894 — The Merchant Shipping Act 1894 required ships over 10,000 tons to carry 16 lifeboats with a total capacity of 990 people.

1902 — The White Star Line was purchased by the International Mercantile Marine Company, a shipping trust headed by U.S. financier J. P. Morgan. While White Star ships still flew the British flag and carried British crews, the company was essentially controlled by American interests.

1904 — J. Bruce Ismay, with Morgan's full support, became president and managing director of International Mercantile Marine. Harland & Wolff chairman William J. Pirrie also became a director of Mercantile Marine.

Planning and Building – 1907 to 1911

1907   At a dinner party in William J. Pirrie's London mansion, Pirrie and J. Bruce Ismay discussed the construction of two huge ships (with a third to be added later) to compete with the luxury, size, and speed of rival lines. These ships were to be known as Olympic class liners, and were intended to beat out the Cunard Line for both the immigrant steerage, and Atlantic luxury passenger trade.

1908   July 29: White Star owners, including Ismay, approved in principle the design plan for the Olympic class ships prepared by builders Harland & Wolff. A contract was signed for construction of *Olympic*, *Titanic*, and later a third ship in the Belfast shipyards.

December 16: Construction of the *Olympic* began.

1909   Alexander Carlisle, Lord Pirrie's brother-in-law and Harland & Wolff's Chief Naval Architect, recommended using davit pairs designed to handle four lifeboats each. With sixteen davit pairs installed, each ship could carry up to four times the number of lifeboats required by British Board of Trade regulations. His design was approved and the davits were built by the Welin Quadrant Davit Company.

March 31: Construction of the *Titanic* began.

1910   June 30: Alexander Carlisle retired and was replaced by Lord Pirrie's nephew, Naval Architect Thomas Andrews.

October 20: *Olympic's* hull was successfully launched.

1911   May 31: *Titanic's* hull was successfully launched and towed by tugs to the fitting-out basin. Outfitting began.

June: *Olympic's* maiden voyage.

July: First projected date agreed on by White Star and Harland & Wolff for *Titanic's* maiden voyage – March 20, 1912.

Origins of Unsinkable Belief

1910   White Star's publicity brochure for their sister ships *Olympic* and *Titanic* stated, "…and as far as it is possible to do so, these two wonderful vessels are designed to be unsinkable."

1911   Articles in the Irish News, the Belfast Morning News, and Shipbuilder magazine contained reports describing the system of watertight compartments and electronic watertight doors. The conclusion was, for all practical and foreseeable sea going calamities, the *Titanic* will be "practically unsinkable."

Origins of Unsinkable Belief

September 20: *Olympic* (with Captain Edward J. Smith) had her hull badly damaged in collision with Royal Navy cruiser *Hawke* but did not sink. *Titanic's* maiden voyage was delayed due to necessary diversion of workers and materials to repair *Olympic*.

On October 11, 1911, White Star announced the new date for *Titanic's* maiden voyage would be April 10, 1912.

High Tides and Icebergs – January 1912

Jan 3rd The earth was at its closest point to the sun during its annual orbit.

Jan 4th The moon was at its closest point to the earth and on the opposite side of earth than the sun. This rare combination of the earth's closeness to the sun and moon created higher than normal tides capable of refloating more than the expected number of large grounded icebergs. The Labrador current carried these icebergs south of Newfoundland and into the North Atlantic shipping lanes.

Preparing for the Maiden Voyage – January to April 1912

Jan Sixteen wooden lifeboats are installed on *Titanic's* Welin davits (designed to handle up to 64 boats total).

Feb *Titanic* successfully dry-docked at Belfast's Thompson Graving Dock.

Mar Engineering crew began assembling in Belfast. Some lived on board the ship. Lifeboats are tested. They were swung out, lowered, and hoisted back into position under the davits

Mar 31 Outfitting completed, making *Titanic* the largest ship in the world.

Apr 1 While taking on coal in Belfast (or possibly later in Southampton) a fire broke out in coalbunker 10 next to the watertight bulkhead that separates Boiler Room 5 from Boiler Room 6. Sea trials were delayed due to high winds.

Apr 2 6:00 a.m.: Sea trials began. All equipment tested, including wireless. Speed and handling trials undertaken, including various turning and stop-start maneuvers. Major stopping test conducted: ran full ahead at 20 knots and then stopped full astern.

Preparing for the Maiden Voyage – January to April 1912

2:00 p.m.: Running test conducted. Traveled for about two hours (about 40 miles) out into the open Irish Sea at an average speed of 18 knots, and then returned to Belfast. All tests met Board of Trade standards.

8:00 p.m.: Left Belfast for Southampton, her port of embarkation.

Apr 4 — 12:05 a.m.: Arrived at Southampton to begin provisioning and staffing for maiden voyage.

Apr 5 — Good Friday: *Titanic* was "dressed" in panoply of flags and pennants for a salute to the people of Southampton.

Apr 6 — Recruitment day for remainder, and majority, of crew.

Apr 8 — Henry T. Wilde was selected as a last minute addition to the *Titanic* as Chief Officer. This resulted in two officers being pushed down a rank and bumped current Second Officer David Blair off the ship.

Sailing Day – April 10, 1912

6:00 a.m. — Chief Officer Wilde reported for duty.

7:30 a.m. — Captain Edward J. Smith boarded *Titanic* with full crew. Most Officers had spent the night on board. Smith received sailing report from Chief Officer Wilde.

8:00 a.m. — Entire crew mustered, followed by a lifeboat drill using starboard boats 11 and 15.

9:30 to 11:30 a.m. — Second and Third Class boat-trains arrived and passengers boarded the ship.

11:30 a.m. — First Class boat-train from London arrived at dockside. First Class passengers boarded and were escorted to their cabins.

Noon — The *Titanic* departed from Southampton assisted by tugboats. The water surge from *Titanic's* propeller caused the laid-up ship *New York* to bob up and down breaking her mooring lines. The *New York's* stern swung out and was drawn toward the passing *Titanic*. Captain Smith quickly ordered, "Full Astern!" to stop *Titanic's* forward motion. The resulting backwash forced the *New York* away from the *Titanic*. At the same time the tug *Vulcan* was able to attach ropes on the stern of the *New York* to help hold her in place. A collision was avoided by about four feet. *Titanic's* departure was delayed for an hour.

1:00 p.m. — *Titanic* resumed 24-mile trip downstream to English Channel en route to Cherbourg, France.

Sailing Day – April 10, 1912

4:00 p.m.   Boat-train from Paris arrived in Cherbourg. Late arrival of *Titanic* announced.

5:30 p.m.   Cherbourg – passengers boarded the tenders and waited to be ferried out to *Titanic*.

6:30 p.m.   While *Titanic* was anchored in Cherbourg harbor 22 cross-Channel passengers disembarked, and some cargo was unloaded.

8:10 p.m.   With 274 Cherbourg passengers aboard the *Titanic* departed for Queenstown, Ireland.

Trans-Atlantic Crossing – April 11 to 13, 1912

Apr 11   Thursday morning: Captain Smith tested *Titanic's* maneuverability by taking her through some additional practice turns en route to Queenstown.

11:30 a.m.: While *Titanic* was anchored in Queenstown harbor, about two miles from land, 113 Third Class and seven Second Class passengers were boarded from tenders along with 1385 bags of mail. Seven passengers disembarked.

1:30 p.m.: *Titanic* departed on her first Transatlantic crossing to New York.

Apr 12   Noon: *Titanic* had covered 464 miles in fine, calm, clear weather.

Apr 13   Noon: *Titanic* covered additional 519 miles. Fine weather continued. Various ice warnings were received, which was not uncommon for April crossings.

10:30 p.m.: Heavy ice pack warning was signaled by passing *Rappahannock*, which had sustained damage coming through the ice field.

Ice Warnings – Sunday, April 14, 1912

9:00 a.m.   *Titanic* picked up a wireless message from *Caronia* warning of field ice and icebergs in 42°N, from 49° to 51°W.

11:40 a.m.   Dutch liner *Noordam* reported "much ice" in about the same position as the *Caronia*.

Noon   Ship's officers calculated daily position with sextants: 546 miles covered since noon Saturday.

Ice Warnings – Sunday, April 14, 1912

1:42 p.m.   A wireless message from the *Baltic* reports icebergs 250 miles ahead but within five miles of *Titanic's* current course and also warns that the *Deutschland* is not under control.

Captain Smith, 'Titanic.' – Have had moderate, variable winds and clear, fine weather since leaving. Greek steamer 'Athenai' reports passing icebergs and large quantities of field ice to-day in lat. 41° 51' N., long. 49° 52' W. Last night we spoke German oiltank steamer 'Deutschland,' Stettin to Philadelphia, not under control, short of coal, lat. 40° 42' N., long. 55° 11' W. Wishes to be reported to New York and other steamers. Wish you and 'Titanic' all success. – Commander.

The message was delivered to Captain Smith. Smith later gave it to J. Bruce Ismay, who put it in his pocket.

1:45 p.m.   The German liner *Amerika* sent a message through *Titanic's* wireless via Cape Race to the US Hydrographic Office in Washington.

'Amerika' passed two large icebergs in 41º 27' N., 50º 8' W., on the 14th of April.

Amerika's message was overheard by the Marconi Operator but wasn't passed on to the Captain or any other officer.

5:50 p.m.   Captain Smith altered course slightly to the South and West of the normal track. This "turning the corner" course alteration to bring the ship from a southwesterly to a westerly course was delayed by 30 minutes taking *Titanic* eight miles south of the original course.

6:00 p.m.   Second Officer Lightoller relieved Chief Officer Wilde on the bridge.

7:00 p.m.   Captain Smith retrieved the *Baltic* message from Bruce Ismay and posted it in the chart room prior to attending a dinner party in his honor.

7:15 p.m.   First Officer Murdoch ordered forward forecastle hatch closed to stop the glow from inside from interfering with crow's nest and bridge watch.

7:30 p.m.   A message from the *Californian* to the *Antillian* was picked up by the *Titanic*. The message gave *Californian's* position as 42º 3' N, 49º 9' W and warned of three large bergs five miles to the south. The message was delivered to the bridge but did not get to Captain Smith who was attending a dinner party. Ice was now only 50 miles ahead.

Ice Warnings – Sunday, April 14, 1912

Air temperature dropped ten degrees over previous two hours to 33ºF.

The Perfect Calm – Sunday, April 14, 1912

8:40 p.m. Lightoller ordered the carpenter to look after ship's fresh water supply, as the outside seawater was now close to freezing.

8:55 p.m. Captain Smith excused himself from the dinner party and went directly to bridge. He discussed the calm and clear weather conditions with Second Officer Lightoller, as well as visibility of icebergs at night.

9:20 p.m. Captain Smith retired for the night with the order to rouse him "if it becomes at all doubtful…"

9:30 p.m. Lightoller had Sixth Officer Moody send a message to the crow's nest "to keep a sharp lookout for ice, particularly small ice and growlers," until daylight.

9:40 p.m. Senior Wireless Operator received this message from the steamship *Mesaba*, *From 'Mesaba' to 'Titanic' and all east-bound ships. Ice report in lat. 42° N. to 41° 25' N., long. 49° to long. 50° 30' W. Saw much heavy pack ice and great number large icebergs. Also field ice. Weather good, clear.*
The message never makes it to the Captain, the bridge, or any officer.

10:00 p.m. Lightoller was relieved on the bridge by First Officer Murdoch. Lookouts in crow's nest also relieved. Warning to watch for icebergs was passed between the watches. Temperature was 32º F, the moonless, starlit sky was cloudless and the air clear.

10:30 p.m. Sea temperature down to 31º F.

The Collision – Sunday, April 14, 1912

10:55 p.m. Just north of *Titanic*, the *Californian* was stopped for the night in an ice field, and sent out warnings to all ships in area. When the *Californian's* wireless operator called up the *Titanic*, his ice warning was interrupted by a blunt "Keep out! Shut up! You're jamming my signal. I'm working Cape Race."

11:30 p.m. *Californian's* wireless operator turned off his set and retired for the night.

Lookouts Fleet and Lee in the crow's nest noted a slight haze that appeared directly ahead of the *Titanic*. This haze was not recognized as an iceberg and not reported to the bridge.

The Collision – Sunday, April 14, 1912

11:40 p.m. With the *Titanic* moving at 21 knots, Lookout Fleet saw an iceberg dead ahead, about 500 yards away, towering some 55-60 feet above the water. He immediately struck three bells and telephoned the bridge. He reported "Iceberg right ahead," and heard "Thank you" in reply. On the bridge Sixth Officer Moody relayed the message to First Officer Murdoch who called "hard-a-starboard" to the helmsman and ordered the engine room to stop engines and then full astern. Murdoch then activated the lever to close the watertight doors below the waterline. The Helmsman spun the wheel as far as it would go and after several seconds the *Titanic* began to veer to port before her bow struck the iceberg on the starboard side. The impact jarred the crew in the forward area but wasn't noticed by many of the passengers.

Immediate Aftermath – Sunday, April 14, 1912

11:40 p.m. to 11:59 p.m. During first ten minutes after impact, water rises 14 feet above the keel, forward. The first five compartments begin to take on water. Boiler room No. 6, five feet above keel, is flooded in eight feet of water.

Immediately after the collision First Officer Murdoch ordered hard-a-port to complete the port-around attempt that was too late to avoid the iceberg.

Captain Smith arrived on the bridge just after the collision and, after learning they had struck an iceberg, sent Fourth Officer Boxhall to inspect the forward part of the ship.

Captain Smith commanded that the ship steam forward at half-ahead speed.

Chief Officer Henry Wilde arrived on the bridge with news that the forepeak ballast tank was taking in seawater.

With the news of this breach Captain Smith ordered the engines stopped.

Captain Smith went to the Marconi room and told Senior Operator Jack Phillips to be ready to send the distress signal for assistance but not to start sending until he gives the order.

Boxhall made his way down to F deck to look for damage and, finding none, returned to the bridge and reported to Captain Smith. He was then sent to find the Carpenter to have him sound the ship (check for damage).

Immediate Aftermath – Sunday, April 14, 1912

After Boxhall left the bridge he met the Carpenter and a Mail Clerk both on their way to find the Captain with news that the forward compartments were flooding with over two feet of water in the mail sorting room on the Orlop Deck. Boxhall left them to go inspect the damage.

Captain Smith ordered the manually operated bulkhead doors closed on the Orlop Deck and other higher decks.

Damage Discovered – Monday, April 15, 1912

12:01 a.m. The Mailroom, 24 feet above keel, began taking on enough water to float mail bags. Boilers shut down and the relief pipes started blowing off huge noisy clouds of steam.

Captain Smith ordered the lifeboats uncovered.

Captain Smith left the bridge to make his own tour and found Thomas Andrews who was already inspecting the damage and flooding.

Andrews informed the Captain that 3 watertight compartments had been breached.

12:05 a.m. The Squash court, 32 feet above keel was flooded.

12:10 a.m. to 12:27 a.m. Captain Smith returned to the bridge while Andrews continued his damage inspection.

Captain Smith gave the order for passengers and crew to get ready with life belts on deck.

Fourth Officer Joseph Boxhall confirmed the flooding in the mailroom.

Captain Smith sent Boxhall to rouse Officers Lightoller and Pitman and then work out the ship's position.

Thomas Andrews arrived on the bridge, informed the Captain that the *Titanic* will sink, and calculated the ship can only stay afloat for one to two hours.

Captain Smith gave the order to start loading the lifeboats with women and children first.

Boxhall worked out their position to be Latitude 41.46 N, Longitude 50.14 W

Captain Smith took *Titanic's* estimated position to the Marconi room and told Senior Wireless Operator Phillips to start sending the distress call.

Distress Calls and Signals – Monday, April 15, 1912

12:27 a.m. Senior Wireless Operator Phillips started sending the *CQD* distress call for assistance over the ship's wireless.

The message was picked up and shared by ships in range.

12:28 a.m. to 1:00 a.m. Phillips realized the position he was sending was wrong and immediately started sending the correct position, a difference of about 5 miles.

Cape Race reported that *Titanic* gave corrected position as 41.46 N 50.14 W. He said "have struck iceberg".

Carpathia calls *Titanic*, hears the *CQD*, and reverses course and heads to her aid.

From *Carpathia*: *CQD* call received from *Titanic* by *Carpathia*. *Titanic* said "Come at once. We have struck a berg. It's a *CQD* Position 41.46 N. 50.14 W."

Mount Temple reported *MGY* (*Titanic's* call letters) still calling *CQD*. *Mount Temple's* captain reversed ship and steamed for *MGY*. They were about 50 miles away.

Mount Temple reported that *Frankfurt* answered *MGY*. *Titanic* gave him his position and asked "Are you coming to our assistance?" *Frankfurt* asked: "What is the matter with you?" *MGY* replies: "We have struck iceberg and sinking; please tell captain to come." "O.K.; will tell the bridge right away." "O.K.; yes; quick."

From *Olympic*: Hear *Titanic* signaling to some ship about striking an iceberg. Am not sure it is the *Titanic* who has struck an iceberg. Am interfered by atmospherics and many stations working.

Phillips began to intersperse *SOS* with the traditional *CQD* call. *Mount Temple* reported *MGY* calling *SOS*.

12:38 a.m. In an attempt to contact a nearby vessel Fourth Officer Joseph Boxhall, Quartermaster George Rowe, and Quartermaster Arthur J. Bright, began firing rockets from the bridge. While Rowe and Bright continued firing rockets, Boxhall attempted to contact the vessel with a Morse lamp.

Launching Lifeboats – Monday, April 15, 1912

Approx. Time of Launch	Launch Order	Capacity/Passengers and Crew Aboard:
12:40 a.m.	Starboard No. 7	65/28
12:45 a.m.	Starboard No. 5	65/36

Approx. Time of Launch	Launch Order	Capacity/Passengers and Crew Aboard:
12:55 a.m.	Starboard No. 3	65/32
1:00 a.m.	Portside No. 8	65/25
1:05 a.m.	Starboard No. 1	40/12
1:10 a.m.	Portside No. 6	65/24
1:20 a.m.	Portside No. 16	65/53
1:25 a.m.	Portside No. 14	65/40
1:30 a.m.	Portside No. 12	65/42
1:30 a.m.	Starboard No. 9	65/40
1:35 a.m.	Starboard No. 11	65/50
1:40 a.m.	Starboard No. 13	65/55
1:41 a.m.	Starboard No. 15	65/68
1:45 a.m.	Portside No. 2	40/17
1:50 a.m.	Portside No. 10	65/30
1:50 a.m.	Portside No. 4	65/30
2:00 a.m.	Collapsible C	47/43
2:05 a.m.	Collapsible D	47/20

Titanic's Last Hour – Monday, April 15, 1912

1:15 a.m. Water reached *Titanic's* name on the bow as she now listed to port and the tilt of the deck grew steeper.

1:20 a.m. The bow pitched and water flooded through anchor-chain holes.

1:30 a.m. *Titanic's* distress calls became more desperate. "We are sinking fast" and "Women and children in boats. Cannot last much longer"

1:40 a.m. The forward Well Deck was awash.

1:50 a.m. Quartermasters Rowe and Bright fired the last distress rocket. A total of eight rockets were fired.

Senior Wireless Operator Phillips sent the the last wireless distress message the *Carpathia* would hear from the *Titanic*, – "...Engine room full up to boilers..."

2:00 a.m. While the bow continued to submerge the stern began to lift out of the water.

2:05 a.m. *Titanic's* forecastle head sank under water and the tilt of her decks grew steeper.

Titanic's Last Hour – Monday, April 15, 1912

2:10 a.m. As the bow continued to submerge the propellers were lifted out of the water. The North Atlantic ocean was now only ten feet below the Promenade Deck.

2:12 a.m. Senior Wireless Operator Phillips sent *Titanic's* last wireless message just minutes before her bow plunged under the sea.

2:15 a.m. to 2:20 a.m. *Titanic's* bow plunged underwater.

Collapsible B floated clear but upside down.

Father Thomas Byles heard confession and gave absolution to over one hundred Second and Third-Class passengers gathered at the aft end of the Boat Deck.

The ship's band stopped playing.

Many passengers and crew jumped overboard.

Titanic's forward funnel collapsed, crushing a number of swimming passengers.

Collapsible A floated free, right side up but swamped. About two dozen people in the water grabbed hold.

A huge roar was heard as all moveable objects inside *Titanic* crashed toward the submerged bow. As the bow sinks, the pressure of the rising stern increased and, when *Titanic's* tilt exceeded 45 degrees, the structure's steel began to rip apart.

The ship's lights blinked once and then went out.

Weighing 16,000 tons, the sinking bow ripped loose and sank.

Titanic's broken-off stern section settled back into the water and righted itself for a few minutes before it again tilted high into the air as it filled with water.

2:20 a.m. The *Titanic* foundered in the North Atlantic ocean.

In the Water or in a Lifeboat – Monday, April 15, 1912

2:20 a.m. to 3:00 a.m. Almost 1500 people struggled and cried out for help in the freezing, 28° F, water.

After about 20 minutes cries for help diminished, then turned to moans, and by 3:00 a.m. all was silent as hypothermia claimed the lives of most of those in the water.

Lifeboats 1, 2, 3, 4, 5, 6, 7, 8, and collapsible D all have room but none returned to pick up survivors.

Lifeboat 12 was tied together with boats 4, 10, 14 and collapsible D.

In the Water or in a Lifeboat – Monday, April 15, 1912

3:00 a.m. to 3:30 a.m.	Fifth Officer Lowe moved survivors from lifeboat 14 to the other boats so he could return to look for any surviving passengers.
	Fifth Officer Lowe and his crew found only four survivors to pull from the water, with one man dying minutes later.
	1503 victims died in the sinking of the *Titanic*.
3:30 a.m.	The *Carpathia's* rockets were sighted by the lifeboats.
4:00 a.m.	The *Carpathia* was sighted.
4:10 a.m.	Boat 2 was the first boat picked up by the *Carpathia*.
4:00 a.m. to 6:30 a.m.	Fifth Officer Lowe rigged a sail on Boat 14 and started towing collapsible D toward the *Carpathia*.
	Fifth Officer Lowe rescued the 12 surviving passengers that were standing knee deep in freezing water, from the swamped Collapsible A. Three bodies were left in the lifeboat.
	As dawn approached swell waves began to replace the flat calm sea.
	On the up-side-down Collapsible B lifeboat Second Officer Lightoller lined the men up into a double column, facing the bow. Then, as the boat swayed, he ordered a lean to the left or right, to counteract the swell, but Collapsible B was slowly sinking.
	Second Officer Lightoller saw Boats 4, 10, and 12 tied together about 400 yards away and signaled the boat with his officer's whistle.
	Boats 4 and 12 rowed over to assist Collapsible B.
	Boat 4 arrived first and took on twelve of the survivors from the foundering collapsible.
	Boat 12 took the remaining sixteen survivors with Second Officer Lightoller the last to leave.
	Second Officer Lightoller took over command of lifeboat 12 from ABS John Poingdestre.
	Lifeboat 12, designed to hold 65, now carried 69 survivors.
8:15 a.m.	All except lifeboat 12 have been rescued by the *Carpathia*.
8:30 a.m.	Lifeboat 12 was picked up by the *Carpathia*. Second Officer Lightoller was the last survivor to come on board.
8:50 a.m.	The *Carpathia* left the area bound for New York with 712 survivors.

Californian Timeline

Sunday, April 14, 1912

7:30 p.m. The *Californian* sent a message to the *Antillian* giving the *Californian's* position as 42° 3' N, 49° 9' W and warned of three large bergs five miles to the south. The message was picked up by the *Titanic*.

8:00 p.m. Third Officer Charles Groves started his watch shift on the bridge.

10:55 p.m. The *Californian* was stopped in an ice field about 10 miles north of the *Titanic*. The *Californian* sent out ice warnings to all ships in area. When the *Californian's* wireless operator called up the *Titanic*, his ice warning was interrupted by the *Titanic's* wireless operator with the message, "Keep out! Shut up! You're jamming my signal. I'm working Cape Race."

11:10 p.m. to 11:25 p.m. Third Officer Groves saw a steamer coming up a little bit abaft (behind the stern) of the *Californian's* starboard beam. He judged the steamer to be 10 to 12 miles away.

Groves believed the steamer was getting closer and coming around slightly to the south and west.

Groves made out two white masthead lights on the steamer.

Groves reported the movement of the steamer to Captain Lord and remarked that she was evidently a passenger steamer based on her many deck lights.

11:30 p.m. Third Officer Groves to attempted to signal the steamer with the Morse light.

11:30 p.m. *Californian's* wireless operator turned off his set and retired for the night.

11:40 p.m. One bell was struck to call the middle watch. Third Officer Groves determined that the steamer had stopped. He saw the lights of the steamer go out or go out of his sight.

11:45 p.m. Captain Lord came to the bridge while Groves was Morsing the steamer and he remarked to Groves, "She does not look like a passenger steamer." Groves replied that it was a passenger steamer but she put her lights out a few minutes ago.

Captain Lord said: "The only passenger steamer near us is the *Titanic*."

Groves got no answer from his Morsing of the steamer.

Monday, April 15, 1912

12:10 a.m.   Third Officer Groves was relieved by Second Officer Stone on deck. Captain Lord told Stone to watch the stopped steamer and let him know if she altered her bearings or got any closer. Captain Lord then went to lie down in the chart room.

1:10 a.m.   By way of the speaktube to the chart room, Second Officer Stone reported to Captain Lord that he had spotted what appeared to be white rockets bursting in the sky from the direction of the steamer that they had been observing. Five white bursts had come at intervals of about three or four minutes. Captain Lord instructed Second Officer Stone to continue Morsing this vessel and to send Apprentice Gibson down to him with any information received.

1:10 a.m. to 1:50 a.m.   Morsing was not answered by the steamer under observation. Three additional rockets were fired from the steamship. Second Officer Stone remarked to Apprentice Gibson that the steamer was slowly steaming away towards the south-west and said, "Look at her now; she looks very queer out of the water; her lights look queer."

Second Officer Stone said to Apprentice Gibson that a ship is not going to fire rockets at sea for nothing.

2:00 a.m.   Second Officer Stone sent Apprentice Gibson to the chart room to notify Captain Lord of the additional rockets. Captain Lord asked about color in the rockets but was half asleep and does not remember the conversation.

2:05 a.m.   The steamship that had been under observation from the bridge of the *Californian* and the subject of conversation between Second Officer Stone and Apprentice Gibson disappeared from sight.

2:40 a.m.   Second Officer Stone informed Captain Lord through the speak tube that the ship they have been watching appears to have disappeared bearing south-west half west. Captain Lord does not remember the conversation.

6:00 a.m.   The *Californian* turned her wireless back on and learned of the *Titanic* disaster from the *Frankfort*. The *Californian* then steamed toward *Titanic's* last reported position.

8:30 a.m.   The *Californian* arrived at side of the *Carpathia*, and then steamed through disaster area to undertake final check for survivors.

Chapter 24

COLLISION WITH AN ICEBERG - ROOT CAUSE ANALYSIS

DMAIC Analyze

In this DMAIC phase the incident or a specific associated problem is analyzed to discover and verify cause-and-effect relationships and determine root cause(s). To aid in the root cause analysis, facts and testimony normally collected during the DMAIC Measure phase, but that are specific to this problem statement, are presented in this Chapter.

Problem Statement:
The *Titanic* collided with an iceberg – This root cause analysis focuses on why the collision with the iceberg occurred.

Desired State:
The goal and acceptable level of improvement is for ships at sea to avoid collisions with icebergs.

Coal Fire – Did Captain Smith maintain the ship's speed as it approached the ice fields in order to use up the smoldering coal and extinguish the fire that had been burning since their departure?

Testimony concerning the coal fire:

> **British Wreck Commissioner's Inquiry** – Testimony of Lead Fireman Frederick Barrett, examined by Mr. Pringle.
> 2330. You told us there was some fire in that bunker?
> Barrett – Yes.
> 2331. Soon after you left port?
> Barrett – Yes.
> 2332. Is it a very uncommon thing for fire to get into a coal bunker in that way?
> Barrett – It is not an uncommon thing.
> 2333. It happens sometimes?
> Barrett – Yes.
> 2334. I suppose the proper order is to have that actual bunker emptied as soon as possible?
> Barrett – Yes.

British Wreck Commissioner's Inquiry – Testimony of Fireman Charles Hendrickson, examined by Mr. Lewis.

5232. Do you remember a fire in a coal bunker on board this boat?
Hendrickson – Yes.
5233. Is it a common occurrence for fires to take place on boats?
Hendrickson – No.
5235. How long have you been on a White Star boat?
Hendrickson – About five years.
5236. When did you last see a fire in a coal bunker?
Hendrickson – I never saw one before.
5237. It has been suggested that fires in coal bunkers are quite a common occurrence, but you have been five years in the White Star line and have not seen a fire in a coal bunker?
Hendrickson – No.
5238. Did you help to get the coal out?
Hendrickson – Yes.
5239. Did you hear when the fire commenced?
Hendrickson – Yes, I heard it commenced at Belfast.
5240. When did you start getting the coal out?
Hendrickson – The first watch we did from Southampton we started to get it out.
5241. How many days would that be after you left Belfast?
Hendrickson – I do not know when she left Belfast to the day.
5242. It would be two or three days, I suppose?
Hendrickson – I should say so.
5243. Did it take much time to get the fire down?
Hendrickson – It took us right up to the Saturday to get it out.

Facts concerning the coal fire:
- A coal fire had been burning in coalbunker 10 since the start of the voyage.
- Once the ship was underway the coal in bunker 10 was used up in order to get to and extinguish the coal fire that had started prior to departure.
- It took until Saturday night to empty the coal bunker and extinguish the fire.

Port-around Attempt – Was First Officer Murdoch's port-around attempt the correct and expected response to the iceberg sighting?

Testimony concerning the port-around attempt:

Quartermaster Hichens was on duty manning the ship's wheel when 3 bells and the lookout's call to the bridge alerted First Officer Murdoch of the iceberg. Murdoch immediately ordered hard-a-starboard in an attempt to port-around the iceberg.

British Wreck Commissioner's Inquiry – Testimony of Quartermaster Robert Hichens, examined by the Attorney General.
952. Did you begin to get the helm over?
Hichens – Yes, the helm was barely over when she struck. The ship had swung about two points.
954. (The Commissioner.) Do let me understand; had she swung two points before the crash came?
Hichens – Yes, my Lord.
955. (The Attorney General.) I am not quite sure that I understand what you had done to the helm before this. You had got an order, "Hard-a-starboard"?
Hichens – "Hard-a-starboard," yes.
956. You proceeded at once to put the wheel hard-a-starboard?
Hichens – Immediately, yes.
957. Before the vessel struck had you had time to get the wheel right over?
Hichens – The wheel was over then, hard over.
958. (The Commissioner.) Before she struck?
Hichens – Oh yes, hard over before she struck.
959. (The Attorney General.) Who gave the order "hard-a-starboard"?
Hichens – Mr. Murdoch, the First Officer.

Quartermaster Alfred Olliver was running messages for the officers and had just returned to the bridge when the collision occurred. He heard First Officer Murdoch's "hard-a-port" order to complete the port-around attempt that caused the stern of the *Titanic* to swing away and disengage from the underwater contact with the iceberg.

United States Senate Inquiry – Testimony of Quartermaster Alfred Olliver, questioned by Senator Burton.
Mr. Olliver – What I know about the wheel – I was stand-by to run messages, but what I knew about the helm is, hard-a-port.
Senator Burton – Do you mean hard-a-port or hard-a-starboard?
Mr. Olliver – I know the orders I heard when I was on the bridge was after we had struck the iceberg. I heard hard-a-port, and there was the man at the wheel and the officer. The officer was seeing it was carried out right.
Senator Burton – What officer was it?
Mr. Olliver – Mr. Moody, the sixth officer, was stationed in the wheelhouse.
Senator Burton – Who was the man at the wheel?
Mr. Olliver – Hichens, quartermaster.

Facts concerning the Collision:
- First Officer Murdoch ordered hard-a-starboard in order to attempt to port-around the iceberg.
- Less than 30 seconds had elapsed from the iceberg sighting to the collision.
- *Titanic's* bow struck the iceberg on the starboard side, causing damage to spots along nearly 300 feet of the hull.
- Immediately after the collision First Officer Murdoch ordered hard-a-port to complete the port-around maneuver. This caused the stern to swing away and disengage from the underwater contact with the iceberg and prevented further damage.

The Perfect Calm – Did the perfectly calm conditions on the North Atlantic result in the iceberg not being seen in time to avoid a collision?

Testimony concerning the conditions prior to the collision:

Sunday night's perfect calm was described by Second Officer Charles Lightoller.

> **British Wreck Commissioner's Inquiry** – Testimony of Charles Lightoller, examined by the Solicitor General.
> 14197. Can you suggest at all how it can have come about that this iceberg should not have been seen at a greater distance?
> Lightoller – It is very difficult indeed to come to any conclusion. Of course, we know now the extraordinary combination of circumstances that existed at that time which you would not meet again once in 100 years; that they should all have existed just on that particular night shows, of course, that everything was against us.
> 14198. (The Commissioner.) ... What were the circumstances?
> Lightoller – ... In the first place, there was no moon.
> 14199. That is frequently the case.
> Lightoller – Very—I daresay it had been the last quarter or the first quarter. Then there was no wind, not the slightest breath of air. And most particular of all in my estimation is the fact, a most extraordinary circumstance, that there was not any swell. Had there been the slightest degree of swell I have no doubt that berg would have been seen in plenty of time to clear it.
> 14200. Wait a minute: No moon, no wind, no swell?
> Lightoller – The moon we knew of, the wind we knew of, but the absence of swell we did not know of. You naturally conclude that you do not meet with a sea like it was, like a tabletop or a floor, a most extraordinary circumstance, and I guarantee that 99 men out of 100 could never call to mind actual proof of there having been such an absolutely smooth sea.
> ...14203. Do not let me interrupt you; you were going to particularise

the circumstances which you say combined to bring about this calamity. There was no moon, no wind, and no swell; is there anything else?

Lightoller – The berg into which we must have run in my estimation must have been a berg which had very shortly before capsized, and that would leave most of it above the water practically black ice.

14204. You think so?

Lightoller – I think so, or it must have been a berg broken from a glacier with the blue side towards us, but even in that case, had it been a glacier there would still have been the white outline that Captain Smith spoke about, with a white outline against, no matter how dark a sky, providing the stars are out and distinctly visible, you ought to pick it out in quite sufficient time to clear it at any time. That is to say, providing the stars are out and providing it is not cloudy. You must remember that all the stars were out and there was not a cloud in the sky, so that at any rate there was bound to be a certain amount of reflected light. Had it been field ice, had we been approaching field ice, of more or less extent, looking down upon it it would have been very visible. You would have been able to see that field ice five miles away, I should think. Had it been a normal iceberg with three sides and the top white with just a glimpse of any of the white sides they would have shown sufficient reflected light to have been noticeable a mile and a half or two miles distant. The only way in which I can account for it is that this was probably a berg which had overturned as they most frequently do, which had split and broken adrift; a berg will split into different divisions, into halves perhaps, and then it becomes top-heavy, and at the same time as it splits you have what are often spoken of as explosions and the berg will topple over. That brings most of the part that has been in the water above the water.

14206. Just let us put that together. It is dark, in the sense that there is no moon, with a bright, starlit sky perfectly clear, but there is no wind or swell, and if there had been there would have been some motion of the water against the bottom iceberg, which would have been noticeable?

Lightoller – Yes.

… 14208. And [the iceberg] was displaying black ice with nothing white about it – that is it, is it not?

Lightoller – That is about it.

14209. Does that, in your opinion, account for the man on the look-out not seeing the iceberg?

Lightoller – Yes.

Lookouts Frederick Fleet and Reginald Lee, the lookouts on duty when the *Titanic* struck the iceberg, testified concerning the appearance of a slight distant haze on the horizon prior to the collision.

British Wreck Commissioner's Inquiry – Testimony of Reginald Lee, examined by the Attorney General.

2401. What sort of a night was it?

Lee – A clear, starry night overhead, but at the time of the accident there was a haze right ahead.

2402. At the time of the accident a haze right ahead?

Lee – A haze right ahead – in fact it was extending more or less round the horizon. There was no moon.

2403. And no wind?

Lee – And no wind whatever, barring what the ship made herself.

2404. Quite a calm sea?

Lee – Quite a calm sea.

... 2407. It was colder that night than ever you had had it that voyage in the "Titanic"?

Lee – Yes, on that trip.

2408. Did you notice this haze which you said extended on the horizon when you first came on the look-out, or did it come later?

Lee – It was not so distinct then—not to be noticed. You did not really notice it then—not on going on watch, but we had all our work cut out to pierce through it just after we started. My mate happened to pass the remark to me. He said, "Well; if we can see through that we will be lucky." That was when we began to notice there was a haze on the water. There was nothing in sight.

British Wreck Commissioner's Inquiry – Testimony of Lookout Frederick Fleet, examined by the Attorney General.

17257. When you saw this haze did it continue right up to the time of your striking the berg?

Fleet – Yes.

17258. Can you give us any idea how long it was before you struck the berg that you noticed the haze?

Fleet – No, I could not.

17259. Can you tell us about how long you had been on duty before you noticed the haze?

Fleet – I could not say. I had no watch.

17260. I want you to give us some idea. You came on duty at 10 o'clock. We know that the berg was struck at about 11:40. That gives us an hour and 40 minutes, during which time you were in the crow's-nest all the time. That is right, is it not?

Fleet – Yes.

You say the first part of the watch it was clear and then there came this change which you have described. I want you to give some idea of when it was you noticed the change – when it got to a haze.

17261. (The Commissioner.) We do not want you to guess, you know;

if you cannot tell us you must not guess.

The Witness: Well, I daresay it was somewhere near seven bells.

17262. (The Attorney General.) Somewhere near seven bells, which would be half-past 11?

Fleet – Yes.

17263. Did you say anything to your mate about it?

Fleet – Well, I told him there was a slight haze coming.

17264. Is that Lee?

Fleet – Lee.

17265. At the time that you noticed the haze was there anything in sight?

Fleet – No.

17266. Did it interfere with your sight ahead of you?

Fleet – No.

17267. Could you see as well ahead and as far ahead after you noticed the haze as you could before?

Fleet – It did not affect us, the haze.

17268. It did not affect you?

Fleet – No, we could see just as well.

17269. You did not report it then, I gather from that?

Fleet – No.

17270. You did not say anything about it to the bridge?

Fleet – No.

17271. The Attorney General reads Reginald Lee's answer to question 2408 to Frederick Fleet (…My mate happened to pass the remark to me. He said, "Well; if we can see through that we will be lucky.")

Fleet – Well, I never said that.

17273. (The Commissioner – To the witness.) I understand you to say that whatever it was, it made no difference to the look-out?

Fleet – Yes, My Lord.

Facts concerning the Environment:
- High tides of January were unusually high due to the closeness of the sun and the moon. These high tides likely refloated grounded icebergs and freed them to drift south resulting in more and larger icebergs in the North Atlantic shipping lanes.
- Sunday night was cold, there was no breeze and the night sky was moonless, starlit and clear.
- The perfectly calm sea was absolutely flat with no swell (very unusual for the North Atlantic).
- From about 7:00 to 9:00 p.m. the air temperature dropped 10º F. By 10:00 p.m. the air temperature was 32º F.

- Without any breeze or ocean swell, an iceberg is harder to spot because there are no water ripples breaking on the base of the iceberg to give early warning of its presence.

PROBLEM SOLVING MODEL

The *Titanic* collided with an iceberg (Figure 24 – 1).

Method/Procedure – Causal factor considered:
– **Alternate Practice** – Was an "Alternate Practice" followed by Captain Smith or First Officer Murdoch instead of the expected standard?

Discussion of Captain Smith's methods:

Captain Smith was following the accepted (and successful) practice of maintaining speed and relying on the crow's nest lookouts when approaching ice in clear weather. Captain Smith's failure to take appropriate preventive measures prior to the collision will be analyzed later in this chapter using the Human Performance Model.

Discussion of First Officer Murdoch's actions:

When he first became aware of the iceberg the immediate actions of First Officer Murdoch were the expected responses. The port-around attempt to avoid a collision was the textbook response method based on current training. There simply wasn't enough time to clear the iceberg. The Lookouts failure to see the iceberg in time will be analyzed using the Human Performance Model.

Conclusion:

The port-around attempt was the expected response and is not a root cause.

Equipment – Causal factor considered:
– **Breakdown** – Was Saturday's "Mechanical Failure" of the *Titanic's* Marconi Wireless a causal factor that led to the collision?

Discussion:

The Marconi Operators diagnosed the problem and had the wireless back up and running by Sunday morning. The Senior Operator was still working on clearing passenger messages from the backlog that had built up while the wireless was out of service when the *Mesaba* ice warning came in at 9:40 p.m.. He put the message aside intending to deliver it to the bridge when he was finished with the backlog, but the message that reported heavy pack ice and icebergs in the immediate area never made it to the Captain, the bridge, or any officer.

Conclusion:

While the failure to deliver the ice warning can easily be attributed to the distraction of clearing the passenger message backlog due to the breakdown of the wireless the previous day, this is a Human Performance issue, not a breakdown/mechanical failure root cause. The mechanical failure root cause would be appropriate if the *Titanic* had not received crucial ice warnings because the wireless was out of service.

Fishbone Diagram

Categories: Method, Equipment, Measurement, Material, Environment

- Breakdown
- Alternate Practice
- Hazardous Conditions
- Outside Environment

Effect: **Titanic collided with an iceberg**

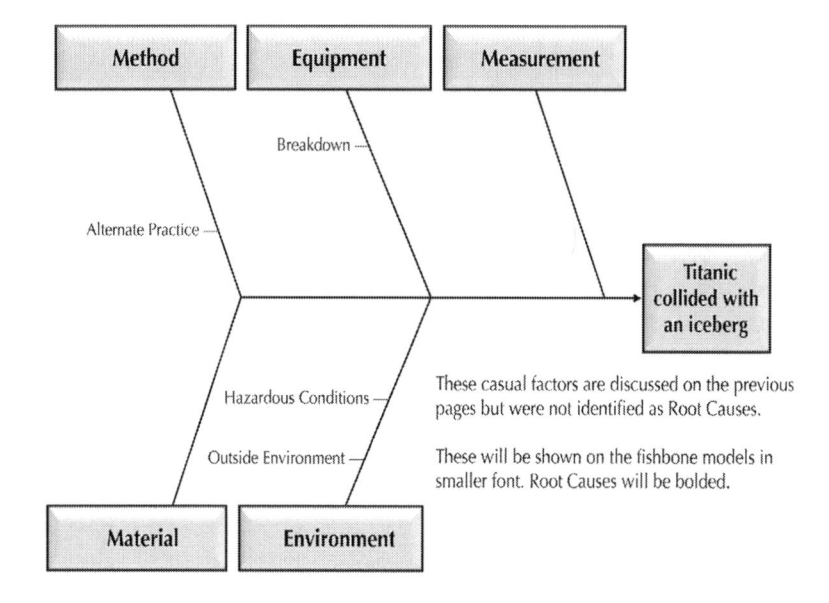

These casual factors are discussed on the previous pages but were not identified as Root Causes.

These will be shown on the fishbone models in smaller font. Root Causes will be bolded.

Figure 24 – 1, Problem Solving Model with selected causal statements

Environment – Causal factors considered:

   – **Hazardous Conditions** – Did the coal fire that was burning in coalbunker 10 prior to departure result in the full speed that was maintained while approaching the ice field?

Discussion:

Once the ship was underway the coal in bunker 10 was used in order to get to and extinguish the coal fire. It took until Saturday night to use the coal and empty the coal bunker.

There was conflicting testimony as to whether the coal fire was a hazardous condition or common place on steamers of the day but even if Captain Smith did maintain high speed during the voyage in order to use the coal faster he no longer needed to maintain that speed on Sunday. The bunker 10 coal had been used up by Saturday night and the fire was out.

Conclusion:

The coal fire is not a root cause for excessive speed prior to striking the iceberg but the damage the fire caused to the transverse bulkhead will be considered in the root cause analysis for why the *Titanic* sank following the collision.

   – **Outside environment** – Were the number of large icebergs in the North Atlantic and the perfect calm on the night of the collision causal factors?

Discussion of icebergs and perfect calm:

There were more and larger icebergs in the North Atlantic than usual, likely due to the January high tides caused by the rare nearness of the earth to both the sun and moon.

With no moonlight, no wind, and absolutely no swell on the North Atlantic, this starlit, perfect calm resulted in the iceberg being difficult to see at a distance because there was no water breaking at its base to give early warning of its presence. This, along with the iceberg displaying its dark ice side, were contributing factors to not seeing the iceberg in time to avoid the collision.

Conclusion:

This fits part of the root cause definition in that more and larger icebergs and the perfect calm could be considered a "most basic initiating cause for the problem being investigated," but these conditions are not correctable and can't be eliminated and therefore are not realistic root causes. The lack of an appropriate response to these conditions is correctable; the conditions as they existed, and may exist in the future, are not.

HUMAN PERFORMANCE

Human Performance Issue:

The Crow's Nest Lookouts failed to see the iceberg in time to avoid the collision.

Less than 30 seconds elapsed from the iceberg sighting to the collision. If the crow's nest lookouts would have had binoculars would the iceberg have been spotted in time to avoid it or would the collision have been less severe?

People associated with the Human Performance issue:
- Mr. William T. Murdoch – First Officer, age 39. Murdoch was the officer in charge of the bridge when the iceberg was struck. Murdoch did not survive.
- Mr. David Blair – Second Officer (replaced). Blair, considered too senior to be 3rd Officer, was bumped off the *Titanic* in Southampton by Wilde's appointment as Chief Officer.
- Frederick Fleet – Lookout, Age 24. Fleet spotted the iceberg, immediately struck three bells and telephoned the bridge with these now famous words, "Iceberg right ahead!"
- Reginald Lee – Lookout, Age 41. Lee was in the crow's nest with Fleet when the iceberg was sighted.

Testimony concerning the availability and use of binoculars:

British Wreck Commissioner's Inquiry – Testimony of Lookout Frederick Fleet, examined by the Attorney General.
17224. Had your eyes been tested by the Board of Trade?
Fleet – Yes.
117226. And got a certificate?
Fleet – I had one, but I lost it.
17227. Lost it?

Fleet – In the "Titanic."
17228. But, at any rate, you had got it before you went on this voyage in the "Titanic"?
Fleet – Yes.

Testimony of Frederick Fleet, examined by Mr. Scanlan.
17401. Do you think if you had had glasses you could have seen the iceberg sooner?
Fleet – Certainly.
17402. How much sooner do you think you could have seen it?
Fleet – In time for the ship to get out of the way.
17403. So that it is your view that if you had had glasses it would have made all the difference between safety and disaster?
Fleet – Yes.
17404. (The Commissioner.) Would it depend upon whether you had the glasses up to your eyes, or not? I suppose having the glasses in the box would not have been any good to you?
Fleet – When I have to keep a sharp look-out I have the glasses in my hand, if there are any there, till my watch is finished.
17405. Glasses in your hand will not help you to see anything unless you had them up to your eyes?
Fleet – I put the glasses before my eyes. I pick things out on the horizon with the glasses.
17406. (Mr. Scanlan.) You were told when you went on watch that you had to keep a sharp look-out. In these circumstances, if there had been glasses in the crow's-nest would you have used them?
Fleet – Yes.
17407. Constantly?
Fleet – Yes.
17408. After all, you are the man who discovered the iceberg?
Fleet – Yes.

Second Officer Lightoller testified concerning the use and effectiveness of glasses at night.

British Wreck Commissioner's Inquiry – Testimony of Charles Lightoller, examined by Solicitor General.
13682. Were you using glasses?
Lightoller – Part of the time, yes.
13683. Do you in practice at night use glasses for the purpose of scanning the track you have to follow? Do you mean it was exceptional to use them?
Lightoller – I mean to say that on this occasion, knowing there were no lights round the icebergs, you would naturally have a pair of glasses in

your hand, but where there are lights about you do not use glasses; you pick them up with your eyes first.

13684. Supposing anybody's duty is to look out for ice at night what is your view as to the usefulness of glasses?

Lightoller – With regard to picking up ice?

13685. Yes?

Lightoller – It is rather difficult to say. I never have picked up ice at nighttime with glasses, so it is really difficult for me to say.

13686. (The Commissioner.) What were you using them for on the bridge?

Lightoller – To assist me in keeping a look-out.

13687. Then you were using them; you were looking out for ice?

Lightoller – I was looking out for ice.

13688. And you were using the glasses?

Lightoller – Occasionally I would raise the glasses to my eyes and look ahead to see if I could see anything, using both glasses and my eyes.

13689. The question I understand is this: Do the glasses help you to detect ice?

Lightoller – Well I should naturally think so, My Lord.

Fleet's lookout mate Reginald Lee also testified concerning the availability and use of glasses.

British Wreck Commissioner's Inquiry – Testimony of Reginald Lee, examined by the Attorney General.

2365. You have had about 15 or 16 years at sea altogether?

Lee – Yes.

2367. Are glasses usually supplied to the lookout man in mail steamers?

Lee – Not that I know.

…2370. Have you ever had glasses for use as look-out man?

Lee – Yes, but I do not know whether they were private or supplied by the company.

2372. Have you found them of use?

Lee – They are better than the ordinary eye-sight.

2373. Are they of use at night at all?

Lee – Certainly, night glasses.

2375. There are different glasses used at night from those used in the day; is that right?

Lee – Well, they are called that by the trade, I believe.

2377. Do you know whether they are supplied in any other vessels of the White Star Line?

Lee – I cannot say they are for certainty, but my mate in the crow's-nest, who was for four years in the "Oceanic" as look-out man, told me they had them there.

2378. Who is your mate in the crow's-nest?
Lee – Fleet.
2379. (The Commissioner.) Fleet told you they were in the "Oceanic"?
Lee – They used them there.
2380. (The Attorney General.) Were there any on the "Titanic?
Lee – No, not for our use anyway.
…2385. Did you look for glasses at all in the crow's-nest?
Lee – We asked for them.
2386. On the "Titanic"?
Lee – Yes. I did not personally ask for them, but one of the other fellows did, and they said there were none for us.
2387. Who was the one of the other fellows who asked for them, do you know?
Lee – Simmons [Symons] or Jewell; I cannot be sure which one it was.
2388. I think we know Simmons was Jewell's mate on the look-out?
Lee – Yes.
2389. Fleet was yours?
Lee – Yes.
2390. And I think Hogg and Evans were the other two?
Lee – Yes.

Lookout George Alfred Hogg, 29, gave this testimony before Senator Perkins at the United States Senate Inquiry:

"We never had night glasses. Just the naked eye. I have always had night glasses in the White Star boats. I asked for the glasses, and I did not see why I should not have them. I had them from Belfast to Southampton; but from Southampton to where the accident occurred we never had them. I asked for the glasses several times."

British Wreck Commissioner's Inquiry – Testimony of Reginald Lee, examined by Mr. Cotter.
2710. If you had had a pair of night binoculars that night, and you were using them, I suggest to you that you would have seen that berg earlier?
Lee – Quite feasible.
2711. And then there would have been a chance of telling the Officer on the bridge that it was ahead before you did.
2712. (The Commissioner.) Can you tell me the difference between day binoculars and night binoculars?
Lee – No, my Lord, except that they are made in the trade for night use and day use.

Testimony of Reginald Lee, examined by Sir Robert Finlay.
2713. Just a few questions. The practice varies a good deal, does not it, about supplying binoculars to the look-out men?
Lee – Well, Sir, I do not know. They are supposed to be. It may be that some companies would supply them and some companies would not supply them.
2714. You know, I daresay, there is some difference of opinion as to whether it is desirable that the men who have to look out all round should have glasses?
Lee – Yes.
2715. That is, I believe, because it leads them to fix their attention on the spot to which they are directing the glasses?
Lee – Yes.

Facts concerning the lack of binoculars (also called glasses at the time) for the Lookouts:
- The Lookouts had glasses to use from Belfast to Southampton but did not have glasses after leaving Southampton.
- When Chief Officer Wilde was selected as a last minute addition to the *Titanic* crew two officers were pushed down a rank and Second Officer David Blair was bumped off the ship. Blair left the ship with the only key to the locker holding the lookout's glasses.
- The Lookouts requested glasses but did not get them.

HUMAN PERFORMANCE MODEL

Crow's Nest Lookouts failed to see the iceberg in time to avoid the collision (Figure 24 – 2).

Tools and Resources – Causal factor considered:
– **Availability** – Binoculars were not available to the Lookouts. Were the binoculars "Required Equipment" that would have prevented the accident or resulted in a less severe collision?
Discussion:
Frederick Fleet, the Lookout in the crow's nest who spotted the iceberg testified that binoculars would have made a difference. The lookout's binoculars, normally supplied by White Star Line, were locked up and not available after the ship departed Southampton. The lookouts requested binoculars but none were forthcoming and they had to do without. It has been argued that binoculars would not have made any difference with the moonless, perfectly calm conditions rendering them almost useless for spotting a distant iceberg. Concerning how he would have used glasses to keep a sharp lookout, Frederick Fleet testified, "I put the glasses before my eyes. I pick things out on the horizon with the glasses." During his testimony Reginald Lee, Fleet's lookout partner,

agreed with the assertion that the use of glasses could lead the Lookout "to fix their attention on the spot to which they are directing the glasses." Fleet was directing his attention straight ahead when he sighted the iceberg with his naked eye and sounded the alarm. The *Titanic* struck the iceberg 30 seconds later. The ship's officers and crew were able to avoid a head on collision and almost missed the iceberg. Would the use of binoculars to "pick things out on the horizon" and fix "attention on the spot," straight ahead, have allowed the berg to be sighted 30 seconds, a minute, or two minutes earlier? Enough time, according to Fleet, "for the ship to get out of the way."

Conclusion:

Binoculars not being available is a root cause for the Lookout's failure to see the iceberg in time to avoid the collision.

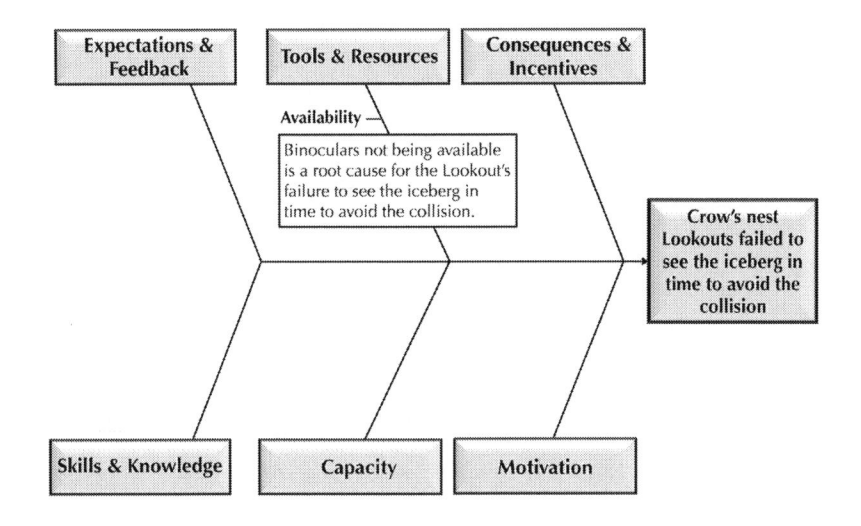

Figure 24 – 2, Human Performance Model with selected causal statements

Discussion of Officer Handoff Process:

The 5-Why example in Chapter 22 identified the Lookouts lack of binoculars as a potential cause for not spotting the iceberg in time and drilled down to a root cause of an inadequate handoff process between the reassigned Second Officer and the officer who left the ship without turning over the key to the binoculars. This implies that the CAPA should be a procedure or other written guidelines to be followed to ensure an adequate handoff in a similar situation. A process with written instructions is often an effective CAPA for a regular, expected activity but a closer examination rightfully questions if a formal process (procedure or checklist) for this unusual, non-emergency, event (replacement officer handoff) would prevent an inadequate handoff in a similar circumstance. The unusual nature of the last minute replacement could find the participants unaware there is a formal process to follow and result in another necessary key being carried away. This exposes the risk of asking "why" too many times when attempting to drill down to a root cause. The resulting root cause may lead to a corrective action that is too specific to prevent the same problem under different circumstances. If the Lookouts needed binoculars and didn't have them, that is a root cause and it is correctable regardless of why they didn't have them.

Conclusion:

An inadequate handoff process between the officers is not a root cause for the *Titanic* colliding with an iceberg six days later.

Human Performance Issue:

> The Captain failed to take adequate preventive measures based on the multiple ice warnings

People associated with the Human Performance issue:
- Captain Edward J. Smith – Ship's Master, Age 62. Smith was an experienced Master with 38 years at sea. Smith went down with his ship.
- Mr. Charles H. Lightoller – Second Officer, Age 38. During U.S. Senate inquiry Lightoller was asked when he left the *Titanic*. He replied, "I did not leave the 'Titanic' sir; the 'Titanic' left me."
- J. Bruce Ismay – A partner in White Star Line, Ismay had ultimate decisions of design and fitting during construction of the *Titanic*. Ismay survived when he took a spot in a lifeboat being lowered with room for additional passengers and no other passengers immediately available.

Unsinkable? – Did the belief that the *Titanic* was unsinkable affect Captain Smith's decisions?

> Facts concerning the Unsinkable Belief:
- In 1910 White Star's publicity brochure for their sister ships *Olympic* and *Titanic* stated, "…and as far as it is possible to do so, these two wonderful vessels are designed to be unsinkable."
- In 1911 – Articles in the Irish News, the Belfast Morning News, and Shipbuilder magazine contained reports describing the system of watertight compartments and electronic watertight doors. The conclusion, for all practical and foreseeable sea going calamities, the *Titanic* will be "practically unsinkable."
- In September, 1911 the *Olympic* (with Captain Edward J. Smith) was in a collision with Royal Navy cruiser *Hawke*, a ship designed to ram and sink other vessels. *Olympic's* hull was badly damaged but she did not sink, bolstering the unsinkable moniker.

Ice Warnings – Did Captain Edward J. Smith fail to take appropriate preventive measures based on the multiple ice warnings that he received?

Testimony concerning the upcoming icebergs:

During his testimony for the British Inquiry Fourth Officer Joseph Boxhall was asked to chart the positions of ice reported to the *Titanic* by other ships. Boxhall charted the ice position reported by the *Caronia* and, while not recalling these subsequent messages, also charted icebergs reported by the *Amerika*, the *Baltic*, and the *Californian*.

British Wreck Commissioner's Inquiry – Testimony of Joseph Boxhall. Questioned by the Solicitor General.

15731. …I am going to ask the Court to look at your calculation to see if it is what they understand. You have been good enough to mark on that chart the place of ice as indicated by the "Caronia," the "Amerika," the "Baltic," and the "Californian"?

Boxhall – I have got the "Amerika," the "Californian" and the "Baltic." I did not put down the "Caronia."

15732. The "Caronia," as we know, is 49º to 51º.

Boxhall – Yes, and 42º N.

15733. Now have you any recollection of the "Californian" message reaching you or being plotted?

Boxhall – No, I have not.

15734. That message, as we see from the evidence, was sent at 7:30 "Californian" ship's time, and the "Californian" on any view was not very far from you. You were on duty from eight till twelve. As far as you know until I called your attention to it, had you ever plotted that message on any chart?

Boxhall – No.

15735. Now that is not the last. I came to another which the Court has not heard of yet. It is a message that was sent from the "Mesaba" to the "Titanic" and all east-bound ships.

The Commissioner: East-bound ships?

The Solicitor General: It was sent to the "Titanic," and it was sent to east-bound ships, and according to the information we have from the Marconi people it was acknowledged by the "Titanic." Of course, that I shall have to prove. This is the message:

"Ice report. In lat. 42 N. to 41.25 N. long. 49 W. to long. 50.30 W. Saw much heavy pack ice, and great number large icebergs, also field ice. Weather good, clear."

The Commissioner: When is that?

The Solicitor General: That is sent at 7:50 p.m., New York time, and if one allows for the difference of two hours – one hour and fifty-five minutes, we were told – that would bring it practically to a quarter to ten that night, about two hours before the accident.

15737. The message gives you an oblong, a parallelogram, does it not? I want you to make the parallelogram.
Boxhall – From 42 north and 49 west to 41.25 and 50.30.
The Commissioner: Am I right in supposing – I have not heard of this message at all – that she was running to a place which was bounded by icebergs on the north and the south. Is that so?
15738. (The Solicitor General.) According to this message it is. I do not know if I might show you and ask your Lordship's Assessors to see it, but I have marked the oblong on that plan and hatched it in pencil. (Showing to his Lordship.) (To the witness.) Have you got the mark there?
Boxhall – I have only the two positions from the "Mesaba," the one position 42 north and 49 west, and the other position, "Mesaba," 41.27 north and 50.30 west.
15739. Let me read it again. The message really gives you, as I understand, an oblong, a parallelogram: "In latitude 42 north to 41.25 north"—in two lines like that (Showing.); "and longitude 49 west to 50.30 west." The message mentions ice there. That means that you want to make an oblong on your chart, does it not? May I show you mine for a moment, because I am anxious to be sure that you do it right. (Showing chart to Witness.) I have given you my chart, and I want you to check it. You notice I have made an oblong on the chart, and I have sketched it in with pencil?
Boxhall – Yes.
15740. Just check it and see if I am not right, that that oblong is latitude 42 N. to 41.25 N., and longitude 49 W. to 50.3 W.?
Boxhall – Yes; that is about right.
15741. In that space the message is "Saw much heavy pack ice and great number large icebergs, also field ice"?
Boxhall – Yes.
15742. Is the space that was referred to by the "Baltic" within that oblong – the southern track between the two longitudes?
Boxhall – What are the two longitudes again?
15743. 49.9 to 50.20?
Boxhall – Yes, that is inside.
15744. The "Baltic's" position is inside that oblong?
Boxhall – Yes.
15745. Is the position that is indicated by the "Caronia," a position that is inside that oblong?
Boxhall – Yes.
15746. Is the position that is indicated by the "Amerika" inside that oblong?
Boxhall – Yes, it is.
15747. Is the position that is indicated by the "Californian" inside that

oblong?
Boxhall – Yes.
15748. And is the space where the disaster happened inside that oblong?
Boxhall – Yes.
15749. (The Commissioner.) Then to sum it up, if these messages were received and were in the terms that have been stated by the Solicitor General, this steamer was steaming a course through an oblong space, having received warning that there were icebergs on the north of her and icebergs on the south of her?
Boxhall – Yes, you are quite right in saying that the steamer sunk in that position. She sunk in that position.
15750. But she steamed through it did not she for some time, until she met with her doom?
Boxhall – Yes, she must have done.
15751. Of course, the whole thing is assumption at present, because we have not had some of these messages proved, but can you give me any explanation of why such navigation should exist?
Boxhall – I do not think for a moment that we had those messages, My Lord.
15752. I am asking you to assume that you did. I said that they have not been proved yet, but we are told they are going to be proved. Assuming that they are proved can you explain how the "Titanic" was allowed to find her way into such a region?
Boxhall – No, Sir, I cannot.

When Captain Smith retired for the night he told Second Officer Lightoller to rouse him "if it becomes at all doubtful…" concerning the weather, the distance he could see, and his ability to spot upcoming ice.

British Wreck Commissioner's Inquiry – Testimony of Charles Lightoller, examined by the Solicitor General.
13639. Now tell me again what this observation of the Captain meant, because I do not understand it.
Lightoller – With regard to the word "doubtful"?
13640. Yes; what did he mean?
Lightoller – It is rather difficult to define. It means to say if I had any doubt at all in my mind.
13641. What about?
Lightoller – About the weather, about the distance I could see – principally those two conditions it would refer to. If there were the slightest degree of haze to arise, the slightest haze whatever, if that were to any degree noticeable, to immediately notify him.
13642. (The Solicitor General.) I will take what you have just said. You said if the slightest degree of haze was to arise – that would be what was

meant – you were to notify him?
Lightoller – Immediately; yes.
13643. And then did you understand, and do you represent, that if the slightest degree of haze arose it would at once become dangerous?
Lightoller – Well, it would render it more difficult to see the ice, though not necessarily dangerous. If we were coming on a large berg there might be a haze, as there frequently is in that position, where warm and cold streams are intermixing. You will very frequently get a little low-lying haze, smoke we call it, lying on the water perhaps a couple of feet.
13644. Do not misunderstand me. I am not suggesting that it would be necessarily dangerous in the sense that there would necessarily be an accident, but there would be a risk of danger, would not there?
Lightoller – If there was any haze?
13645. Yes?
Lightoller – Undoubtedly.
13646. The slightest haze?
Lightoller – The slightest haze would render the situation far more difficult.
13647. Far more dangerous?
Lightoller – Far more dangerous if there were ice.
13653. I think I must press you a little about this. The Captain leaves you and says, "If it becomes at all doubtful let me know at once"?
Lightoller – Yes.
13654. Surely that had reference to the risk of ice had it not?
Lightoller – Yes, undoubtedly; undoubtedly that was referring to ice.

Facts concerning Icebergs, Warnings, and Precautions:
- An iceberg is a detached portion of a freshwater polar glacier carried out to sea. Only about one-ninth of its mass floats above the surface of sea water.
- A "Growler" is a term applied to icebergs of small mass. It is frequently a berg which has turned over, and is therefore showing what has been termed "black ice."
- Ice warnings received on Sunday by the Captain or an Officer:
    - 9:00 a.m.: message from the *Caronia* warned of field ice and icebergs in 42ºN, from 49º to 51ºW.
    - 11:40 a.m.: *Noordam* reported "much ice" in about the same position as the *Caronia*.
    - 1:42 p.m.: message from the *Baltic* reports icebergs 250 miles ahead but within five miles of *Titanic's* current course and also provides the position of the *Deutschland* and warns that she is short of coal and not under control.

- o   7:30 p.m.: message picked up by the *Titanic* from the *Californian* to the *Antillian* gave *Californian's* position as 42º 3' N, 49º 9' W and warned of three large bergs five miles to the south.
- Captain Smith gave the *Baltic's* message to Bruce Ismay who kept it until Smith retrieved it and posted it in the chart room shortly after 7:00 p.m..
- Seven ice warnings on Sunday (three of which were not received by the Captain or an Officer) showed a huge field of ice some 78 miles long directly ahead of *Titanic's* path on Sunday night.
- At 5:50 p.m. on Sunday evening Captain Smith altered *Titanic's* course slightly south and west of the normal course (likely as a precaution to avoid the ice reported by the *Baltic* but still stay north of the drifting *Deutschland*).
- 9:30 p.m.: Second Officer Lightoller had a message sent to the crow's nest "to keep a sharp lookout for ice, particularly small ice and growlers," until daylight.
- Second Officer's conversation with Captain Smith concerning conditions and ability to spot ice was passed on when Second Officer Lightoller was relieved by First Officer Murdoch.
- No extra lookouts were posted on Sunday night as the *Titanic* approached known ice positions
- The message to crow's nest "to keep a sharp lookout for ice, particularly small ice and growlers," was passed on when the crow's nest lookouts were relieved.

Speed – Was Captain Smith attempting to make record crossing time or arrive in New York early on *Titanic's* maiden voyage?

Testimony concerning conditions and the ship's speed:

British Wreck Commissioner's Inquiry – Testimony of Second Officer Charles Lightoller, examined by the Solicitor General.
13723. The captain had said to you only half-an-hour or 35 minutes before that if it got at all doubtful you were to send for him, and that he would be close by?
Lightoller – Yes.
13724. Did you tell Mr. Murdoch of that message?
Lightoller – Oh, undoubtedly.
13725. The captain's room, I think, is just at the side of the bridge there?
Lightoller – On the side of the bridge, and the window facing right on to the bridge. The bridge is in clear view from his chart room.
13726. You have had great experience of the North Atlantic at all times

of the year. Just tell me, when a liner is known to be approaching ice is it, or is it not in your experience usual to reduce speed?

Lightoller – I have never known speed to be reduced in any ship I have ever been in in the North Atlantic in clear weather, not on account of ice.

The inquiry also solicited testimony from White Star Line's J. Bruce Ismay concerning the ship's speed.

> **British Wreck Commissioner's Inquiry** – Testimony of J. Bruce Ismay, examined by the Attorney General.
>
> 18432. ... if you were approaching ice in the night it would be desirable, would it not, to slow down?
>
> Ismay – I am not a navigator.
>
> 18433. (The Commissioner.) Answer the question.
>
> Ismay – I say no. I am not a navigator.
>
> The Attorney General – You are not quite frank with us, Mr. Ismay.
>
> Sir Robert Finlay – The Attorney General will forgive me; I do not think there is the slightest justification for that remark.
>
> 18434. (The Attorney General.) You have told me now what your answer is. What was your answer?
>
> Ismay – I should say if a man can see far enough to clear ice, he is perfectly justified in going full speed.
>
> 18435. Then apparently you did not expect your Captain to slow down when he had ice reports?
>
> Ismay – No, certainly not.

Facts concerning the ship's speed and potential arrival time:
- After leaving Queenstown the *Titanic* averaged 21 knots in clear weather and covered 464 miles by noon on Friday
- The *Titanic* covered an additional 519 miles by noon on Saturday
- *Titanic* covered another 546 miles by noon Sunday.
- The ship's progress led to some passengers speculating that they may arrive in New York on Tuesday night instead of Wednesday morning.
- Prior to the collision the *Titanic* had not slowed down and was moving at 21.5 knots when the iceberg was spotted.

HUMAN PERFORMANCE MODEL

The Captain failed to take adequate preventive measures based on the multiple ice warnings (Figure 24 – 3).

Consequences and Incentives – Causal factor considered:
– **Initial Incentive** – Should Captain Smith have recognized the risk the perfect calm presented for spotting icebergs and taken additional precautions?

Discussion:

This was Captain Smith's retirement trip. All he had to do was get the *Titanic* to New York. Captain Smith knew the *Titanic* was approaching an ice field and he discussed with his Second Officer the difficulty that the flat calm sea and no wind would pose in spotting upcoming ice, but took no extra precautions. Additional lookouts were not posted nor did the Captain call for the ship to slow down or stop for the night. He also recognized that changes in the conditions might warrant extra precautions and told his Second Officer "If it becomes at all doubtful let me know at once. I will be just inside."

There is no doubt that avoiding icebergs while navigating the North Atlantic is a value-added and necessary activity. Captain Smith's initial consideration concerning the upcoming ice does show he understood the importance of avoiding it. Captain Smith's judgement on how to avoid the ice was in line with the commonly accepted practice of maintaining speed and relying on the Crow's Nest Lookouts. Based on his belief that icebergs would be spotted in time by the Lookouts, Captain Smith determined that posting additional Lookouts in the ship's bow and/or slowing down were not value-added and unnecessary.

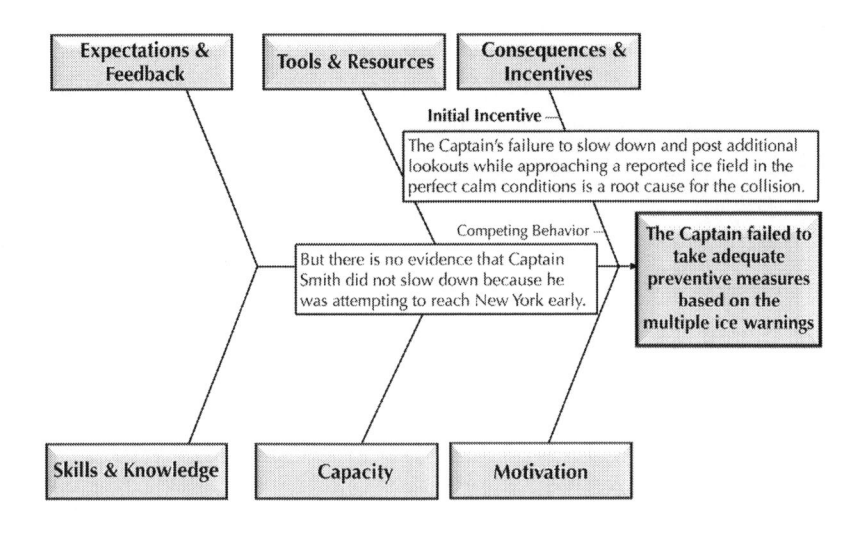

Figure 24 – 3, Human Performance Model with selected causal statements

In making this determination Captain Smith underestimated the difficulty of spotting icebergs in the perfect calm—a rarely encountered condition on the North Atlantic.

Conclusion:

Posting additional Lookouts with a different sight angle in the bow may have resulted in spotting the iceberg's silhouette against the starlit horizon sooner than it was seen from the Crow's Nest. Slowing down would have allowed more time to clear the iceberg after it was spotted. The Captain's failure to slow down and post additional Lookouts in the perfect calm while approaching the reported icefield is a root cause for the collision with the iceberg.

Whether or not Captain Smith's confidence in the Lookouts was bolstered by the belief that the *Titanic* was unsinkable can not be determined and therefore is not a contributing factor.

– Competing Behavior – Did an "Alternate Priority" of reaching New York early cause Captain Smith to maintain speed through the ice field? If so was Captain Smith unduly influenced by Bruce Ismay?

Discussion:

The fact that Captain Smith did not slow down has already been identified as a root cause but there is no evidence that the Captain was trying to reach New York early.

Captain Smith did give the *Baltic*'s ice warning to Bruce Ismay, and allowed him to hold it until 7:00 p.m., but this is not enough evidence to conclude that Bruce Ismay influenced Captain Smith's navigation of the *Titanic*.

Conclusion:

There are no competing behavior root causes.

Human Performance Issue:

> The Senior Wireless Operator failed to deliver crucial ice warning messages to the Captain or Officers

People associated with the Human Performance issue:
- Jack Phillips – Senior Wireless Operator, Age 25. Phillips was on duty nearing the end of his shift at the time of impact. Phillips failed to deliver a crucial ice warning to the bridge two hours prior to the collision. He managed to make it to the overturned Collapsible B but died before being rescued.
- Harold Bride – Junior Wireless Operator, Age 22. Bride was sleeping in the adjoining cabin when the collision occurred. Bride survived after reaching Collapsible B.

A message received in the *Titanic* Marconi Wireless room at 9:40 p.m. from the steamer *Mesaba* clearly indicated the presence of ice in the immediate vicinity of the *Titanic*. A later warning from the nearby *Californian* was abruptly cut off by the Wireless Operator. If the messages had reached the bridge would the navigation of the vessel have been altered and the collision avoided?

Testimony:

On his Sunday night shift, Jack Phillips was busy catching up on the message backlog while Harold Bride slept prior to his midnight shift.

> **British Wreck Commissioner's Inquiry** – Testimony of Wireless Operator Harold Bride, examined by Sir Robert Finlay.
> 16695. I think you saw Phillips about 10 minutes before the collision, did you not?
> Bride – No; after the collision.
> ...16702. You know Phillips was engaged in communicating with Cape Race right on from half-past 8 to 10 minutes before the collision?
> Bride – Apparently so, yes.
> 16703. Well, have you any doubt about it?
> Bride – No. I do not think so. I am judging by the amount of work that was got through.
> 16704. He was engaged during these hours from half-past 8 to 10 minutes before the collision in communicating with Cape Race these trade and private messages?
> Bride – Yes.

Facts concerning ice warnings not conveyed to the Captain or an Officer:
- The Wireless Operators report to, and are accountable to, the Marconi Company. They are required to inform the crew, usually an officer, of emergency messages and messages that pertain to the navigation of the ship. The Operators also relay messages picked up from other ships, essentially networking to extend the reach of wireless communication, but their main concern is sending and receiving paid messages for the passengers.
- The *Titanic's* Marconi Wireless wasn't working Saturday. The Operators worked seven hours to diagnose the problem and had it back up and running by Sunday morning. A large backlog of passenger messages accumulated while the wireless was down and messages continued to come in as passengers anticipated the ship being in wireless transmission range of the Cape Race, Newfoundland station.
- Ice warnings that were *not* received by the Captain or an officer
  o Sunday, 1:45 p.m.: The German liner *Amerika* sent this message through *Titanic's* wireless via Cape Race to the US Hydrographic Office in Washington: '*Amerika*' passed two large icebergs in 41º 27' N., 50º 8' W., on the 14th of April. (*Amerika's* message is overheard by the Marconi Operator but isn't passed on to the Captain or any other officer).

- 9:40 p.m.: Senior Wireless Operator received this message from steamship *Mesaba*: *From 'Mesaba' to 'Titanic' and all east-bound ships. Ice report in lat. 42° N. to 41° 25' N., long. 49° to long. 50° 30' W. Saw much heavy pack ice and great number large icebergs. Also field ice. Weather good, clear.*
- 10:55 p.m.: The *Californian* was stopped in an ice field about 10 miles north of the *Titanic*, and sent out warnings to all ships in area. When the *Californian's* wireless operator called up the *Titanic*, his ice warning was interrupted and he was told, "Keep out! Shut up! You're jamming my signal. I'm working Cape Race."
- The Senior Operator was working on clearing passenger messages from the backlog that had built up while the wireless was out of service and put the *Mesaba* ice warning aside. He intended to deliver it to the bridge when he was finished with the backlog but the message reporting heavy pack ice and icebergs in the immediate area never made it to the Captain, the bridge, or any officer.

HUMAN PERFORMANCE MODEL

Senior Wireless Operator failed to deliver crucial ice warning messages to the Captain or officers (Figure 24 – 4)

Expectations and Feedback – Causal factor considered:
– Complex Process/Distractions – Was the Marconi Wireless Operator distracted or overloaded causing his failure to deliver crucial ice warnings to the Captain? Would these ice warnings have made a difference?
Discussion:
While clearing a backlog of passenger messages a distracted Marconi Wireless Operator failed to report the 9:40 p.m. ice warning from the *Mesaba* to the *Titanic* and all eastbound ships. This warning reported "great number large icebergs" but never reached the Captain or the bridge. While still working the backlog through the Cape Race station the 10:55 p.m. message from the *Californian*, stopped in an ice field about 10 miles north of the *Titanic*, was cut off by *Titanic's* Marconi Wireless Operator before the ice warning was received.

The *Titanic's* Captain and officers already knew they were approaching previously reported ice and had already determined that it would be spotted by the lookouts in the current conditions without reducing speed. Captain Smith's remark to Second Officer Charles Lightoller, "If it becomes at all doubtful let me know at once," was in reference to the distance that they could see and spot ice in the current conditions. There was no doubt that they were approaching an icefield and icebergs, but the warnings from the *Mesaba* and the *Californian* would have provided additional detail about the location of the upcoming icebergs.

Conclusion:

It is unknown if the course or speed of the ship would have been altered based on the additional ice warnings from the *Mesaba* and the *Californian* but without this information the Captain or the officer in charge did not have the opportunity to consider it.

The Senior Wireless Operator's failure to deliver crucial ice warning messages to the Captain or to any of the officers due to being overloaded with a backlog of passenger messages is a root cause for the *Titanic* striking the iceberg.

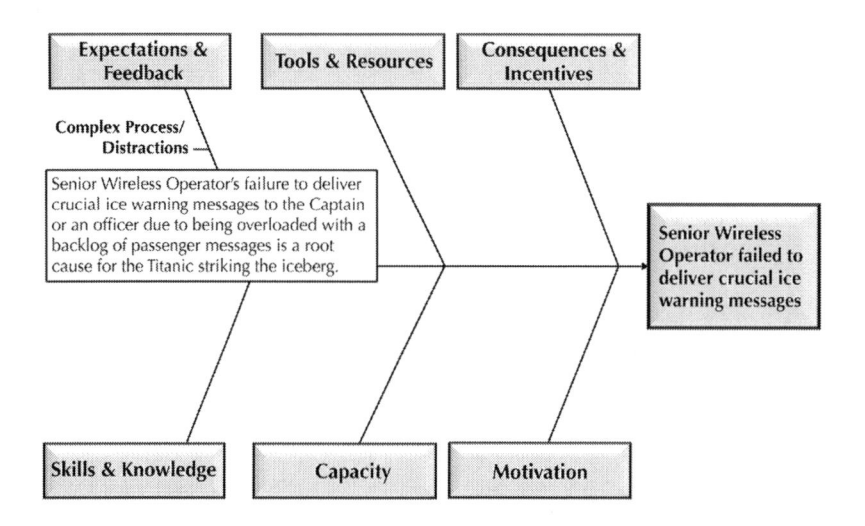

Figure 24 – 4, Human Performance Model with selected causal statements

Root Cause Summary

Root causes and contributing factors for the Problem Statement:

The *Titanic* collided with an iceberg.

Contributing Factor: The unusual perfect calm of that night on the North Atlantic ocean—no moonlight, no wind, and absolutely no swell—is a contributing factor. This environment resulted in the iceberg being difficult to see at a distance because there was no water breaking at the base of the iceberg to give early warning of its presence.

Human Performance

The Crow's Nest Lookouts failed to see the iceberg in time to avoid the collision.

Root Cause: Binoculars not being available to the crow's nest Lookouts is a root cause for the Lookout's failure to see the iceberg in time to avoid the collision.

The Captain failed to take adequate preventive measures based on the multiple ice warnings

Root Cause: Captain Smith underestimated the difficulty of spotting icebergs in the perfect calm—a rarely encountered condition on the North Atlantic. His subsequent failure to slow down and post additional lookouts while approaching the reported icefield is a root cause for the collision with the iceberg.

Senior Wireless Operator failed to deliver crucial ice warning messages to the Captain or officers

Root Cause: An backlog of passenger messages, overloaded and distracted the Senior Wireless Operator resulting in his failure to deliver crucial ice warning messages to the Captain or to any of the officers. This is a root cause for the *Titanic* striking the iceberg.

Chapter 25

THE TITANIC SANK AFTER THE COLLISION - ROOT CAUSE ANALYSIS

DMAIC Analyze

In this DMAIC phase the incident or a specific associated problem is analyzed to discover and verify cause-and-effect relationships and determine root cause(s). To aid in the root cause analysis, facts and testimony normally collected during the DMAIC Measure phase, but that are specific to this problem statement, are presented in this Chapter.

Problem Statement:

The *Titanic* **sank after the collision** – This root cause analysis focuses on why the *Titanic* sank following the collision with an iceberg.

Desired State:

The goal is to prevent ships from sinking following a collision at sea.

Ship's Design – Did design flaws cause the *Titanic* to sink following the collision?

Testimony concerning White Star Line's shipbuilding arrangement with Harland & Wolff:

> **British Wreck Commissioner's Inquiry** – Testimony of J. Bruce Ismay, examined by the Attorney General.
>
> 18281. ... Now one other general question with regard to the construction of vessels by Harland & Wolff; are they constructed under contract at a lump sum in the ordinary course, or are they constructed at cost price plus a percentage?
>
> Ismay – Cost price, plus a percentage. We build no ships by contract at all.
>
> 18282. So that what it amounts to, if I follow you correctly, is, that there is no limit placed by you upon the cost of the vessel?
>
> Ismay – Absolutely none. All we ask them to do is to produce us the very finest ship they possibly can; the question of money has never been considered at all.
>
> ... 18287. And the "Olympic" and "Titanic" were both built upon those terms?
>
> Ismay – Exactly.

Facts concerning design:
- The *Titanic* was built with a cellular double-bottom hull with five feet between the inner and outer steel skins.
- The *Titanic's* hull was subdivided with fifteen transverse bulkheads, creating sixteen compartments from the bow to the stern. The first two of these vertical bulkheads in the bow and the last six in the stern of the ship divided the E Deck reaching the Saloon Deck above. The remaining bulkheads were one deck lower in the middle portion of the ship with those watertight compartments dividing the F Deck.
- The watertight compartments extended above the waterline but were open at the top.
- Large watertight doors were built into each bulkhead so each compartment could be isolated in the event of an emergency. At the lowest level the watertight doors could be closed electronically from the bridge. The watertight doors on the other decks were closed manually using a special key.
- With the watertight doors closed the *Titanic* was designed to stay afloat with the first four compartments flooded or with any two of her larger amidship compartments flooded.
- The bulkheads creating "watertight" compartments, along with the double bottom hull, are the design features that led to the "unsinkable" designation for sister ships *Olympic* and *Titanic*.

Damaged Bulkhead – Did the coal fire damage a watertight bulkhead, causing it to collapse while the *Titanic* was taking on water?

Testimony concerning the coal fire and bulkhead:

British Wreck Commissioner's Inquiry – Testimony of Fireman Charles Hendrickson, examined by Mr. Lewis.
5232. Do you remember a fire in a coal bunker on board this boat?
Hendrickson – Yes.
... 5238. Did you help to get the coal out?
Hendrickson – Yes.
... 5244. How long did it take to put the fire itself out?
Hendrickson – The fire was not out much before all the coal was out.
5246. The bulkhead forms part of the bunker—the side?
Hendrickson – Yes, you could see where the bulkhead had been red hot.
5247. You looked at the side after the coal had been taken out?
Hendrickson – Yes.
5248. What condition was it in?
Hendrickson – You could see where it had been red hot; all the paint

and everything was off. It was dented a bit.
5249. It was damaged, at any rate?
Hendrickson – Yes, warped.

British Wreck Commissioner's Inquiry – Testimony of Lead Fireman Frederick Barrett, examined by Mr. Lewis.
2292. Now, with regard to the bunker, you have said this bunker referred to just now was empty—the coal bunker?
Barrett – Yes.
… 2296. Why was it emptied?
Barrett – My orders were to get it out as soon as possible.
2297. When did you receive those orders?
Barrett – Not very long after the ship left Southampton.
2299. What was wrong?
Barrett – The bunker was a-fire.
2300. Shortly after you left Southampton—
The Commissioner:
Now how is this relevant to this Inquiry?
2301. I'll put another question or two, and you will see why I think it is relevant. (To the Witness.) How long did it take them to work the coal out?
Barrett – Saturday.
2302. The whole Saturday. What condition was the watertight bulkhead in?
Barrett – It was the idea to get the bunker out. The chief engineer, Mr. Bell, gave me orders: "Builder's men wanted to inspect that bulkhead."
2303. The bulkhead forms the side of the bunker.
2304. What was the condition of the bulkhead running through the bunker?
Barrett – It was damaged from the bottom.
2305. Badly damaged?
Barrett – The bottom of the watertight compartment was dinged aft and the other part was dinged forward.
2306. (The Commissioner.) What do you attribute that to?
Barrett – The fire.
2307. Do you mean to say the firing of the coal would dinge the bulkhead?
Barrett – Yes.
2308. (Mr. Lewis.) This is the bulkhead between sections 5 and 6?
Barrett – Yes.

Following the collision Lead Fireman Frederick Barrett was working under the direction of Senior Assistant Second Engineer Bertie Wilson and Junior Assistant Second Engineers Herbert Harvey and Jonathan Shepherd. The room was full of steam from water used to put out the furnaces and Shepard fell through an open manhole and broke his leg.

British Wreck Commissioner's Inquiry – Testimony of Lead Fireman Frederick Barrett, examined by the Solicitor General.

2036. And then you attended to Mr. Shepherd as best you could. Did you stay there after that?
Barrett – Just about a quarter of an hour after that.
2037. And during that quarter of an hour did No. 5 keep free from water?
Barrett – Yes.
2038. Then tell us what happened at the end of a quarter of an hour?
Barrett – A rush of water came through the pass—the forward end.
2039. You say the forward end of the pass. What is the pass?
Barrett – It is a space between the boilers where we walk through.
2044. Supposing that the bulkhead which is the fore-end of No. 5 had given way, would water come through it and through this pass?
Barrett – Yes.
2045. Do you know yourself where it was the water came from, whether it had got through the bulkhead or not?
Barrett – I did not stop to look.
2046. Can you tell us, up to this time, was the ship lying on an even keel?
Barrett – No, she was sloping down by the head.
2049. And had it been getting worse?
Barrett – Yes.
2050. Had you ever remarked on it to Mr. Shepherd, or any of them?
Barrett – No, we never passed any remarks, the engineers never had time to pass any remarks; they were working all the time.
2053. Then you said there was a quarter of an hour, about, before this rush of water?
Barrett – After the fires were drawn.
2056. And you say it got worse. Now can you give me any idea whether the water came from over the top of the bulkhead or through it?
Barrett – I do not see how it could come over the top.
2057. You do not think it did come over the top?
Barrett – No.
2058. Now, when it came through this pass between the boilers, did it come with a rush?
Barrett – Yes.
The Commissioner: I suppose he means by that as if something had given way.
2059. (The Solicitor General.) Do you hear my Lord's question? He is asking whether, when you said that, you got the impression that

something had given way?
Barrett – That was my idea.
2060. (The Commissioner.) Something that had been holding the water back gave way?
Barrett – That is my idea, my Lord.
2061. (The Solicitor General.) So it came with a rush? How fast did it fall?
Barrett – I never stopped to look. I went up the ladder. Mr. Harvey told me to go up.
2062. (The Commissioner.) Could it have been a bunker bulkhead that gave way, do you think?
Barrett – I have no idea on that, but that is the bunker that was holding the water back.

Was the sinking *Titanic* down by the head enough for the water to spill over the top of the bunker?

> **British Wreck Commissioner's Inquiry** – Testimony of Lead Fireman Frederick Barrett, examined by Mr. Laing.
> 2348. When this rush of water came from the pass, you went up and got in the alleyway?
> Barrett – Yes.
> 2349. You have told us that was about ten minutes past one, I think?
> Barrett – That is as near as I can recollect.
> 2350. Was there water on the alleyway?
> Barrett – Just a little.
> 2351. I do not know whether you know – do you know where that must have come from?
> Barrett – No. In my idea, the cause of that water being in the alleyway was some of the lower deck ports being open, and the water reached them and came through the ports.
> 2352. But to be on the alleyway the water must have been above the level of the watertight bulkhead?
> Barrett – The water was coming down the alleyway from forward.
> 2353. If there was water on the alleyway it must have been above the watertight bulkhead?
> Barrett – I cannot say; I do not know how high the watertight bulkhead is.

Facts concerning the impact of the coal fire:
- A coal fire was burning in coalbunker 10 next to the watertight bulkhead that separates Boiler Room 5 from Boiler Room 6.
- This bulkhead was damaged by the long burning fire that wasn't extinguished until the bunker was cleared of coal on Saturday.

PROBLEM SOLVING MODEL

The *Titanic* sank after the collision (Figure 25 – 1)

Equipment – Causal factor considered:

– **Breakdown** – Mechanical Failure. Did the watertight bulkhead that separates Boiler Room 5 from Boiler Room 6 collapse due to the damage caused by the coal fire? If so, did the collapse hastened the inevitable sinking by any significant degree?

Discussion:

Lead Fireman Frederick Barrett's testimony that "A rush of water came through the pass—the forward end" supports the notion that the bulkhead between Boiler Rooms 5 and 6 collapsed while the *Titanic* was taking on water. It is also possible the bulkhead did not collapse but that the water had reached the top of the bulkhead and started pouring over into Boiler Room 5—the scenario that was inevitable and eventually sunk the ship. If the damaged bulkhead did collapse, the question to consider is if the consequences would have been less severe if the bulkhead held.

Conclusion:

If the bulkhead collapsed, Boiler Room 5 would have filled very quickly but this is not enough evidence to identify the bulkhead failure as a root cause for the *Titanic* sinking faster than she otherwise would have.

– **Design** – After striking the iceberg the damage was done but were there design flaws that doomed the giant liner causing the unsinkable ship to sink?

Discussion:

White Star Line and shipbuilder Harland & Wolff did not set out to design an unsinkable ship—they did set out to design and build the world's largest and safest passenger liners. The design included a double bottom hull and transverse bulkheads, creating sixteen compartments from the bow to the stern. The bulkheads contained watertight doors that could be closed on the lowest deck electronically from the bridge. With the watertight doors closed these compartments were horizontally watertight from each other up to the height of the bulkhead but the bulkheads did not extend all the way up to the higher decks because there was also a passenger liner to design. The bulkheads were thought to be high enough to keep the ship afloat in an emergency involving any conceivable sea going mishap—if the ship collided with a rocky shoreline it would still float with the first four compartments breached; if it was rammed in a collision the ship would stay afloat with any two of the largest midship compartments breached (proven when the *Hawke* rammed the *Olympic*); and if the ship's bottom scraped a reef the double bottom hull would limit the damage to the outer hull. The sea going mishap that wasn't planned for was sideswiping an iceberg and breaching the first five compartments. After inspecting the damage, Thomas Andrews, the ship's designer, immediately knew this was one compartment too many for the *Titanic* to survive. As the bow sank, the five compartments filled with water faster than it could be pumped out. When the water reached the top of the dividing bulkhead it spilled over and started filling the next compartment. The bulkheads were high enough above the waterline to stop this domino effect if the first four compartments were breached but with five compartments filling there was no way to stop the spillover to unaffected compartments, one after another, as the bow settled in the water.

Conclusion:

The design of the ship, specifically the height of the transverse bulkheads, is a root cause for the *Titanic* sinking following the collision.

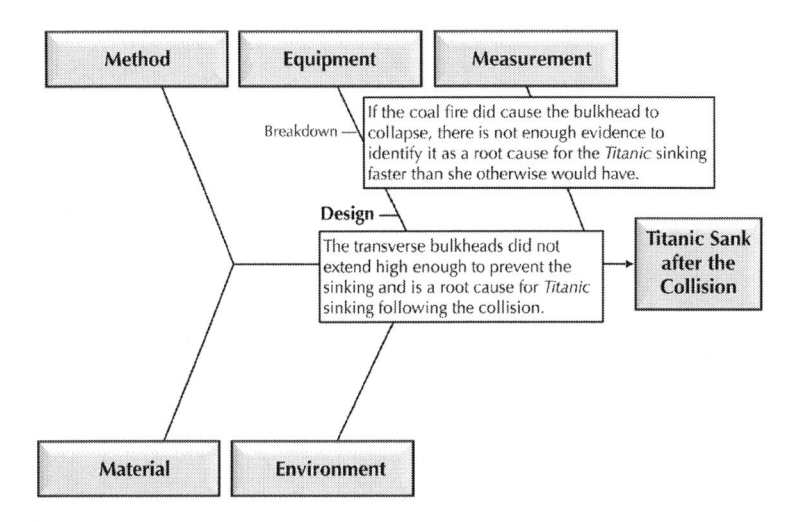

Figure 25 – 1, Problem Solving Model with selected causal statements

Materials – Causal factor considered:

– **Physical Properties** – Did unexpected or unusual physical properties of the materials used to build the *Titanic* contributed to the incident?

Discussion:

Modern day testing and analysis of the 2.5 inch thick steel hull plates used to construct the *Titanic* indicate the steel had a high sulphur content. This, along with the very cold water and high impact loading of the collision, may have caused the steel to break rather than bend when the ship struck the iceberg. This is known as brittle fracture and is a failure that occurs in structural materials without prior plastic deformation. Crack an egg on the side of a frying pan and you get brittle fracture, try it with a rubber ball and you get plastic deformation.

It was also discovered that wrought iron rivets used to hold *Titanic's* hull plates together contained almost three times more slag particles than expected for rivet-quality wrought iron, and also contained large slag particle sizes. This compromised the strength of the rivets causing some to fail and allow hull plate seams to open during the impact.

Conclusion:

Recent evidence points to a combination of metallurgical issues concerning the hull steel and the iron rivets causing the cracks and/or split seams that resulted when the *Titanic* struck the iceberg. Today's higher quality steel and iron would likely have resulted in less severe damage but when the *Titanic* was constructed the metals used were the best available at the time and their physical properties were not unexpected or known to be unusual. While the discovery of these issues could be considered a root cause today, they were not a root cause for the *Titanic* sinking after it struck the iceberg in 1912.

HUMAN PERFORMANCE

Human Performance Issue:

After the collision Captain Smith ordered the ship to move forward at "half-ahead" speed.

Did Captain Smith's half-ahead order after cause the *Titanic* to take on water faster and sink sooner than it otherwise would have?

Person associated with the human performance issue:

- Captain Edward J. Smith – Ship's Master. Smith was an experienced Master with 38 years at sea. Smith went down with the ship.

Testimony concerning Captain Smith's half-ahead order:
Quartermaster Alfred Olliver was the stand-by quartermaster when Captain Smith ordered the ship to steam half-speed ahead.

United States Senate Inquiry – Testimony of Alfred Olliver, questioned by Senator Burton.

Senator Burton – Were the engines reversed; was she backed?

Mr. Olliver – Not whilst I was on the bridge; but whilst on the bridge she went ahead, after she struck; she went half speed ahead.

Senator Burton – The engines went half speed ahead, or the ship?

Mr. Olliver – Half speed ahead, after she hit the ice.

Senator Burton – Who gave the order?

Mr. Olliver – The captain telegraphed half speed ahead.

Senator Burton – Had the engines been backing before he did that?

Mr. Olliver – That I could not say, sir.

Senator Burton – Did she have much way on?

Mr. Olliver – When?

Senator Burton – When he put the engines half speed ahead?

Mr. Olliver – No, sir. I reckon the ship was almost stopped.

Senator Burton – He must have backed the engines, then.

Mr. Olliver – He must have done so, unless it was hitting the iceberg stopped the way of the ship.

... Senator Burton – How long did he go ahead half speed?

Mr. Olliver – Not very long, sir.
Senator Burton – One minute, two minutes, five minutes?
Mr. Olliver – I could not say the number of minutes, because I had messages in the meantime.
Senator Burton – But you know he went ahead half speed?
Mr. Olliver – Yes, sir; I know he went ahead half speed.

HUMAN PERFORMANCE MODEL

After the collision Captain Smith ordered the ship to move forward at "half-ahead" speed (Figure 25 – 2).

Consequences and Incentives – Causal factor considered:
– **Competing Behavior – Alternate Priorities** – Was Captain Smith's half-ahead order given to reassure passengers and/or to start making progress toward the nearest port? Did this order cause the *Titanic* to sink sooner than it otherwise would have?

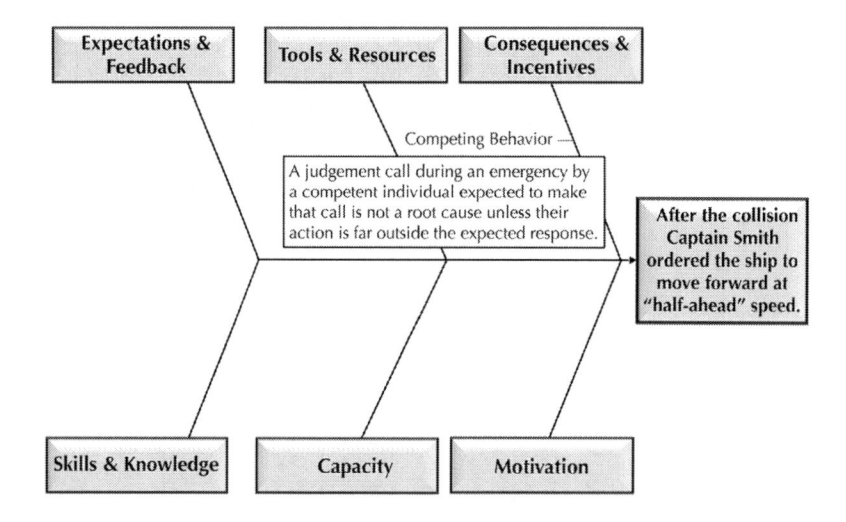

Figure 25 – 2, Human Performance Model with selected causal statements

Discussion:

After the collision with the iceberg the damage was done and the *Titanic* was going to sink. Captain Smith ordered the ship forward at half-ahead speed before knowing the full extent of the damage. This forward movement inevitably forced water through the hull breaches at a faster rate and used up some of the precious little time the *Titanic* had left. In retrospect, whatever the reason for the half-ahead order was, it was a mistake by Captain Smith but wasn't the reason the *Titanic* sank after striking the iceberg.

Conclusion:

A judgement call during emergency situations by a competent individual that is expected to make judgement calls is not a root cause unless the action is far outside of the expected response. This was not the case with Captain Smith's half-ahead order. He may have hastened the inevitable but his ship was sinking and nothing he did or didn't do was going to change that.

Root Cause Summary

The problem statement, "The *Titanic* sank following the collision with an iceberg," assumes there is a root cause to discover for the sinking other than the damage caused by striking the iceberg. *Titanic's* unsinkable mantra was certainly a factor in that assumption. Why did she sink – wasn't she designed to be unsinkable? Her designers believed they had designed the *Titanic* to stay afloat in the event of any conceivable sea going mishap.

The *Titanic's* transverse bulkheads did not reach high enough above the waterline to prevent her from sinking with five forward compartments breached. This design flaw is the root cause that sealed the fate of the *Titanic* following the collision.

Chapter 26

1503 Perish - Root Cause Analysis

DMAIC Analyze

In this DMAIC phase the incident or a specific associated problem is analyzed to discover and verify cause-and-effect relationships and determine root cause(s). To aid in the root cause analysis, facts and testimony normally collected during the DMAIC Measure phase, but that are specific to this problem statement, are presented in this Chapter.

Problem Statement:

1503 people perished when the *Titanic* sank – This root cause analysis focuses on how more people could have been saved after the collision and subsequent sinking.

Desired State:

The goal and acceptable level of improvement is to prevent or minimize loss of life in future shipwrecks.

Testimony concerning how the victims perished:

United States Senate Inquiry – Testimony of Seaman Edward Buley, questioned by Senator Fletcher.
Senator Fletcher – You were then with Lowe in his boat and went back to where the *Titanic* sank?
Mr. Buley – Yes, sir; and picked up the remaining live bodies.
Senator Fletcher – How many did you get?
Mr. Buley – There were not very many there. We got four of them. All the others were dead.
Senator Fletcher – Were there many dead?
Mr. Buley – Yes, sir; there were a good few dead, sir. Of course you could not discern them exactly on account of the wreckage; but we turned over several of them to see if they were alive. It looked as though none of them were drowned. They looked as though they were frozen. The life belts they had on were that much (indicating) out of the water, and their heads were laid back, with their faces on the water, several of them. Their hands were coming up like that (indicating).

Facts concerning the North Atlantic environment:
- By 10:00pm on Sunday night, April 14th, the air temperature had dropped to 32°F.
- When the *Titanic* sank the sea temperature of the North Atlantic was about 28° F.
- Hypothermia is a potentially dangerous drop in body temperature, caused by prolonged exposure to cold temperatures. If cold exposure is due to being immersed in cold water, the movement of the water can increase the rate of heat loss up to 50%. Water temperatures near freezing can cause death in as little as 15 minutes.
- Most of the people that ended up in the water after the *Titanic* sank died of hypothermia.

PROBLEM SOLVING MODEL

1503 people perished when the *Titanic* sank (Figure 26 – 1)

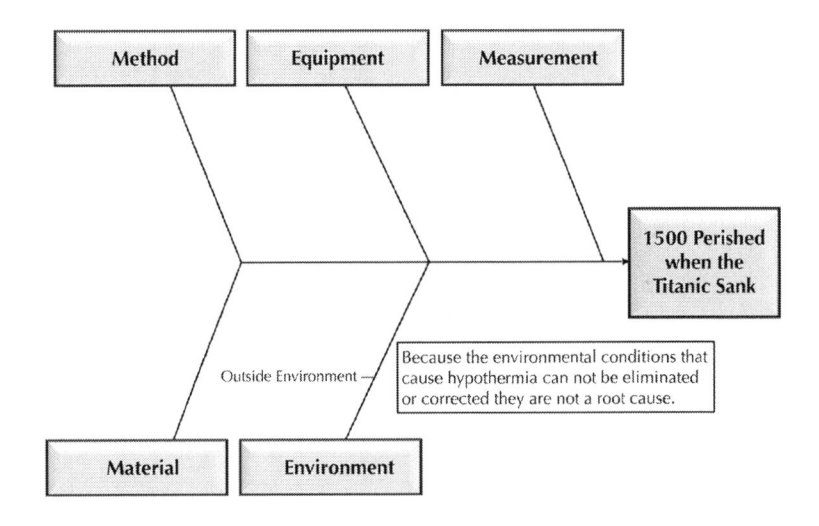

[Fishbone diagram with branches: Method, Equipment, Measurement, Material, Environment, Outside Environment, leading to "1500 Perished when the Titanic Sank". Note: "Because the environmental conditions that cause hypothermia can not be eliminated or corrected they are not a root cause."]

Figure 26 – 1, Problem Solving Model with considered causal statement

Environment – Causal factor considered:
Was the outside environment a root cause for the large loss of life?
Discussion:
The extremely cold water of the North Atlantic caused hypothermia and death in 15 to 30 minutes for most of those who went into the water when the *Titanic* sank.
Conclusion:
The outside environment causal factor fits part of the root cause definition in

that the severely cold water temperature was a, "most basic initiating cause" for the large loss of life after the ship went down. But because this condition can't be eliminated or corrected it is not a realistic (solvable) root cause.

HUMAN PERFORMANCE

Human Performance Issue:

The *Titanic* did not carry enough lifeboats for the passengers and crew.

People involved with ship design and fitting decisions:
- Alexander Carlisle – General Manager and Chairman of the Managing Directors at Harland & Wolff. He was also their Chief Naval Architect until his retirement in June, 1910.

- Harold A. Sanderson – Sanderson was a member of the firm of Messrs. Ismay, Imrie and Company, the managers of the White Star Line and a Director of the company that owns White Star and the *Titanic*. He was *Titanic's* first and only passenger on the delivery trip from Belfast to Southampton.

- J. Bruce Ismay – Ismay was a partner in White Star Line and had ultimate decisions of design and fitting during construction of the *Titanic*. Ismay survived when he took a spot in a lifeboat being lowered with room for additional passengers and no other passengers immediately available.

- Sir Alfred Chalmers – Chalmers held a Master's certificate and served at sea in various classes of vessels for 18 years. He joined the Board of Trade in 1877 and in 1896 was appointed Professional Member of the Marine Department serving as the Nautical Adviser. Chalmers served in that capacity until his retirement in August, 1911.

Could more lives have been saved if the *Titanic* had carried more lifeboats? Testimony concerning the number of lifeboats installed:

Alexander Carlisle recommended lifeboat davits that were designed to hold four boats each because he "expected the Board of Trade and the Government would require much larger boat accommodation on these large ships."

British Wreck Commissioner's Inquiry – Testimony of Alexander Carlisle, examined by Mr. Butler Aspinall.

21267. I will direct your attention to statements in the interview which were suggested and cross-examined to, in the case of one or more of the witnesses who were called. This is the statement: "When working out the designs of the 'Olympic' and the 'Titanic' I put my ideas before the davit constructors, and got them to design me davits which would allow me to place, if necessary, four lifeboats on each pair of davits, which would have meant a total of over 40 boats. Those davits were fitted in both ships, but though the Board of Trade did not require anything more than the 16 lifeboats 20 boats were supplied." I will stop there for one moment. The paragraph opens thus: "When working out the designs of the 'Olympic' and the 'Titanic.'" At that time did you occupy a position in the builder's firm?

Carlisle – I was chairman of the managing directors and general manager of the whole works.

21268. At the present moment I think you have retired from the business?

Carlisle – I retired on the 30th of June, 1910.

21269. Did you take part in working out the designs of the "Olympic" and the "Titanic"? Deal with the "Titanic."

Carlisle – Yes, they were entirely designed practically by Lord Pirrie. The details, the decorations, the equipments, and general arrangements all came under me.

21270. Did you put your ideas before the davits constructors?

Carlisle – I did.

21271. Who would that be?

Carlisle – Welin's Quadrant Davit Company.

…(The witness explained the plan to the Commissioner.)

21280. (The Commissioner.) What I understand Mr. Carlisle to say is this: He was of opinion, or thought it possible, that, having regard to the size of the "Titanic," the Board of Trade might require greater lifeboat accommodation; and he mentioned this to Lord Pirrie and to other people connected with Messrs. Harland & Wolff, and he was then told to prepare plans for the installment of larger lifeboat accommodation, and he accordingly prepared this plan. Now this plan provides for, as I understand, four boats upon one set of davits. (To the witness.) Is not that so?

Carlisle – Yes.

21281. Later on he prepared another plan, which is this, which provides for two boats to each set of davits, instead of one, but neither plan was utilised because the Board of Trade did not require any increased accommodation beyond that which was originally contemplated before these plans came into existence. That is right?

Carlisle – That is so.

The Attorney General – May I see the plans?

The Commissioner – Yes; (Handing same.) and then, Mr. Attorney, I did not tell you what he said and what has come out already; it is already in evidence. The davits on the "Titanic" were of the kind that would have been required if the larger number of boats, double the boats, had been provided.

The Attorney General – That is the welin's.

The Commissioner – Yes, and they were installed when the "Titanic" went down. Of course, the boats were not there.

21282. (Mr. Butler Aspinall.) Were these plans ever submitted to the White Star Company?

Carlisle – Two or three times.

21283. (The Commissioner.) To whom were they submitted – the individual, I mean?

Carlisle – Mr. Ismay and his co-director; but Mr. Ismay was the only one who spoke or said anything about it.

21285. Who was the other director?

Carlisle – Mr. Sanderson was present at one or two interviews.

…21293. Now will you tell us what was said?

Carlisle – It was said they thought it would be desirable to fit them in the ship.

21294. But what did you say first?

Carlisle – I showed them the advantage, and that it would put them to no expense or trouble in case the Board of Trade called upon them to do something at the last minute.

21295. Then it was your view, was it, that it was desirable to have these on board the ship, so that if the Board of Trade made greater lifeboat requirements than you were intending to give, you could easily comply with them?

Carlisle – Yes.

21296. That was the object?

Carlisle – That is it.

21297. (Mr. Butler Aspinall.) When did this interview take place?

Carlisle – One took place in October, 1909, and the other in January, 1910.

21298. Was the interview in respect of the "Titanic" alone, or was it in respect of the "Olympic" as well?

Carlisle – Everything was taken to be doubled. It always meant the two ships. Anything which was taken up for one applied to the second ship the same.

…21303. The scheme which will carry four – does that commend itself to you as being a good working scheme?

Carlisle – Yes.

21304. And would you, as a constructor, have any difficulty in putting boats upon the decks – four boats, which the one set of davits could work and serve?

Carlisle – I see no difficulty.

21305. (The Commissioner.) There is one which could never be on the deck at all; that is so, is it not?

Carlisle – One would be hanging outboard by the spar.

21306. Always?

Carlisle – Yes, the same as the P. and O. Company generally carry their boats.

21309. Would there be any difficulty in filling all these boats with passengers?

Carlisle – A great deal would depend upon the weather; in bad weather the boats would be little or no use.

21310. You are talking generally about lifeboats?

Carlisle – Yes.

21311. Well, I was not talking generally about lifeboats, but I was thinking about these four boats. Assume that four boats had been placed upon the davits according to your first design?

Carlisle – Well, I consider the whole of those boats ought to have been lowered into the water inside of an hour without any trouble.

21313. (The Commissioner.) You say Lord Pirrie designed this ship?

Carlisle – Yes, what I call the design of the ship is the length, the breadth, the depth, and the modelling.

21314. Who was responsible for the supply of the lifeboats?

Carlisle – The supply of lifeboats comes entirely practically under the Board of Trade.

21315. Oh, no, because we know this ship was supplied with considerably more lifeboats than the Board of Trade required?

Carlisle – But we always do that. We always give something more.

21316. I want to know who was the person at Harland & Wolff's responsible for saying, "So far with lifeboats and no further." I am going to ask another question: Were you?

Carlisle – If I had been there I very likely might—

21317. Were you?

Carlisle – Was I?

21318. Yes?

Carlisle – No.

21319. Well, that seems to me to be a grudging "No"?

Carlisle – Not in the very least.

21320. Well, who was?

Carlisle – The owners, in the first place, who would have to pay for them, would be consulted.

21321. We know perfectly well the owners left the whole thing to Harland & Wolff. Now, who was responsible for saying, "So many lifeboats shall be put on this boat and no more"?

Carlisle – The White Star and other friends give us a great deal of liberty, but at the same time we cannot build a ship any bigger than they order, or put anything in her more than they are prepared to pay for. We have a very free hand, and always have had; but I do not think that we could possibly have supplied any more boats to the ship without getting the sanction and the order of the White Star Line.

21322. Did you try?
Carlisle – You must remember that I retired on the 30th of June, 1910, prior to the ship being launched.
21323. Yes, but I suppose the boats were made, or ordered, before the ship was launched?
Carlisle – Oh, no, they are very often, and in that case they would be left—a great many of them—till after the launch, because it takes so many months to finish a big ship.
21324. Do you suggest that there were not, according to the views which were entertained at that time, a sufficient number of boats on board the "Titanic"?
Carlisle – Personally I consider there were not enough.
21326. Did you ever say so?
Carlisle – I have said so over and over again.
…21338. …Will you tell me to which of the representatives of the White Star Line you ever said: "The 'Olympic' and the 'Titanic' are going away with an insufficient supply of boats"?
Carlisle – To no person, as I was not there.
21339. But did you never say it? Did you never say to them, "If we are to supply only the boats that we have hitherto supplied, she will not have enough"?
Carlisle – I showed them the plans of my proposals; I could not do any more.
21340. I know you did, and you have told us the reason, because it was thought that the Board of Trade would require more?
Carlisle – Yes.
21341. And therefore it was thought advisable to have the davits prepared?
Carlisle – Yes.
21342. Yes, that is a very good reason and quite intelligible, but I want to know from you whether I am to understand that you knew these two ships were going to sea with these boats, you thought they were insufficient, and you said nothing?
Carlisle – I was never on board them, My Lord. I had nothing to do with the finishing.
21343. I suppose you knew about the boats?
Carlisle – I knew nothing about the boats that she was leaving with.
21344. Whose business is it to know about the boats?
Carlisle – It is the owners'.

Examined by Mr. Thomas Scanlan.
…21363. So that it stands in this way. You made the plans in 1909; you left Harland & Wolff in 1910; you went to the Board of Trade in 1911 and took these plans with you?

Carlisle – I did.

21365. Now, I want to make this clear. At the time of submitting your plans to the White Star Line Directors Mr. Ismay was present?
Carlisle – Yes.

21366. And I suppose we may take it from you that the object of submitting the plans was to give the White Star people an opportunity of deciding for themselves whether those plans suited them?
Carlisle – Certainly.

21367. And with reference to the boats, giving them an opportunity of seeing whether they would have 20 boats or 64 boats which you could show them could be provided?
Carlisle – Yes.

…21370. I suppose on the occasion of this long discussion you had with the Directors various changes and alterations were made in the details of the decorations and otherwise?
Carlisle – Yes.

21371. And there was no reason why, if the White Star people wanted more boats, they could not have ordered you to go ahead and install 64?
Carlisle – Certainly.

21372. (The Commissioner.) Am I to understand you advised them to install 64?
Carlisle – I merely put my ideas before them.

21375. Did you think there ought to be 64 [lifeboats]?
Carlisle – I thought there ought to be three on each set of davits.

21376. How many would that make altogether?
Carlisle – Forty-eight boats.

21378. Whereas, in point of fact, how many were there?
Carlisle – Sixteen.

21379. You thought there ought to be three times the number. Did you say so?
Carlisle – I believe I did, but I could not swear.

21380. But it is a very important matter, is it not?
Carlisle – You see I never put my ideas on paper unless I thought they were what should be carried out.

21381. You do not answer my question. You were there apparently discussing this matter. Did you say, as the chairman of the managing directors of Harland & Wolff's, "I think there ought to be three times as many boats on that deck as we are at present contemplating putting there"?
Carlisle – No, I would not say that I did.

21382. Did you think it?
Carlisle – I thought there ought to have been.

21383. Why did you not say so?

Carlisle – Because I have always been accustomed to put the plans before the owners and let them judge. Unless they asked questions I did not give them an answer.

21384. Do you mean to tell me that on this important matter, having formed the opinion, and the matter being discussed and you being the chairman of the managing directors of the builders, you did not say that?

Carlisle – Certainly not.

Examined by Mr. Clement Edwards.

21385. You recalled an occasion when you produced that plan at a meeting at which Lord Pirrie was present, and Mr. Sanderson, and Mr. Ismay?

Carlisle – Yes.

…21402. Now do you remember what Mr. Ismay said in regard to this proposal that there should be equipment for this number of boats?

Carlisle – He quite agreed that it would be a good thing to make preparations for supplying the larger number of boats.

21403. (The Commissioner.) Now do be accurate. Do you mean to say that he thought it was desirable that a larger number of boats should be supplied, or that there should be what Mr. Edwards correctly calls an equipment for a larger number of boats? They are two different things.

Carlisle – I take it at that first interview it was merely the davits for carrying four boats.

…21407. Was anything said at that interview as to the advisability, or otherwise, of carrying a larger number of boats?

Carlisle – Nothing.

21408. Not at that interview. Now then, when you attended the second interview in January, 1910, is that the occasion when four hours were occupied?

Carlisle – Yes.

21409. Was Mr. Ismay, and also was Mr. Sanderson, present on that occasion?

Carlisle – Yes.

21411. Did you have any discussion at that time with regard to the number of boats, as apart from the question of the character of the davits?

Carlisle – No.

21413. Was there any decision arrived at at that interview in regard to what equipment for the boats you should fix up?

Carlisle – Nothing.

21414. Was there any arrangement arrived at by which some decision some later time should be come to in regard to the number of boats?

Carlisle – No, that was not considered at that time; I did not hear anything.

21415. Was the whole thing treated as quite tentative and simply just allowed to pass?

Carlisle – There is the ship and there are the boats shown on it, and that part was settled, as far as that goes; but how many boats would ultimately be fitted in the ship before she left Liverpool, Belfast, or Southampton was not settled when I was present, nor did I hear it.

21416. If it was not settled, was there any circumstance discussed or any time mentioned at which it should be decided what should be the number of boats?

Carlisle – Not that I heard of.

21417. Now then, from January, 1910, when this interview took place, until June, 1910, when you left, was there anything more said in your presence by the White Star directors or any member of the White Star Company?

Carlisle – No.

21418. Nothing?

Carlisle – No. I merely ordered the davits after that—the same month.

21419. That is to say, you ordered davits that should each take how many boats?

Carlisle – Four.

21420. And was there, while you were still connected with the firm, any decision arrived at to your knowledge with regard to the number of boats?

Carlisle – None that I know of.

21421. Do you know what you were waiting for at that time; that is to say, do you know why no definite decision had been arrived at up to June, 1910, as to the number of boats?

Carlisle – I would say they were entirely waiting to see what the Board of Trade would require.

The Commissioner – Of course. They were living in hopes that the Board of Trade would not ask for any more.

British Wreck Commissioner's Inquiry – Testimony of J. Bruce Ismay, examined by Mr. Scanlan

18661. … Did you personally examine the designs for the lifeboats?

Ismay – I did not.

18662. Who of your Company did examine the designs?

Ismay – The design would be submitted to us by the shipbuilders.

18663. Will you tell me who, amongst your officials, would be responsible for accepting or rejecting a design of this kind?

Ismay – I never saw any such design and I do not know that anybody connected with the White Star Line saw such a design.

18664. If there was a question of accepting or rejecting a design which provided for greater lifeboat accommodation than you had on the "Titanic," I want to ask you whether it is you yourself or some subordinate of yours, or some associate of yours—?

Ismay – It would be done jointly between the shipbuilders and the managers of the White Star Line.

18665. Evidently you were not the manager who was responsible for examining this design?

Ismay – I saw the design I have no doubt; I saw the design with the rest of the ship.

18666. I suggest to you that a design was submitted which would have provided sufficient lifeboats to take off everybody on board, and was rejected by the White Star Line.

Ismay – I tell you I have never seen any such design.

18667. (The Commissioner.) Have you ever heard of it before?

Ismay – No, I have not.

18668. (Mr. Scanlan.) Of course, I take it this is what you say, that you have no recollection of seeing the design at all?

Ismay – No; I have no recollection of seeing any design which showed the "Titanic" fitted up for 40 boats.

Testimony of J. Bruce Ismay, examined by Mr. Harbinson:

18754. Did you give any special consideration to the question of providing additional lifeboat accommodation to cope with the additional number of passengers that you proposed to carry?

Ismay – I do not think any special attention was given to that.

18755. Would not that have been a consideration that should have specially engaged you?

Ismay – I think the position was taken up that the ship was looked upon as practically unsinkable; she was looked upon as being a lifeboat in herself.

18756. That is owing to the transverse bulkheads?

Ismay – No; to the bulkheads and the power of flotation she had in case of accident.

18757. I understand that you considered that either of these steamers would float with two adjacent watertight compartments full?

Ismay – Two of the largest compartments full.

18758. If that were so, and you considered those boats practically as lifeboats themselves and unsinkable, on that theory it was not necessary to carry any lifeboats at all?

Ismay – Yes, because we might have to use them to pick up a crew from another ship.

18759. It was practically for that purpose you carried lifeboats?

Ismay – Or landing, in the case of the ship going ashore.
18760. You did not consider having them for the purpose of saving the crew and passengers carried?
Ismay – No, I do not think so.

Testimony of J. Bruce Ismay, examined by Mr. Clement Edwards:
18843. If you had not taken the view that the "Titanic" was unsinkable, would you or would you not have insisted upon provision being made for a larger number of boats?
Ismay – I do not think so.
18844. So that the number of boats, in your view, had nothing at all to do with the relative sinkability of the "Titanic"?
Ismay – The "Titanic" had more boats than were necessary by the Board of Trade regulations.
18845. Will you answer the question?
Ismay – What is the question?
18846. The question was this, that according to your view the number of boats had nothing to do with the relative sinkability of the "Titanic"?
Ismay – No; I do not think so.
18847. So that if you had taken the view that the "Titanic" was not unsinkable you would not have had more boats provided?
Ismay – No, I do not think so.

British Wreck Commissioner's Inquiry – Testimony of Harold A. Sanderson, examined by the Solicitor General:
19130. We had just been comparing the provision of boats in the "Titanic" with the maximum regulations of the Board of Trade. I want to ask you now the view of your Company as to the expediency of providing more boats than were on this ship?
Sanderson – I think, to answer that question, I should have to divide the subject into two. I should have to tell you what was in our minds before the "Titanic" accident happened, and then modify it by the result of experience.
19131. If you please?
Sanderson – I do not think it had ever been in our minds, nor do I think it had been in the minds of any of the experts who had been responsible for framing the existing regulations, that the whole ship's company of a ship like the "Titanic" could under any conceivable circumstances be required to be put afloat in boats; nor do I think, if provision were made for that, that in fact we ever would, 19 times out of 20, or even perhaps 99 times out of a hundred, succeed in utilising those boats by filling them and launching them. The weather conditions in the Atlantic are such that I should look upon it as a very remote contingency, and

one to be avoided at all costs. Therefore, in my judgment, I would rather devote myself to accomplishing in fact what we thought we had done with the "Titanic"; in other words, to make her so safe that we would not have to consider the possibility of putting all these people afloat, and, having regard to the extraordinary nature of the accident which happened to the "Titanic," I still do not feel that it would be a wise or a necessary provision to make; that is to say, to provide boats for everybody on board the ship. I do think, however, that we might advantageously increase the boat accommodation somewhat. But I am looking forward to the recommendation that will be made by this Court for our guidance, and I am quite certain that the public will accept it gratefully and we shall do so likewise. In the meanwhile, in order to satisfy the public, on whom we are dependent for our living, we are putting on the ships more boats than I think it is wise to do.

19132. I should just like to follow one thing about that. You speak of the wisdom of the course of adding to the number of boats. Of course I can quite understand it involves more expense, and I can quite understand that it would occupy more space, but why is it an unwise thing to add substantially to the number of boats?

Sanderson – It is all a question of degree. I think if we were to carry boats on the boat deck of all our ships which would be equal in capacity to the total number of people on board we should, in fact, have those boat decks so crowded with boats that it would materially interfere with the efficiency of a great many of them, that is to say, the men would not have proper room to work to get them over the side.

…19187. Can you help us at all as to this suggestion that at one time they had contemplated to double the boats on the davits?

Sanderson – I can only help you by telling you what I learned after I saw this story in the newspapers.

19188. Well, I think you may tell us?

Sanderson – When I saw that I expressed great surprise. I enquired of the builders what it meant. I told them that, to the best of my recollection, I had been present at practically all the discussions which had taken place with them with regard to the building of the "Olympic" and the "Titanic," and that I never heard, to the best of my knowledge, of any such suggestion as was referred to in that paper. I was told that the builders, when they heard that the Board of Trade was reconsidering the matter of boating for ships communicated with Mr. Welin, who was the designer of the particular davit which was on the "Titanic," and is on the "Olympic," and they asked him to what extent he could increase the arrangements for putting boats under davits on these ships; and I believe that Mr. Welin did submit a sketch or a plan showing how these additional boats could be arranged for. Whether the builders have still got that sketch I do not know, but I am quite clear, in my own mind, that the managers of the White Star Line never saw it and never heard of it until after the "Titanic" accident. I have not the faintest recollection of ever hearing a word about it.

…The Commissioner – Will you ask him whether the number they determined to put on this boat was fixed according to any principle?

19194. (The Solicitor General – To the witness.) You heard the question?

Sanderson – I find that rather a difficult question to answer. I believe there are certain requirements for deckhands which are based upon the boating arrangements. There are requirements for firemen in regard to their service and the amount of coal which a man has to handle on the watch.

19195. Certainly there are?

Sanderson – But over and above that we are guided by the recommendations of our various superintendents, and I fancy that the "Titanic" would be found to be manned very largely in excess of any requirements.

19196. (The Commissioner.) I was not talking about the manning. You did provide the "Titanic" with considerably more boats than you were bound to provide her with under the Board of Trade Rules?

Sanderson – Yes.

19197. Now what I want to know is, upon what principle did you proceed, if any, when you fixed the number of boats that you would provide. Why did you stop at the number which you stopped at?

Sanderson – I do not think there was anything more definite in our minds than that we should comply with the requirements, and, as is our usual practice, go a little in excess of them, without any particular theory as to what that excess should be.

19198. You went a great deal in excess of them?

Sanderson – I do not think we went on any theory; I think it was mere guess or rule of thumb.

Sir Alfred Chalmers joined the Board of Trade in 1877 and in 1896 was appointed Professional Member of the Marine Department serving as the Nautical Adviser. He testified at the British Wreck Commissioner's Inquiry concerning the The Merchant Shipping Act 1894 and defended the scale used for the lifeboat requirement.

> **British Wreck Commissioner's Inquiry** – Testimony of Sir Alfred Chalmers, examined by Mr. Butler Aspinall:
>
> 22870. You have told us that you became a professional member in 1896, and we know that in 1894 the Rules which have been referred to were enacted?
>
> Chalmers – The 1894 Rules were in force.
>
> 22871. They were in force when you came into office?

Chalmers – That is the case.

22872. But I believe they have been the subject matter of your consideration from time to time?

Chalmers – Yes.

22873. We were told by Sir Walter Howell that it was in 1904 that he specially consulted you with regard to that matter?

Chalmers – Yes, that is the case.

22874. ... Lord Mersey yesterday asked Sir Walter Howell this question. He was pointing out to the witness that the Rules came into force in 1894, and that we are now in 1912, that is a difference of 18 years, and that there had been no alteration in the scale. The question that Lord Mersey put to the witness, having pointed those facts out to him, was "Why has it never been altered?" and Sir Walter Howell answered thus, "I can only just indicate to your Lordship. That will be explained by the professional Officers." You are the gentleman I think he had in his mind. Can you give my Lord the reason why it was that no alteration was made in the table?

Chalmers – Yes, I can.

22875. Will you give it, please?

Chalmers – I considered the matter very closely from time to time. I first of all considered the record of the trade—that is to say, the record of the casualties—and to see what immunity from loss there was. I found it was the safest mode of travel in the world, and I thought it was neither right nor the duty of a State Department to impose regulations upon that mode of travel as long as the record was a clean one. Secondly, I found that, as ships grew bigger, there were such improvements made in their construction that they were stronger and better ships, both from the point of view of watertight compartments and also absolute strength, and I considered that that was the road along which the shipowners were going to travel, and that they should not be interfered with. I then went to the maximum that is down in the table—16 boats and upwards, together with the supplementary boats, and I considered from my experience that that was the maximum number that could be rapidly dealt with at sea and that could be safely housed without encumbering the vessel's decks unduly. In the next place, I considered that the traffic was very safe on account of the routes—the definite routes being agreed upon by the different companies, which tended to lessen the risk of collision, and to avoid ice and fog. Then, again, there was the question of wireless telegraphy which had already come into force on board of these passenger ships. I was seized of the fact that in July, 1901, the "Lucania" had been fitted with wireless telegraphy, and the Cunard Line, generally, fitted it during that year to all their ships. The Allan Line fitted it in 1902, and I am not sure that in 1904 it had not become quite general on the trans-Atlantic ships. That, of course, entered into my consideration as well. Then another point was the manning. It was quite evident to me that if you went on crowding the ship with boats you would require a crew which were not required otherwise for the safe navigation of the ship, or for the proper upkeep of the ship, but you are providing a crew which would be carried uselessly across the ocean, that never would be required to man the boats. Then the last point, and not the least, was this, that the voluntary action of the owners was carrying them beyond the requirements of our scale, and when voluntary action on the part of shipowners is doing that, I think that any State Department should hold its hand before it steps in to make a hard-and-fast scale for that particular type of shipping. I considered that that scale fitted all sizes of ships that were then afloat, and I did not consider it necessary to increase it, and that was my advice to Sir Walter Howell.

22876. You have now left the Department, but in view of the disaster that happened to the "Titanic," could you give us the benefit of any opinion you may have as to whether it would not be reasonably practicable to at any rate extend the scale?

Chalmers – No, I would not extend it.

22877. You would not?

Chalmers – No. I would not personally. I consider you would be putting an undue strain upon the masters and Officers—that they could never possibly get people into the boats in case of a disaster.

The Commissioner – I do not understand that answer.

22878. (Mr. Butler Aspinall.) First of all I gather, in view of what you have been saying, that you wish to convey the opinion that you do not think it would be practicable to have boats for all on these large steamers?

Chalmers – Certainly not.

22879. But you do not even go as far as this—you do not think that it would be expedient to extend the scale in existence at the present moment?

Chalmers – I do not.

Mr. Butler Aspinall – Why would not it be practicable to have more boats than are required under the existing Rules?

The Commissioner – If you will allow me to say so, that is not the question to put. The question, I think, is: Why is it not expedient?

Mr. Butler Aspinall – Why is it not expedient to have more boats?

22880. (The Commissioner.) No, to extend the scale?

Chalmers – Because if you extend the scale, if the Board of Trade by their one man power, as is suggested, that is to say, the professional Officer alone completes the scale without referring it to an Advisory committee, it could be fallen foul of. If you refer it to an advisory committee I hold that you will get a smaller quantity than you will by

the voluntary action of the shipowner, and that scale proves it.
22881. Let me see that I understand what you mean. Do you mean that in your view it is better to leave it to the discretion of the shipowners than to lay down by a scale a hard-and-fast Rule?
Chalmers – I do.
…22884. If that is so, why have a scale at all—any scale?
Chalmers – The reason of this scale, My Lord, was that up to 1890, when these life-saving appliances came into force, the scale was a very antiquated one, and no matter what ship was built the highest tonnage was 1,500 tons and upwards, and if you sent an 8,000 ton ship to sea in those days she only had boats equal to 216 people.
22885. That is not an answer that appears to me to be satisfactory.
Chalmers – What I mean to say is there was a necessity for this scale then, but there is no necessity, in my opinion, to extend it now.
22886. Then does your evidence lead up to this, that there is no occasion now to have a scale at all?
Chalmers – No. I admit that this scale is good, as far as it goes, and it goes as far as I want it to go, because I say that when you have provided for 10,000 ton ships that boat capacity is sufficient for a 50,000 ton ship for all practical purposes, and I quote the record of the trade, which proves that it is sufficient.
…22896. (The Commissioner.) I am afraid—I do not want to criticise you adversely, I am sure—that your opinion flies in the face of the conduct of British shipowners—I mean shipowners sailing boats of this kind, and flies in the face of the practice on German boats of a similar kind?
Chalmers – As far as the German boats are concerned, I do consider that they are encumbering their decks unduly, and in case of a disaster I am afraid the consequences would be very bad. I say that advisedly.

Facts concerning the number of lifeboats:
- The Merchant Shipping Act of 1894 was in effect and based the requirements for the number of lifeboats on the tonnage of a ship. Ships over 10,000 tons were required to carry 16 lifeboats with a minimum capacity of 1040 people.
- The British Board of Trade failed to extend the scale to keep the lifeboat requirements in line with the expanding size and capacity of passenger ocean liners.
- *Titanic's* 16 Welin davit pairs were designed to handle four lifeboats each, 64 total. The total capacity of 64 lifeboats is 4160 people.
- 16 wooden lifeboats (one on each davit pair) plus 4 additional "collapsible" canvas-sided lifeboats were installed on the *Titanic*.

- *Titanic's* 20 lifeboats exceeded British Board of Trade capacity requirements by about ten percent.
- Maximum capacity of the *Titanic* was 3547 people.
- Full capacity of the lifeboats was 1178 people.

HUMAN PERFORMANCE MODEL

The *Titanic* did not carry enough lifeboats for the passengers and crew (Figure 26 – 2).

Consequences and Incentives – Causal factor considered:
– **Initial Incentive** – Did White Star Line consider additional lifeboats (above those required by the Board of Trade) unnecessary and not value-added?

If the *Titanic* carried more lifeboats:
- Could they have been launched in the time available?
- Would the Captain have been more inclined to have a boat drill?
- Would more men have been allowed in partially filled boats when no women were immediately available?
- With more people in lifeboats and fewer in the water, would the partially filled boats have returned to rescue those struggling in the water?

These questions can only be answered with after-the-fact speculation because the lifeboats weren't there.

Discussion:

White Star Line's perception that the *Titanic* was "practically unsinkable" and "was looked upon as being a lifeboat in herself" demonstrates that they considered as value-added only the lifeboats necessary to "comply with the requirements, and, as is our usual practice, go a little in excess of them." White Star agreed to davits that would hold more boats but only to be ready in case the British Board of Trade raised the requirement.

Conclusion:

White Star Line's failure to supply an adequate number of lifeboats is a root cause for the large loss of life when the *Titanic* sank.

– **Competing Behavior** – Were there alternate priorities or practices competing with the desired performance of equipping the *Titanic* with enough lifeboats for all aboard?

Discussion:

If the desired performance was to equip the *Titanic* with enough lifeboats for all aboard (or substantially more than the 20 she carried) the Competing Behavior was White Star's practice of supplying enough lifeboats to, "comply with the requirements" of the British Board of Trade and "go a little in excess of them."

When the requirements were set by the British Board of Trade in 1894 ships the size of those later put in service for the immigrant trade, not to mention the Olympic class liners being built for White Star line, did not exist. The ships got larger but the top end of the Board of Trade's scale for required lifeboats did not keep up. The *Titanic*, with a capacity of 3547, carried 20 lifeboats with a capacity of 1178 and this was 10% more than the Board of Trade requirement. Shipbuilder Harland & Wolff's Alexander Carlisle recommended outfitting the *Titanic* with 16 lifeboat davits pairs, capable of holding 4 boats each, making 64 lifeboats possible. Carlisle's plan suggested 48 lifeboats (3 per davit pair) but White Star Line only agreed with the plan for the davit pairs so they would be prepared to supply additional lifeboats if the Board of Trade raised the required minimum.

Conclusion:

The British Board of Trade's failure to update the lifeboat requirements for larger ships in general and the Olympic class liners specifically is a root cause for the large loss of life when the *Titanic* sank.

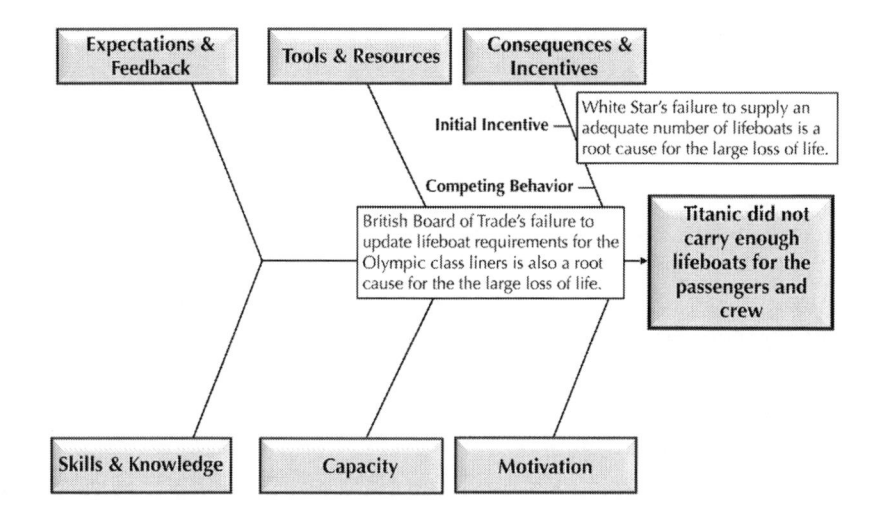

Figure 26 – 2, Human Performance Model with selected causal statements

Human Performance Issue:

The Titanic's Crew failed to utilize the full capacity of the lifeboats.

The vessel was equipped with enough lifeboats for 1,178 persons, but only 712 were saved.

The Captain and Officers of the *Titanic*:
- Captain Edward J. Smith – Ship's Master, age 62. Smith was an experienced Master with 38 years at sea. Smith went down with his ship.

- Mr. Henry T. Wilde – Chief Officer Wilde transferred from the *Olympic* due to his familiarity Olympic class liners. Wilde did not survive.

- Mr. William T. Murdoch – First Officer Murdoch also transferred from the *Olympic* and was bumped to First Officer when Wilde transferred. Murdoch did not survive

- Mr. Charles H. Lightoller – Second Officer Lightoller survived after staying on board the sinking ship until waist deep in water.

- Mr. Herbert Pitman – Third Officer Pitman was off duty at the time of the collision. He survived in command of lifeboat 5.

- Mr. Joseph Boxhall – Fourth Officer Boxhall fired rockets and used the Morse lamp in an attempt to contact a nearby ship. He survived commanding lifeboat 2.

- Mr. Harold T. Lowe – Fifth Officer Lowe was able to complete a survivor transfer at sea to clear a boat and return to pick up additional survivors.

- Mr. James Moody – Sixth Officer Moody was not ordered to command a lifeboat, as were the other Junior Officers. He did not survive.

Would the first boats launched have been full if the passengers had been alerted to the ship's fate sooner?

Testimony concerning loading and launching the lifeboats:

British Wreck Commissioner's Inquiry – Testimony of J. Bruce Ismay, examined by Mr. Scanlan.
18679. ... I want to know, were you told at any time before you left the ship, by the Chief Engineer or the Captain, or by any of the Officers of the ship that the ship was doomed?
Ismay – No, I was not.
18680. We have heard a good deal in the course of this Enquiry of people being unwilling to leave the ship in the lifeboats. Do not you think if those in charge of the ship knew that she was doomed, and was about sinking, that they should have given this information to all the passengers?
The Commissioner: That is not a question to ask him. That is a question for me.
18681. (Mr. Scanlan.) So far as you know, I take it from your evidence that there was no general intimation conveyed to the passengers that the "Titanic" was sinking, and could not be kept afloat?
Ismay – Not that I know of.

Second Officer Charles Lightoller was in charge of loading the even-numbered port side boats and strictly enforced the "women and children" general order. First Officer William Murdoch took charge of loading the starboard boats with women and children "first" but then allowed men aboard when there were no other women available. The first lifeboats to depart carried First Class passengers and crew and weren't filled to capacity.

> **British Wreck Commissioner's Inquiry** – Testimony of Seaman William Lucas, examined by Mr. Rowlatt.
> 1479. Had you received the order that women were to be put in the boats?
> Lucas – Yes.
> 1480. Whom did you receive that from?
> Lucas – Mr. Moody, the Sixth Officer.
> 1482. And you called out for women and there were no more?
> Lucas – That is right, Sir.
> 1483. That was right at the afterend was it?
> Lucas – Yes, the afterend of all.
> 1499. Did you know what the passengers were on the boat deck – First Class, Second Class, or Third Class?
> Lucas – The majority First Class.
> 1501. How many boats did you see filled. How many boats did you take notice of as they were being filled?
> Lucas – About nine.
> 1502. Could you see whether they were all filled to the full capacity?
> Lucas – They were not all filled.
> 1503. Why was that?
> Lucas – Because there were no women knocking about.

> **United States Senate Inquiry** – Testimony of Helen Bishop, questioned by Senator Smith:
> Mrs. Bishop – ... we went up onto the boat deck on the starboard side. We looked around, and there were so very few people up there that my husband and I went to the port side to see if there was anyone there. There were only two people, a young French bride and groom, on that side of the boat, and they followed us immediately to the starboard side. ... About five minutes later the boats were lowered, and we were pushed in. At the time our lifeboat was lowered I had no idea that it was time to get off.
> Senator Smith: Was that a large lifeboat?
> Mrs. Bishop – Yes; it was a wooden lifeboat.
> Senator Smith: And there were 28 people in it?
> Mrs. Bishop – Yes. We counted off after we reached the water.

Lifeboat 3, with a capacity of 65 people, was lowered away at 12:55 a.m. with 26 First Class passengers, including 12 men, and a crew of 6. Seaman George Moore took charge and manned the tiller when the boat reached the sea.

> **United States Senate Inquiry** – Testimony of George Moore, questioned by Senator Newlands.
> Senator Newlands: …Go on and tell what happened.
> Mr. Moore – I went on the starboard side of the boat deck and helped clear the boats; swung three of the boats out; helped to lower No. 5 and No. 7. When we swung No. 3 out, I was told to jump in the boat and pass the ladies in. I was told that by the first officer. After we got so many ladies in, and there were no more about, we took in men passengers. We had 32 in the boat, all told, and then we lowered away.
> Senator Newlands: Why did you not take more than 32 in that boat?
> Mr. Moore – That is not up to me, sir; that was for the officer on top.
> Senator Newlands: Did you not think at the time that it ought to have been more heavily loaded?
> Mr. Moore – It seemed pretty full, but I dare say we could have jammed more in. The passengers were not anxious to get in the boats; they were not anxious to get in the first lot of boats.
> Senator Newlands: What was your feeling at the time?
> Mr. Moore – I thought, myself, that there was nothing serious the matter until we got away from the ship and she started settling down.

Lightoller put Seaman Thomas Jones in command of lifeboat 8. With a capacity 65, she was lowered away with 25 aboard.

> **United States Senate Inquiry** – Testimony of Thomas Jones, questioned by Senator Newlands.
> Senator Newlands: How many men do you regard it as safe to load in a boat of that kind from the upper deck, the boat deck?
> Mr. Jones – According to what sort of falls there are. With good ropes you could take 50 or more.
> Senator Newlands: Would there be any danger of the boats buckling?
> Mr. Jones – Oh, no, sir.
> Senator Newlands: Those boats are supposed to accommodate 60, are they not?
> Mr. Jones – Yes, sir.
> Senator Newlands: Or 65?
> Mr. Jones – Yes, sir.
> Senator Newlands: Would that crowd them?
> Mr. Jones – Oh, no. They were floating quite light, with what we had aboard.
> Senator Newlands: When you got on the boat did you think the ship was sinking?

Mr. Jones – No, sir; I would not believe it.
Senator Newlands: You thought the ship was unsinkable, did you?
Mr. Jones – Yes, sir; I thought so.
Senator Newlands: Was that the view of the crew, generally?
Mr. Jones – Yes, sir.

Lightoller placed Quartermaster Robert Hichens in command of lifeboat 6 and, with a capacity of 65, she was lowered away with 24 aboard including Mrs. Rothschild's Pomeranian.

British Wreck Commissioner's Inquiry – Testimony of Robert Hichens, examined by the Attorney-General.
1118. Who gave orders for her to be pushed off?
Hichens – The Second Officer, Mr. Lightoller, ordered the boat to be lowered away.
1124. Were there any other passengers on the deck so far as you could see when you got the order to lower away—when the order was given to lower away?
Hichens – Yes, there were some passengers there.
1125. Women?
Hichens – I think there were one or two women, Sir, besides gentlemen as well. They felt half inclined—they did not care about getting into the boat.
1126. Who felt half inclined?
Hichens – Why, the passengers, Sir.
1127. They did not like getting into the boat?
Hichens – They did not like to get into the small boat—no.
1128. Who is "they" that you are speaking of?
Hichens – Why, the passengers that were standing there on the deck that I heard talking.

British Wreck Commissioner's Inquiry – Testimony of Second Officer Charles H. Lightoller, examined by the Solicitor General.
13876. Now, we can take No. 6. You say you went to that?
Lightoller – Yes.
13877. You saw that boat filled, did you?
Lightoller – Yes.
13878. It was filled under your supervision?
Lightoller – Yes.
13879. Now, tell us about the way in which it was done and the orders given as to who should get into it?
Lightoller – As a matter of fact, I put them in myself. There were no orders. I stood with one foot on the seat just inside the gunwale of the boat, and the other foot on the ship's deck, and the women merely held

out their wrist, their hand, and I took them by the wrist and hooked their arm underneath my arm.

…13882. And then was No. 6 lowered away?

Lightoller – No. 6 was lowered away.

13883. Was boat No. 6 filled?

Lightoller – It was filled with a reasonable regard to safety. I did not count the people going in.

13884. But you exercised your judgment about it?

Lightoller – Yes.

13885. It was filled as much as you thought was safe in the circumstances?

Lightoller – Yes.

13886. In your judgment is it possible to fill these lifeboats when they are hanging as full as you might fill them when they are water borne?

Lightoller – Most certainly not.

13887. (The Commissioner.) Is that due to the weak construction of the lifeboats or to the insufficiency of the falls?

Lightoller – A brand new fall, I daresay, would have lowered the boats down and carried the weight, but it would hardly be considered a seamanlike proceeding as far as the sailor side of it goes, but I certainly should not think that the lifeboats would carry it without some structural damage being done—buckling, or something like that.

13888. And had you those considerations in mind in deciding how many people should go in the boat?

Lightoller – Yes.

…13896. Did you give any orders with the object of getting more people into it when it was in the water?

Lightoller – Yes, I see what you are alluding to now, the gangway doors. I had already sent the boatswain and 6 men or told the boatswain to go down below and take some men with him and open the gangway doors with the intention of sending the boats to the gangway doors to be filled up. So with those considerations in mind I certainly should not have sent the boats away.

13897. That is what I meant. Did you give any order or direction to the man in charge of boat No. 6 that he was to keep near or was to go to the gangway doors?

Lightoller – Not that I remember. The boats would naturally remain within hail.

…13900. Now let us pursue the two things you have mentioned. You say you gave those orders to the boatswain to go down with some men and open the gangway doors?

Lightoller – Yes.

…13904. Were your orders general, or did they refer to one set of gangway doors in particular?

Lightoller – General.

...13910. Did the boatswain execute those orders?

Lightoller – That I could not say. He merely said "Aye, aye, sir," and went off.

13911. Did not you see him again?

Lightoller – Never.

...13913. I had better just put it. As far as you know, were any of those gangway doors open at any time?

Lightoller – That I could not say. I do not think it likely, because it is most probable the boats lying off the ship would have noticed the gangway doors, had they succeeded in opening them.

Facts concerning capacity and utilization of the lifeboats
- There were 2,215 people on board the *Titanic* for the maiden voyage. Only 712 survived the disaster.
- The capacity of the lifeboats launched by the crew was 1084 people. A total of 668 people were aboard.
- Likely lifeboat launch order, approximate time of launch, and lifeboat capacity with total aboard (based on adjusted witness accounts to reflect the number of people saved by the *Carpathia*):

Boat No.	Time	Capacity/Total aboard
Starboard No. 7	12:40 a.m.	65/28
Starboard No. 5	12:45 a.m.	65/36
Starboard No. 3	12:55 a.m.	65/32
Portside No. 8	1:00 a.m.	65/25
Starboard No. 1	1:05 a.m.	40/12
Portside No. 6	1:10 a.m.	65/24
Portside No. 16	1:20 a.m.	65/52
Portside No. 14	1:25 a.m.	65/40
Portside No. 12	1:30 a.m.	65/42
Starboard No. 9	1:30 a.m.	65/40
Starboard No. 11	1:35 a.m.	65/50
Starboard No. 13	1:40 a.m.	65/55
Starboard No. 15	1:41 a.m.	65/68
Portside No. 2	1:45 a.m.	40/17
Portside No. 10	1:50 a.m.	65/57
Portside No. 4	1:50 a.m.	65/30

Boat No.	Time	Capacity/Total aboard
Collapsible C	2:00 a.m.	47/43
Collapsible D	2:05 a.m.	47/17

Collapsible lifeboats A and B were washed off the deck. Total capacity of these lifeboats was 94 people.

HUMAN PERFORMANCE MODEL

The *Titanic's* Crew failed to utilize the full capacity of the lifeboats (Figure 26 – 3).

Tools and Resources – Causal factor considered:
– **Inadequate Time** – Did the crew have adequate time to utilize the full capacity of the lifeboats?

Discussion:

Collapsible lifeboats A and B were not launched by the crew but were washed off the deck when *Titanic's* bow plunged beneath the sea. This supports a causal factor of inadequate time available to launch all the boats but the boats that were launched by the crew had room for over 400 more passengers. Much of that available capacity was in the first boats launched. When considering inadequate time as a causal factor the hour of time between the collision and the first boat launched needs to be considered. If loading and launching the lifeboats would have started sooner, there may have been time to launch boats A and B.

Conclusion:

Inadequate time is a causal factor for not using the 94 spaces available in lifeboats A and B but is not a root cause for the crew's failure to utilize the full capacity of the lifeboats they did launch.

Consequences and Incentives – Causal factors considered:
– **Initial Incentive** – Were passengers initially averse to getting into a lifeboat resulting in fewer being saved?

Discussion:

This causal factor applies to the passengers unwillingness to board the lifeboats when there was no apparent danger. The passengers did not know the *Titanic* was sinking and many did not believe it was necessary to leave an unsinkable ship for a small boat dangling on davits 70 feet above the water.

Conclusion:

Had more passengers been willing to board the first boats to leave the *Titanic*, more would have been saved. The unwillingness of some passengers to board a lifeboat is a root cause for the crew's failure to utilize the full capacity of the lifeboats.

– **Competing Behavior** – Divulge *Titanic's* fate so passengers would willingly board a lifeboat or keep quiet to avoid panic?

Discussion:

If the desired performance should have been announcing to the passengers that the *Titanic* was sinking the competing behavior was not doing it to avoid a panic. If avoiding a panic was the desired performance it was initially accomplished but with the consequence of lifeboats being launched with empty seats. When it did become apparent to the passengers that the *Titanic* was sinking the lifeboats were launched at close to full capacity. Disclosing that the *Titanic* was sinking before it became obvious likely would have resulted in the first lifeboats being launched with more passengers aboard.

Conclusion:

Failure to disclose to the passengers that the *Titanic* was sinking is a root cause for not utilizing the full capacity of the lifeboats.

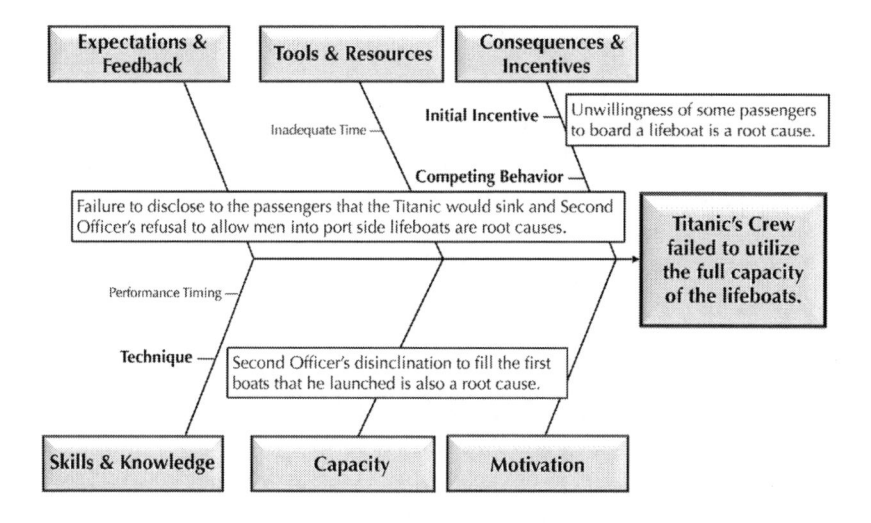

Figure 26 – 3, Human Performance Model with selected causal statements

– **Competing Behavior** – Women and children "first" or women and children "only"?

Discussion:

On the port side Second Officer Charles Lightoller strictly enforced the Captain's general order by *only* allowing women and children passengers to board lifeboats. On the starboard side First Officer William Murdoch loaded the lifeboats with women and children *first* then allowed men aboard when there were no more women immediately available. The first two starboard boats launched with 66 empty seats but included 30 men that would not have been allowed to board on the port side. The first two port side boats were launched with 81 empty seats. When lifeboat 4 was finally launched from the A Deck, 30 minutes before the *Titanic* foundered, Lightoller did not allow the men to join their wives and children and lowered the boat away with room for 35 more.

Conclusion:

The Second Officer's refusal to allow men into port side lifeboats is a root cause for not utilizing the full capacity of the lifeboats.

Skills and Knowledge – Causal factors considered:

– **Performance Timing** – Did Captain Smith give the order to load and launch lifeboats in a timely manner?

Discussion:

After learning the *Titanic* had struck ice and was taking on water, Captain Smith ordered the lifeboats uncovered and made ready. Later there was a small delay when Chief Officer Henry Wilde, not wanting to start undue panic, did not seek the Captain's order to start loading the lifeboats. The delay was short lived when Second Officer Charles Lightoller directly requested the order from Captain Smith. At 12:30 a.m., fifty minutes after the collision and right after learning the full extent of the damage, Smith gave the order to start loading and launching the boats.

Conclusion:

The timing of Captain Smith's order to load and launch the lifeboats is a causal factor for not using the 94 spaces available in lifeboats A and B but is not a root cause for the crew's failure to utilize the full capacity of the lifeboats they did launch.

Technique – Allowable flexibility (worker technique) – Did Second Officer Charles Lightoller's concern over the safety of lowering full boats from the boat deck result in fewer being saved?

Discussion:

Lightoller did not believe it was safe to fill the boats to capacity on the Boat Deck before lowering them to the sea. He intended that the partially filled boats return to the side of the *Titanic* and pick up additional passengers from the gangway doors. The crew did not succeed in opening these doors and only boat 4 picked up additional passengers (found swimming in the ocean). Some boats were successfully launched near capacity and lifeboat 15 was lowered away with 3 over capacity.

Conclusion:

Lightoller's disinclination to fill the first boats that he launched is a root cause for not utilizing the full capacity of the lifeboats.

Human Performance Issue:

After the Titanic sank, most of the lifeboats with room did not return to pick up survivors.

After the *Titanic* sank many of the 1503 people that died struggled for survival in the frigid North Atlantic until they succumbed to hypothermia. Could more lives have been saved if lifeboats with room had returned to pick up survivors?

The Perfect Calm

Testimony concerning lifeboats with room not picking up survivors:

Emergency Clipper 1 – Seaman George Symons was in command of lifeboat 1 with a capacity of 40 people and holding only 12.

> **British Wreck Commissioner's Inquiry** – Testimony of George Symons, examined by the Attorney General.
>
> 11526. When you saw the "Titanic" go down did you hear any cries from the people that went down with the boat?
> Symons – Yes.
> 11527. Did you try to rescue them?
> Symons – I thought at the time, being Master of the situation, it was not safe in any case to go back at that time.
> ...11538. The boat's complement is 40, and you had 12?
> Symons – If there were 40 in that boat there would not be room.
> 11541. Do you tell my Lord that you determined, without consultation with anybody, that you would not go back?
> Symons – I determined by my own wish, as I was Master of the situation, to go back when I thought that most of the danger was over.
> ...11545. Never mind, it had disappeared, and had gone down to the bottom, two miles down, or something like that. What were you afraid of?
> Symons – I was afraid of the swarming.
> 11546. Of what?
> Symons – Of the swarming of the people—swamping the boat.
> ...11555. Then, if I understand correctly what you say, your story to my Lord is; the vessel had gone down; there were the people in the water shrieking for help; you were in the boat with plenty of room; nobody ever mentioned going back; nobody ever said a word about it; you just simply lay on your oars. Is that the story you want my Lord to believe?
> Symons – Yes, that is the story.

Emergency Clipper 2 – Fourth Officer Joseph G. Boxhall was in command of lifeboat 2 with a capacity of 40 people and carrying 17. Saloon Steward James Johnson was one of the crewmembers aboard.

> **British Wreck Commissioner's Inquiry** – Testimony of James Johnson, examined by Mr. Scanlan.
>
> 3564. Is it your evidence that instead of the Fourth Officer, who was in charge of your boat, deciding for himself as to whether it was possible for him to go and rescue the people from whom he heard shrieks, he consulted the lady passengers on the boat?
> Johnson – He asked the lady passengers.
> ...3568. Do you know yourself how many additional people you could have accommodated in your boat?
> Johnson – I have no idea—they might have crammed in.

3569. For the benefit of the Court, give us the best of your belief?
Johnson – I think if they had got five or six more in it would have been quite enough to pull, and if it had been heavy weather I do not suppose there would be anybody here to tell the tale.
3570. In the weather conditions which you had, I take it to be your view that you could at all events have accommodated five or six more?
Johnson – Certainly.

Lifeboat 5 – Third Officer Herbert Pitman was in command of boat 5 with 36 people aboard and room for 29 more.

United States Senate Inquiry – Testimony of Herbert Pitman, questioned by Senator Smith.

Mr. Pitman – They commenced pulling toward the ship, and the passengers in my boat said it was a mad idea on my part to pull back to the ship, because if I did, we should be swamped with the crowd that was in the water, and it would add another 40 to the list of drowned, and I decided I would not pull back.

Senator Smith – Officer, you really turned this No. 5 boat around to go in the direction from which these cries came?

Mr. Pitman – I did.

Senator Smith – And were dissuaded from your purpose by your crew—

Mr. Pitman – No, not crew; passengers.

Senator Smith – One moment; by your crew and by the passengers in your boat?

Mr. Pitman – Certainly.

Senator Smith – Then did you turn the boat toward the sea again?

Mr. Pitman – No; just simply took our oars in and lay quiet.

Lifeboat 7 – Lookout George Hogg was in command of boat 7 with 28 people aboard and room for 37 more.

United States Senate Inquiry – Testimony of George Hogg, questioned by Senator Perkins.

Mr. Hogg – … As soon as she went down, I went to try to assist them in picking up anybody if I could. I met another boat on my way, and they said to pull away. They said: "We have done all in our power and we can not do any more." I can not remember the number of the boat or who the man was who spoke to me. I laid off, then, until I saw the lights of the "Carpathia."

Senator Perkins – But you pulled around in search of other people?

Mr. Hogg – I pulled around in search of other people before I could pull to the wreck. One man said: "We have done our best. There are no more people around. We have pulled all around." I said: "Very good. We will get away now."

Lifeboat 9 – Boatswain Albert Haines was in command of boat 9 with 40 people aboard and room for 25 more.

United States Senate Inquiry – Testimony of Albert Haines, questioned by Senator Smith.
Senator Smith – Did you hear any cries for help?
Mr. Haines – Yes, sir; we heard some cries after the ship went down.
Senator Smith – Did anybody in your boat urge you to return?
Mr. Haines – No, sir. I called the sailors aft, and I passed the remark to them: "There is people in the water." I said, "Do you think it advisable?" I said, "We can't do nothing with this crowd we have in the boat," because we had no room to row, let alone do anything else, sir; and it was no good of our going back. By the time we got back there, we could not have done anything. We could not move in the boat, let alone row. I thought it unsafe to go back there, sir, having so many in the boat.

Lifeboat 3 – Seaman George Moore was in command of boat 3 with 32 people aboard and room for 33 more.

United States Senate Inquiry – Testimony of George Moore, questioned by Senator Newlands.
Senator Newlands – Did your boat make any effort to go back?
Mr. Moore – No, sir.
Senator Newlands – Why not?
Mr. Moore – All the people in the boat wanted to get clear of the ship. They did not want to go near her. They kept urging me to keep away; to pull away from her. In fact, they wanted to get farther away.
Senator Newlands – Why did you not go back and attempt to rescue some of the people who were sinking?
Mr. Moore – Well, sir, we were about a quarter of a mile away, and the cries did not last long. I do not think anybody could live much more than 10 minutes in that cold water. If we had gone back, we would only have had the boat swamped.
Senator Newlands – Do you think it would have been swamped?
Mr. Moore – Yes; if there were any alive. Five or six pulling on that boat's gunwales would no doubt have capsized the boat.

Lifeboat 8 – Seaman Thomas Jones was in command of boat 8 with 25 people aboard and room for 40 more.

United States Senate Inquiry – Testimony of Thomas Jones, questioned by Senator Newlands.
Jones – …I pulled for the light, and I found that I could not get near the light, and I stood by for a little while. I wanted to return to the ship, but the ladies were frightened, and I had to carry out the captain's orders and pull for that light; so I did so. I pulled for about two hours, and then it started to get daybreak, and we lost the light; and then all

of a sudden we saw the "Carpathia" coming, and we turned right back and made for the "Carpathia". That is all I know, sir.
Senator Newlands – Who was the officer on the port side who gave you your directions?
Jones – The captain.

Lifeboat 6 – Quartermaster Robert Hichens was in command of boat 6 with 24 people aboard and room for 41 more. Major Arthur Peuchen was allowed on board while the boat was being lowered to help man the understaffed boat.

United States Senate Inquiry – Testimony of Major Arthur Godfrey Peuchen, questioned by Senator Smith.
Maj. Peuchen – …It seemed to be one, two, or three rumbling sounds, then the lights went out. Then the dreadful calls and cries.
Senator Smith – For help?
Maj. Peuchen – We could not distinguish the exact cry for assistance; moaning and crying; frightful. It affected all the women in our boat whose husbands were among these; and this went on for some time, gradually getting fainter, fainter. At first it was horrible to listen to.
Senator Smith – How far was it away?
Maj. Peuchen – I think we must have been five-eighths of a mile, I should imagine, when this took place. It was very hard to guess the distance. There were only two of us rowing a very heavy boat with a good many people in it, and I do not think we covered very much ground.
Senator Smith – While these cries of distress were going on, did anyone in the boat urge the quartermaster to return?
Maj. Peuchen – Yes; some of the women did. But, as I said before, I had had a row with him [Quartermaster Robert Hichens], and I said to the women, "It is no use you arguing with that man, at all. It is best not to discuss matters with him." He said it was no use going back there, there was only a lot of stiffs there, later on, which was very unkind, and the women resented it very much. I do not think he was qualified to be a quartermaster.
Senator Smith – As a matter of fact, you did not return to the boat?
Maj. Peuchen – We did not return to the boat.

Lifeboat 4 – Quartermaster Walter Perkis is in command of Lifeboat 4 with 40 people aboard after picking up six surviving swimmers shortly after being launched.

United States Senate Inquiry – Testimony of Walter J. Perkis, questioned by Senator Perkins.
Mr. Perkis – No. 4 was the boat I got away in; the last big boat on the port side to leave the ship.
Senator Perkins – You picked up eight in the water?

Mr. Perkis – Yes; and two died afterwards, in the boat.
Senator Perkins – Were they passengers or men of the crew?
Mr. Perkis – No, sir; one was a fireman and one was a steward.
Senator Perkins – The others were all passengers?
Mr. Perkis – Yes, sir.
Senator Perkins – Tell us what you did after that.
Mr. Perkis – After that, after we had picked up the men, I could not hear any more cries anywhere. Everything was over. I waited then until daylight, or just before daylight, when we saw the lights of the "Carpathia".

Collapsible D – The last boat launched by the crew of the *Titanic* was the collapsible D. With Quartermaster Arthur J. Bright in charge it left with 20 people aboard and picked 1 person out of the water.

United States Senate Inquiry – Testimony of Quartermaster Arthur J. Bright, questioned by Senator Smith.
Senator Smith – You did not go back to the scene of this disaster after you pulled out into the sea, away from the *Titanic*?
Mr. Bright – No; by the time we got clear we did not have time to go back. We were told to keep together, you see—
Senator Smith – You kept together and did not return again to the scene of the disaster?
Mr. Bright – No, sir. Mr. Lowe, who gave us the order to stay together, went back.

Lifeboat 14 – Fifth Officer Harold Lowe gathered and tied together lifeboat 4, collapsible D, boat 10 and boat 12. He then redistributed the survivors from his boat 14 to the other boats. When the cries substantially subsided Lowe deemed it safe to return. Lifeboat 14 is the only boat that returned to pick up survivors but Lowe's timing was called into question at the British Inquiry.

British Wreck Commissioner's Inquiry – Testimony of Harold G. Lowe, examined by Mr. Harbinson.
15943. Did you return to the wreckage immediately after the "Titanic" had disappeared?
Lowe – I did not.
15944. Had you any reason for not doing so?
Lowe – I had.
15945. Would you mind telling me what it was?
Lowe – Because it would have been suicide to go back there until the people had thinned out.
15946. Your boat at that time was empty except for the crew?
Lowe – It was.
15947. And it was one of the ordinary lifeboats, with the gunwale a considerable distance above the water?

Lowe – Yes.

15948. I put it to you, as an experienced seaman, would not it be impossible for people who were struggling in the water to get into the boat without the assistance of those who were in the boat?

Lowe – No, it would not.

15949. They could not get in without help?

Lowe – Yes.

15950. Therefore if you had gone back to where the "Titanic" had sunk, it would have been impossible for these people who were floating about to have swamped your boat, because you could have detached them? Is not that so?

Lowe – How could you detach them?

15951. How could they get into the boat without you helped them in?

Lowe – Could not a man hold his weight on the side like that (Showing.) without help from me?

15952. Is not the gunwale three or four feet above the level of the water?

Lowe – No, the boat only stands up like that (Showing.)

15953. About what height would the gunwale of the boat be above the water?

Lowe – There are lifelines round the lifeboat too and they could get hold of those and hang on the rail.

15954. Do not you think it would have been possible for the crew of your boat to have got a considerable number of people out of the water?

Lowe – No, it would have been useless to try it, because a drowning man clings at anything.

Likely lifeboat launch order:

Boat No.	Time	Capacity/ Total aboard	Crew member in charge
Starboard No. 7	12:40 a.m.	65/28	Lookout George Hogg
Starboard No. 5	12:45 a.m.	65/36	Third Officer Herbert Pitman
Starboard No. 3	12:55 a.m.	65/32	ABS George Moore
Portside No. 8	1:00 a.m.	65/25	ABS Thomas Jones
Starboard No. 1	1:05 a.m.	40/12	ABS George Symons
Portside No. 6	1:10 a.m.	65/24	Quartermaster Robert Hichens
Portside No. 16	1:20 a.m.	65/52	Master-at-arms Joseph Bailey

Boat No.	Time	Capacity/Total aboard	Crew member in charge
Portside No. 14	1:25 a.m.	65/40	Fifth Officer Harold Lowe
Portside No. 12	1:30 a.m.	65/42	ABS John Poingdestre
Starboard No. 9	1:30 a.m.	65/40	Boatswain Albert Haines
Starboard No. 11	1:35 a.m.	65/50	Quartermaster Sidney Humphries
Starboard No. 13	1:40 a.m.	65/55	Lead Fireman Frederick Barrett
Starboard No. 15	1:41 a.m.	65/68	Fireman Frank Dymond
Portside No. 2	1:45 a.m.	40/17	Fourth Officer Joseph Boxhall
Portside No. 10	1:50 a.m.	65/57	ABS Edward Buley
Portside No. 4	1:50 a.m.	65/36*	Quartermaster Walter Perkis
Collapsible C	2:00 a.m.	47/43	Quartermaster George Rowe
Collapsible D	2:05 a.m.	47/20**	Quartermaster Arthur Bright

* after picking up six swimmers from the water shortly after being launched

** after picking up one swimmer from the water

Collapsible A and B were washed off the sinking *Titanic*.

HUMAN PERFORMANCE MODEL

After the *Titanic* sank, most of the lifeboats with room did not return to pick up survivors (Figure 26 – 4).

Consequences and Incentives – Causal factor considered:
– **Competing Behavior** – Were fear and survival instinct competing with the desired performance of returning to pick up survivors struggling in the water?
Discussion:
The passengers and/or the commanders of lifeboats that realistically could have returned for survivors were afraid their boats would be swamped by the vast number of desperate people struggling in the water. They did not risk returning, choosing instead the relative safety of their underfilled lifeboats. Fifth Officer Harold Lowe did return after transferring his passengers to other lifeboats but

he had the same concern and waited "because it would have been suicide to go back there until the people had thinned out." Lowe waited too long and only pulled four survivors out of the water with one dying soon after being pulled into the boat. With about 350 spaces available in 12 underfilled lifeboats, it is conceivable that the over a thousand people struggling for life in the frigid water could have swamped and sank a lifeboat if it was immediately available. It is also apparent that if more than one lifeboat had returned and not been swamped, more would have been rescued.

Conclusion:

The failure of nearby lifeboats to return and pick up survivors is one of many contributing factors for the large loss of life. Whether or not the fear of being swamped was valid, that fear and the associated lack of action can not be eliminated or corrected and therefore this competing behavior is not a root cause.

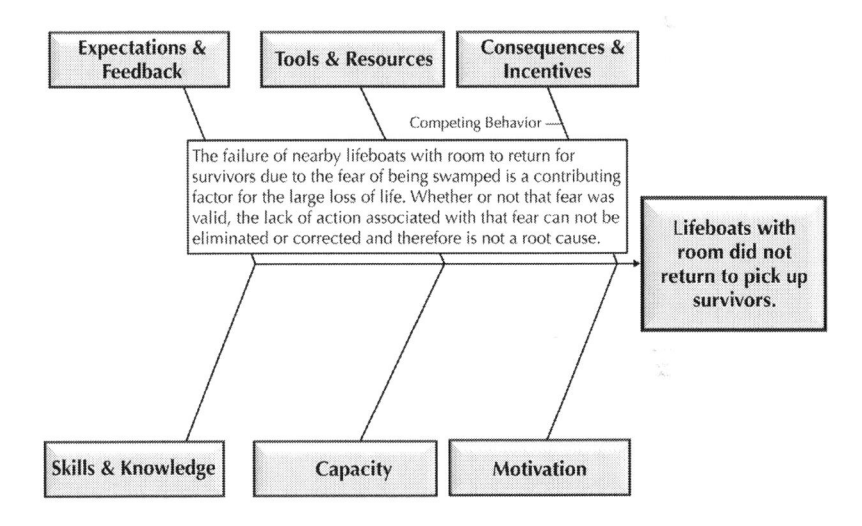

Figure 26 – 4, Human Performance Model with selected causal statements

Human Performance Issue:

The Captain and Officers of the *Californian* failed to respond to Titanic's distress calls or rockets and come to her aid.

The Captain and Officers of the *Californian*:
- Captain Stanley Lord – Stanley Lord's ship had stopped for the night about 10 miles from the *Titanic*.
- Third Officer Charles Groves – Groves was on the 8:00 p.m. to Midnight watch on Sunday night, April 14th.

- Second Officer Herbert Stone – Stone relieved Third Officer Groves at 12:10 a.m. on the morning of April 15th, thirty minutes after the *Titanic* had struck the iceberg.
- James Gibson – Gibson was an apprentice aboard the *Californian*. He was on the Midnight to 4:00 a.m. watch with Second Officer Stone on the morning of April 15th.

The Officers on watch reported seeing rockets being fired from a big liner but Captain Stanley Lord did not recognize these as distress rockets. If Captain Lord or one of his Officers had summoned their Marconi Operator would she have been able to reach the *Titanic* in time to save some of the passengers and crew?

Testimony concerning the *Californian*'s response:

> **British Wreck Commissioner's Inquiry** – Testimony of Stanley Lord, examined by the Attorney General.
> 6801. … Is it the fact—am I right in supposing that this vessel, the name of which you apparently do not know, from which a rocket appeared, was at the time that the rocket was sent up in the position in which probably the "Titanic" was?
> Lord – No.
> 6802. Well, then, you have conveyed to me an erroneous impression. How did this rocket bear to you?
> Lord – I have never heard the exact bearing of it.
> The Commissioner: What is in my brain at the present time is this, that what they saw was the "Titanic."
> The Attorney General: I know.
> The Commissioner: That is in my brain, and I want to see whether I am right or not.
> The Attorney General: It certainly must have been very close.
> The Commissioner: Clear it up if you can.
> The Attorney General: I think it will clear up as we go on—at least, as far as it can be cleared up. It is a point your Lordship will probably have to determine on the evidence.
> The Commissioner: Yes, and therefore I want the evidence put before me as clearly as possible.
> 6805. (The Attorney General – To the Witness.) Can you tell us whether you saw one or two masthead lights?
> Lord – I only saw one.
> 6806. You only saw one?
> Lord – The Third Officer said he saw two.
> The Attorney General: Now that is important.
> The Commissioner: That is very important, because the "Titanic" would have two.
> 6807. (The Attorney General.) Yes, that is it – two masthead lights.

(To the Witness.) You only saw one, but the Third Officer said he saw two?

Lord – And the Second Officer said he saw one.

The Attorney General: Very well; we will hear their accounts from them.

…6810. Were you on deck when he (Third Officer) told you this?

Lord – He told me the following day, I think; I do not think it was mentioned that night.

6811. He told you next day he had seen two white lights when on deck about 12 o'clock?

Lord – Yes, two masthead lights.

6812. Is the Third Officer still in the ship?

Lord – Yes.

6813. Will you tell me his name?

Lord – Mr. Groves.

The Attorney General: My Lord, I think it very desirable that the other Witnesses from the "Californian" should be out of Court whilst this Witness is giving evidence.

The Commissioner: By all means.

The Attorney General: If your Lordship will direct it.

The Commissioner: Where are the other Witnesses from the "Californian"? (The Officers of the "Californian" stood up in Court.) Well, gentlemen, I think you had better leave the Court at present. (The Officers retired.)

British Wreck Commissioner's Inquiry – Testimony of Third Officer Charles Groves, examined later by Mr. S. A. T. Rowlatt.

8146. Did you then see more lights than one?

Groves – About 11:25 I made out two lights—two white lights.

8147. Two masthead lights?

Groves – Two white masthead lights.

…8167. Did you report that to the captain?

Groves – Yes, because, as I said before, he left orders to let him know if I saw any steamers approaching.

8172. Did you say what sort of a steamer you thought she was?

Groves – Captain Lord said to me, "Can you make anything out of her lights?" I said, "Yes, she is evidently a passenger steamer coming up on us."

8176. Did you say why you thought she was a passenger steamer?

Groves – Yes. I told him that I could see her deck lights and that made me pass the remark that she was evidently a passenger steamer.

8178. How many deck lights had she? Had she much light?

Groves – Yes, a lot of light. There was absolutely no doubt her being a passenger steamer, at least in my mind.

...8211. Now you said something about the lights going out; what was it?
Groves – Well he said to me, "It does not look like a passenger steamer." I said, "Well, she put her lights out at 11:40"—a few minutes ago that was.
8212. Then had she put her lights out before the captain came on the bridge?
Groves – Yes, my Lord.
8214. And you told the captain this, did you?
Groves – Yes.
8215. What did he say to that; did he say anything?
Groves – When I remarked about the passenger steamer he said: "The only passenger steamer near us is the 'Titanic.'"
8217. What makes you fix the time 11:40 for her lights going out?
Groves – Because that is the time we struck one bell to call the middle watch.
8218. Do you remember that bell was struck at that time?
Groves – Most certainly.
8219. Did the steamer continue on her course after that?
Groves – No, not so far as I could see.
8220. She stopped?
Groves – She stopped.
8221. Was that at the time when her lights appeared to go out?
Groves – That was at the time that her lights appeared to go out.
8222. Were the lights you saw on her port side or her starboard side?
Groves – Port side.
8223. I want to ask you a question. Supposing the steamer whose lights you saw turned two points to port at 11.40, would that account to you for her lights ceasing to be visible to you?
Groves – I quite think it would.

British Wreck Commissioner's Inquiry – Testimony of Second Officer Herbert Stone, examined by Mr. Butler Aspinall.
7849. You had been keeping this vessel under close observation and saw five rockets go up in fairly quick succession. What did you think at the time they meant? You applied your mind to the matter, did you not?
Stone – Yes.
7850. Now, what did you think at the time?
Stone – I knew they were signals of some sort.
7851. I know; of course—signals of what sort did you think?
Stone – I did not know at the time.
7852. (The Commissioner.) Now try to be frank?
Stone – I am.
7853. If you try, you will succeed. What did you think these rockets

were going up at intervals of three or four minutes for?
Stone – I just took them as white rockets, and informed the Master and left him to judge.
7854. Do you mean to say you did not think for yourself? I thought you told us just now that you did think.
[No Answer.]
7855. (Mr. Butler Aspinall.) You know they were not being sent up for fun, were they?
Stone – No.
7856. (The Commissioner.) You know, you do not make a good impression upon me at present.
7856a. (Mr. Butler Aspinall.) Did you think that they were distress signals?
Stone – No.
7857. Did not that occur to you?
Stone – It did not occur to me at the time.
7858. When did it occur to you? Did it occur at some later time to you?
Stone – Yes.
7859. When?
Stone – After I had heard about the "Titanic" going down.

British Wreck Commissioner's Inquiry – Testimony of Apprentice James Gibson, examined by the Solicitor General.
7609. …I want to be quite sure first of all that I have got accurately the message that you were told to give to the Captain after the ship had disappeared about five minutes past two. Just tell us again exactly, what it was the Second Officer told you to tell the Captain?
Gibson – To call the Captain and tell him that the ship has disappeared in the S.W., that we were heading W.S.W., and that she has fired altogether eight rockets.
The Commissioner: Will you ask him what he understood by the word "disappeared"?
7611. (The Solicitor General.) Yes, my Lord. (To the Witness.) You say you were told to report that the ship had disappeared. What did you understand by "disappeared"?
Gibson – We could not see anything more of her.
7612. (The Commissioner.) Did it convey to you, and did the man who was speaking to you, in your opinion, intend to convey that the ship had gone down? That is what I understand by disappearing. Did you understand him to mean that?
Gibson – No, my Lord.
7613. What did you understand him to mean that she had steamed away through the ice?

Gibson – That she had gone out of sight.

7614. Oh, yes. A ship goes out of sight when she goes down to the bottom. What did you understand by the word "disappeared"?

Gibson – That is all I could understand about it.

7615. A ship that had been sending up rockets; then you are told to go to the Captain and say, "That ship which has been sending up rockets has disappeared." What did you understand the Second Officer to mean? Did not you understand him to mean that she had gone to the bottom?

Gibson – No.

7616. Then what did you understand, that she had steamed away through the ice?

Gibson – [No Answer.]

7617. (The Solicitor General.) I want to follow out this last message and see what it means. You were to tell the Captain, and you did tell him, that this ship had disappeared to the S.W.?

Gibson – Yes.

British Wreck Commissioner's Inquiry – Testimony of Captain Stanley Lord, Examined by the Attorney General .

7274. Mr. Stone is your Second Officer, is he not?

Lord – Yes.

7275. Did Mr. Stone send the Apprentice to report to you at any time?

Lord – Did he on this morning?

7276. I am speaking of this morning.

Lord – He told me afterwards that he had done so.

7277. At about 2 o'clock?

Lord – At about 2 o'clock.

7278. Did he tell you that there had been rockets sent up?

Lord – He did. That was the message the boy was supposed to have delivered to me. I heard it the next day.

7279. That is rather important, you see—that is the message which the boy was supposed to have delivered to you which you heard next day?

Lord – Yes.

7280. I want to put this to you. Did not the boy deliver the message to you, and did not you inquire whether they were all white rockets?

Lord – I do not know; I was asleep.

7281. Think. This is a very important matter.

Lord – It is a very important matter. I recognise that.

7282. It is much better to tell us what happened, Captain.

Lord – He came to the door, I understand. I have spoken to him very closely since. He said, I opened my eyes and said, "What is it"? and he gave the message; and I said, "What time is it"? and he told me, and then I think he said I asked him whether there were any colours in the light.

7283. That is what the boy has said to you. You have questioned him a good many times since?

Lord – Yes, I have questioned him since.

7284. Is he still an Apprentice in your ship?

Lord – He is.

The Commissioner: Is he telling the truth?

Lord – Is the boy telling the truth?

7285. Yes.

Lord – I do not know. I do not doubt it for a moment.

7286. (The Attorney General.) Just think. You say you do not doubt it for a moment. Do you see what that means? That means that the boy did go to the chart room to you. He did tell you about the rockets from the ship and you asked whether they were white rockets, and told him that he was to report if anything further occurred?

Lord – So he said. That is what he said.

7287. Have you any reason to doubt that is true?

Lord – No; I was asleep.

7288. Then do you mean you said this in your sleep to him, that he was to report?

Lord – I very likely was half awake. I have no recollection of this Apprentice saying anything to me at all that morning.

7289. Why did you ask whether they were white rockets?

Lord – I suppose this was on account of the first question they asked, whether they were Company's signals.

7290. Do just think?

Lord – Company signals usually have some colours in them.

7291. So that if they were white it would make it quite plain to you they were distress signals?

Lord – No, I understand some companies have white.

7292. Do really try and do yourself justice?

Lord – I am trying to do my best.

7293. Think you now. Mr. Lord, allow me to suggest you are not doing yourself justice. You are explaining, first of all, that you asked if they were white rockets, because companies' signals are coloured. I am asking you whether the point of your asking whether they were all white rockets was not in order to know whether they were distress signals? Was not that the object of your question, if you put it?

Lord – I really do not know what was the object of my question.

7294. And you think that is why you asked about it?

Lord – I think that is why I asked about it.

7295. I must ask you something more. Do you remember Mr. Stone reporting at twenty minutes to three to you that morning through the tube?

Lord – I do not.

7302. Listen to this—he reported to you at twenty minutes to three through the tube and told you that the steamer had disappeared bearing south-west half west. Do you remember that?

Lord – I do not remember it. He has told me that since.

7303. Have you any reason to doubt it?

Lord – I do not know anything at all about it.

7304. Have you any reason to doubt that Mr. Stone, the Officer, is speaking the truth?

Lord – I do not see why he should not tell me the truth.

…7307. Listen to this:—"The Captain again asked me if I was sure there were no colours in the lights that had been seen." Do you remember that?

Lord – I do not.

7308. "And that he"—Mr. Stone—"assured you that they were white lights"?

Lord – He has told me all about this since, but I have not the slightest recollection that anything happened that way.

…7312. This is what he says: "I assured him that they were white lights, and he"—that is you—"said 'All 'right.'" Have you no recollection of that conversation?

Lord – I have no recollection of any conversation between half-past one and half-past four that I had with the Second Officer.

7313. There is only one thing further I want to ask you, who is Mr. Stewart?

Lord – The Chief Officer.

7314. Was it he who called you at half-past four?

Lord – Yes.

7315. And was it he who told you that the second mate had seen rockets?

Lord – Yes.

7316. And did you reply "Yes, I know."?

Lord – I said, Yes, they certainly had told me something about a rocket.

7317. Do you observe the difference in the question I put to you and your answer?

Lord – You mentioned rockets; I mentioned rocket.

7318. That the second mate had said he had seen rockets, and you replied, "Yes, I know." Very well. Now I want to ask you something further. When you were not satisfied that the rocket which you had seen was a company's signal, there was no difficulty in your calling your Marconi operator, was there?

Lord – None whatever.

7319. If you had called him you would have been in communication with the "Titanic," as I understand it?

Lord – Yes, I believe she was sending out signals.

7320. And you would have received the "Titanic's" messages?

Lord – Yes.

Facts concerning the *Californian's* response:
- The *Californian* had one Marconi Wireless Operator and did not man the wireless overnight.
- The *Californian's* wireless was off before the *Titanic* collided with the iceberg.
- A total of eight rockets were fired from the *Titanic* and eight rockets were seen from the *Californian*.
- The Captain or Officers of the *Californian* did not call for the Marconi Operator to determine if there was a problem with the unidentified ship they were observing.

SIGNALS OF DISTRESS – When a vessel is in distress and requires assistance from other vessels or from the shore, the following shall be the signals to be used or displayed by her, either together or separately.

AT NIGHT:
1. A gun or other explosive signal fired at intervals of about a minute.
2. Flames on the vessel (as from a burning tar barrel, oil barrel, etc.).
3. Rockets or shells, throwing stars of any color or description, fired one at a time at short intervals.
4. A continuous sounding with any fog-signal apparatus.

HUMAN PERFORMANCE MODEL

The Captain and Officers of the *Californian* failed to respond to *Titanic's* distress calls or rockets and come to her aid (Figure 26 – 5).

Tools and Resources – Causal factor considered:
– Availability – Was the required equipment available?
Discussion:

The required equipment to ascertain the identity of the ship, and the reason she was firing rockets, was the Marconi Wireless and while the equipment was available it was useless without a Marconi Wireless Operator. Without a Marconi Operator on duty the *Californian* did not pick up the *Titanic's* call for help. Had the wireless been manned around the clock the *Californian* would likely have already been on the way to aid the *Titanic* before the distress rockets were fired.

Conclusion:

Lack of around the clock Marconi Wireless coverage is a root cause for the failure of the *Californian* to respond to *Titanic's* distress calls.

Consequences and Incentives – Causal factor considered:

– Competing Behavior – Were there alternate priorities, practices or procedures competing with the desired performance?

Discussion:

When the *Titanic* began firing distress rockets the initial desired performance on the part of the Captain and Officers of the *Californian* was to find out why. Summoning the Marconi Wireless Operator to attempt contact with the ship would have identified the *Titanic's* peril but the half-asleep Captain did not grasp the significance of what he had been told. The Bridge Officers only did what the Captain ordered, even as one remarked to the other that a ship was "not going to fire rockets at sea for nothing."

Conclusion:

The practice of only doing what the Captain ordered, even as he slept through the midnight watch, did not leave open other options for the ranking Bridge Officer. No officer woke the Marconi Operator without the Captain's order and this behavior is a root cause for not determining the reason the rockets were being fired, and responding.

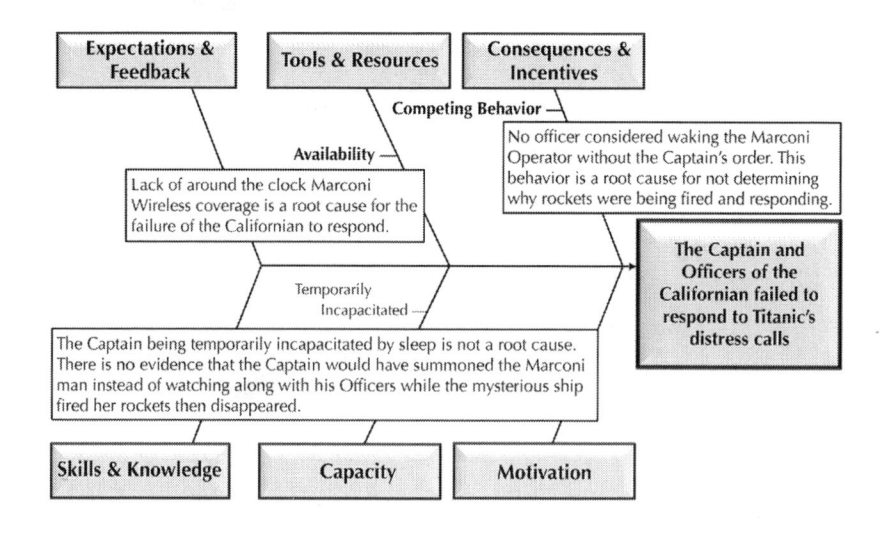

Figure 26 – 5, Human Performance Model with selected causal statements

Capacity – Causal factor considered:

– Temporarily Incapacitated – Was the Captain impaired due to being overly tired and sleeping on the job?

Discussion:

Captain Stanley Lord testified that he was asleep or only half awake when he received messages about the ship that was being observed and he had no recollection of the conversations the next morning. While the Captain was lying down in the chart room and still awake he was told about white rockets but remembered hearing about a single white rocket. The Captain's orders were to keep Morsing the vessel and to send the Apprentice down with any information.

Conclusion:

The Captain being temporarily incapacitated by sleep may be a contributing factor but is not a root cause for failing to respond to the *Titanic's* distress calls or rockets.

With knowledge of at least one rocket having been fired from the unidentified ship Captain Lord did not change his orders or have the Marconi Operator summoned. It is possible, had the Captain been fully awake and aware, that he may have decided to wake the Marconi man but it is also possible that he would have watched along with his Officers while the mysterious ship fired her rockets then disappeared.

Root Cause Summary

Root causes and contributing factors for the Problem Statement:

1503 people perished when the *Titanic* sank.

Contributing Factor: The sea temperature of the North Atlantic had dropped below freezing the night of the collision. Most of the 1503 people that ended up in the water after the *Titanic* sank died of hypothermia. Because this condition can't be eliminated or corrected it is not a root cause.

Human Performance

The *Titanic* did not carry enough lifeboats for the passengers and crew.

Root Cause: White Star Line's failure to supply an adequate number of lifeboats is a root cause for the large loss of life when the *Titanic* sank.

Root Cause:– The British Board of Trade's failure to update the lifeboat requirements for larger ships in general and the Olympic class liners specifically is a root cause for the large loss of life when the *Titanic* sank.

The *Titanic's* Crew failed to utilize the full capacity of the lifeboats.

Root Cause: The unwillingness of some passengers to board a lifeboat is a root cause for the crew's failure to utilize the full capacity of the lifeboats.

Root Cause: Failure to disclose to the passengers that the *Titanic* would sink is a root cause for not utilizing the full capacity of the lifeboats.

Root Cause: On the starboard side First Officer William Murdoch loaded the lifeboats with women and children "first" then allowed men aboard. On the port side Second Officer Charles Lightoller strictly enforced "women and children" by only allowing women and children passengers to board lifeboats. Lightoller's refusal to allow men into port side lifeboats is a root cause for not utilizing the full capacity of the lifeboats.

Root Cause: Second Officer Lightoller did not believe it was safe to fill the boats to capacity on the Boat Deck before lowering them to the sea. His disinclination to fill the first boats that he launched is a root cause for not utilizing the full capacity of the lifeboats.

Contributing Factor: Inadequate time is a contributing factor for not using the 94 spaces available in Collapsible lifeboats A and B but is not a root cause for the crew's failure to utilize the full capacity of the lifeboats they did launch.

After the *Titanic* sank most of the lifeboats with room did not return to pick up survivors.

Contributing Factor: The failure of nearby lifeboats to return and pick up survivors is a contributing factor for the large loss of life. Whether or not the initial fear of being swamped by swimming passengers was valid, that fear, and the associated lack of action, can not be eliminated or corrected and is not a root cause.

The Captain and officers of the *Californian* failed to respond to *Titanic's* distress calls or rockets and come to her aid.

Root Cause: Without an operator on duty the *Californian's* Marconi Wireless did not pick up the *Titanic's* call for help and was not used by the Captain or officers to determine if there was a problem with the unidentified ship they were observing. Lack of around the clock Marconi Wireless coverage is a root cause for the failure of the *Californian* to respond to *Titanic's* distress calls.

Root Cause: No officer aboard the *Californian* considered waking the Marconi Operator without the Captain's order and this behavior is a root cause for not determining the reason the rockets were being fired and responding.

Contributing Factor: Captain Stanley Lord testified that he was only half awake when he received messages about the ship that was being observed and he had no recollection of the conversations the next morning. There is no evidence that Captain Lord would have changed his orders or summoned the Marconi Operator if he had been awake. The Captain being temporarily incapacitated by sleep may be a contributing factor but is not a root cause for failing to respond to the *Titanic's* distress calls or rockets.

Chapter 27

IMPROVE AND CONTROL

DMAIC Improve and Control

The DMAIC Define, Measure, and Analyze phases were detailed for each problem statement in the preceding Chapters. This Chapter will discuss the Improve and Control phases and summarize the changes that resulted from the *Titanic* disaster and the subsequent American and British inquiries.

Improve – Corrective and Preventive Actions – Identified root causes should be addressed with corrective and preventive actions (CAPAs). In some cases it is possible that a single CAPA will address multiple root causes while in other cases multiple CAPAs are necessary to address a single root cause. To be effective the CAPAs should be comprehensive and address all identified root causes in order to prevent a recurrence of the incident or result in less severe consequences if there is a recurrence.

Control – Implement and Monitor – In the Control phase of the DMAIC process a plan is formulated to verify the identified CAPAs are appropriately implemented and are effective in preventing a repeat or similar problem. One of the preventive actions resulting from the *Titanic* disaster was the formation of the International Ice Patrol which still charts the location of icebergs in the North Atlantic. Monitoring this CAPA following implementation has demonstrated its effectiveness—since the formation of the ice patrol there has not been any lives lost due to collisions with icebergs.

Broad application of CAPAs should be considered if any of the root causes are identified as generic problems. CAPAs specific to the *Titanic* itself would be applicable to the *Olympic*, her sister ship, and the *Britannic* the third Olympic class liner that was under construction at Harland & Wolff. CAPAs that address root causes pertaining to the shipbuilding industry or the passenger shipping trade would have broader application than the Olympic class liners or White Star Line and would likely be implemented by way of regulation.

The CAPAs and control plan should align to address the root causes identified and achieve the Desired State identified in the Define phase for each problem statement.

CAPA Is Not A Four Letter Word

CAPA is, of course, an acronym for Corrective And Preventive Action but is often thought of in the world of business and profit as something nasty (read costly) to be avoided rather than an investment (often a small one) in a safer and more productive workplace. There were opposing opinions on the effectiveness of binoculars in the moonless, perfect calm encountered by the *Titanic* as she sped toward her meeting with the iceberg, but it is clear that the lookouts – the men doing the work – believed they were needed and could have prevented the accident. In cases of disagreement on the effectiveness of a proposed CAPA, the people doing the work are usually right.

The CAPA for some root causes are obvious and are simply fixes that reverse the root cause itself. For the root cause of binoculars not being available for the lookouts, the obvious corrective action is to supply the binoculars. Other CAPAs are less obvious but equally as important. The obvious corrective action of supplying the binoculars, also needs to include the less obvious preventive action of providing a backup pair in case the pair in use is lost, broken, or locked away.

After CAPAs are identified for the root causes of the specific incident it is necessary to determine if those CAPAs have broader applications. Supplying binoculars for the lookouts on the *Olympic* only helps that ship avoid icebergs. Application of the CAPA to all White Star ships that travel the North Atlantic would help to achieve the desired state of avoiding collisions with icebergs, but even that broader application is still limited to the White Star Line. The desired application of this generic CAPA to all shipping lines could be suggested by the White Star Line or be required by regulation.

The Gift of a Near-Miss

Near-miss is defined as a narrowly avoided collision or other accident, but too often a near-miss is seen as a free-pass to skip an investigation and avoid identifying root causes. It is common for near-misses to go unreported when management openly or otherwise discourages near-miss reports. When they are reported they may not be fully investigated leaving root causes undiscovered and CAPAs not identified and unimplemented. When the uncorrected root causes that led to the near-miss eventually result in an actual incident with real consequences, the near-miss (and the lost opportunity to prevent the incident) is often forgotten history.

The British Inquiry identified excess speed as one of the causes of the *Titanic* accident but did not find Captain Smith at fault because he was following the accepted and proven course of action that had been proven effective for over a quarter century.

> Excerpt from the British Wreck Commissioner's Inquiry Report issued on July 30, 1912:
> ... Why, then, did the Master persevere in his course and maintain his

speed? The answer is to be found in the evidence. It was shown that for many years past, indeed, for a quarter of a century or more, the practice of liners using this track when in the vicinity of ice at night had been in clear weather to keep the course, to maintain the speed and to trust to a sharp look-out to enable them to avoid the danger. This practice, it was said, had been justified by experience, no casualties having resulted from it. I accept the evidence as to the practice and as to the immunity from casualties which is said to have accompanied it. But the event has proved the practice to be bad. Its root is probably to be found in competition and in the desire of the public for quick passages rather than in the judgment of navigators. But unfortunately experience appeared to justify it. In these circumstances I am not able to blame Captain Smith. He had not the experience which his own misfortune has afforded to those whom he has left behind, and he was doing only that which other skilled men would have done in the same position.

A quarter century of experience with no casualties justified an unsafe practice until that unsafe practice was a root cause for a collision that claimed 1503 lives. If there had been near-misses over that 25 years there was no incentive for captains to report them and shine a light on the navigation of their ship. With an unmarred record of success and a "we have always done it this way" attitude, Captain Smith provided the experience and the consequence necessary to change the practice.

A near-miss should be considered a gift to the family, community, business or other entity that cares and is relieved that something that almost happened—didn't happen. The root cause analysis techniques offered in this book also work for investigating a near-miss but are not often used for that purpose even when near-miss reporting is encouraged. The reason may be that while it is easy to measure the time spent on root cause investigations, and the dollars spent on implemented CAPAs, it is difficult to measure the cost avoidance of a problem, incident, or catastrophe that was prevented.

Titanic Root Cause Scrutiny

Analysis of the three problem statements identified for the *Titanic* disaster yielded a total of twelve root causes. Three root causes were identified for the *Titanic* striking the iceberg, one for her sinking following the collision, and eight were associated with the large loss of life. Each root cause should address the identified Desired State and align with the root cause definition from Chapter 22, meeting the test that it is "correctable" and "if eliminated, would have prevented the problem or resulted in less severe consequences." If a root cause does not meet the definition scrutiny it should be revisited prior to identifying CAPAs although in some cases it is desirable to identify CAPAs for contributing factors that, while not a root cause, need be addressed. The formation of the

International Ice Patrol is an example of a preventive action for a contributing factor.

Scrutinizing the twelve root causes identified:

> The *Titanic* collided with an iceberg – The Desired State is for ships at sea to avoid collisions with icebergs.

Root Cause: Binoculars were not available for the lookouts.

Eliminating this root cause is only accomplished by supplying binoculars for the crow's nest lookouts but would they have helped prevent the collision in the perfect calm that prevailed that night? There was no moon to cast light on the iceberg and there was no swell causing ripples at the base of the berg, both early warning signs that weren't present to be picked up by binoculars or the naked eye. The *Titanic* struck the iceberg 30 seconds after it was first spotted. The ship avoided a head on collision and almost missed the iceberg. If the use of binoculars would have allowed the berg to be sighted just a little sooner the ship may have been able to avoid the collision or a less severe collision may have resulted in less than fatal damage.

Root Cause: The Captain relied on accepted navigation practices instead of slowing down and posting additional lookouts.

The Captain relied on common, accepted navigation practices in what he recognized to be the uncommon condition of a perfectly calm, glass-like ocean. Additional lookouts would likely have resulted in spotting the iceberg sooner and slower speed would have allowed more time to avoid the iceberg. If the ship did strike the iceberg, a less severe collision may have resulted.

Root Cause: The Senior Wireless Operator failed to deliver crucial ice warning messages due to being distracted and overloaded with a backlog of passenger messages.

The Crow's Nest Lookouts did not have binoculars, no additional lookouts were posted, and the ship's speed was maintained even as it approached known ice fields. With this scenario the failure to deliver the ice warning from the *Mesaba*, identifying icebergs in the immediate vicinity, two hours before the collision, may seem inconsequential. It may not have made any difference in the navigation of the ship but just before the message was picked up by the Marconi Operator the Captain had told the Second Officer, "If it becomes at all doubtful let me know at once." This in reference to the distance that they could see and spot ice in the current conditions. The ice warning from the *Mesaba*, if delivered to the bridge, may have provided the doubt needed for the Second Officer to alert the Captain, slow down, or post additional lookouts.

> The *Titanic* sank after the collision – The Desired State is that ships do not sink following a collision at sea.

Root Cause: The equipment design root cause identified that the transverse bulkheads did not reach high enough above the waterline to prevent the sinking.

If the bulkheads had reached the B Deck the *Titanic* would not have sunk following the collision.

> 1503 people perished when the *Titanic* sank – The Desired State is preventing or minimizing loss of life in future shipwrecks.

Without speculating on how many lives could have been saved, eliminating any of the eight root causes identified would have resulted in the less severe consequence of fewer lives being lost.

Root Cause: White Star Line failed to supply an adequate number of lifeboats.

Root Cause: The British Board of Trade failed to update the lifeboat requirements for the Olympic class liners.

If the Board of Trade had compelled White Star to equip the *Titanic* with enough lifeboats for all on board, or if White Star had chosen to do so, more of the large wooden lifeboats could have been launched from each of the sixteen sets of lifeboat davits. More lives would have been saved if more lifeboats would have been available.

Root Cause: Some passengers were unwilling to board a lifeboat.

Root Cause: Officers failed to disclose to the passengers that the *Titanic* was sinking.

Root Cause: On the port side only women and children were allowed to board lifeboats.

Root Cause: The Second Officer did not believe it was safe to fill the boats to capacity.

Eliminating any or all of these root causes for not utilizing the full capacity of the lifeboats would have resulted in more people being saved in the lifeboats that were available.

Root Cause: Without an operator on duty the *Californian's* Marconi Wireless did not pick up the *Titanic's* call for help.

Root Cause: No officer aboard the *Californian* considered waking the Marconi Operator without the Captain's order.

After rockets were observed the Captain, half-asleep and not recognizing the reason they were being fired, did not order the Marconi Operator to contact the ship and no other Officer took the initiative to do so. Had the Marconi been manned around the clock or the operator been roused the *Californian* would have come to the aid of the *Titanic*.

Chapter 28

FINDINGS OF THE AMERICAN AND BRITISH INQUIRIES

United States Senate Inquiry

Senator Smith's committee presented their final report to the United States Senate on May 28, 1912, only 43 days after the *Titanic* sank in the North Atlantic. The nineteen page report also contained 44 pages of exhibits, and summarized over 1100 pages of testimony and affidavits.

The report's key findings included:
- Captain Edward Smith's "indifference to danger was one of the direct and contributing causes of this unnecessary tragedy."
- The inadequate number of lifeboats was the fault of the British Board of Trade, "to whose laxity of regulation and hasty inspection the world is largely indebted for this awful tragedy."
- The *SS Californian* had been "much nearer [to *Titanic*] than the captain is willing to admit" and the British Government should take "drastic action" against him for his actions.
- J. Bruce Ismay had not ordered Captain Smith to put on extra speed, but Ismay's presence on board may have contributed to the captain's decision to do so.
- Third Class passengers had not been prevented from reaching the lifeboats, but had in many cases not realized until it was too late that the ship was sinking.

The report was strongly critical of established seafaring practices but it did not find White Star Line or the International Mercantile Marine Company negligent under existing maritime law. They had followed standard accepted practices and the disaster was therefore categorized as an "act of God."

British Wreck Commissioner's Inquiry

The Wreck Commissioner's final report was published on July 30, 1912. The report included a detailed description of the ship, an account of the ship's journey, a description of the damage caused by the iceberg, an account of the evacuation and rescue, and a section devoted to the *Californian*.

The British report found that *Titanic's* sinking was solely the result of colliding with the iceberg and not due to any inherent flaws with the ship. The report also stated:

> "The Court, having carefully inquired into the circumstances of the above mentioned shipping casualty, finds, for the reasons appearing in the annex hereto, that the loss of the said ship was due to collision with an iceberg, brought about by the excessive speed at which the ship was being navigated."

The British Inquiry also concluded:

- An inadequate lookout was being kept for the navigational hazards being faced.
- There were not enough lifeboats available and they had not been properly filled or manned with trained seamen.
- The *Californian* "could have pushed through the ice to the open water without any serious risk and so have come to the assistance of the *Titanic*."
- The Duff-Gordons were not guilty of any wrongdoing but should have acted more tactfully.

While the report found that Captain Smith was at fault for not changing course or slowing down, it concluded that he had not been negligent because he had followed long-standing practice which had not previously been shown to be unsafe.

Speed a Primary Cause

Both inquiries identified the speed of the ship as it approached reported ice as a primary cause of the accident.

The U.S. Senate Inquiry report detailed the ice warnings received by the *Titanic* prior to the accident then discussed the lack of response.

United States Senate Inquiry Report:

ICE BOTH TO NORTHWARD AND SOUTHWARD OF STEAMSHIP "TITANIC'S" TRACK.

This enables the committee to say that the ice positions so definitely reported to the *Titanic* just preceding the accident located ice on both sides of the track or lane which the *Titanic* was following, and in her immediate vicinity. No general discussion took place among the officers; no conference was called to consider these warnings; no heed was given to them. The speed was not relaxed, the lookout was not increased, and the only vigilance displayed by the officer of the watch was by instructions to the lookouts to keep "a sharp lookout for ice." It should be said, however, that the testimony shows that Capt. Smith remarked to Officer Lightoller, who was the officer doing duty on the bridge until 10 o'clock ship's time, or 8:27 o'clock New York time, "If it was in a slight degree hazy there would be no doubt we should have to go very slowly", and "If in the slightest degree doubtful, let me know." The evidence is that it was exceptionally clear. There was no haze, and the ship's speed was not reduced.

The British inquiry identifies the speed of the ship as a cause for the accident but stops short of blaming Captain Smith.

British Wreck Commissioner's Inquiry Report – Action That Should Have Been Taken:

The question is what ought the Master to have done. I am advised that with the knowledge of the proximity of ice which the Master had, two courses were open to him: The one was to stand well to the southward instead of turning up to a westerly course; the other was to reduce speed materially as night approached. He did neither. The alteration of the course at 5:50 p.m. was so insignificant that it cannot be attributed to any intention to avoid ice. This deviation brought the vessel back to within about two miles of the customary route before 11:30 p.m. And there was certainly no reduction of speed. Why, then, did the Master persevere in his course and maintain his speed? The answer is to be found in the evidence. It was shown that for many years past, indeed, for a quarter of a century or more, the practice of liners using this track when in the vicinity of ice at night had been in clear weather to keep the course, to maintain the speed and to trust to a sharp look-out to enable them to avoid the danger. This practice, it was said, had been justified by experience, no casualties having resulted from it. I accept the evidence as to the practice and as to the immunity from casualties which is said to have accompanied it. But the event has proved the practice to be bad. Its root is probably to be found in competition and in the desire of the public for quick passages rather than in the judgment of navigators. But unfortunately experience appeared to justify it. In these circumstances I am not able to blame Captain Smith. He had not the experience which his own misfortune has afforded to those whom he has left behind, and he was doing only that which other skilled men would have done in the same position. It was suggested at the bar that he was yielding to influences which ought not to have affected him; that the presence of Mr. Ismay on board and the knowledge which he perhaps had of a conversation between Mr. Ismay and the Chief Engineer [Bell] at Queenstown about the speed of the ship and the consumption of coal probably induced him to neglect precautions which he would otherwise have taken. But I do not believe this. The evidence shows that he was not trying to make any record passage or indeed any exceptionally quick passage. He was not trying to please anybody, but was exercising his own discretion in the way he thought best. He made a mistake, a very grievous mistake, but one in which, in face of the practice and of past experience, negligence cannot be said to have had any part; and in the absence of negligence it is, in my opinion, impossible to fix Captain Smith with blame. It is, however, to be hoped that the last has been heard of the practice and that for the future it will be abandoned for what we now know to be more prudent and wiser measures. What was a mistake in the case of the "Titanic" would without doubt be negligence in any similar case in the future.

The *Californian*

Both inquiries harshly criticized the *Californian's* Captain and officers for not responding to the *Titanic's* distress.

> **United States Senate Inquiry Report** – Pleas For Help
> STEAMSHIP "CALIFORNIAN'S" RESPONSIBILITY.
> The committee is forced to the inevitable conclusion that the *Californian*, controlled by the same company, was nearer the *Titanic* than the 19 miles reported by her Captain, and that her officers and crew saw the distress signals of the *Titanic* and failed to respond to them in accordance with the dictates of humanity, international usage, and the requirements of law. The only reply to the distress signals was a counter signal from a large white light which was flashed for nearly two hours from the mast of the *Californian*. In our opinion such conduct, whether arising from indifference or gross carelessness, is most reprehensible, and places upon the commander of the *Californian* a grave responsibility. The wireless operator of the *Californian* was not aroused until 3:30 a.m., New York time, on the morning of the 15th, after considerable conversation between officers and members of the crew had taken place aboard that ship regarding these distress signals or rockets, and was directed by the Chief Officer to see if there was anything the matter, as a ship had been firing rockets during the night (p. 736). The inquiry thus set on foot immediately disclosed the fact that the *Titanic* had sunk. Had assistance been promptly proffered, or had wireless operator of the *Californian* remained a few minutes longer at his post on Sunday evening, that ship might have had the proud distinction of rescuing the lives of the passengers and crew of the *Titanic*.

> **British Wreck Commissioner's Inquiry Report**
> Circumstances in Connection with the *SS Californian* (excerpt)
>
> There are contradictions and inconsistencies in the story as told by the different witnesses. But the truth of the matter is plain. The "Titanic"

collided with the berg 11.40. The vessel seen by the "Californian" stopped at this time. The rockets sent up from the "Titanic" were distress signals. The "Californian" saw distress signals. The number sent up by the "Titanic" was about eight. The "Californian" saw eight. The time over which the rockets from the "Titanic" were sent up was from about 12:45 to 1:45 o'clock. It was about this time that the "Californian" saw the rockets. At 2:40 Mr. Stone called to the Master that the ship from which he'd seen the rockets had disappeared.

At 2:20 a.m. the "Titanic" had foundered. It was suggested that the rockets seen by the "Californian" were from some other ship, not the "Titanic." But no other ship to fit this theory has ever been heard of.

These circumstances convince me that the ship seen by the "Californian" was the "Titanic," and if so, according to Captain Lord, the two vessels were about five miles apart at the time of the disaster. The evidence from the "Titanic" corroborates this estimate, but I am advised that the distance was probably greater, though not more than eight to ten miles. The ice by which the "Californian" was surrounded was loose ice extending for a distance of not more than two or three miles in the direction of the "Titanic." The night was clear and the sea was smooth. When she first saw the rockets the "Californian" could have pushed through the ice to the open water without any serious risk and so have come to the assistance of the "Titanic." Had she done so she might have saved many if not all of the lives that were lost.

American and British Inquiry Recommendations

Lifeboats – Based on their findings both the American and British Inquiries made recommendations concerning the number of lifeboats ships need to carry, mandatory lifeboat drills, and lifeboat inspections.

The United States Senate Inquiry proposed:

- Every ship carry sufficient lifeboats to hold all passengers and crew.
- No less than four crew members with knowledge of handling boats would be assigned to every lifeboat.
- Lifeboat drills for the crew would be conducted a minimum of twice a month and the drills noted in the ship's log.
- Both crew and passengers would be assigned to lifeboats before the start of the voyage and the assignments would be allocated as to provide passengers the shortest route possible to a lifeboat.
- Lifeboat assignments and directions to the lifeboats would be posted in each stateroom.

The British Inquiry proposed plans that were far more detailed:
- Lifeboat accommodation on passenger ships would be based on the projected number of passengers to be carried, rather than tonnage, and such accommodations would be considered independently of the subdivision of the ship into watertight components. (Striking down Rule 12 of the Life-Saving Appliance Rules of 1902.)
- In special cases where the Board of Trade believed the provision of lifeboats for all on board to be impractical, requirements would be altered accordingly. This could include changing the sizes and types of lifeboats used, changing how they were stowed, or setting aside an entire deck to the storage of lifeboats and the drilling of the crew.
- All lifeboats would be on board before any ship commenced a voyage, and be equipped with lamps and pyrotechnics for signaling, as well as compasses and provisions.
- All lifeboats would be marked to easily indicate the maximum capacity of adult individuals when being lowered.
- All lifeboats would be fitted with a "protective fender" or bumper, to prevent damage when being lowered.
- The Board of Trade should be empowered to require that one or more lifeboats be fitted with "some form of mechanical propulsion"—i.e. an engine.
- The Board of Trade inspection of lifeboats should be more strict and searching in the future.

The British Inquiry also proposed recommendations for the conduct of lifeboat drills:
- If a ship did not carry enough deckhands to man all the lifeboats, other members of the crew should be trained and tested in boat work to take up the slack. To accomplish this the committee recommended that steps be taken to encourage boys to train in the merchant service.
- More frequent drills should be conducted in all ships as soon as possible upon leaving port;
    - a lifeboat drill
    - a fire drill
    - a watertight door drill
- Drills should be repeated during the voyage at intervals lasting no longer than a week.
- All the drills should be recorded in the ship's log.
- Before a ship leaves port the Board of Trade should be satisfied that

all requirements have been met and that each officer knows the plan for efficiently working the lifeboats.

Many of these recommendations were incorporated into the International Convention for the Safety of Life at Sea passed in 1914.

24 hour Marconi Watch – Following the inquiries, the United States government passed the Radio Act of 1912. This act and the International Convention for the Safety of Life at Sea, stated that passenger ship radio communication would be operated 24 hours a day and radios would include a secondary power supply. The Radio Act of 1912 also required ships to maintain contact with vessels in their vicinity as well as coastal onshore radio stations.

Distress Rockets – The International Convention for the Safety of Life at Sea determined that the firing of red rockets from a ship must be interpreted as a sign of distress and request for help. After the Radio Act of 1912 was passed it was agreed that all rockets at sea would be interpreted as distress signals only, removing any possible misinterpretation.

Ship Design – The *Titanic* disaster also demonstrated the design deficiencies and the need to revise shipbuilding regulations.

The U.S. Senate Inquiry made the following recommendations in their final report:

- All steel ships carrying more than one hundred passengers should have an interior watertight skin in the form of bottom or longitudinal bulkheads extending no less than ten percent of the load draft above the full-load waterline.
- The watertight skin should run from the forward collision bulkhead to no less than two-thirds the length of the ship.
- Bulkheads should be spaced so that any two adjacent compartments could be flooded without destroying the stability or "floatability" of the ship.
- Watertight transverse bulkheads should extend between each side of the ship and attach to the outside hull.
- Transverse bulkheads surrounding the ship's machinery should continue vertically to the uppermost continuous structural deck, which should be made watertight as well.
- Bulkheads in the vicinity of the machinery should extend no less than twenty-five percent of the ship above the load waterline, and all should end at a watertight deck.
- All watertight decks and bulkheads should be able to withstand water pressure equal to five feet more than the full height of the bulkhead without critical damage, and smaller bulkheads should be tested by subjection to actual water pressure.

The British, also very thorough in their outline for new shipbuilding regulations, made several similar proposals:

- A Bulkhead Committee was to report on the "desirability and practicality" of providing ships with a number of new protections.

- Ships should have a double skin carried up above the waterline; longitudinal and vertical watertight bulkheads extending as far forward and aft as convenient on each side of the ship; or a combination of both. All of this was to be in addition to watertight transverse bulkheads.

- Inquiries were also to be made as to the feasibility of fitting ships with watertight decks above the waterline, and a report made as to how such decks should be made watertight.

- It was recommended that the Board of Trade consider their proposals and, if it chose to approve of them, seek legislation to enforce them.

- The committee also recommended that the Board of Trade be given legislative powers to require future construction of passenger ships to adhere to the new guidelines.

Other – Both the American and British Inquiries resulted in a number of general recommendations for further improvement of safety at sea.

The U.S. Senate committee's final report pointedly stated "the accident clearly indicates the need for additional legislation to secure safety of life at sea." Their general recommendations included:

- By then current law, the United States accepted the inspection certificates of foreign ships whose home countries had similar inspection laws. One of the committee's recommendations for the revision of maritime law proposed that unless other nations saw fit to alter their inspection laws accordingly as well, such "reciprocal arrangements" would end.

- No ship would be licensed to carry passengers from American ports until it conformed to the rules and regulations set forth by United States law.

- Each steamship carrying a hundred or more passengers should be equipped with two electric searchlights to aid in the detection of ice and other potential obstacles.

- Firing rockets or other distress signals for any reason other than to communicate an emergency should be made a misdemeanor.

General recommendations from the British Wreck Commissioner's Inquiry Report included:

- All lookouts should undergo sight tests at regular intervals.

- A police system should be devised to ensure control on board in times of emergency.
- All steamship companies should include in their regulations that when ice has been sighted near or in the path of a ship, the ship should either alter its course to steer well clear of the danger or proceed at moderate speeds during nighttime.
- All ship captains should be made aware that under the Maritime Conventions Act of 1911, it is considered a misdemeanor to not aid a ship in distress when it is possible to do so.
- All regulations required of emigrant ships should also apply to all foreign-bound passenger liners.
- An international conference should be convened to establish common laws concerning construction of ships, provision of lifeboats, installation and operation of wireless sets, courses of action in regards to ice, and the use of searchlights.

Part Two Epilogue

PREVENTING ANOTHER DISASTER

After the *Titanic* disaster White Star Line made several changes before the American and British inquiries issued their findings.

Lifeboats – White Star immediately added lifeboats to the *Olympic* but not without problems.

When the *Titanic* sank, the *Olympic*, her sister ship, was 500 miles away and traveling in the opposite direction en route to Southampton. The *Olympic* arrived in Southampton on April 21st and, with only a few days before her next scheduled voyage, the lifeboat capacity was increased with the addition of 24 collapsible boats. Extra crew were brought on in case the lifeboats were actually needed.

The collapsibles were secondhand boats from troop ships but Captain Maurice Clarke of the Board of Trade inspected the boats and oversaw lifeboat drills that averaged 12.5 minutes to lower each boat. Duly impressed he passed the *Olympic* for her next voyage scheduled for April 24th. Captain Clarke may have been impressed but the crew wasn't—demanding that White Star provide the conventional wooden lifeboats instead of the collapsibles that they did not deem reliable for long periods of time in the water.

White Star refused. The crew's response was to strike and White Star's response was to find a new crew. While recruiting a crew to replace the strikers their trade union offered a compromise—a union delegation would check out the safety of the collapsibles in the water. Six collapsible boats were lowered and after two hours five were dry inside and the sixth had just started leaking but slowly enough that bailing would have kept it afloat. The leaking boat was replaced but now the original crew refused to sail with the new, inexperienced, strikebreaking crew members. After White Star refused to dismiss the replacements, 54 sailors left the ship and were immediately charged with mutiny. Already two days behind schedule White Star was forced to cancel the April voyage. With the next trip scheduled for May 15th, White Star had time to sort out their union crew problems.

On May 4th the mutiny charge against the 54 deserting sailors was found to be proved, but the Portsmouth magistrate refused to impose fines or jail time. With a keen sense of public opinion, White Star allowed the men to return to work on the *Olympic*.

Marconi Wireless Operators – The *Titanic* and the *Olympic* both carried two Marconi operators for around the clock coverage but some other White Star Line vessels did not. The *Californian* demonstrated what can happen when the wireless is shut down for the night and White Star learned the tragic lesson.

> **British Wreck Commissioner's Inquiry** – Testimony of Harold A. Sanderson, examined by the Solicitor General:
> 19259. There were as we know, two operators on this ship so that you had a continuous Marconi service?
> Sanderson – We had.
> 19260. Have you also got two on the "Olympic"?
> Sanderson – Yes.
> 19261. What is your practice with regard to the rest of your fleet?
> Sanderson – With few exceptions in the Atlantic trade we have two, but those exceptions cease to exist. We have made two on all the ships.
> ...19263. As far as regards your North Atlantic service today as I follow you, you have two operators on every single ship?
> Sanderson – We have.
> 19264. Was that change made in consequence of the disaster?
> Sanderson – Yes.
> 19265. And it is one which I suppose you intend to persist in?
> Sanderson – Absolutely.

Binoculars – Although not entirely convinced it would have made a difference on the *Titanic*, White Star Line also supplied binoculars to all their lookouts following the disaster.

> **British Wreck Commissioner's Inquiry** – Testimony of Harold A. Sanderson, examined by the Solicitor General:
> 19356. (The Solicitor General.) About the binoculars, I meant to have asked you this. Since this disaster has your company taken any steps to provide binoculars for the crow's-nest?
> – We have.
> 19357. For all your vessels?
> – We have ordered binoculars to be given to all the look-outs for much the same reason that we have put all these extra boats on. There is a popular cry that they want to have glasses, and we are going to satisfy them.

Refitting the *Olympic*

After the American and British Inquiry recommendations were issued, many ships were refitted for increased safety including the *Olympic* when White Star Line withdrew her from service in October 1912.

The *Olympic* was returned to Belfast to be refitted as follows:

- The number of lifeboats was increased from twenty to sixty-four with extra davits installed along the boat deck to accommodate them.
- An inner watertight skin was added in the boiler rooms and engine rooms to create a double hull.
- Five of the watertight bulkheads were extended the entire height of the hull to the B Deck, correcting the design flaw that had these bulkheads only going up as far as E or D-Deck, a short distance above the waterline.
- An extra bulkhead was added to divide the electrical dynamo room increasing the total number of watertight compartments to seventeen.
- Improvements were also made to the *Olympic*'s pumping apparatus.

The same modifications would also be applied to the *Britannic* which was under construction at the time. The modifications would allow the *Olympic* and the *Britannic* to survive a collision and remain afloat if the first six compartments are breached whereas five breached compartments doomed the *Titanic*.

Navigation

First Officer Murdoch's port-around attempt to miss the iceberg was the 'textbook' response to the fast approaching danger he was faced with but that approach led to the sideswipe damage that doomed the ship. The *Titanic*'s fate and testimony of her possible survival had she struck the berg head on, rewrote the seamanship best practice in the unlikely event of a recurrence. Two years later the unlikely event did occur. From the *London Times*, June 1, 1914:

"The steamship *Royal Edward*, of the Canadian Northern Company, docked safely at Avonmouth Docks, Bristol, on Friday night, from Montreal and Quebec.

"On her voyage across the Atlantic she struck an iceberg, but received very little damage beyond a twisted stem and a few buckled plates. The collision occurred last Friday week in a dense fog while the vessel was proceeding dead slow.

"The berg was sighted only two ship's lengths away, and not more than a minute elapsed before the vessel struck, despite the fact that the engines were reversed with remarkable promptitude.

"The passengers speak very highly of Commander Wotton's nerve and coolness. When he saw that it was impossible to avoid the berg, he took it end-on instead of starboarding the helm and risking extensive damage alongside...."

Hitting an unavoidable iceberg head-on and damaging the bow rather than sideswiping it with the hull is now the accepted rule of navigation included in the International Regulations for Preventing Collisions at Sea (COLREGs).

The International Ice Patrol

After the *Titanic* disaster, the U.S. Navy assigned the scout cruisers *Chester* and *USS Birmingham* to ice patrol duty in the North Atlantic shipping lanes for the remainder of 1912. In 1913, the Navy could not spare ships for this purpose, so the Revenue Cutter Service (forerunner of the United States Coast Guard) assumed responsibility, assigning the cutters *Seneca* and *Miami* to conduct the ice patrol.

The first International Convention for the Safety of Life at Sea (SOLAS) was convened in London, in November 1913 and a treaty was signed in January 1914 that resulted in the formation and international funding of the International Ice Patrol (IIP). The IIP was set up to monitor and report the location of North Atlantic Ocean icebergs that could pose a threat to transatlantic sea traffic. The United States Coast Guard assumed the responsibility of running the IIP in February 1914. After initially using cutters to monitor the area between the 52nd parallel (near northern Newfoundland) to the 40th parallel (equal to Philadelphia) during the February-July ice season, the Coast Guard switched to aircraft after World War II.

Flights are made an average of five days a week every other week, and ice reports are updated twice a day with information on the location of icebergs, their courses, and rates of speed. Based in Groton, Connecticut the IIP is comprised of a fifteen-member unit of active Coast Guardsmen and civilians.

Every year, on April 15th, the chart transmissions sent out by the IIP mark not only the positions of icebergs but also that of the *Titanic's* final resting place. The IIP drop two wreaths over the spot from a Hercules C-130 airplane— their own and one from the Titanic Historical Society.

Index

1503 Perished When The *Titanic* Sank 292, 306, 360, 361, 411
  Californian failed to respond 395, 403, 406
  Lifeboats with room did not return to pick up survivors 387, 394, 406
  North Atlantic environment 361
  Root Cause Summary 405
  The *Titanic* did not carry enough lifeboats 377, 405
  Titanic's Crew failed to utilize the full capacity of the lifeboats 378, 405
Abelseth, Olaus 36, 115, 159, 194, 195, 273, 274
Adriatic 20, 75, 250
Amerika 40, 78, 312, 338, 339, 346
Andrew, Samuel 37
Andrews, Thomas 15, 27, 32, 117, 118, 159, 188, 252, 253, 308, 315, 355
Archer, Seaman Ernest 159, 160, 212
Astor, Colonel John Jacob IV 44, 68, 82, 108, 121, 122, 150, 173, 188, 193, 232, 233, 239, 243, 257, 258
  Photo 59
Astor, Madeleine 44, 68, 82, 121, 122, 150, 167, 173, 232, 257, 259, 273
  Photo 59
Ballard, Dr. Robert 274, 275
Baltic 14, 15, 76, 77, 78, 79, 131, 132, 220, 229, 230, 234, 312, 338, 339, 341, 342
Barrett, Lead Fireman Frederick 27, 28, 99, 100, 105, 106, 112, 113, 114, 169, 170, 212, 322, 352, 353, 354, 355, 394
Beauchamp, Fireman George 100, 101, 104, 105, 212
Beesley, Lawrence 36, 64, 110, 112, 119, 168, 213, 273
Behr, Karl 47, 48, 70, 148, 149, 270, 271
Belfast, Ireland 13, 15, 26, 27, 70, 71, 72, 308, 309, 310, 323, 334
Bell, Chief Engineer Joseph 43, 116, 352, 414
Binoculars 30, 70, 71, 286, 288, 289, 290, 293, 331, 334, 335, 336, 337, 408, 410, 422. *See also* Glasses
Bishop, Dickinson 49, 68, 108, 121, 147, 207, 242, 267, 268, 274
Bishop, Helen 49, 68, 108, 121, 147, 148, 207, 242, 259, 267, 268, 274, 380
Blair, David 29, 30, 70, 91, 248, 288, 289, 310, 331, 335
Board of Trade 21, 22, 23, 24, 26, 31, 34, 35, 244, 246, 247, 257, 308, 310, 331, 362, 363, 364, 365, 366, 369, 371, 372, 373, 375, 376, 377, 378, 405, 411, 412, 417, 419, 421
Boxhall, Fourth Officer Joseph 31, 94, 103, 115, 116, 117, 124, 128, 129, 130, 172, 181, 206, 224, 245, 249, 250, 314, 315, 316, 338, 339, 340, 379, 388, 394
Bremen 238
Brice, Seaman Walter 209
Bride, Junior Wireless Operator Harold 74, 75, 81, 127, 128, 131, 132, 133, 188, 190, 191, 193, 220, 253, 281, 345, 346
Bright, Quartermaster Arthur John 129, 176, 215, 216, 316, 392, 394
Britannic 14, 423
British Board of Trade Regulations 21. *See also* Board of Trade

Brown, Margaret 44, 121, 154, 210, 267
  Photo 60
Buckley, Daniel 50, 114, 115, 155, 156, 167, 273
Buley, Seaman Edward John 172, 173, 198, 199, 214, 215, 218, 219, 360, 394
Butt, Major Archibald 39, 46, 57, 66, 68, 69, 82, 83, 122, 188, 232, 233, 235, 236, 243, 261, 262, 263
Californian 81, 92, 131, 178, 179, 181, 183, 186, 199, 225, 232, 247, 287, 312, 313, 320, 321, 338, 339, 342, 345, 347, 348, 395, 396, 397, 403, 404, 406, 411, 412, 413, 415, 416, 422
CAPA (Corrective And Preventative Action) 300, 336, 407, 408
Captain Lord 178, 182, 186, 395, 396, 400, 404, 406
Captain Rostron 134, 135, 137, 138, 139, 140, 141, 223, 224, 225, 226, 267, 270
Captain Smith 10, 34, 35, 40, 43, 62, 69, 70, 75, 76, 78, 79, 81, 82, 86, 92, 102, 103, 115, 116, 117, 119, 124, 128, 129, 130, 144, 151, 152, 158, 181, 188, 242, 248, 250, 253, 310, 311, 312, 313, 314, 315, 322, 326, 329, 330, 337, 340, 342, 344, 345, 347, 357, 358, 359, 387, 408, 409, 412, 413, 414, 415
Carlisle, Alexander 15, 22, 24, 308, 362
Caronia 75, 78, 79, 311, 338, 339, 341
Carpathia 128, 131, 132, 133, 134, 135, 141, 199, 201, 207, 209, 214, 219, 220, 222, 223, 224, 225, 226, 227, 231, 232, 236, 241, 242, 243, 247, 248, 249, 250, 259, 261, 265, 267, 268, 269, 270, 271, 272, 273, 274, 316, 317, 319, 321
Carter, Lucile 42, 121, 173, 258
Carter, William 42, 82, 83, 106, 121, 173, 175, 227, 258
Chalmers, Sir Alfred (Nautical Advisor to the British Board of Trade) 362, 373, 374, 375, 376
Cherbourg, France 35, 37, 39, 43, 44, 46, 47, 48, 49, 165, 310, 311
Clarke, Captain Maurice 34, 421
Coal Fire 71, 322, 323, 330, 351, 354, 355
Collision
  Hard-a-Port 97, 98, 103, 180, 314, 324, 325
  Iceberg Right Ahead 93, 96, 249, 250, 251, 284, 304, 314, 331
  Just a trembling of the ship 101, 102
  She Hit Us 98, 99
  Shut All Dampers 99
  Slight Haze 95, 304, 313, 328
Collision Aftermath
  A Rush of Water 112, 113, 353
  Assessing the Damage 115
  Boiler Room 5 27, 105, 309, 354, 355
  Boiler Room 6 27, 104, 309, 354, 355
  Bread for the Boats 119
  First Class Passengers 106, 118, 120, 121, 122, 145, 149, 150, 163, 193, 204, 259, 272, 380, 381
  Half Speed Ahead 103, 357
  making water in the forepeak tank 110
  Second Class Passengers 110, 160, 272
  Third Class Passengers 114, 159, 170

Index

Titanic's position 124, 128
Warm Clothing and Life Belts 120
Cottam, Wireless Operator Harold 135, 136, 137, 141, 142, 143
Countess of Rothes 38, 152, 209, 267
Crawford, First Class Bedroom Steward Alfred 120, 121, 151, 152
Curse of Princess of Amen-Ra 83, 84
Davidson, Orian 42, 150, 259, 260
Davidson, Thornton 42, 260
Dillon, Coal Trimmer Thomas P. 195, 196
Distress Calls
   CQD and SOS 124, 125, 126, 127, 128, 131, 136, 186, 316
   Distress Rockets 21, 128, 131, 181, 396, 403, 404
DMAIC Model
   Analyze 293
   Control 300
   Define 291
   Improve 300
   Measure 292
Duff-Gordon, Lady Lucile 43, 82, 153, 154, 201, 202, 204, 205, 247, 266
Duff-Gordon, Sir Cosmo 43, 82, 153, 154, 201, 202, 204, 205, 247, 266
Etches, Bedroom Steward Henry 116, 117, 263, 264
Evans, Seaman Frank 68, 71, 176, 217, 218, 219, 334
Farrell, Maurice L. 228, 229, 230, 231, 232, 233, 234
First Class 16, 17, 18, 19, 33, 36, 37, 38, 40, 42, 43, 44, 46, 47, 48, 49, 50, 54, 63, 65, 66, 67, 68, 69, 72, 82, 83, 106, 118, 120, 121, 122, 145, 148, 150, 155, 160, 163, 165, 169, 172, 175, 193, 204, 227, 255, 257, 259, 263, 272, 305, 310, 380, 381
Fleet, Lookout Frederick 71, 91, 92, 94, 95, 96, 97, 155, 210, 211, 250, 251, 265, 284, 289, 303, 304, 313, 314, 326, 327, 328, 331, 332, 333, 334, 335, 336
Frankfurt 131, 132, 141, 316
Franklin, Phillip A. S. 228, 229, 230, 231, 232, 235, 242
Futrelle, Jacques 42, 82, 176, 233
Futrelle, May 42, 82, 176
Gatti, Luigi 38, 66, 67, 70, 82, 165, 166, 255
Gibson, Apprentice James 183
Gibson, Dorothy 46, 68, 69, 82, 107, 147, 269
Gigantic 14
Glasses 70, 71, 87, 91, 92, 289, 332, 333, 334, 335, 336, 422. *See also* Binoculars
Gracie, Colonel Archibald 39, 45, 68, 109, 151, 173, 176, 188, 191, 192, 193, 220, 265
Groves, Third Officer Charles 179, 180, 181, 320, 321, 395, 396, 397, 398
Guggenheim, Benjamin 48, 82, 121, 149, 163, 233, 263, 264, 269
Haines, Boatswain Albert 163, 164, 208, 390, 394
Harland & Wolff 13, 14, 15, 20, 22, 27, 52, 307, 308, 355, 362
Hart, Third Class Steward John 122, 123, 156, 157, 158, 170, 171, 214
Hays, Charles 42, 150, 259, 260
Hays, Clara 42, 150, 259, 260
Hays, Margaret 272

Hemming, Lamp Trimmer Samuel 110, 118, 174
Hendrickson, Lead Fireman Charles 71, 72, 201, 202, 204, 323, 351, 352
Hichens, Quartermaster Robert 89, 90, 96, 97, 98, 154, 155, 210, 265, 266, 323, 324, 382, 391, 393
Hogg, Lookout George Alfred 71, 146, 148, 207, 334, 389, 393
Horswell, Seaman Albert E. J. 204
Hosono, Masabumi 37, 172, 215, 273
Human Performance Model
  Capacity 299
  Consequences and Incentives 298
  Expectations and Feedback 298
  Motivation 299
  Skills and Knowledge 298
  Tools and Resources 298
Iceberg 73, 75, 83, 84, 86, 93, 95, 96, 97, 98, 245, 284, 285, 288, 289, 290, 314, 322, 323, 324, 325, 326, 329, 330, 331, 332, 335, 336, 337, 410, 412, 413, 423, 424
Ice Warnings 10, 63, 244, 247, 290, 292, 311, 320, 329, 337, 338, 342, 344, 346, 347, 348, 349, 413
Inquiry Recommendations 416, 422
Isaacs, Sir Rufus 14, 246, 247, 285
Ismay, Bruce 13, 14, 23, 38, 42, 44, 51, 76, 77, 79, 106, 116, 117, 148, 149, 159, 164, 175, 199, 227, 243, 255, 256, 257, 258, 260, 270, 282, 307, 312, 337, 342, 343, 345, 362, 412
Johnson, Saloon Steward James 101, 118, 165, 166, 388, 389
Jones, Seaman Thomas 68, 152, 153, 209, 210, 229, 233, 234, 267, 381, 382, 390, 391, 393
Joughin, Chief Baker Charles 72, 94, 119, 120, 171, 196, 197, 220, 221, 222, 252
Keep a Sharp Lookout for Ice 87
Lee, Lookout Reginald 70, 71, 91, 94, 95, 97, 98, 99, 169, 251, 303, 304, 313, 327, 328, 331, 333, 334, 335
Lifeboat Davits 31, 70, 362, 378, 411. *See also* Welin Quadrant Davits
Lifeboats 17, 22, 23, 24, 25, 67, 112, 116, 119, 144, 145, 151, 154, 155, 162, 164, 167, 171, 201, 206, 207, 208, 209, 210, 212, 214, 216, 218, 219, 220, 223, 224, 225, 226, 227, 292, 307, 308, 309, 315, 316, 319, 362, 363, 365, 367, 369, 370, 376, 377, 378, 379, 380, 383, 384, 385, 386, 387, 388, 392, 393, 394, 395, 405, 406, 411, 412, 413, 416, 417, 418, 420, 421, 423
Lightoller, Second Officer Charles 29, 30, 31, 75, 76, 79, 80, 81, 84, 85, 86, 87, 88, 89, 91, 117, 144, 145, 151, 152, 154, 155, 158, 162, 163, 173, 176, 188, 189, 190, 191, 193, 199, 220, 222, 227, 248, 249, 257, 258, 266, 267, 303, 312, 313, 315, 319, 325, 326, 332, 333, 337, 340, 341, 342, 343, 347, 379, 380, 381, 382, 383, 384, 386, 387, 405, 406, 414
Loading and Launching Lifeboats 144, 316, 317, 384, 385, 393, 394
  Collapsible C 175, 176, 213, 227, 274, 317, 385, 394
  Portside No. 10 172, 317, 384, 394
  Portside No. 12 162, 317, 384, 394
  Portside No. 14 160, 317, 384, 394
  Portside No. 16 159, 317, 384, 393

Portside No. 2 172, 317, 384, 394
Portside No. 4 173, 317, 385, 394
Portside No. 6 154, 317, 384, 393
Portside No. 8 151, 317, 384, 393
Starboard No. 1 153, 317, 384, 393
Starboard No. 11 164, 317, 384, 394
Starboard No. 13 167, 317, 384, 394
Starboard No. 15 170, 317, 384, 394
Starboard No. 3 149, 317, 384, 393
Starboard No. 5 148, 316, 384, 393
Starboard No. 7 146, 316, 384, 393
Starboard No. 9 163, 317, 384, 394
Lord, Captain Stanley 178, 182, 186, 396, 400, 404, 406
Lowe, Fifth Officer Harold 31, 146, 147, 148, 149, 160, 161, 162, 216, 218, 219, 222, 223, 240, 241, 245, 250, 319, 360, 379, 392, 393, 394, 395
Lucas, Seaman William 145, 146, 176, 177, 380
Mackay-Bennett 263
Marconi, Guglielmo 74, 125
Marconigram 62, 75, 77, 78, 79, 80, 81, 88, 236, 242, 269. *See also* Wireless Message
Mauge, Paul 166, 167, 168
Mesaba 87, 313, 329, 338, 339, 345, 347, 348, 410
Millet, Francis 39, 45, 68, 69, 82, 122, 131, 188, 233, 240, 261, 263, 272
Minia 238, 240, 255, 260
Miss Gladys Cherry 39, 107, 152, 210, 267
Moody, Sixth Officer James 31, 80, 81, 87, 89, 96, 98, 146, 151, 159, 163, 170, 250, 251, 304, 313, 314, 324, 379, 380
Moore, Clarence 39, 82, 83, 122, 149, 150, 188, 208, 263, 381, 390, 393
Moore, Seaman George 149, 381, 390, 393
Morgan, J.P. 13, 307
Mount Temple 128, 131, 316
Murdoch, First Officer William 29, 30, 75, 88, 89, 96, 97, 102, 103, 116, 145, 146, 148, 149, 153, 158, 163, 164, 167, 170, 171, 172, 175, 191, 248, 249, 250, 266, 284, 303, 304, 312, 313, 314, 323, 324, 325, 329, 331, 342, 379, 380, 386, 405, 423
Myths and Legends 305
Near-Miss 42, 408, 409
Newsom, Helen 48, 70, 148, 270, 271
New York, passenger ship 76, 310, 312
Oliver, Quartermaster Alfred 89, 90, 116
Olympic 12, 14, 15, 17, 19, 20, 21, 22, 23, 24, 26, 27, 29, 30, 40, 43, 49, 62, 66, 67, 69, 72, 91, 130, 131, 132, 141, 142, 220, 230, 232, 245, 248, 249, 251, 271, 300, 301, 308, 309, 316, 337, 350, 351, 355, 362, 363, 364, 366, 372, 378, 379, 405, 407, 411, 421, 422, 423
Orchestra 33, 67, 254
Perfect Calm 82, 84, 313
Perkis, Quartermaster Walter John 174, 214, 391, 392, 394
Peuchen, Major Arthur 40, 155, 210, 211, 212, 265, 266, 391

Phillips, Senior Wireless Operator Jack 74, 75, 87, 92, 115, 124, 127, 128, 131, 132, 133, 188, 190, 193, 220, 233, 253, 314, 315, 316, 317, 318, 345, 346
Pirrie, Lord 13, 14
Pitman, Third Officer Herbert 30, 31, 39, 117, 149, 206, 207, 249, 315, 379, 389, 393
Poingdestre, Seaman John 101, 102, 162, 163, 197, 198, 216, 217, 218, 222, 319, 394
Postal Clerks 33, 115, 188, 253
Problem Solving Model
  Environment 295
  Equipment 295
  Materials 295
  Measurement 295
  Method/Procedure 294
Pusey, Fireman Robert 204, 205
Queenstown, Ireland 30, 35, 37, 43, 47, 49, 50, 62, 69, 70, 311, 343, 414
Raynor, Senator Isidor 187
Restaurant Staff 165, 237, 255
Root Cause 285
Root Cause Analysis
  5-Whys Method 287
  Basic Concepts 286
  Desired State 292
  Human Error 287
  Human Performance 286
Root Cause Scrutiny 409
Rostron, Captain Arthur Henry 134, 135, 137, 138, 139, 140, 141, 223, 224, 225, 226, 267, 270
Rowe, Quartermaster George 129, 130, 175, 213, 316, 394
Russell, Edith 47, 164, 268
Ryerson, Arthur 77, 173, 174, 258
Ryerson, Emily 77, 258
Ryerson, John 173, 258
Sanderson, Harold A. (White Star Director) 23, 362, 364, 368, 371, 372, 373, 422
Scarrott, Seaman Joseph 102, 160, 161, 162
Second Class 17, 18, 36, 37, 42, 43, 48, 49, 63, 64, 65, 67, 72, 110, 111, 122, 160, 168, 172, 213, 270, 272, 311
Senior, Fireman Harry 256
Smith, Clinch 45, 151, 191, 216, 265
Smith, Edward 412. *See also* Captain Smith
Smith, Eloise 49, 68, 82, 106, 154, 259
Smith, Lucian 49, 68, 82, 83, 106, 154, 259
Smith, Senator William Alden 61, 242
Southampton, England 26, 27, 29, 30, 34, 35, 36, 37, 38, 70, 251, 253, 309, 310, 323, 334, 335, 421
Stanley, Amy 115, 175, 213, 236
Stead, William 40, 41, 58, 82, 83, 84, 122, 188, 200, 233, 245, 248, 254, 260, 261, 305, 307

Steerage 14, 18, 35, 36, 43, 49, 63, 114, 139, 156, 167, 172, 191. *See also* Third Class

Stone, Second Officer Herbert 181, 182, 183, 184, 237, 321, 396, 398, 399, 400, 401, 402, 416

Straus, Ida
  40, 82, 121, 151, 152, 188, 260

Straus, Isidor
  40, 82, 121, 188, 233, 260
  Photo 57

Symons, Seaman George 90, 91, 92, 154, 197, 202, 203, 204, 206, 334, 388, 393

Taft, President William Howard 39, 41, 66, 82, 235, 236, 243, 260, 261, 262

Taylor, Fireman James 67, 204, 254

Thayer, Jack 48, 193, 222, 227, 258

Thayer, John 48, 82, 121, 173, 188, 258
  Photo 60

Thayer, Marian 48, 77, 82, 121, 173, 227, 258
  Photo 60

Third Class 18, 19, 35, 36, 43, 49, 50, 63, 64, 65, 71, 72, 114, 115, 122, 155, 156, 159, 160, 167, 170, 172, 214, 273, 310, 311. *See also* Steerage

Tip of the Iceberg 284

Titanic
  Below Deck 71
  Coalbunker Fire 27. *See also* Coal Fire
  First Class Maps 38
  Hull Launch 23
  Provisioning in Southampton 27
  RMS Titanic 16, 61
  Sea Trials 26

Titanic Collided with an iceberg 292, 297, 306, 322, 329, 348
  Captain failed to take adequate preventive measures 337, 344, 349
  Crow's nest Lookouts failed to see the iceberg in time 331, 335, 348
  Discussion of Officer Handoff Process 336
  Perfect Calm Conditions 325, 330, 331, 335, 344, 345, 349, 408, 410
  Root Cause Summary 348
  Wireless Operator failed to deliver crucial ice warning 345, 347, 349, 410
  port-around attempt 97, 314, 323, 324, 329, 423
  The Coal Fire 71, 322, 323, 330, 351, 354, 355

Titanic Crew and Staff
  Captain and Officers 248
  Deck Crew 31
  Engineering Crew 32
  Guarantee Group 32
  Non-White Star Staff 33
  Victualling Crew 32

Titanic Decks
  A Decks 17, 107, 121, 145, 151
  B Deck 17, 18, 33, 38, 66, 165

Boat Deck 16, 17, 38, 55, 64, 67, 68, 69, 120, 121, 144, 159, 168, 172, 176, 188, 318
C Deck 18, 35, 36, 64, 65
D Deck 18, 63
E Deck 16, 18, 20, 63, 65, 71, 117, 351
F Deck 18, 19, 20, 63, 351
G Deck 19, 115
Orlop Deck 315
Tank Top 19, 104
Titanic Sank After The Collision 350
  Captain Smith's half-ahead order 357, 358, 359
  Design Flaws 350, 355
  Impact of the Coal Fire 354
  Physical Properties of the Materials 356
  Root Cause Summary 359
Titanic Timeline
  Background 307
  Damage Discovered 315
  Distress Calls and Signals 316
  High Tides and Icebergs 309
  Ice Warnings 311, 320
  Immediate Aftermath 314
  In the Water or in a Lifeboat 318
  Launching Lifeboats 316
  Origins of Unsinkable Belief 308
  Preparing for the Maiden Voyage – January to April 309
  Sailing Day 310
  The Collision 313
  The Perfect Calm 313
  Titanic's Last Hour 317, 318
  Trans-Atlantic Crossing 311
Touma, Hanna 49, 175, 242, 274
Transverse Bulkheads 20, 25, 351, 355, 356, 370, 410, 418, 419
Unsinkable 9, 10, 20, 21, 24, 25, 26, 47, 84, 93, 119, 135, 150, 228, 230, 231, 233, 245, 249, 284, 308, 337, 345, 351, 355, 359, 370, 371, 377, 382, 385
Watertight Compartments 9, 20, 21, 25, 26, 93, 117, 245, 308, 315, 337, 351, 370, 374, 423
Watertight Doors 16, 18, 19, 20, 21, 96, 100, 101, 102, 103, 104, 105, 116, 308, 314, 337, 351, 355
Welin Quadrant Davits 22, 24. *See also* Lifeboat Davits
Whiteley, Saloon Steward Thomas 301, 302, 303, 304
  Root Cause Analysis of Whiteley's Account 301
White Star Line 13, 14, 20, 22, 24, 26, 29, 30, 31, 33, 37, 38, 42, 74, 178, 234, 235, 236, 238, 242, 246, 247, 248, 307, 337, 350, 355, 362, 365, 366, 367, 370, 373, 377, 378, 412, 421, 422
Widener, Eleanor 48, 79, 82, 121, 173, 258
  Photo 59

Widener, George 48, 69, 70, 79, 82, 121, 173, 188, 233, 258
  Photo 59
Widener, Harry 48, 82, 83, 121, 173, 188, 233, 258
Widener Dinner Party 79, 81, 82
Wilde, Chief Officer Henry 29, 30, 31, 34, 69, 70, 80, 110, 115, 116, 144, 145, 151, 158, 160, 161, 162, 171, 172, 175, 176, 188, 189, 248, 249, 250, 310, 312, 314, 331, 335, 379, 387
Williams, Charles D. 48, 83, 193, 271
Williams, Charles E. 36, 160, 270, 272
Williams, R. Norris 48, 83, 193, 271
Wireless Message 76, 188, 311, 312, 318. *See also* Marconigram

Made in the USA
Columbia, SC
26 January 2021